Thomas Hastings

Church Melodies

A collection of Psalms and hymns, with appropriate music

Thomas Hastings

Church Melodies
A collection of Psalms and hymns, with appropriate music

ISBN/EAN: 9783337038694

Printed in Europe, USA, Canada, Australia, Japan

Cover: Foto ©Lupo / pixelio.de

More available books at **www.hansebooks.com**

CHURCH MELODIES:

A

COLLECTION OF PSALMS AND HYMNS,

WITH APPROPRIATE MUSIC.

FOR THE USE OF CONGREGATIONS.

BY

THOMAS HASTINGS, Mus. Doc.,

AND

Rev. THOMAS S. HASTINGS.

NEW-YORK:

PUBLISHED BY ANSON D. F. RANDOLPH,

No. 770 BROADWAY.

CHICAGO: WILLIAM TOMLINSON. CINCINNATI: GEORGE CROSBY.
BOSTON: HENRY HOYT.

—

1865.

PREFACE.

THE object of the present work is to promote congregational and social singing. It is intended to be used in the church, in the lecture-room, and in the family. It is not designed to supersede books already introduced, but rather to be used in connection with them ; yet its contents are sufficiently varied and full to meet the wants of congregations that have not been previously supplied, or that desire a change. Great care has been exercised to avoid adding to the endless variety of readings which unhappily prevail in the current Psalmody. The selection of Psalms and Hymns has been made with much study and labor. Those which have already secured a hold upon the affections of the church have been carefully gathered ; and numerous additions from recent sources, it is thought, will add greatly to the value of the work. The variety of topics is ample and rich. The hymns could not be arranged according to their subjects, without neglecting the imperative claims of musical adaptation. The number and character of indices will obviate the apparent inconvenience of such an arrangement. Much labor has been bestowed upon the *Index of Subjects*, which will be found specially copious and available.

. In the selection of the music, the aim has been to *avoid extremes*, and to secure adaptation, variety, and availability. Large numbers in our congregations can read plain music at sight, and will gladly join in the exercises of praise if the tunes are before them. A choir is needed to lead the congregation. It is desirable that during the winter months, the congregation should have occasional rehearsals, with such instruction as they shall seem to require. That the work may be useful in promoting the spirit of praise in the church, and in the home circle, is the earnest hope of

THE COMPILERS.

CHURCH MELODIES.

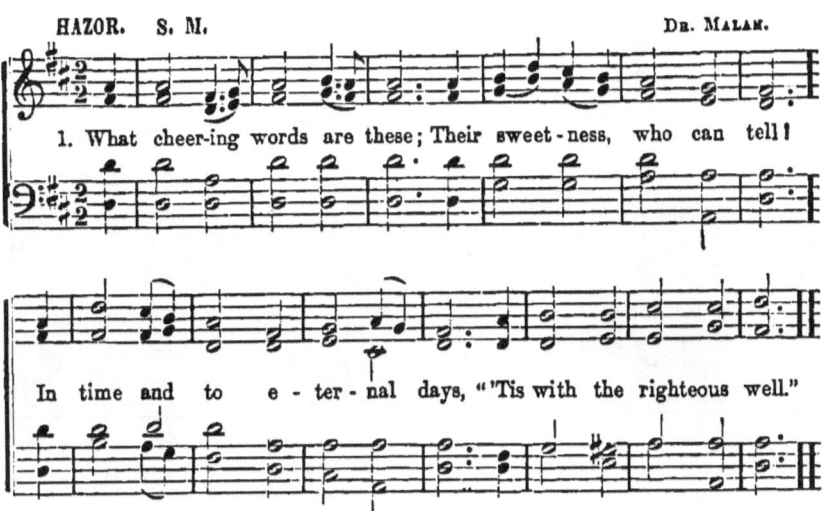

HAZOR. S. M.   DR. MALAN.

1. What cheer-ing words are these; Their sweet-ness, who can tell!

In time and to e-ter-nal days, " 'Tis with the righteous well."

1.   *Well with the Righteous.*

1. WHAT cheering words are these;
    Their sweetness who can tell?
In time and to eternal days,
    " 'Tis with the righteous well."

2. Well when they see His face,
    Or sink amidst the flood;
Well in affliction's thorny maze,
    Or on the mount with God.

3. 'Tis well when joys arise,
    'Tis well when sorrows flow,
'Tis well when darkness veils the skies,
    And strong temptations grow.

4. In every state secure,
    Kept as Jehovah's eye,

· 'Tis well with them while life endures,
    And well when called to die.

2.   *Sanctifying Influence.*

1. COME, Holy Spirit, come,
    With energy divine,
And on this poor benighted soul
    With beams of mercy shine.

2. Melt, melt this frozen heart;
    This stubborn will subdue;
Each evil passion overcome,
    And form me all anew.

3. Mine will the profit be,
    But thine shall be the praise
And unto thee will I devote
    The remnant of my days.

MORAVIAN. C. M. Double.   GERMAN

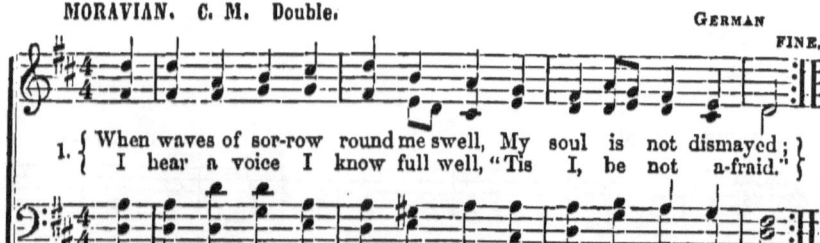

When waves of sor-row round me swell, My soul is not dismayed;
I hear a voice I know full well, "'Tis I, be not a-fraid."

D. C. voice shall tranquil - ize each fear, "'Tis I, be, not a - fraid.

When black the threatening clouds appear, And storms my path invade, That

3.   *Christian Courage.*

1. WHEN waves of sorrow round me swell,
My soul is not dismayed ;
I hear a voice I know full well—
"'Tis I, be not afraid."

2. When black the threatening clouds appear,
And storms my path invade,
That voice shall tranquilize each fear,—
"'Tis I, be not afraid."

3. There is a gulf that must be crossed,—
Saviour! be near to aid;
Whisper, when my frail bark is tossed,
"'Tis I, be not afraid."

4. There is a dark and fearful vale,
Death hides within its shade;
Oh! say, when flesh and heart shall fail,
"'Tis I, be not afraid."

4.   *Christian Assurance.*

1. I'M not ashamed to own my Lord,
Or to defend his cause;
Maintain the honor of his word,
The glory of his cross.

2. Jesus, my God!—I know his name—
His name is all my trust;
Nor will he put my soul to shame,
Nor let my hope be lost.

3. Firm as his throne, his promise stands,
And he can well secure
What I've committed to his hands,
Till the decisive hour.

4. Then will he own my worthless name
Before his Father's face,
And in the new Jerusalem
Appoint my soul a place.

5.   *Christian Soldier.*

1. AM I a soldier of the cross !
A follower of the Lamb ?
And shall I fear to own his cause,
Or blush to speak his name ?

2. Must I be carried to the skies
On flowery beds of ease ?
While others fought to win the prize,
And sailed through bloody seas ?

3. Are there no foes for me to face ?
Must I not stem the flood ?
Is this vile world a friend to grace,
To help me on to God ?

4. Sure I must fight, if I would reign;
Increase my courage, Lord !
I'll bear the toil, endure the pain,
Supported by thy word.

5. Thy saints, in all this glorious war,
   Shall conquer, though they die;
   They view the triumph from afar,
   And seize it with their eye.

6. When that illustrious day shall rise,
   And all thy armies shine
   In robes of victory thro' the skies,
   The glory shall be thine.

6. *The Church our Delight and Safety.*

1. THE Lord of glory is my light,
   And my salvation too;
   God is my strength, nor will I fear
   What all my foes can do.

2. One privilege my heart desires:
   Oh grant me mine abode
   Among the churches of thy saints,
   The temples of my God.

3. There shall I offer my requests,
   And see thy beauty still;
   Shall hear thy messages of love,
   And there inquire thy will.

4. When troubles rise and storms appear,
   There may his children hide;
   God has a strong pavilion where
   He makes my soul abide.

7. *Christ's first and second Coming.*

1. SING to the Lord, ye distant lands,
   Ye tribes of every tongue;
   His new-discovered grace demands
   A new and nobler song.

2. Say to the nations, Jesus reigns,
   God's own Almighty Son;
   His power the sinking world sustains,
   And grace surrounds his throne.

3. Let now seraphic joy surprise
   The islands of the sea;
   Ye mountains, sink; ye valleys, rise;
   Prepare the Lord his way.

4. Behold he comes! he comes to bless
   The nations as their God,
   To show the world his righteousness,
   And send his truth abroad.

5. But when his voice shall raise the dead,
   And bid the world draw near,
   How will the guilty nations dread
   To see their Judge appear!

8. *Prayer for the Reign of Christ.*

1. ARISE, O King of grace, arise,
   And enter to thy rest;
   Behold, thy church, with longing eyes,
   Waits to be owned and blest.

2. Enter with all thy glorious train,
   Thy Spirit and thy Word;
   All that the ark did once contain
   Could no such grace afford.

3. Here, mighty God, accept our vows;
   Here let thy praise be spread;
   Bless the provisions of thy house,
   And fill thy poor with bread.

4. Here let the Son of David reign,
   Let God's Anointed shine:
   Justice and truth his court maintain,
   With love and power divine.

5. Here let him hold a lasting throne;
   And, as his kingdom grows,
   Fresh honors shall adorn his crown,
   And shame confound his foes.

9. *The everlasting Song.*

1. EARTH has engrossed my love too long:
   'Tis time I lift my eyes
   Upward, dear Father, to thy throne,
   And to my native skies.

2. Seraphs, with elevated strains,
   Circle the throne around;
   And move and charm the starry plains
   With an immortal sound.

3. Jesus, the Lord, their harps employs,
   Jesus, thy love they sing;
   Jesus, the life of all our joys,
   Sounds sweet from every string.

4. Now let me mount and join their song;
   And be an angel too;
   My hand, my heart, my ear, my tongue,
   Here's joyful work for you.

5. I would begin the music here,
   And so my soul should rise;
   Oh for some heavenly notes to bear
   My passions to the skies!

6. There ye that love my Saviour sit,
   There I would fain have place,
   Among your thrones, or at your feet,
   So I might see his face.

HEPHER. 11s.   GERMAN.

1. Delay not, delay not, O sinner, draw near, The waters of life are now flow-ing for thee; No price is de-mand-ed, the Sa-viour is here; Re-demp-tion is purchased, sal-va-tion is free.

10.   *Dangers of Delay.*

1. DELAY not, delay not, O sinner draw near,
   The waters of life are now flowing for thee;
   No price is demanded, the Saviour is here;
   Redemption is purchased, salvation is free.

2. Delay not, delay not, why longer abuse
   The love and compassion of Jesus thy God?
   A fountain is open, how canst thou refuse
   To wash and be cleansed in his pardoning blood?

3. Delay not, delay not, O sinner, to come,
   For Mercy still lingers and calls thee to-day:
   Her voice is not heard in the vale of the tomb;
   Her message unheeded will soon pass away.

4. Delay not, delay not, the Spirit of grace
   Long grieved and resisted may take his sad flight,
   And leave thee in darkness to finish thy race,
   To sink in the vale of eternity's night!

5. Delay not, delay not, the hour is at hand,
   The earth shall dissolve, and the heavens shall fade;
   The dead, small and great, in the judgment shall stand;
   What power then, O sinner, will lend thee its aid!

11. *Promises.*

1. How firm a foundation, ye saints of the Lord,
Is laid for your faith in his excellent word;
What more can he say than to you he hath said—
Who unto the Saviour for refuge have fled.

2. Fear not, I am with thee, oh! be not dismayed;
. For I am thy God, and will still give thee aid:
I'll strengthen thee, help thee, and cause thee to stand,
Upheld by my righteous, omnipotent hand.

3. When through the deep waters I call thee to go,
The rivers of sorrow shall not overflow;
For I will be with thee, thy trials to bless,
And sanctify to thee thy deepest distress.

4. When through fiery trials thy pathway shall lie,
My grace, all sufficient, shall be thy supply,
The flame shall not hurt thee; I only design
Thy dross to consume, and thy gold to refine.

5. E'en down to old age all my people shall prove
My sovereign, eternal, unchangeable love;
And then, when gray hairs shall their temples adorn,
Like lambs they shall still in My bosom be borne.

6. The soul that on Jesus hath leaned for repose,
I will not—I will not desert to his foes:
That soul—though all hell should endeavor to shake,
I'll never—no never—no never forsake!

12. *Our Shepherd.*

1. THE Lord is my Shepherd, no want shall I know;
I feed in green pastures, safe folded to rest;
He leadeth my soul where the still waters flow,
Restores me when wandering, redeems when oppressed.

2. Through the valley and shadow of death though I stray,
Since Thou art my Guardian, no evil I fear;
Thy rod shall defend me, thy staff be my stay;
No harm can befall, with my Comforter near.

3. In the midst of affliction my table is spread;
With blessings unmeasured my cup runneth o'er;
With perfume and oil thou anointest my head;
O what shall I ask of thy providence more.

4. Let goodness and mercy, my bountiful God!
Still follow my steps till I meet thee above;
I seek—by the path which my forefathers trod,
Through the land of their sojourn—thy kingdom of love.

LIBNAH, 7s. Double.

FROM "SELAH." BY PERMISSION.

Je - sus, lov - er of my soul, Let me to thy bo - som fly,
While the bil - lows near me roll, While the tem - pest still is high:

Hide me, O my Sa - viour hide, Till the storm of life be past:

Safe in - to the ha - ven guide; O, re - ceive my soul at last.

13.   *Jesus the Refuge.*

1. JESUS, lover of my soul,
    Let me to thy bosom fly,
  While the billows near me roll,
    While the tempest still is high:
  Hide me, O my Saviour, hide,
    Till the storm of life be past:
  Safe into the haven guide;
    O, receive my soul at last.

2. Other refuge have I none,
    Hangs my helpless soul on thee;
  Leave ah! leave me not alone,
    Still support and comfort me:
  All my trust on thee is stayed,
    All my help from thee I bring?
  Cover my defenseless head
    With the shadow of thy wing.

3. Plenteous grace with thee is found;
    Grace to pardon all my sin: .
  Let the healing streams abound,
    Make and keep me pure within:
  Thou of life the fountain art;
    Freely let me take of thee:
  Spring thou up within my heart,
    Rise to all eternity.

14.   *Expostulation with Sinners.*

1. SINNERS, turn, why will ye die?
  God your Maker asks you why;
  God who did your being give,
  Made you with himself to live:
  He the fatal cause demands,
  Asks the work of his own hands;
  Why, ye thankless creatures, why
  Will ye cross his love, and die?

2. Sinners turn, why will ye die?
God your Saviour asks you why:
He who did your souls retrieve,
Died himself that ye might live;
Will you let him die in vain?
Crucify your Lord again?
Why, ye ransomed sinners, why
Will ye slight his grace, and die?

3. Sinners, turn, why will ye die?
God the Spirit asks you why;
Many a time with you He strove,
Wooed you to embrace His love
Will ye not His grace receive?
Will ye still refuse to live?
Why will ye for ever die,
O ye guilty sinners, why?

15. *The Redeemed in Heaven.*

1. WHO are these in bright array,
This exulting, happy throng,
Round the altar night and day,
Hymning one triumphant song?—
"Worthy is the Lamb, once slain,
Blessing, honor, glory, power,
Wisdom, riches, to obtain,
New dominion every hour."

2. These through fiery trials trod;
These from great affliction came;
Now, before the throne of God,
Sealed with his almighty name:
Clad in raiment pure and white,
Victor-palms in every hand,
Through their great Redeemer's might,
More than conquerors they stand.

3. Hunger, thirst, disease, unknown,
On immortal fruits they feed;
Them the Lamb, amidst the throne,
Shall to living fountains lead:
Joy and gladness banish sighs;
Perfect love dispels all fears;
And for ever from their eyes
God shall wipe away their tears.

16. *Portion with the People of God*

1. PEOPLE of the living God,
I have sought the world around,
Paths of sin and sorrow trod,

Peace and comfort no where found;
Now to you my spirit turns,
Turns a fugitive unblest;
Brethren, where your altar burns,
O! receive me into rest.

2. Lonely I no longer roam,
Like the cloud, the wind, the wave;
Where you dwell shall be my home.
Where you die shall be my grave :
Mine the God whom you adore;
Your Redeemer shall be mine;
Earth can fill my soul no more,
Every idol I resign.

17. *Praise of the Redeemed in Heaven.*

1. HIGH in yonder realms of light,
Dwell the raptured saints above,
Far beyond our feeble sight,
Happy in Immanuel's love:
Pilgrims in this vale of tears,
Once they knew like us below,
Gloomy doubts, distressing fears,
Torturing pain, and heavy woe.

2. Oft the big unbidden tear,
Stealing down the furrowed cheek,
Told in eloquence sincere,
Tales of woe they could not speak.
But these days of weeping o'er,
Past this scene of toil and pain,
They shall feel distress no more,
Never, never weep again.

3. Mid the chorus of the skies,
Mid the angelic lyres above,
Hark! their songs melodious rise,
Songs of praise to Jesus' love.
Happy spirits, ye are fled,
Where no grief can entrance find:
Lulled to rest the aching head,
Soothed the anguish of the mind.

4. All is tranquil and serene,
Calm and undisturbed repose,
There no cloud can intervene,
There no angry tempest blows.
Every tear is wiped away,
Sighs no more shall heave the breast,
Night is lost in endless day,
Sorrow, in eternal rest.

HANDEL.

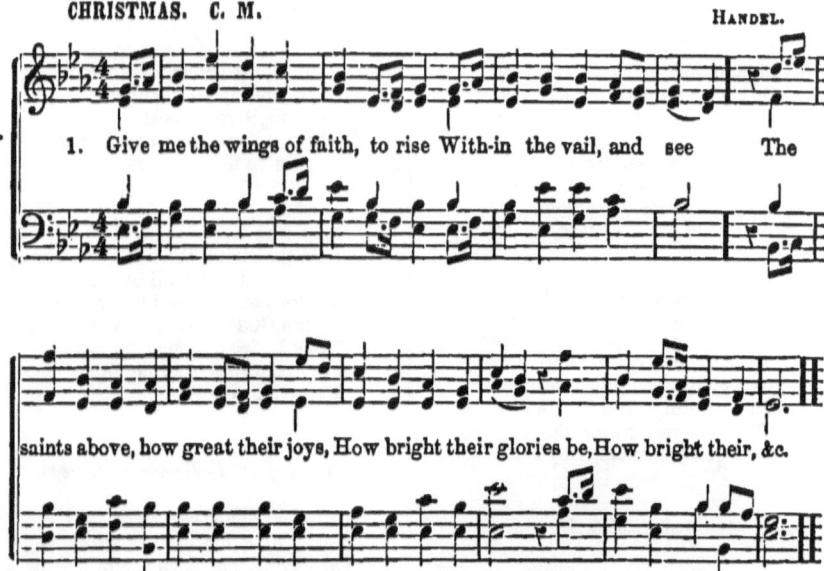

1. Give me the wings of faith, to rise With-in the vail, and see The

saints above, how great their joys, How bright their glories be, How bright their, &c.

18. *The Examples of Christ and the Saints.*

1. GIVE me the wings of faith, to rise
    Within the vail, and see
The saints above, how great their joys,
. How bright their glories be!

2. Once they were mourning here below,
    And wet their couch with tears;
They wrestled hard, as we do now,
    With sins, and doubts, and fears.

3. I ask them, whence their vict'ry came?
    They, with united breath,
Ascribe their conquest to the Lamb,
    Their triumph, to his death.

4. They mark'd the footsteps that he trod,
    (His zeal inspired their breast:)
And, following their incarnate God,
    Possess'd the promis'd rest.

5. Our glorious Leader claims our praise
    For his own pattern given,
While the long cloud of witnesses
    Show the same path to heaven.

19. *The new Song to the Lamb*

1. BEHOLD the glories of the Lamb
    Amidst his Father's throne;
Prepare new honors for his name,
    And songs before unknown.

2. Let elders worship at his feet,
    The church adore around,
With vials full of odors sweet,
    And harps of sweeter sound.

3. Those are the prayers of all the saints,
    And these the hymns they raise:
Jesus is kind to our complaints;
    He loves to hear our praise.

4. Now to the Lamb, that once was slain,
    Be endless blessings paid;
Salvation, glory, joy, remain
    For ever on thy head.

5. Thou hast redeemed our souls with blood,
    Hast set the prisoner free,
Hast made us kings and priests to God,
    And we shall reign with thee.

20. *Protection from spiritual Enemies.*

1. ARISE, my soul, my joyful powers,
And triumph in my God;
Awake, my voice, and loud proclaim
His glorious grace abroad.

2. The arms of everlasting love
Beneath my soul he placed,
And on the Rock of Ages set
My slippery footsteps fast.

3. The city of my blest abode
Is walled around with grace;
Salvation for a bulwark stands
To shield the sacred place.

4. Arise, my soul; awake, my voice,
And tunes of pleasure sing;
Loud hallelujahs shall address
My Saviour and my King.

21. *Heaven in Prospect.*

1. ON Jordan's rugged banks I stand,
And cast a wishful eye
To Canaan's fair and happy land,
Where my possessions lie.

2. O the transporting, rapturous scene,
That rises to my sight!—
Sweet fields arrayed in living green,
And rivers of delight.

3. O'er all those wide-extended plains
Shines one eternal day;
There God the Son for ever reigns,
And scatters night away.

4. No chilling winds, nor poisonous breath,
Can reach that healthful shore;
Sickness and sorrow, pain and death,
Are felt and feared no more.

5. When shall I reach that happy place,
And be for ever blest?
When shall I see my Father's face,
And in his bosom rest?

22. *Praise from all Nature.*

1. BEGIN the high, celestial strain,
My raptured soul, and sing
A sacred hymn of grateful praise.
To heaven's almighty King.

2. Ye curling fountains, as ye roll
Your silver waves along,
Repeat to all your verdant shores
The subject of the song.

3. Bear it, ye breezes, on your wings,
To distant climes away,
And round the wide-extended world
The lofty theme convey.

4. Take up the burden of his name,
Ye clouds, as ye arise,
To deck with gold the opening morn,
Or shade the evening skies.

5. While we, with sacred rapture fired,
The blest Creator sing,
And chant our consecrated lays
To heaven's eternal King.

23. *The Glory of the latter Day.*

1. BEHOLD, the mountain of the Lord,
In latter days, shall rise
Above the mountains and the hills,
And draw the wondering eyes.

2. To this the joyful nations round,
All tribes and tongues, shall flow:
"Up to the hill of God," they say,
"And to his house, we'll go."

3. The beam that shines on Zion's hill
Shall lighten every land:
The King who reigns in Zion's towers
Shall all the world command.

4. No strife shall vex Messiah's reign,
Or mar the peaceful years;
To ploughshares men shall beat their swords,
To pruning-hooks their spears.

5. Come then, O, come from every land,
To worship at his shrine;
And, walking in the light of God,
With holy beauty shine.

Doxology.

LET God the Father and the Son,
And Spirit be adored,
Where there are works to make him known,
Or saints to love the Lord.

HOW CALM. C. L. M.

Gentle—Legato.

1. How calm and beau-ti-ful the morn, That gilds the sa-cred tomb, Where Christ the cru-ci-fied was borne, And veiled in mid-night gloom! O weep no more the Saviour slain, The Lord is risen, he lives a-gain.

24. *The Sepulchre on Sabbath Morning.*

1. How calm and beautiful the morn,
   That gilds the sacred tomb,
   Where Christ the crucified was borne,
   And veiled in midnight gloom!
   O weep no more the Saviour slain,
   The Lord is risen, he lives again.

2. Ye mourning saints, dry every tear
   For your departed Lord,
   "Behold the place, he is not here!"
   The tomb is all unbarr'd:
   The gates of death were closed in vain,
   The Lord is risen, he lives again.

3. Now cheerful to the house of prayer,
   Your early footsteps bend;
   The Saviour will himself be there,
   Your Advocate and Friend:
   Once by the law, your hopes were slain,
   But now in Christ, ye live again

4. How tranquil now the rising day!
   'Tis Jesus still appears,
   A risen Lord, to chase away
   Your unbelieving fears:
   O weep no more your comforts slain,
   The Lord is risen, he lives again.

5. And when the shades of evening fall,
   When life's last hour draws nigh,
   If Jesus shines upon the soul,
   How blissful then to die!
   Since he hath risen that once was slain,
   Ye die in Christ to live again.

25.   *Christ's Agony.*

1. He knelt, the Saviour knelt and prayed,
   When but his Father's eye
   Looked thro' the lonely garden's shade,
   On that dread agony;
   The Lord of all above, beneath,
   Was bowed with sorrow unto death.

2. The sun set in a fearful hour,
   The skies might well grow dim,
When this mortality had power
So to o'ershadow him!
That he who gave man's breath, might
   know
The very depths of human woe.

3. He knew them all; the doubt, the
   strife,
The faint, perplexing dread,
The mists that hang o'er parting life,
All darkened round his head;
And the Deliverer knelt to pray;
Yet passed it not, that cup, away.

4. It passed not, though the stormy wave
   Had sunk beneath his tread;
It passed not, though to him the
   grave
Had yielded up its dead.
But there was sent him from on high,
A gift of strength for man to die.

5. And was his mortal hour beset
   With anguish and dismay?
How may *we* meet our conflict yet,
In the dark, narrow way?
How but through him, that path who
   trod?
Save or we perish, Son of God.

MANOAH. C. M.
QUICK, BUT GENTLE.

SEE GREATOREX'S COLL.

1. How glo-rious is the land we seek, A land with-out a tomb,

An ev - er - last - ing rest - ing-place, A sure and qui - et home.

26. *Heaven.*

1. How glorious is the land we seek,
   A land without a tomb,
An everlasting-resting place,
   A sure and quiet home.

2. Far sunnier than the hills of time
   Are its eternal hills;
Far fresher than the rills of earth
   Are its eternal rills.

3. No blight can fall upon its flowers,
   No darkness fill its air,
It has a day for ever bright,
   For Christ, its sun, is there.

4. O Sun of love, and peace, arise,
   Thy light upon us beam;
For all this life is but a sleep,
   And all this world a dream.

27. *Love to God.*

1. GOD only is the creature's home,
   Though long and rough the road;
Yet nothing less can satisfy
   The love that longs for God.

2. O utter but the name of God
   Down in your heart of hearts,
And see how from the world at once
   All tempting light departs.

3. A trusting heart, a yearning eye,
   Can win their way above;
If mountains can be moved by faith,
   Is there less power in love?

4. How little of that road, my soul!
   How little hast thou gone!
Take heart, and let the thought of God
   Allure thee further on.

SPAULDING. L. M.*   FAWCET—ARRANGED.

1. Just as   I   am, with-out one plea, Save that thy blood was shed for
me, And that thou bid'st me come to Thee! O Lamb of God, I come, I come!

* See also Hamburg. Repeat a portion of the last line, when it is short, as shown in the
first stanza of each hymn. See "Just as I am." p. 290.

28.   *John vi. 37.*

1. JUST as I am, without one plea,
   Save that thy blood was shed for me,
   And that thou bidst me come to Thee,
   O, Lamb of God, I come! [I come!]

2. Just as I am,, and waiting not
   To rid my soul of one dark blot, [spot,
   To Thee, whose blood can cleanse each
   O Lamb of God, I come.

3. Just as I am, though tossed about
   With many a conflict, many a doubt,
   With fears within and foes without,
   O Lamb of God, I come.

4. Just as I am, poor, wretched, blind,
   Sight, riches, healing of the mind,
   Yea, all I need, in Thee to find,
   O Lamb of God, I come.

5. Just as I am—Thou wilt receive,
   Wilt welcome, pardon, cleanse, relieve,
   Because thy promise I believe—
   O Lamb of God, I come.

6. Just as I am—Thy love unknown
   Has broken every barrier down ;
   Now to be thine, yea, thine alone—
   O Lamb of God, I come.

29.   *Christ's Intercession.*

1. O THOU, the contrite sinner's Friend!
   Who loving, lov'st them to the end,
   On this alone my hopes depend,
   That Thou wilt plead for me. [for me.]

2. When weary in the Christian race,
   Far off appears my resting place,
   And, fainting, I mistrust Thy grace,
   Then, Saviour, plead for me.

3. When Satan, by my sins made bold,
   Strives from Thy cross to loose my hold.
   Then with thy pitying arms enfold,
   And plead, oh! plead for me.

4. And when my dying hour draws near,
   Darkened with anguish, guilt, and fear,
   Then to my fainting sight appear,
   Pleading in heaven for me.

5. When the full light of heavenly day,
   Reveals my sins in dread array,
   Say Thou hast washed them all away—
   O! say thou plead'st for me.

30.   *Acquiescence.*

1. MY God, my Father, while I stray,
   Far from my home, on life's rough way
   Oh! teach me from my heart to say,
   "Thy will be done, [Thy will be done."]

2 If Thou should'st call me to resign
What most I prize—it ne'er was mine;
I only yield Thee what was Thine;
"Thy will be done."

3. E'en if again I ne'er should see
The friend more dear than life to me,
Ere long we both shall be with Thee;
"Thy will be done."

4. Should pining sickness waste away
My life in premature decay,
My Father, still I strive to say,
"Thy will be done."

5. If but my fainting heart be blest
With Thy sweet Spirit for its guest,
My God, to Thee I leave the rest—
"Thy will be done."

6. Renew my will from day to day,
Blend it with Thine, and take away
All that now makes it hard to say,
"Thy will be done."

7. Then when on earth I breathe no more
The prayer oft mixed with tears before,
I'll sing upon a happier shore,
"Thy will be done."

31.   *Clinging to God.*

1. THOUGH far from home, fatigued, opprest,
Here we have found a place of rest;
As exiles still, yet not unblest,
   Because we cling to Thee, [to Thee.]

2. What though the world deceitful prove,
And earthly friends and hopes remove,
With patient, uncomplaining love,
   Still can we cling to Thee.

3. Though oft we seem to tread alone
Life's dreary waste with thorns o'er-
   grown,
Thy voice of love, in gentlest tone,
   Whispers, "Still cling to Me."

4. Though faith and hope are often tried,
We ask not, need not, aught beside,
So safe, so calm, so satisfied
   The souls that cling to Thee.

32.   • *The Grave.*

1. THERE is a calm for those who weep,
A rest for weary pilgrims found:
They softly lie, and sweetly sleep,
   Low in the ground,[low in the ground.]

2. The storm that sweeps the wintry sky
No more disturbs their deep repose,
Than summer evening's latest sigh,
   That shuts the rose.

3. Then, traveler, in the vale of tears,
To realms of everlasting light,
Through time's dark wilderness of years,
   Pursue thy flight.

4. Thy soul, renewed by grace divine,
In God's own image, freed from clay,
In heaven's eternal sphere shall shine,
   A star of day.

33.   *Consecration in View of the Cross.*

1. WHEN I survey the wondrous cross,
On which the Prince of glory died,
My richest gain I count but loss,
   And pour contempt on all my pride.

2. Forbid it, Lord, that I should boast,
Save in the death of Christ, my God;
All the vain things that charm me most,
   I sacrifice them to his blood.

3. See from his head, his hands, his feet,
Sorrow and love flow mingled down:
Did e'er such love and sorrow meet,
   Or thorns compose so rich a crown?

4. Were the whole realm of nature mine,
That were a present far too small;
Love so amazing, so divine,
   Demands my soul, my life, my all.

34.   *The Indwelling of God desired.*

1. COME, gracious Lord, descend and dwell
By faith and love, in every breast;
Then shall we know, and taste, and feel
   The joys that can not be expressed.

2. Come, fill our hearts with inward
   strength,
Make our enlargéd souls possess,
And learn the height, and breadth, and
   length
Of thine eternal love and grace.

3. Now to the God whose power can do
More than our thoughts and wishes
   know,
Be everlasting honors done,
   By all the church, through Christ, his
   Son.

WATCHMAN. S. M.

LEACH.

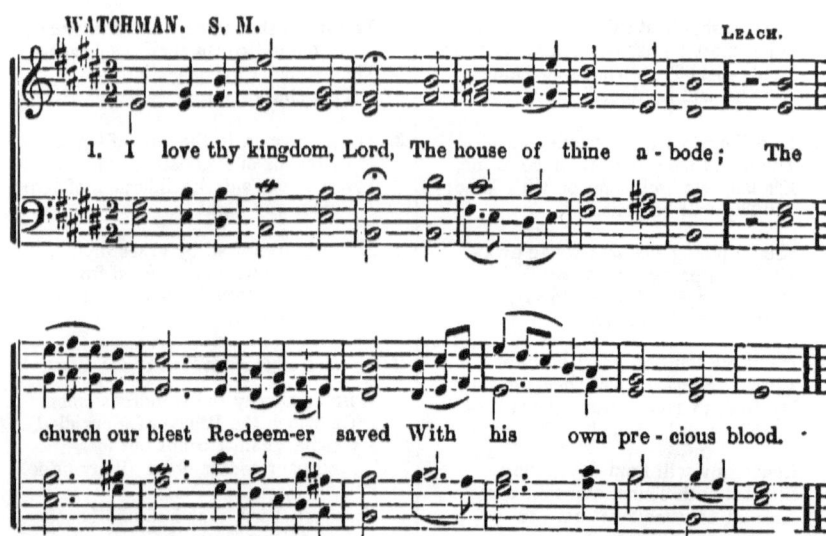

1. I love thy kingdom, Lord, The house of thine a-bode; The church our blest Re-deem-er saved With his own pre-cious blood.

35.   *Love to the Church.*

1. I LOVE thy kingdom, Lord,
    The house of thine abode,
The church our blest Redeemer saved
    With his own precious blood.

[2. I love thy church, O God,
    Her walls before thee stand
Dear as the apple of thine eye,
    And graven on thy hand.]

3. If e'er to bless thy sons
    My voice or hands deny,
These hands let useful skill forsake,
    This voice in silence die.

4. If e'er my heart forget
    Her welfare or her woe,
Let every joy this heart forsake,
    And every grief o'erflow.

5. For her my tears shall fall,
    For her my prayers ascend:
To her my cares and toils be given,
    Till toils and cares shall end.

6. Beyond my highest joy
    I prize her heavenly ways;
Her sweet communion, solemn vows,
    Her hymns of love and praise.

36.   *Confession and Forgiveness.*

1. OH, blessed souls are they,
    Whose sins are covered o'er;
Divinely blest, to whom the Lord
    Imputes their guilt no more.

2. They mourn their follies past,
    And keep their hearts with care;
Their lips and lives without deceit,
    Shall prove their faith sincere

3. While I concealed my guilt,
    I felt the fest'ring wound;
Till I confessed my sins to thee,
    And ready pardon found.

4. Let sinners learn to pray,
    Let saints keep near the throne;
Our help, in times of deep distress,
    Is found in God alone.

37.   *Praise for Mercies, Spiritual and
         Temporal.*

1. OH bless the Lord my soul;
    Let all within me join
To bless his great and holy name,
    Whose favors are divine.

2. Oh bless the Lord, my soul,
    Nor let his mercies lie
Forgotten in unthankfulness,
    And without praises die.

3. 'Tis he forgives thy sins,
   'Tis he relieves thy pain ;
   'Tis he that heals thy sicknesses,
   And makes thee young again.

4. He crowns thy life with love
   When ransomed from the grave:
   He that redeemed my soul from hell
   Hath sovereign power to save.

5. He fills the poor with good,
   He gives the sufferers rest :
   The Lord hath judgments for the proud,
   And justice for th' oppressed.

6. Oh bless the Lord, my soul ;
   Let all within me join
   To bless his great and holy name,
   Whose favors are divine.

38. *Committing the Soul to Jesus.*

1. MY spirit on thy care
   Blest Saviour, I recline,
   Thou wilt not leave me to despair :
   For thou art Love divine.

2. In thee I place my trust,
   On thee I calmly rest :
   I know thee good, I know thee just,
   And count thy choice the best.

3. Whate'er events betide,
   Thy will they all perform,
   Safe in thy breast, my head I hide,
   Nor fear the coming storm.

4. Let good or ill befall,
   It must be good for me,
   Secure in having thee in all,
   And having all in thee.

39. *Trust in God.*

1. "MY times are in thy hand ;"
   My God I'd have them there,
   My life, my friends, my soul, I leave
   Entirely to thy care.

2. "My times are in thy hand ;"
   Whatever they may, be,
   Pleasing or painful, dark or bright,
   As best they seem to thee.

3. "My times are in thy hand," |
   Why should I doubt or fear?
   My Father's hand will never cause
   A child a needless tear.

4. "My times are in thy hand,"
   I'll always trust in thee,
   And after death at thy right hand
   I shall for ever be.

40. *Christ our Shepherd.*

1. JESUS my Shepherd is,
   'Twas He that loved my soul,
   'Twas He that washed me in His blood,
   'Twas He that made me whole.

2. 'Twas He that sought the lost,
   That found the wandering sheep :
   'Twas He that brought me to the fold,
   'Tis He that still doth keep.

3. I was a wandering sheep,
   I would not be controlled ;
   But now I love the Shepherd's voice,
   I love, I love the fold !

4. I was a wayward child,
   I once preferred to roam ;
   But now I love my Father's voice,
   I love, I love his home !

41. *Divine Condescension.*

1. O LORD, our heavenly King,
   Thy name is all divine ;
   Thy glories round the earth are spread,
   And o'er the heavens they shine.

2. Lord, what is worthless man,
   That thou should'st love him so ?
   Next to thine angels is he placed,
   And lord of all below.

3. How rich thy bounties are,
   How wondrous are thy ways,
   That, from the dust, thy power should frame
   A monument of praise !

42. *Ark of Safety*

1. O, CEASE, my wandering soul,
   On restless wing to roam ;
   All this wide world, to either pole,
   Has not for thee a home.

2. Behold the ark of God ;
   Behold the open door ;
   O, haste to gain that dear abode,
   And rove, my soul, no more.

3. There safe thou shalt abide,
   There sweet shall be thy rest,
   And every longing satisfied,
   With full salvation blest.

Doxology.

LET God the Father, Son,
And Spirit be adored,
Where there are works to make him known
Or saints to love the Lord.

O WEEP NOT. C. M. D.*   ARR. FROM "SPIRITUAL SONG S."

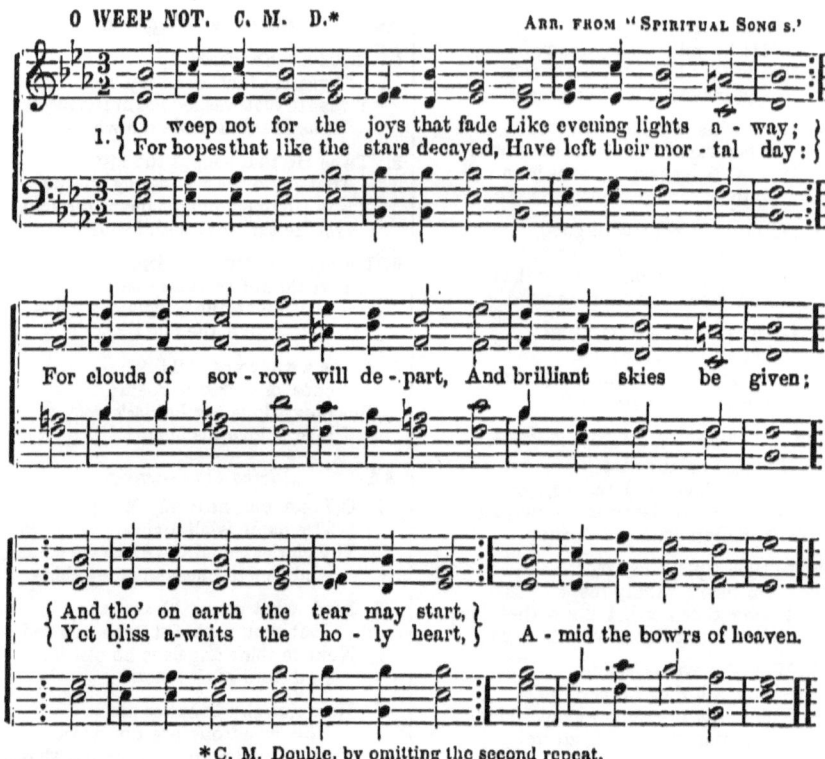

1. { O weep not for the joys that fade Like evening lights a - way; }
{ For hopes that like the stars decayed, Have left their mor - tal day: }

For clouds of sor - row will de - part, And brilliant skies be given;

{ And tho' on earth the tear may start, }
{ Yet bliss a-waits the ho - ly heart, } A - mid the bow'rs of heaven.

*C. M. Double, by omitting the second repeat.

43. "The Things which are not seen are Eternal."

1. O! WEEP not for the joys that fade
  Like evening lights away;
For hopes that like the stars decayed
  Have left their mortal day:
For clouds of sorrow will depart,
  And brilliant skies be given;
And tho' on earth the tear may start,
  Yet bliss awaits the holy heart,
  Amid the bowers of heaven.

2. O weep not for the joys that pass
  Into the lonely grave,
As breezes sweep the withered grass,
  Along the restless wave:
For, tho' thy pleasure may depart,
  And mournful days be given,
And lonely though on earth thou art,
  Yet bliss awaits the holy heart,
  When friends rejoice in heaven.

44.   *A Funeral*

1. I HEAR the deep-toned solemn bell
  Its mournful music pour,
Some spirit now hath bid farewell,
  To this terrestial shore,
And taken a returnless flight,
  Beyond the silent tomb
Hath risen to heaven's beatic height,
Or sunk to hell's eternal night,
  Where hope can never come

2. I listen to each dying tone,
  And mark each fearful pause;
Reflection, while I sit alone,
  · Her solemn inference draws:
How fast the precious moments roll,
  How soon the hour will come!
Ah, soon for me that bell may toll,
  Where then will my departed soul
  Find its eternal home!

45. *The Man of Sorrows.*

1. A PILGRIM through this lonely world,
   The blesséd Saviour passed :
   A mourner all his life was He,
   A dying Lamb at last.
2. That tender heart that felt for all,
   For all its life-blood gave ;
   It found on earth no resting-place,
   Save only in the grave.

3. Such was our Lord ; and shall we fear
   The cross, with all its scorn ?
   Or love a faithless, evil world,
   That wreathed his brow with thorn ?
4. No ; facing all its frowns or smiles,
   Like Him, obedient still,
   We homeward press, through storm or
   To Zion's blessed hill.   [calm,

46.   *Charity.*

1. BLEST is the man whose softening heart
   Can feel another's pain ;
   To whom the supplicating eye
   Was never raised in vain :
2. Who spreads his kind, supporting arms
   To every child of grief ;
   While secret bounty largely flows
   To bring unsought relief.

3. To gentle offices of love
   His feet are never slow ;
   He views, through mercy's melting eye,
   A brother in a foe.
4. He from the bosom of his God
   Shall present peace receive ;
   And when he kneels before the throne,
   His trembling soul shall live.

47. *The cheering Prospect of Heaven.*

1. THERE is a land of pure delight,
   Where saints immortal reign ;
   Infinite day excludes the night,
   And pleasures banish pain.
2. There, everlasting spring abides,
   And never-withering flowers ;
   Death, like a narrow sea, divides
   This heavenly land from ours.

3. Sweet fields, beyond the swelling flood,
   Stand dressed in living green ;
   So to the Jews old Canaan stood,
   While Jordan rolled between.
4. But timorous mortals start and shrink
   To cross this narrow sea ;
   And linger, shivering on the brink,
   And fear to launch away.

5. Oh! could we make our doubts remove,
   Those gloomy doubts that rise,
   And see the Canaan, that we love,
   With unbeclouded eyes ;—
6. Could we but climb where Moses stood,
   And view the landscape o'er,—
   Not Jordan's stream, nor death's cold
   flood,
   Should fright us from the shore.

48.   *The Earnest of Heaven.*

1. WHY should the children of a King
   Go mourning all their days ?
   Great Comforter, descend, and bring
   Some tokens of thy grace.
2. Dost thou not dwell in all thy saints,
   And seal them heirs of heaven ?
   When wilt thou banish my complaints,
   And show my sins forgiven ?

3. Assure my conscience of her part
   In my Redeemer's blood,
   And bear thy witness, with my heart,
   That I am born of God.
4. Thou art the earnest of his love,
   The pledge of joys to come ;
   And thy soft wings, celestial Dove,
   Will safely bear me home.

49. *The Church in the Wilderness.*

1. IN the waste, howling wilderness
   The church is wandering still,
   Because we would not onward press
   When close to Zion's hill.

2. Back to the faithless world we turned,
   And far along the wild,
   With labor lost, and sorrow earned,
   Our steps have been beguiled.

3. Yet full before us, all the while,
   The shadowing pillar stays,
   The living waters brightly smile,
   Th' eternal turrets blaze—

4. Yet heaven is raining angel's bread
   To be our daily food,
   And fresh, as when it first was shed,
   Springs forth the Saviour's blood.

5. When in thy love, and Israel's sin,
   We read our story true,
   May we not all too late begin
   To form our hopes anew.

ST. ANN'S.* C. M.

BOLD AND JOYOUS.

DR. CROFT.

1. The Lord our God is full of might, The winds o - bey his will; .

He speaks, and in his heavenly height, The roll - ing sun stands still.

* See also the tune on the opposite page.

50. *The Power of God.*

1. THE Lord our God is full of might,
   The winds obey his will;
   He speaks, and in his heavenly height,
   The rolling sun stands still.

2. Rebel, ye waves, and o'er the land
   With threatening aspect roar:
   The Lord uplifts his awful hand,
   And chains you to the shore.

3. Howl, winds of night, your force com-
       bine:
   Without his high behest,
   Ye shall not, in the mountain pine,
   Disturb the sparrow's nest.

4. His voice sublime is heard afar,
   In distant peals it dies;
   He yokes the whirlwinds to his car,
   And sweeps the howling skies.

5. Ye nations, bend—in reverence bend;
   Ye monarchs, wait his nod;
   And bid the choral song ascend
   To celebrate your God.

51. *God the Creator.*

1. ETERNAL Wisdom, Thee we praise,
   Thee the creation sings;
   With thy loved name, rocks, hills, and
       seas,
   And heaven's high palace rings.

2. Thy hand—how wide it spread the sky!
   How glorious to behold!
   Tinged with a blue of heavenly dye,
   And starred with sparkling gold.

3. Thy glories blaze all nature round,
   And strike the gazing sight,
   Through skies, and seas, and solid
       ground,
   With terror and delight.

4. Infinite strength and equal skill,
   Shine through the worlds abroad;
   Our souls with vast amazement fill,
   And speak the builder—God.

5. But still the wonders of thy grace
   Our softer passions move;
   Pity divine in Jesus' face,
   We see, adore, and love.

MAESTOSO.

1. The Lord our God is full of might, The winds o-bey his will; He speaks, and in his heaven-ly height, The roll-ing sun stands still, The roll-ing sun stands still.

52. *Prayer for the Enlargement of the Church.*

1. SHINE, mighty God, on Zion shine,
   With beams of heavenly grace;
   Reveal thy power through every land,
   And show thy smiling face.

2. When shall thy name, from shore to shore,
   Sound through the earth abroad,
   And distant nations know and love
   Their Saviour and their God?

3. Sing to the Lord, ye distant lands;
   Sing loud, with joyful voice;
   Let every tongue exalt his praise,
   And every heart rejoice.

4 Earth shall obey his high command,
   And yield her full increase;
   And God will crown each chosen land
   With fruitfulness and peace.

53.   *A Song of Praise.*

1 IN God's own house pronounce his praise,
   His grace he there reveals;
   To heaven your joy and wonder raise,
   For there his glory dwells.

2. Let all your sacred passions move,
   While you rehearse his deeds;
   But the great work of saving love,
   Your highest praise exceeds.

3. All that have motion, life, and breath,
   Proclaim your Maker blest;
   Yet, when my voice expires in death,
   My soul shall praise him best.

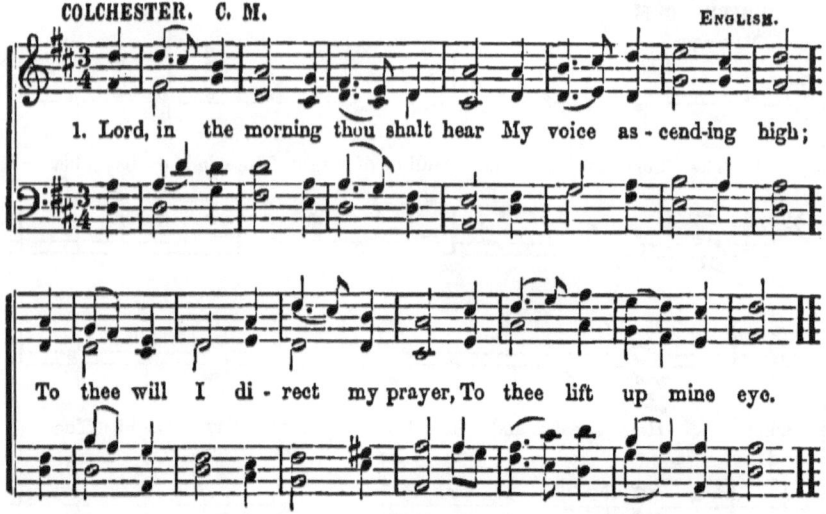

COLCHESTER. C. M.   ENGLISH.

1. Lord, in the morning thou shalt hear My voice as-cend-ing high;

To thee will I di - rect my prayer, To thee lift up mine eye.

---

54. *For the Lord's Day Morning.*

1. LORD, in the morning thou shalt hear
My voice ascending high;
To thee will I direct my prayer,
To thee lift up mine eye:

2. Up to the hills where Christ is gone
To plead for all his saints,
Presenting at his Father's throne
Our songs and our complaints.

3. Thou art a God before whose sight
The wicked shall not stand;
Sinners shall ne'er be thy delight,
Nor dwell at thy right hand.

4. But to thy house will I resort,
To taste thy mercies there;
I will frequent thy holy court,
And worship in thy fear.

5. Oh may the Spirit guide my feet
In ways of righteousness;
Make every path of duty straight
And plain before my face.

55.   *Going to Church.*

1. How did my heart rejoice to hear
My friends devoutly say,
"In Zion let us all appear,
And keep the solemn day!"

2. I love her gates, I love the road!
The church, adorned with grace,
Stands like a palace built for God,
To show his milder face.

3. Up to her courts, with joys unknown,
The holy tribes repair;
The Son of David holds his throne,
And sits in judgment there.

4. He hears our praises and complaints;
And while his awful voice
Divides the sinners from the saints,
We tremble, and rejoice!

5. Peace be within this sacred place
And joy a constant guest!
With holy gifts and heavenly grace
Be her attendants blest.

6. My soul shall pray for Zion still
While life or breath remains;
Here my best friends, my kindred, dwell,
Here God, my Saviour, reigns.

56.   *God Present in his Churches.*

1. MY soul, how lovely is the place
To which thy God resorts!
'Tis heaven to see his smiling face,
Though in his earthly courts.

2. With his rich gifts the heavenly Dove
Descends, and fills the place;
While Christ reveals his wondrous love,
And sheds abroad his grace.

3. My heart and flesh cry out for Thee,
While far from thine abode;
When shall I tread thy courts, and see
My Saviour and my God?

4. To sit one day beneath thine eye,
And hear thy gracious voice,
Exceeds a whole eternity
Employed in carnal joys.

5. Lord! at thy threshold I would wait,
While Jesus is within,
Rather than fill a throne of state,
Or live in tents of sin.

57. *Joy of Worship.*

1. WITH joy we hail the sacred day
Which God has called his own;
With joy the summons we obey,
To worship at his throne.

2. Thy chosen temple, Lord, how fair!
Where willing vot'ries throng
To breathe the humble, fervent prayer,
And pour the choral song.

3. Spirit of grace, Oh, deign to dwell
Within thy church below;
Make her in holiness excel,
With pure devotion glow.

4. Let peace within her walls be found;
Let all her sons unite
To spread, with grateful zeal, around,
Her clear and shining light.

5. Great God! we hail the sacred day
Which thou hast called thine own;
With joy the summons we obey,
To worship at thy throne.

58. *The Glory of Redemption.*

1. FATHER, how wide thy glory shines!
How high thy wonders rise!
Known through the earth by thousand signs,
By thousands through the skies.

2. But when we view thy strange design
To save rebellious worms,
Where justice and compassion join
In their divinest forms:

3. Here the whole Deity is known,
Nor dares a creature guess

Which of the glories brightest shone—
The justice or the grace.

4. Now the full glories of the Lamb
Adorn the heavenly plains;
Bright seraphs learn Immanuel's name,
And try their choicest strains.

5. Oh, may I bear some humble part
In that immortal song!
Wonder and joy shall tune my heart,
And love command my tongue.

59. *The Lamb of God worshiped.*

1. COME, let us join our cheerful songs
With angels round the throne;
Ten thousand thousand are their tongues,
But all their joys are one.

2. "Worthy the Lamb that died," they cry,
"To be exalted thus:"
"Worthy the Lamb," our lips reply,
"For he was slain for us."

3. Jesus is worthy to receive
Honor and power divine;
And blessings, more than we can give,
Be, Lord, forever thine.

4. Let all that dwell above the sky,
And air, and earth, and seas,
Conspire to lift thy glories high,
And speak thy endless praise.

5. The whole creation join in one
To bless the sacred name
Of Him who sits upon the throne,
And to adore the Lamb.

60. *Psalm 96.*

1. SING to the Lord Jehovah's name,
And in his strength rejoice;
When his salvation is our theme,
Exalted be our voice.

2. With thanks approach his awful sight,
And psalms of honor sing;
The Lord's a God of boundless might,
The whole creation's King.

3. Earth, with its caverns dark and deep,
Lies in his spacious hand;
He fixed the seas what bounds to keep,
And where the hills must stand.

4. Come, and with humble souls adore:
Come, kneel before his face;
Oh may the creatures of his power
Be children of his grace!

BYEFIELD. C. M.   FROM "PSALMODIST." BY PERMISSION.

1. Prayer is the soul's sincere de-sire, Uttered or un-ex-pressed;

The mo-tion of a hid-den fire, That trembles in the breast.

---

61. *The Nature of Prayer.*

1. PRAYER is the soul's sincere desire,
   Uttered or unexpressed;
   The motion of a hidden fire
   That trembles in the breast.

2. Prayer is the burden of a sigh,
   The falling of a tear,
   The upward glancing of an eye
   When none but God is near.

3. Prayer is the simplest form of speech
   That infant lips can try;
   Prayer the sublimest strains that reach
   The Majesty on high.

4. Prayer is the Christian's vital breath,
   The Christian's native air,
   His watchword at the gates of death,
   He enters heaven with prayer.

5. Prayer is the contrite sinner's voice
   Returning from his ways;
   While angels in their songs rejoice,
   And cry, "Behold, he prays!"

6. In prayer on earth, the saints are one—
   They're one in word and mind
   When, with the Father and the Son,
   Sweet fellowship they find.

7. O Thou, by whom we come to God,
   The life, the truth, the way,
   The path of prayer thyself hast trod—
   Lord teach us how to pray.

62. *"Watch and Pray."*

1. THE Saviour bids thee watch and pray
   Through life's momentous hour,
   And grants the Spirit's quickening ray
   To those who seek his power.

2. The Saviour bids thee watch and pray,
   Maintain a warrior's strife;
   O Christian! hear his voice to-day:
   Obedience is thy life.

3. The Saviour bids thee watch and pray,
   For soon the hour will come
   That calls thee from the earth away
   To thy eternal home.

4. The Saviour bids thee watch and pray,
   O hearken to his voice,
   And follow where he leads the way,
   To heaven's eternal joys!

63. *In Distress Pleading with God.*

1. O, THAT I knew the secret place
   Where I might find my God!
   I'd spread my wants before his face,
   And pour my woes abroad.

2. I'd tell him how my sins arise,
What sorrows I sustain,
How grace decays, and comfort dies,
And leaves my heart in pain.

3. He knows what arguments I'd take
To wrestle with my God:
I'd plead for his own mercy's sake,
And for my Saviour's blood.

4. [My God will pity my complaints,
And heal my broken bones;
He takes the meaning of his saints,
The language of their groans.]

5. Arise, my soul, from deep distress,
And banish every fear;
He calls thee to his throne of grace,
To spread thy sorrows there.

64. *Retirement and Meditation.*

1. FAR from the world, O Lord, I flee,
From strife and tumult far;
From scenes where Satan wages still
His most successful war.

2. The calm retreat, the silent shade,
With prayer and praise agree;
And seem by thy sweet bounty made
For those who follow thee.

3. There, if thy Spirit touch the soul,
And grace her mean abode,
Oh, with what peace, and joy, and love,
She communes with her God!

4. Author and Guardian of my life,
Sweet Source of light divine,
And (all harmonious names in one)
My Saviour, Thou art mine.

5. What thanks I owe thee, and what love,
A boundless, endless store
Shall echo through the realms above
When time shall be no more.

65. *The Holy Scriptures.*

1. LADEN with guilt and full of fears,
I fly to Thee, my Lord;
And not a glimpse of hope appears,
But in thy written word.

2 The volume of my Father's grace
Does all my grief assuage;

Here I behold my Saviour's face
Almost in every page.

3. [This is the field where hidden lies,
The pearl, of price unknown;
That merchant is divinely wise
Who makes the pearl his own.]

4. Oh! may thy counsels, mighty God,
My roving feet command;
Nor I forsake the happy road
That leads to thy right hand.

66. *The Soul.*

1. WHAT is the thing of greatest price
The whole creation round?
That which was lost in paradise,
That which in Christ is found.

2. The soul of man—Jehovah's breath!
That keeps two worlds at strife;
Hell moves beneath to work its death,
Heaven stoops to give it life.

3. God, to reclaim it did not spare
His well-beloved Son;
Jesus, to save it deigned to bear
The sins of all in one.

4. And is this treasure borne below,
In earthly vessels frail?
Can none its utmost value know
Till flesh and spirit fail?

5. Then let us gather round the cross,
This knowledge to obtain,
Not by the soul's eternal loss,
But everlasting gain.

67. *The Chief and only Good.*

1. NOT all the good which earth bestows
Can fill the craving mind:
Its highest joys have mingled woes,
And leave a sting behind.

2. Should boundless wealth increase my store,
Can wealth my cares beguile?
I should be wretched still, and poor,
Without thy blissful smile.

3. Grant, gracious God, this one request—
Oh! be Thy love alone
My ample portion—here I rest,
For heaven is in the boon.

GENTLY.

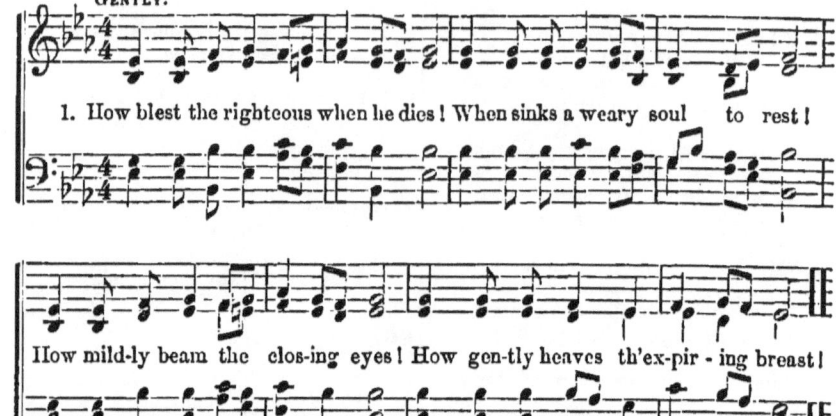

1. How blest the righteous when he dies! When sinks a weary soul to rest!

How mild-ly beam the clos-ing eyes! How gen-tly heaves th'ex-pir-ing breast!

68. *Death of the Righteous.*

1. How blest the righteous when he dies!
   When sinks a weary soul to rest!
   How mildly beam the closing eyes!
   How gently heaves th' expiring breast!

2. So fades a summer cloud away;
   So sinks the gale when storms are o'er;
   So gently shuts the eye of day;
   So dies a wave along the shore.

3. A holy quiet reigns around,
   A calm which life nor death destroys;
   And nought disturbs that peace profound
   Which his unfettered soul enjoys.

4. Farewell, conflicting hopes and fears,
   Where lights and shades alternate dwell;
   How bright th' unchanging morn appears!
   Farewell, inconstant world, farewell;

5. Life's labor done, as sinks the clay,
   Light from its load the spirit flies,
   While heaven and earth combine to say,
   "How blest the righteous when he dies!"

69. *Death of an Infant.*

1. So fades the lovely, blooming flower,
   Frail smiling solace of an hour;
   So soon our transient comforts fly,
   And pleasure only blooms to die.

2. Is there no kind, no lenient art,
   To heal the anguish of the heart?
   Spirit of grace, be ever nigh:
   Thy comforts are not made to die!

3. Bid gentle patience smile on pain,
   Till dying hope shall live again;
   Hope wipes the tear from sorrow's eye,
   And faith points upward to the sky.

70. *Death of the Righteous.*

1. Go, spirit of the sainted dead,
   Go to thy longed-for, happy home;
   The tears of man o'er thee are shed,
   The voice of angels bids thee come.

2. If life be not in length of days,
   In silvered locks and furrowed brow,
   But living to the Saviour's praise,
   How few have lived so long as thou!

3. Though earth may boast one gem the less,
   May not e'en heaven the richer be?
   And myriads on thy footsteps press
   To share thy blest eternity?

71. *Sinners invited to immediate Repentance.*

1. While life prolongs its precious light
   Mercy is found, and peace is given;
   But soon, ah! soon approaching night
   Shall blot out every hope of heaven.

4 While God invites, how blest tho day!
How sweet tho gospel's charming
sound!
Come, sinners, haste, O haste away,
While yet a pard'ning God is found.

3. Soon, borne on times most rapid wing,
Shall death command you to the grave;
Before his bar your spirits bring,
And none be found to hear or save.

4. In that lone land of deep despair,
No Sabbath's heav'nly light shall rise;
No God regard your bitter prayer,
No Saviour call you to the skies.

5. While God invites how blest the day!
How sweet the gopel's charming
sound!
Come, sinners, haste, O haste away,
While yet a pard'ning God is found.

72. *Christ the Physician of Souls.*

1. DEEP are the wounds which sin hath
made
Where shall the sinner find a cure?
In vain, alas! is nature's aid,
The work exceeds her utmost power.

2. And can no sovereign balm be found?
And is no kind physician nigh,
To ease the pain, and heal the wound,
Ere life and hope for ever fly?

3. There is a great Physician near;
Look up, O fainting soul, and live!
See, in His heav'nly smiles appear
Such case as nature cannot give!

4. See, in the Saviour's precious blood,
Life, health, and bliss, abundant flow!
Sinner, approach that sacred flood,
And cleanse thy heart and heal thy
woe.

73. *Christ our Life.*

1. WHEN sins and fears, prevailing rise,
And fainting hope almost expires,
To Thee, O Lord, I lift my eyes;
To Thee I breathe my soul's desires.

2. Art thou not mine, my living Lord?
And can my hope, my comfort die?
'Tis fixed on thine almighty word—
That word which built the earth and
sky.

3. If my Immortal Saviour lives,
Then my immortal life is sure;
His word a firm foundation gives;
Here I may build, and rest secure.

4. Here let my faith unshaken dwell;
For ever sure the promise stands;
Not all the powers of earth or hell
Can e'er dissolve the sacred bands.

5. Here, O my soul, thy trust repose;
If Jesus is for ever mine,
Not death itself—that last of foes—
Shall break a union so divine.

74. *Fruits of Affliction.*

1. "I BLESS Thee, Lord, for sorrows sent
To break the dream of human power
For now my shallow cistern's spent
I find thy fount and thirst no more.

2. I take thy hand and fears grow still;
Behold thy face, and doubts remove;
Who would not yield his wav'ring will
To perfect truth and boundless love!

3. That love this restless soul doth teach
The strength of thine eternal calm,
And tune its sad and broken speech,
To join on earth the angels' psalm.

75. *Presence of the Spirit.*

1. SURE the blest Comforter is nigh;
'Tis he sustains my fainting heart;
Else would my hopes for ever die,
And every cheering ray depart.

2. When some kind promise cheers my
soul,
Do I not find his healing voice
The tempest of my fears control,
And bid my drooping powers rejoice?

3. What less than thine almighty word
Can raise my heart from earth and
dust;
And bid me cleave to thee, my Lord,
My life, my treasure, and my trust?

4. And when my cheerful hope can say,
"I love my God and taste his grace;
Lord, is it not thy blissful ray,
Which brings this dawn of sacred
peace?

5. Let thy kind Spirit in my heart
For ever dwell, O God of love;
And light and heav'nly peace impart,
Sweet earnest of the joys above.

Doxology.

To God the Father, God the Son,
And God the Spirit, Three in One
Be honor, praise, and glory given,
By all on earth, and all in heaven.

THE BETTER LAND. *L. M.* Double.   KNECHT—ARRANGED.

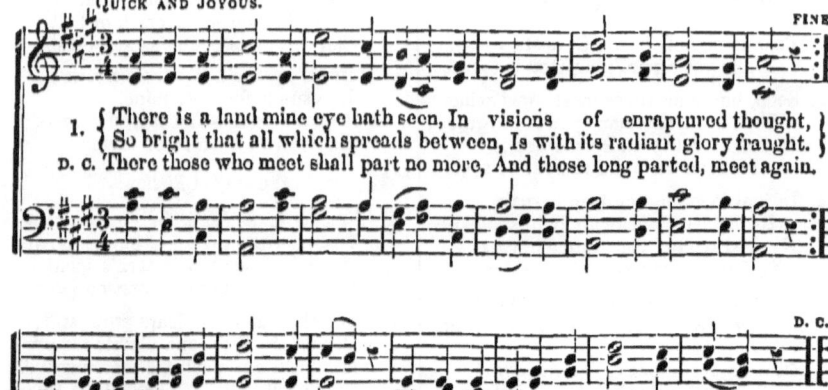

1. { There is a land mine eye hath seen, In visions of enraptured thought, }
{ So bright that all which spreads between, Is with its radiant glory fraught. }
D. C. There those who meet shall part no more, And those long parted, meet again.

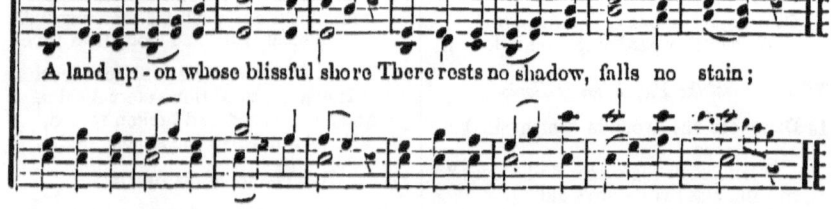

A land up-on whose blissful shore There rests no shadow, falls no stain;

---

76.   *Heaven.*

1. THERE is a land mine eye hath seen
In visions of enraptured thought,
So bright that all· which spreads between
Is with its radiant glory fraught.

2. A land upon whose blissful shore
There rests no shadow, falls no stain;
There those who meet shall part no more,
And those long parted meet again.

3. Its skies are not like earthly skies,
With varying hues of shade and light;
It hath no need of suns to rise,
To dissipate the gloom of night.

4. There sweeps no desolating wind
Across that calm, serene abode;
The wanderer there a home may find,
Within the paradise of God.

77.   *Prospect of Heaven.*

1. As when the weary trav'ler gains
The height of some o'erlooking hill,
His heart revives, if 'cross the plains,
He sees his home, tho' distant still.
Thus when the Christian pilgrim views
By faith his mansion in the skies,

The sight his fainting strength renews,
And wings his speed to reach the prize.

2. 'Tis there, he says, I am to dwell,
With Jesus in the realms of day,
There I shall bid my cares farewell,
And he will wipe my tears away.
Jesus, on Thee our hope depends
To lead us on to thy abode,
Assured our home will make amends
For all our toil while on the road.

78.   *Latter Day.*

1. YE visions bright of heav'nly birth,
Ye glories of the latter day,
Descend upon the fallen earth
And chase the shades of night away
Bid streams of love and mercy flow
Through ev'ry vale of human woe,
Till sin, and care, and sorrow cease,
And all the world is hushed to peace.

2. How long amid the dying race
Shall desolation hold her reign?
How long shall men despise the grace
And love of him who once was slain?
How long shall heathen bow the knee
To gods that neither hear nor see?
Ye scenes of bliss, so long foretold,
When will your radiant hues unfold?

3. The gospel of the living God
  Shall echo the wide earth around,
  Till every place of man's abode
  Shall know the joy-inspiring sound:
  Who shall that heav'nly scene portray?
  Who can describe the glorious day?
  We hail its glimm'rings from afar,
  We hail the bright, the Morning Star!

79. *Blessedness of Worshiping God in his Temple.*

1. How pleasant, how divinely fair,
  O Lord of hosts, thy dwellings are!
  With long desire my spirit faints
  To meet th' assemblies of thy saints.

2. My flesh would rest in thine abode;
  My panting heart cries out for God;
  My God, my King, why should I be
  So far from all my joys and thee?

3. Blest are the saints, who dwell on high,
  Around thy throne, above the sky;
  Thy brightest glories shine above,
  And all their work is praise and love.

4. Blest are the souls who find a place
  Within the temple of thy grace;
  There they behold thy gentler rays,
  And seek thy face, and learn thy praise.

5. Blest are the men whose hearts are set
  To find the way to Zion's gate;
  God is their strength, and, through the road,
  They lean upon their helper, God.

6. Cheerful they walk, with growing strength,
  Till all shall meet in heaven at length;
  Till all before thy face appear,
  And join in nobler worship there.

80. *Voice of Creation.*

1. There seems a voice in every gale,
  A tongue in every opening flower,
  Which tells, O Lord, the wondrous tale
  Of thy indulgence, love, and power.
  The birds that rise on quiv'ring wing,
  Appear to hymn their Maker's praise,
  And all the mingling sounds of spring
  To thee one general chorus raise.

2. And shall my voice, great God, alone,
  Be mute midst nature's loud acclaim?
  No, let my heart with answ'ring tone,
  Breathe forth in praise thy holy name,

And nature's debt is small to mine,
  Thou bad'st her being bounded be,
  But—matchless proof of love divine—
  Thou gavest immortal life to me.

3. The Saviour left his heavenly throne,
  A ransom for my soul to give;
  Man's suffering state he made his own,
  And deign'd to die that I might live.
  But thanks and praise for love so great
  No mortal tongue can e'er express,
  Then let me, bowed before thy feet,
  In silence love thee, Lord, and bless.

81. *Invocation.*

1. Jesus, where'er thy people meet,
  There they behold thy mercy-seat;
  Where'er they seek thee, thou art found,
  And every place is hallowed ground.

2. For Thou, within no walls confined,
  Inhabitest the humble mind;
  Such ever bring Thee where they come,
  And going, take Thee to their home.

3. Great Shepherd of thy chosen few!
  Thy former mercies here renew;
  Here to our waiting hearts proclaim
  The sweetness of thy saving name.

82. *A Sabbath Evening in Summer.*

1. Is there a time when moments flow
  More peacefully than all beside?
  It is, of all the times below,
  A Sabbath eve in summer's tide.

2. Delightful scene! a world at rest,
  A God all love, no grief, no fear,
  A heavenly hope, a peaceful breast,
  A smile unsullied by a tear.

3. If heaven be ever felt below,
  A scene so heavenly, sure, as this,
  May cause a heart on earth to know
  Some foretaste of celestial bliss.

4. Delightful hour! how soon will night,
  Spread her dark mantle o'er thy reign!
  And soon the morn's returning light
  Will call us to the world again.

5. Yet will there dawn, at last, a day—
  A sun that never sets, shall rise:
  Night will not vail his glorious ray,
  The heavenly Sabbath never dies.

LATOUR. C. M. FROM "SACRED LYRE." BY PERMISSION.
WITH VARIED EXPRESSION.

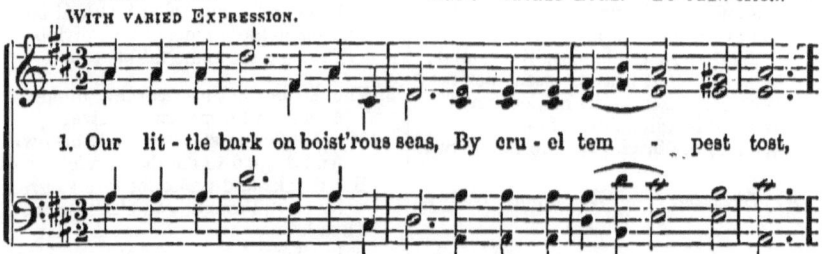

1. Our lit-tle bark on boist'rous seas, By cru-el tem - pest tost,

Coda for last verse.

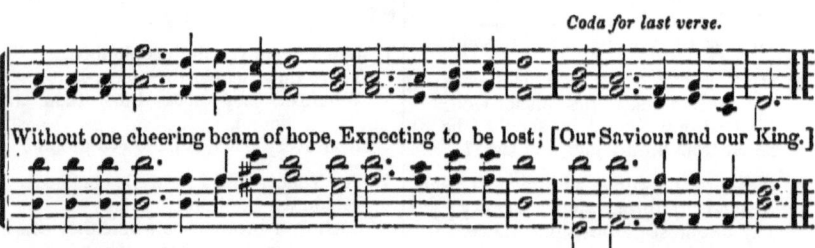

Without one cheering beam of hope, Expecting to be lost; [Our Saviour and our King.]

83.   *Deliverence in a Storm*

1. OUR little bark, on boisterous seas,
   By cruel tempest tost,
   Without one cheering beam of hope,
   Expecting to be lost;

2. We to the Lord, in humble prayer,
   Breathed out our sad distress;
   Though feeble, yet with contrite hearts,
   We sought returning peace.

3. The stormy winds thy voice obeyed,
   The waves no more did roll;
   At thy command a placid sea
   Spake comfort to the soul.

4. Well may our grateful, trembling hearts,
   Sweet hallelujahs sing,
   To Him who hath our lives preserved,
   Our Saviour and our King.

84.   *The Incarnation*

1. MORTALS awake, with angels join,
   And chant the solemn lay :
   Joy, love and gratitude combine
   To hail th' auspicious day.

2. In heaven the rapt'rous song began;
   And sweet seraphic fire,
   Through all the shining legions ran,
   And strung and tuned the lyre.

3. Swift through the vast expanse it flew,
   And loud the echo rolled;
   The theme, the song, the joy was new,
   'Twas more than heaven could hold

4. Down through the portals of the sky,
   The heavenly tidings ran ;
   And angels flew with eager joy,
   To bear the news to man.

5. With joy the chorus we'll repeat—
   " Glory to God on high;
   Good will and peace to men complete,
   Jesus is born to die."

85.   *Gospel Invitation.*

1. THE Saviour calls; let every ear
   Attend the heavenly sound;
   Ye doubting souls, dismiss your fear,
   Hope smiles reviving round.

2. For every thirsty, longing heart.
   Here streams of bounty flow,
   And life, and health, and bliss impart,
   To banish mortal woe.

3. Ye sinners, come; 'tis mercy's voice;
   That gracious voice obey ;
   'Tis Jesus calls to heavenly joys;
   And can you yet delay ?

4. Dear Saviour, draw reluctant hearts;
To Thee let sinners fly,
And take the bliss Thy love imparts,
And drink, and never die.

86. *Christ's Ministry.*

1. HARK—the glad sound!—the Saviour
comes?
The Saviour promised long!
Let every heart prepare a throne—
And every voice a song.

2. On him the Spirit, largely poured,
Exerts its sacred fire;
Wisdom and might, and zeal and love,
His holy breast inspire.

3. He comes—the prisoners to release,
In Satan's bondage held;
The gates of brass before him burst—
The iron fetters yield!

4. He comes from thickest films of vice
To clear the mental ray;
And on the eye-balls of the blind
To pour celestial day.

5. He comes—the broken heart to bind—
The bleeding soul to cure;
And, with the treasures of his grace,
T' enrich the humble poor.

6. Our glad hosannas, Prince of Peace,
Thy welcome shall proclaim;
And heaven's eternal arches ring
With thy beloved name.

87. *Parting with all for Christ.*

1. YE glittering toys of earth, adieu;
A nobler choice be mine;
A heavenly prize attracts my view,
A treasure all divine.

2. Jesus, to multitudes unknown,—
O name divinely sweet!—
Jesus, in Thee, in Thee alone,
True wealth and honor meet.

3. Should earth's vain treasures all depart,
Of this dear gift possessed,
I'd clasp it to my joyful heart,
And be for ever blest.

4. Dear portion of my soul's desires,
Thy love is bliss divine;
Accept the wish that love inspires,
And let me call thee mine.

88. *Praise for Creation and Providence.*

1. LORD, when my raptured thought surveys
Creation's beauties o'er;
All nature joins to teach thy praise,
And bid my soul adore.

2. Where'er I turn my gazing eyes,
Thy radiant footsteps shine;
Ten thousand pleasing wonders rise,
And speak their source Divine.

3. On me thy providence has shone
With gentle smiling rays;
Oh let my lips and life make known
Thy goodness and thy praise.

4. All bounteous Lord, thy grace impart,
Oh teach me to improve
Thy gifts with humble, grateful heart,
And crown them with thy love.

89. *Salvation.*

1. SALVATION! O, the joyful sound!
'Tis pleasure to our ears,
A sovereign balm for every wound,
A cordial for our fears.

2. Buried in sorrow, and in sin,
At hell's dark door we lay;
But we arise, by grace divine,
To see a heavenly day.

3. Salvation! let the echo fly
The spacious earth around,
While all the armies of the sky
Conspire to raise the sound.

90. *Sacramental.*

1. LORD, at Thy table we behold
The wonders of Thy grace;
But most of all admire, that we
Should find a welcome place!

2. "Eat, O my friends!" the Saviour cries,
"The feast was made for you;
For you, I groaned and bled, and died,
And rose in triumph too."

3. With trembling faith and contrite hearts,
Lord, we accept Thy love;
'Tis a rich banquet we have here,
What will it be above!

Doxology.

To Father, Son, and Holy Ghost,
The God whom we adore,
Be glory as it was, is now,
And shall be evermore.

ANDREA. C. M.

BOLD—STACCATO.

1. Blest morning, whose first opening rays Be - held our ris - ing God;

That saw him triumph o'er the dust, And leave his last a - bode.

91. *The Resurrection of Christ.*

1. BLEST morning, whose first opening
   rays
   Beheld our rising God;
   That saw him triumph o'er the dust,
   And leave his last abode.

2. In the cold prison of a tomb
   The great Redeemer lay,
   Till the revolving skies had brought
   The third, th' appointed day.

3. Hell and the grave unite their force
   To hold our Lord in vain;
   The sleeping Conqueror arose,
   And burst their feeble chain.

4. To thy great name, almighty Lord,
   These sacred hours we pay;
   And loud hosannas shall proclaim
   The triumph of the day.

5. Salvation and immortal praise
   To our victorious King!
   Let heaven and earth, and rocks and
   seas
   With glad hosannas ring.

92. *The Lord's Day.*

1. THIS is the day the Lord hath made;
   He calls the hours his own;
   Let heaven rejoice, let earth be glad,
   And praise surround his throne.

2. To-day he rose and left the dead,
   And Satan's empire fell;
   To-day the saints his triumphs spread,
   And all his wonders tell.

3. Hosanna to the Anointed King!
   To David's holy Son;
   Help us, O Lord, descend and bring
   Salvation from thy throne.

4. Blest be the Lord, who comes to men
   With messages of grace;
   Who comes in God his Father's name,
   To save our sinful race.

5. Hosanna in the highest strains
   The church on earth can raise;
   The highest heavens, in which He
   reigns,
   Shall give him nobler praise.

93. *A Morning Song.*

1. ONCE more, my soul, the rising day
   Salutes my waking eyes:
   Once more, my voice, thy tribute pay
   To Him who rules the skies.

2. Night unto night his name repeats,
   The day renews the sound;
   Wide as the heaven on which He sits,
   To turn the seasons round.

3. 'Tis He supports my mortal frame,
   My tongue shall speak his praise;
   My sins would rouse his wrath to flame,
   And yet his wrath delays.

4 A thousand wretched souls are fled,
   Since the last setting sun;
And yet thou length'nest out my thread,
   And yet my moments run.

5. O God, let all my hours be thine,
   While I enjoy the light:
Then shall my sun in smiles decline,
   And bring a pleasant night.

94.   *Obligation to Christ.*

1. ALL that I *was*, my sin, my guilt,
   My death, was all my own:
All that I *am*, I owe to thee,
   My gracious God, alone.

2. The evil of my former state
   Was mine, and only mine;
The good in which I now rejoice
   Is thine, and only thine.

3. The darkness of my former state,
   The bondage, all was mine;
The light of life in which I walk,
   The liberty is thine.

4 All that I am e'en here on earth,
   All that I hope to be,
When Jesus comes, and glory dawns,
   I owe it, Lord, to thee.

95.   *The Inspired Volume.*

1. How precious is the book divine,
   By Inspiration given!
Bright as a lamp its doctrines shine,
   To lead our souls to heaven.

2. O'er all the strait and narrow way
   Its radiant beams are cast;
A light whose never-weary ray
   Grows brightest at the last.

3. It sweetly cheers our drooping hearts,
   In this dark vale of tears;
Life, light, and joy, it still imparts,
   And quells our rising fears.

4. This lamp, through all the tedious
     night
Of life, shall guide our way,
Till we behold the clearer light
   Of an eternal day.

96.   *Invitation to the Young.*

1. YE hearts, with youthful vigor warm,
   In smiling crowds draw near,
And turn from every mortal charm,
   A Saviour's voice to hear.

2. He, Lord of all the worlds on high,
   Stoops to converse with you;
And lays his radiant glories by,
   Your friendship to pursue.

3. What object, Lord, my soul should
     move,
If once compared with thee?
What beauty should command my love
   Like what in Christ I see?

4. Away, ye false, delusive toys,
   Vain tempters of the mind;
'Tis here I fix my lasting choice,
   And here true bliss I find.

97. *Christ the Foundation of his Church.*

1. BEHOLD the sure Foundation-stone,
   Which God in Zion lays,
To build our heavenly hopes upon,
   And his eternal praise.

2. The foolish builders, scribe and priest,
   Reject it with disdain,
Yet on this Rock the church shall rest,
   And envy rage in vain.

3. What though the gates of hell with-
     stood,
Yet must this building rise;
'Tis thine own work, almighty God,
   And wondrous in our eyes.

98.   *The Book of Nature.*

1. THERE is a book that all may read,
   Which heavenly truth imparts,
And all the lore its scholars need,
   Pure eyes and Christian hearts.

2. The works of God above, below,
   Within us and around,
Are pages in that book, to show
   How God himself is found.

3. The glorious sky, embracing all,
   Is like the Maker's love,
Wherewith encompassed, great and small
   In peace and order move.

4. The dew of heaven is like thy grace,
   It steals in silence down;
But where it lights, the favored place
   By richest fruits is known.

5. Thou, who hast given me eyes to see,
   And love this sight so fair,
Give me a heart to find out Thee,
   And read Thee everywhere.

1. How sweet the name of Je - sus sounds In a be -
liev - er's ear! It soothes his sor - rows, heals his wounds, And
Last line p
drives a - way his fear, And drives a - way his fear.

BALERMA may occasionally be preferred p. 178.

99.   *Christ Precious.*

1. How sweet the name of Jesus sounds
In a believer's ear!
It soothes his sorrows, heals his wounds,
And drives away his fear.

2. It makes the wounded spirit whole,
And calms the troubled breast;
'Tis manna to the hungry soul,
And to the weary, rest.

3. Weak is the effort of my heart,
And cold my warmest thought:
But when I see thee as thou art,
I'll praise thee as I ought.

4. Till then, I would thy love proclaim
With every fleeting breath;
And may the music of thy name
Refresh my soul in death.

100.   *Love to Christ.*

1. Do not I love thee, O my Lord?
Behold my heart and see;

And cast each worthless idol out,
That dares to rival thee.

2. Is not thy name melodious still
To my attentive ear?
Doth not each pulse with pleasure bound
My Saviour's voice to hear?

3. Do I not love thee from my soul?
Then let me nothing love:
Dead be my heart to every joy,
When Jesus can not move.

4. Hast thou a lamb in all thy flock
I would disdain to feed?
Hast thou a foe before whose face
I fear thy cause to plead?

5. Could not my heart pour forth its blood
In honor of thy name?
And challenge the cold hand of death
To damp th' immortal flame?

6. Thou know'st I love thee, dearest Lord,
But O, I long to soar
Far from the sphere of mortal joys,
And learn to love thee more.

101. *Heaven Anticipated.*

1. COME, Lord, and warm each languid
heart,
Inspire each lifeless tongue,
And let the joys of heaven impart
Their influence to our song.

2. Then to the shining realms of bliss
The wings of faith shall soar,
And all the charms of Paradise
Our raptured thoughts explore.

3. There shall the followers of the Lamb
Join in immortal songs;
And endless honors to his name
Employ their tuneful tongues.

4. Lord, tune our hearts to praise and love,
Our feeble notes inspire;
Till in thy blissful courts above,
We join the heavenly choir.

102. *Condescension of Christ.*

1. THE Saviour! O, what endless charms
Dwell in that blissful sound!
Its influence every fear disarms,
And spreads sweet peace around.

2. Here pardon, life, and joy divine,
In rich profusion flow,
For guilty rebels, lost in sin,
And doomed to endless woe.

3. The mighty Former of the skies
Descends to our abode,
While angels view with wond'ring eyes,
And hail th' incarnate God.

4. How rich the depths of love divine!
Of bliss, a boundless store!
Dear Saviour, let me call Thee mine;
I can not wish for more.

5. On thee alone my hope relies;
Beneath thy cross I fall,
My Lord, my life, my sacrifice,
My Saviour, and my all.

103. *A Name above every Name*

1. JESUS, in thy transporting name
What glories meet our eyes!
Thou art the seraphs' lofty theme,
The wonder of the skies.

2. Well might the heavens with wonder
view
A love so strange as thine;
No thought of angels ever knew
Compassion so divine.

3. And didst thou, Saviour, leave the sky,
To sink beneath our woes?
Didst thou descend to bleed and die
For thy rebellious foes?

4. O, may our willing hearts confess
Thy sweet, thy gentle sway;
Glad captives of thy matchless grace
Thy righteous rule obey.

104. *Christ our Refuge.*

1. YE humble souls, approach your God,
With songs of sacred praise;
For he is good, supremely good;
And kind are all his ways.

2. He gave his Son, his only Son,
To ransom rebel worms;
'Tis here he makes his goodness known
In its diviner forms.

3. To this dear refuge, Lord, we come,
'Tis here our hope relies;
A safe defence, a peaceful home,
When storms of trouble rise.

4. Thine eye beholds, with kind regard,
The souls who trust in thee;
Their humble hope thou wilt reward,
With bliss divinely free.

5. Great God, to thy almighty love,
What honors shall we raise?
Not all th' angelic songs above
Can render equal praise.

105. *The watchful Shepherd.*

1. MY Shepherd will supply my need;
Jehovah is his name;
In pastures fresh he makes me feed,
Beside the living stream.

2. He brings my wandering spirit back
When I forsake his ways,
And leads me, for his mercy's sake,
In paths of truth and grace.

3. When I walk through the shades of
death,
Thy presence is my stay;
A word of thy supporting breath
Drives all my fears away.

4. Thy hand, in sight of all my foes,
Doth still my table spread;
My cup with blessings overflows;
Thine oil anoints my head.

5. The sure provisions of my God,
Attend me all my days;
O may thine house be mine abode,
And all my work be praise.

6. There would I find a settled rest,
While others go and come—
No more a stranger or a guest,
But like a child at home.

ZEPHYR. L. M.
GENTLY

W. B B. BY PERMISSION

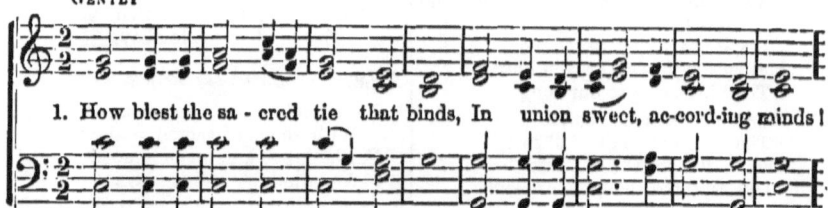

1. How blest the sa - cred tie that binds, In union sweet, ac-cord-ing minds!

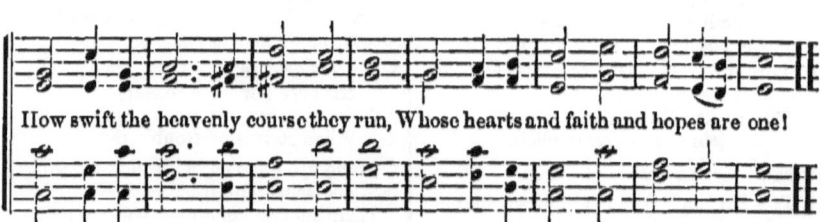

How swift the heavenly course they run, Whose hearts and faith and hopes are one!

106.   *Christian Fellowship.*

1. How blest the sacred tie that binds,
In union sweet, according minds!
How swift the heav'nly course they run,
Whose hearts and faith and hopes are
one!

2. To each, the soul of each how dear!
What tender love, what holy fear!
How doth the gen'rous flame within
Refine from earth, and cleanse from sin!

3. Their streaming eyes together flow,
For human guilt, and mortal woe;
Their ardent prayers together rise,
Like mingling flames in sacrifice.

4. Together oft they seek the place,
Where God reveals his awful face;
At length they meet in realms above,
A heav'n of joy—a heav'n of love.

107.   *Sense of Sin.*

1. JESUS demands this heart of mine,
Demands my love, my joy, my care;
But, ah, how dead to things divine,
How cold my best affections are!

2. 'Tis sin, alas! with dreadful power,
Divides my Saviour from my sight
Or for one happy, shining hour
Of sacred freedom, sweet delight!

3. Come, gracious Lord; thy love can
raise
My captive powers from sin and
death,
And fill my heart and life with praise,
And tune my last, expiring breath.

108.   *Return of Joy.*

1. WHEN darkness long has veiled my
mind,
And smiling day once more appears,
Then, my Redeemer, then I find
The folly of my doubts and fears.

2. I chide my unbelieving heart,
And blush that I should ever be
Thus prone to act so base a part,
Or harbor one hard thought of thee.

3. O, let me, then, at length be taught
(What I am still so slow to learn)
That God is Love, and changes not,
Nor knows the shadow of a turn.

4. Sweet truth, and easy to repeat!
But, when my faith is sharply tried,
I find myself a learner yet—
Unskillful, weak, and apt to slide.

5. But, O my Lord, one look from thee
Subdues the disobedient will,
Drives doubt and discontent away,
· And thy rebellious worm is still.

⤙ Thou art as ready to forgive,
As I am ready to repine ;
Thou therefore all the praise receive;
Be shame and self-abhorrence mine.

109. *Enjoyment in the Service.*

1. FAR from my thoughts, vain world, be
gone ;
Let my religious hours alone ;
Fain would my eyes my Saviour see ;
I wait a visit, Lord, from thee.

2. O, warm my heart with holy fire,
And kindle there a pure desire :
Come sacred Spirit, from above,
And fill my soul with heavenly love.

3. Blest Saviour, what delicious fare !
How sweet thy entertainments are !
Ne'er did the angels taste above
Redeeming grace and dying love.

4. Hail, great Immanuel, all divine !
In thee thy Father's glories shine ;
Thy glorious name shall be adored,
And every tongue confess thee, Lord.

110. *Security in the Cross.*

1. HERE at thy cross, incarnate God,
I lay my soul beneath thy love—
Beneath the droppings of thy blood—
Nor shall it, Jesus, e'er remove.

2. Should worlds conspire to drive me
thence,
Unmoved and firm this heart should
lie ;
Resolved, for that's my last defence—
If I must perish, there to die.

3. But speak, my Lord, and calm my fear
Am I not safe beneath thy shade ?
Thy justice will not strike me here,
Nor Satan dare my soul invade.

4. Yes, I'm secure beneath thy blood,
And all my foes shall lose their aim;
Hosanna to my Saviour God,
And my best honors to his name.

111. *Man mortal, and God eternal.*

1. THROUGH every age, eternal God,
Thou art our rest, our safe abode ;
High was thy throne, ere heaven was
made,
Or earth, thy humble footstool, laid.

2. Long hadst thou reigned, ere time be-
gan,
Or dust was fashioned into man ;
And long thy kingdom shall endure,
When earth and time shall be no more.

3. But man, weak man, is born to die,
Made up of guilt and vanity ;
Thy dreadful sentence, Lord, was just—
" Return, ye sinners, to the dust."

4. A thousand of our years amount
Scarce to a day in thine account;
Like yesterday's departed light,
Or the last watch of ending night.

112. *Waiting at the Mercy-Seat.*

1. FROM deep distress, and troubled
thoughts,
To thee, my God, I raise my cries;
If thou severely mark our faults,
No flesh can stand before thine eyes.

2. But thou hast built thy throne of grace,
Dispensing pardons freely there,
That sinners may approach thy face,
And hope and love, as well as fear.

3. As the benighted pilgrims wait,
And long and wish for breaking day,
So waits my soul before thy gate ;
When will my God his face display ?

4. My trust is fixed upon thy word,
Nor shall I trust thy word in vain ;
Let mourning souls address the Lord,
And find relief from all their pain.

5. His love is great, and large his grace,
Through the redemption of his Son ;
He turns our feet from sinful ways,
And pardons what our hands have
done.

113. *Trusting in God in times of Des-
pondency.*

1. MY spirit sinks within me, Lord ;
But I will call thy grace to mind,
And times of past distress record,
When I have found my God was
kind.

2. Yet will the Lord command his love,
When I address his throne by day,
Nor in the night his grace remove;
The night shall hear me sing and
pray.

3. I'll chide my heart, that sinks so low;
Why should my soul indulge in
grief?
Hope in the Lord, and praise him too;
He is my rest, my sure relief.

4. O God, thou art my hope, my joy ;
Thy light and truth shall guide me
still :
Thy word shall my best thoughts em-
ploy,
And lead me to thy heavenly hill.

RETREAT. L. M.

Very Gently.

HASTINGS.

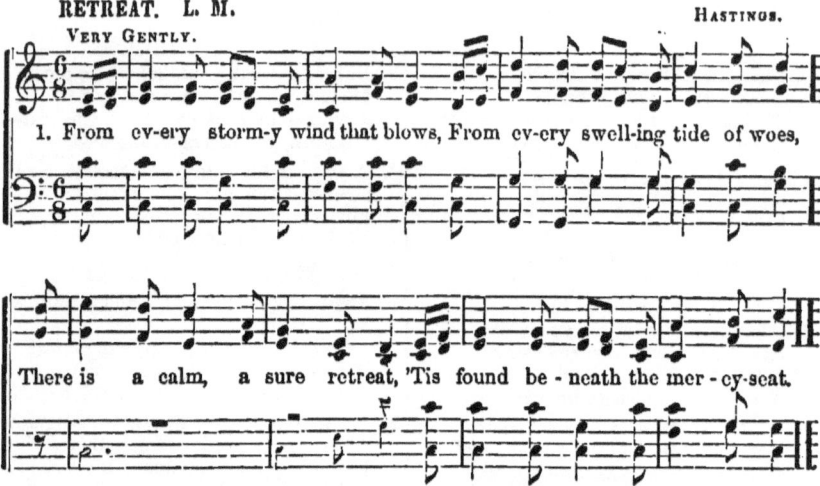

1. From ev-ery storm-y wind that blows, From ev-ery swell-ing tide of woes,

There is a calm, a sure retreat, 'Tis found be-neath the mer-cy-seat.

114. *Mercy-Seat.*

1. FROM every stormy wind that blows,
   From every swelling tide of woes,
   There is a calm, a sure retreat,
   'Tis found beneath the mercy-seat.

2. There is a place where Jesus sheds
   The oil of gladness on our heads,
   A place of all on earth most sweet;
   It is the blood-bought mercy-seat.

3. There is a scene where spirits blend,
   Where friend holds fellowship with friend;
   Though sundered far, by faith we meet
   Around one common mercy-seat.

4. There, there, on eagle wings we soar,
   And sense and sin becloud no more;
   And heaven comes down our souls to greet.
   And glory crowns the mercy-seat.

5. Oh! let my hand forget her skill,
   My tongue be silent, cold, and still,
   This throbbing heart forget to beat,
   If I forget the mercy-seat.

115. *Teach me to pray.*

1. O GOD, I would look up to thee,
   I would address thy throne to-day,
   And this my one request shall be,
   Teach me to pray, [teach me to pray.]

2. A heartless form will not suffice,
   The self-deemed rich are sent away,
   The heart must bring the sacrifice,
   Teach me to pray.

3. To whom shall I Thy creature turn
   Whom else address, whom else obey?
   Teach me the lesson I would learn,
   Teach me to pray.

4. In every hour of trouble deign
   To bow my spirit to thy sway:
   O let me ask thee not in vain,
   Teach me to pray.

5. To thee alone my eyes look up,
   Turn not, O God, thy face away,
   Prayer is my only door of hope:
   Teach me to pray.

116. *Light of the Soul.*

1. LIGHT of the soul! O, Saviour blest!
   Soon as thy presence fills the breast,
   Darkness and guilt are put to flight,
   And all is sweetness and delight.

2. Son of the Father! Lord most high!
   How glad is he who feels Thee nigh!
   Come in Thy hidden majesty;
   Fill us with love, fill us with Thee.

3. Jesus is from the proud concealed,
   But evermore to babes revealed,
   Through Him, unto the Father be
   Glory and praise eternally.

117. *Evening.*

1. 'TIS gone, that bright and orbéd blaze,
Fast fading from our wistful gaze,
Yon mantling cloud has hid from sight
The last faint pulse of quivering light.

2. Sun of my soul! Thou Saviour dear,
It is not night if Thou be near;
Oh! may no earth-born cloud arise
To hide Thee from thy servant's eyes.

3. When the soft dews of kindly sleep,
My wearied eyelids gently steep,
Be my last thought, how sweet to rest
For ever on my Saviour's breast.

4. Abide with me from morn till eve,
For, without Thee, I can not live;
Abide with me when night is nigh,
For without Thee I dare not die.

5. Watch by the sick, enrich the poor
With blessings from thy boundless store
Be every mourner's sleep to-night
Like infant's slumbers, pure and bright.

6. Come near and bless us when we wake,
Ere through the world our way we take,
Till in the ocean of thy love,
We lose ourselves in heaven above.

118. *Heaven.*

1. WITH tearful eyes I look around,
Life seems a dark and stormy sea;
Yet 'midst the gloom, I hear a sound,
A heavenly whisper, "Come to Me."

2. It tells me of a place of rest—
It tells me where my soul may flee;
O! to the weary, faint, oppressed,
How sweet the bidding, "Come to Me."

3. When nature shudders, loth to part
From all I love, enjoy, and see;
When a faint chill steals o'er my heart,
A sweet voice utters, "Come to Me."

4. "Come, for all else must fail and die;
Earth is no resting place for thee;
Heavenward direct thy weeping eye,
I am thy portion, "Come to Me."

5. O, voice of mercy! voice of love!
In conflict, grief, and agony,
Support me, cheer me from above!
And gently whisper, "Come to Me."

119. *A Psalm for the Lord's Day.*

1. SWEET is the work, my God, my King,
To praise thy name, give thanks, and
sing;
To show thy love by morning light,
And talk of all thy truth at night.

2. Sweet is the day of sacred rest;
No mortal cares shall seize my breast;
O may my heart in tune be found,
Like David's harp of solemn sound!

3. My heart shall triumph in my Lord,
And bless his works, and bless his word;
Thy works of grace, how bright they
shine!
How deep thy counsels! how divine!

4. Fools never raise their thoughts so high;
Like brutes they live, like brutes they
die;
Like grass they flourish, till thy breath
Blast them in everlasting death.

5. But I shall share a glorious part,
When grace hath well refined my heart;
And fresh supplies of joy are shed,
Like holy oil, to cheer my head.

6. Then shall I hear, and see, and know
All I desired or wished below:
And every power find sweet employ
In that eternal world of joy.

120. *Glory surrounding All.*

1. ERE to the world again we go,
Its pleasures, cares and idle show,
Thy grace, once more, O God, we crave,
From folly and from sin to save.

2. May the great truths we here have
heard—
The lessons of Thy holy word—
Dwell in our inmost bosoms deep,
And all our souls from error keep.

3. O, may the influence of this day
Long as our memory with us stay,
And as an angel guardian prove,
To guide us to our home above.

RETURN. C. M. With a Coda.*   HASTINGS.
WITH PATHOS.

1. Re-turn, O wanderer, to thy home, Thy Fa-ther calls for thee:

No longer now an ex-ile roam In guilt and mis - e - ry. Return, return.

Coda p

* For the first three hymns only. For the others, see also DUNDEE 168

121. *Invitation to Wanderers.*

1. RETURN, O wand'rer to thy home,
 Thy Father calls for thee:
 No longer now an exile roam
 In guilt and misery.

2. Return, O wand'rer, to thy home;
 'Tis Jesus calls for thee:
 "The Spirit and the bride say, come;"
 O now for refuge flee!

3. Return, O wand'rer, to thy home,
 'Tis madness to delay:
 There are no pardons in the tomb;
 And brief is mercy's day!

122. *The Same.*

1. RETURN, O wanderer, return,
 And seek thy Father's face;
 Those new desires which in thee burn
 Were kindled by his grace.

2. Return, O wanderer, return;
 He hears thy humble sigh:
 He sees thy softened spirit mourn,
 When no one else is nigh.

3. Return, O wanderer, return;
 Thy Saviour bids thee live:
 Come to his cross, and, grateful, learn
 How Jesus can forgive.

4. O Wretched wanderer, now return,
 And wipe the falling tear:
 Thy Father calls—no longer mourn;
 'Tis love invites thee near.

5. From all thy wanderings, now return,
 Regain thy long-sought rest:
 The Saviour's melting mercies yearn
 To clasp thee to his breast.

123. *The Shadow of the Cross.*

1. OPPRESSED with noon-day's scorching
   heat,
 To yonder cross I flee;
 Beneath its shelter take my seat;
 No shade like this for me. [for me.]

2. Beneath that cross clear waters burst,
 A fountain sparkling free;
 And there I quench my desert thirst;
 No spring like this for me.

3. A stranger, here I pitch my tent
 Beneath this spreading tree;
 Here shall my pilgrim life be spent;
 No home like this for me.

4. For burdened ones a resting-place,
 Beside that cross I see,
 Here I cast off my weariness;
 No rest like this for me.

124. *Invitation.*

1. COME, sinner, to the Gospel feast;
 O, come without delay;
 For there is room in Jesus' breast
 For all who will obey.

2. There 's room in God's eternal love
 To save thy precious soul;
 Room in the Spirit's grace above
 To heal and make thee whole.

3. There 's room within the church, re-
 deemed
 With blood of Christ divine;
 Room in the white-robed throng con-
 vened;
 For that dear soul of thine.

4. There 's room in heaven among the choir,
 And harps and crowns of gold,
 And glorious palms of victory there,
 And joys that ne'er were told.

5. There 's room around thy Father's board
 For thee and thousands more:
 O, come and welcome to the Lord;
 Yea, come this very hour.

125. *Imitation of Christ.*

1. IN duties and in sufferings too,
 Thy path, my Lord, I'd trace;
 As thou hast done, so would I do,
 Depending on thy grace.

2. Inflamed with zeal, 't was thy delight
 To do thy Father's will;
 O, may that zeal my soul excite
 Thy precepts to fulfil.

3. Unsullied meekness, truth, and love,
 Through all thy conduct shine;
 O, may my whole deportment prove
 A copy, Lord, of thine.

126. *Prayer for Children's Conversion.*

1. O LORD, behold us at thy feet,
 A needy, sinful band;
 As suppliants round thy mercy-seat,
 We come at thy command.

2. 'Tis for our children we would plead,
 The offspring thou hast given;
 Where shall we go, in time of need,
 But to the God of heaven?

3. We ask not for them wealth or fame,
 Amid the worldly strife;
 But, in the all-prevailing Name,
 We ask eternal life.

4. We seek the Spirit's quickening grace,
 To make them pure in heart,
 That they may stand before thy face,
 And see thee as thou art.

127. *Jehovah Jireh.*

1. WHEN earthly joys glide swift away,
 When hopes and comforts flee,
 When foes beset, and friends betray,
 I turn, my God, to thee.

2. Thy nature, Lord, no change can know,
 Thy promise still is sure;
 And ills can ne'er so hopeless grow,
 But thou canst find a cure.

3. Deliverance comes, most bright and
 blest,
 At danger's darkest hour;
 And man's extremity is best
 To prove Almighty power.

4. High as thou art, thou still art near
 When suppliants succor crave;
 And if thy car is swift to hear,
 Thy arm is strong to save.

128. *Exhortation to Sinners.*

1. SINNERS, the voice of God regard,
 'Tis mercy speaks to-day:
 He calls you, by his sovereign word,
 From sin's destructive way.

2. Like the rough sea, that can not rest,
 You live devoid of peace;
 A thousand stings within your breast
 Deprive your soul of ease.

3. [Your way is dark, and leads to hell!
 Why will you persevere?
 Can you in endless torments dwell,
 Shut up in black despair?]

4. Why will you in the crooked ways
 Of sin and folly go?
 In vain you travail all your days,
 To reap immortal woe.

5. But he that turns to God shall live,
 Through his abounding grace;
 His mercy will the guilt forgive
 Of those who seek his face.

6. Bow to the sceptre of his word,
 Renouncing every sin;
 Submit to him, your sovereign Lord,
 And learn his will divine.

7. His love exceeds your highest thoughts,
 He pardons like a God:
 He will forgive your num'rous faults,
 Through a Redeemer's blood.

NEW HAVEN.   6s & 4s.   HASTINGS.
CHANT-LIKE.

1. Sa-viour, I look to thee; Be not thou far from me, 'Mid storms that low'r: On me thy grace be-stow, Thy lov-ing kind-ness show, Thine arms a-round me throw, This try-ing hour.

129.   *Looking to Christ.*

1. SAVIOUR, I look to thee,
  Be not thou far from me,
   'Mid storms that lower :
  On me thy care bestow,
  Thy loving kindness show,
  Thine arms around me throw,
   This trying hour.

2 Saviour, I look to thee,
  Feeble as infancy,
   Gird up my heart :
  Author of life and light,
  Thou hast an arm of might,
  Thine is the sovereign right,
   Thy strength impart.

3. Saviour, I look to thee,
  Let me thy fullness see,
   Save me from fear :
  While at thy cross I kneel,
  All my backslidings heal,
  And a free pardon seal,
   My soul to cheer.

4. Saviour, I look to thee,
  Thine shall the glory be,
   Hearer of prayer :
  Thou art my only aid,
  On thee my soul is staid,
  Naught can my heart invade,
   While thou art near.

OLIVET. 6s & 4s.   Dr. L Mason.

1. My faith looks up to thee, Thou Lamb of Cal - va - ry,

Sa - viour di - vine: Now hear me while I pray; Take all my

guilt a - way; O, let me, from this day, Be whol - ly thine.

130.   *Christ our Confidence.*

1. My faith looks up to thee,
   Thou Lamb of Calvary,
     Saviour divine:
   Now hear me while I pray;
   Take all my guilt away;
   O, let me, from this day,
     Be wholly thine.

2. May thy rich grace impart
   Strength to my fainting heart;
     My zeal inspire:
   As thou hast died for me,
   O, may my love to thee
   Pure, warm, and changeless be—
     A living fire.

3. While life's dark maze I tread,
   And griefs around me spread,
     Be thou my Guide;
   Bid darkness turn to day,
   Wipe sorrow's tear away,
   Nor let me ever stray
     From thee aside.

4. When ends life's transient dream,
   When death's cold sullen stream
     Shall o'er me roll,
   Blest Saviour, then in love,
   Fear and distress remove;
   O, bear me safe above,—
     A ransomed soul.

MEMORIAL. 7s & 6s. MANHATTAN—REVISED.

TENDERLY.

1. Lamb of God, whose bleeding love We now re - call to mind,
Send the an-swer from a - bove, And let us mer - cy find:

Think on us who think on thee; Ev - ery burdened soul re-lease;

O! re - mem-ber Cal - va - ry, And bid us go in peace.

131. *Pleading by the Cross.*

1. LAMB of God, whose bleeding love
We now recall to mind,
Send the answer from above,
And let us mercy find:
Think on us who think on thee;
Every burdened soul release;
O! remember Calvary,
And bid us go in peace.

2. Through thy blood by faith applied,
Let us thy pardon feel;
Speak us freely justified,
And all our sickness heal:
By thy passion on the tree,
Let our griefs and troubles cease;
O! remember Calvary,
And bid us go in peace.

3. Can we ever hence depart
Till thou our wants relieve?

Write forgiveness on our heart,
And all thine image give:
Still our souls shall cry to thee,
Till renewed by holiness;
Oh remember Calvary,
And bid us go in peace.

132. *Pleading for Recovering Grace.*

1. WRETCHED, helpless, and distressed,
Ah whither shall I fly?
Ever panting after rest,
Where shall I turn mine eye?
Naked, sick, and poor, and blind,
Bound in sin and misery:
Friend of sinners, let me find
My help, my all in thee.

2. Jesus, full of truth and grace,
Oh hear my sad complaint;
Be the wand'rer's resting-place,
A cordial for the faint:

AMSTERDAM. 7s & 6s.
QUICK AND ENERGETIC.
ENGLISH.

1. Rise, my soul, and stretch thy wings, Thy bet-ter por-tion trace;
Rise from tran-si-to-ry things Tow'rd heav'n, thy na-tive place:

Sun, and moon, and stars de-cay, Time shall soon this earth re-move;

Rise, my soul, and haste a-way, To seats pre-pared a-bove.

Make me rich, for I am poor;
 Let me now thy presence find:
To the dying health restore,
 And eyesight to the blind.

3. Fill my soul with heavenly grace,
 With pure humility:
Clothe me with thy righteousness:
 Endue my heart with thee:
Let thine image be restored;
 Let me thy forgiveness prove;
Fill me with thy fullness, Lord,
 For boundless is thy love.

133. *The Pilgrim's Song.*

1. RISE, my soul, and stretch thy wings,
 Thy better portion trace;
Rise from transitory things
 Tow'rd heaven, thy native place:

Sun, and moon, and stars decay,
 Time shall soon this earth remove;
Rise, my soul, and haste away,
 To seats prepared above.

2. Rivers to the ocean run,
 Nor stay in all their course;
Fire ascending, seeks the sun;
 Both speed them to their source.
So a soul that 's born of God
 Pants to view his glorious face;
Upward tends to his abode
 To rest in his embrace.

3. Cease, ye pilgrims, cease to mourn,
 Press onward to the prize;
Soon your Saviour will return,
 Triumphant in the skies:
Yet a season, and you know
 Happy entrance will be given;
All your sorrows left below,
 And earth exchanged for heaven.

STILLINGFLEET. S. M.*

SWISS COLL.

1. My God, per-mit my tongue This joy. to call thee mine;

And let my ear - ly cries pre-vail To taste thy love di - vine.

* See also Watchman and Boylston 18. 52.

134. *Seeking God.*

1. My God, permit my tongue
This joy to call thee mine;
And let my early cries prevail
To taste thy love divine.

2. My thirsty, fainting soul
Thy mercy doth implore:
Not travelers in desert lands
Can pant for waters more.

3. Within thy churches, Lord,
I long to find a place,
Thy power and glory to behold,
And feel thy quick'ning grace.

4. For life without thy love
No relish can afford;
No joy can be compared with this,
To serve and please the Lord.

5. To thee I'll lift my hands;
I'll praise thee, while I live;
Not the rich dainties of a feast
Such food or pleasures give.

135. *Night Watching.*

1. In wakeful hours of night,
I call my God to mind;
I think how wise thy counsels are
And all thy dealings kind.

2. Since thou hast been my help,
To thee my spirit flies;
And on thy watchful providence
My cheerful hope relies.

3. The shadow of thy wings
My soul in safety keeps;
I follow where my Father leads,
And he supports my steps.

136. *Hearken to the Word.*

1. Come, sound his praise abroad,
And hymns of glory sing;
Jehovah is the sovereign God,
The universal King.

2. He formed the deeps unknown,
He gave the seas their bound;
The watery worlds are all his own,
And all the solid ground.

3. Come, worship at his throne;
Come, bow before the Lord:
We are his work, and not our own,
He formed us by his word.

4. To-day attend his voice,
Nor dare provoke his rod;
Come, like the people of his choice,
And own your gracious God.

5. But if your ears refuse
The language of his grace,
And hearts grow hard, like stubborn Jews,
That unbelieving race ·

6. The Lord in vengeance dressed,
Will lift his hand and swear —
"You that despise my promised rest,
Shall have no portion there."

137. *Invitation to the House of God.*

1. COME to the house of prayer,
   O thou afflicted, come;
   The God of peace shall meet thee there;
   He makes that house his home.

2. Come to the house of praise,
   Ye who are happy now;
   In sweet accord your voices raise,
   In kindred homage bow.

3. Ye aged, hither come,
   For ye have felt his love;
   Soon shall your trembling tongues be
       dumb,
   Your lips forget to move.

4. Ye young, before his throne,
   Come, bow; your voices raise;
   Let not your hearts his praise disown,
   Who gives the power to praise.

5. Thou, whose benignant eye
   In mercy looks on all,
   Who sees the tear of misery,
   And hears the mourners call—

6. Up to thy dwelling place
   Bear our frail spirits on,
   Till they outstrip time's tardy pace,
   And heaven on earth be won

138. *The Sabbath welcomed.*

1. WELCOME, sweet day of rest,
   That saw the Lord arise;
   Welcome to this reviving breast,
   And these rejoicing eyes.

2. The King himself comes near,
   And feasts his saints to-day;
   Here we may sit, and see him here,
   And love, and praise, and pray.

3. One day amidst the place
   Where my dear Lord hath been,
   Is sweeter than ten thousand days
   Of pleasurable sin.

4. My willing soul would stay
   In such a frame as this,
   And sit and sing herself away
   To everlasting bliss.

139. *Active Effort to do Good.*

1. Sow in the morn thy seed;
   At eve hold not thy hand;
   To doubt and fear give thou no heed;
   Broadcast it o'er the land;—

2. And duly shall appear,
   In verdure, beauty, strength,
   The tender blade, the stalk, the ear,
   And the full corn at length.

3. Thou canst not toil in vain;
   Cold, heat and moist, and dry,
   Shall foster and mature the grain
   For garners in the sky.

4. Thence, when the glorious end,
   The day of God shall come,
   The angel-reapers shall descend,
   And heaven cry, "Harvest home!"

140. *Rev. xxii. 17–20.*

1. THE Spirit in our hearts
   Is whispering, Sinner, come!
   The bride, the Church of Christ proclaims
   To all his children, come.

2. Let him that heareth, say
   To all about him, Come!
   Let him that thirsts for righteousness,
   To Christ, the fountain, come!

3. Yes! whosoever will,
   Oh! let him freely come,
   And freely drink the stream of life;
   'Tis Jesus bids him Come;

4. Lo! Jesus, who invites,
   Declares, "I quickly come;"
   Lord, even so! I wait Thy hour:
   Jesus, my Saviour, come!

141. *Prayer for the Spirit.*

1. BLEST Comforter divine,
   Let rays of heavenly love
   Amid our gloom and darkness shine,
   And guide our souls above.

2. Turn us, with gentle voice,
   From every sinful way,
   And bid the mourning saint rejoice,
   Though earthly joys decay.

3. By thine inspiring breath
   Make every cloud of care,
   And e'en the gloomy vale of death,
   A smile of glory wear.

4. O, fill thou every heart
   With love to all our race;
   Great Comforter, to us impart
   These blessings of thy grace.

MODERATO.

1. My God, how end-less is thy love! Thy gifts are ev-ery evening new;

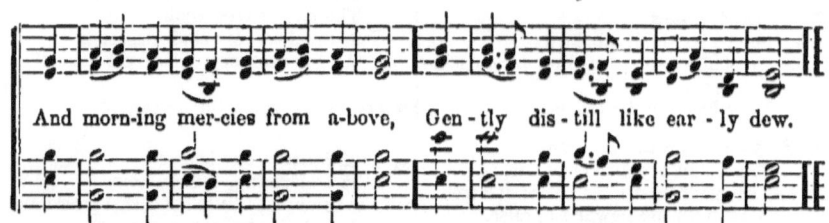

And morn-ing mer-cies from a-bove, Gen - tly dis - till like ear - ly dew.

142. *A Song for Morning and Evening.*

1. My God, how endless is thy love!
Thy gifts are every evening new;
And morning mercies from above,
Gently distill like early dew.

2. Thou spread'st the curtains of the night,
Great Guardian of my sleeping hours;
Thy sovereign word restores the light,
And quickens all my drowsy powers.

3. I yield my powers to thy command;
To thee I consecrate my days;
Perpetual blessings from thine hand
Demand perpetual songs of praise.

143. *A Morning Hymn.*

1. GOD of the morning, at whose voice
The cheerful sun makes haste to rise,
And like a giant doth rejoice,
To run his journey to the skies;—

2. Oh, like the sun may I fulfill
The appointed duties of the day;
With ready mind, and active will,
March on and keep my heavenly way.

3. (But I shall rove and lose the race,
If God my Sun should disappear,
And leave me in this world's wide maze,
To follow every wandering star).

4. Lord, thy commands are clear and pure,
Enlightening our beclouded eyes;

Thy threatenings just, thy promise sure,
Thy gospel makes the simple wise.

5. Give me thy counsel for my guide,
And then receive me to thy bliss:
All my desires and hopes beside
Are faint, and cold, compared with
this.

144. *Morning Gratitude.*

1. IN sleep's serene oblivion laid,
I safely passed the silent night;
Again I see the breaking shade,
I drink again the morning light.

2. New-born I bless the waking hour,
Once more, with awe, rejoice to be:
My conscious soul resumes her power,
And springs, my guardian God, to
thee!

3. Oh guide me through the various maze
My doubtful feet may this day tread;
And spread thy shield's protecting blaze
Where dangers press around my head.

4. A deeper shade will soon impend,
A deeper sleep mine eyes oppress;
Yet then thy strength shall still defend,
Thy goodness still delight to bless.

5. That deeper shade shall break away,
That deeper sleep shall leave mine
eyes;
Thy light shall give eternal day,
Thy love, the rapture of the skies.

145. *Praise for Divine Goodness.*

1. BLESS, O my soul, the living God,
Call home thy thoughts that roam
abroad;
Let all the powers within me join
In work and worship so divine.

2. Bless, O my soul, the God of grace,
Whose favors claim the highest praise;
Why should the wonders he hath
wrought
Be lost in silence, and forgot?

3. 'Tis he, my soul, that sent his Son
To die for crimes which thou hast done;
He owns the ransom, and forgives
The hourly follies of our lives.

4. Let the whole earth his power confess,
Let the whole earth adore his grace;
Let every living creature join
In work and worship so divine.

146. *Communion with God.*

1. BLEST hour when mortal man retires
To hold communion with his God,
To send to heaven his warm desires,
And listen to the sacred word.

2. Blest hour, when earthly cares resign
Their empire o'er his anxious breast,
While all around the calm divine
Proclaims the holy day of rest.

3. Blest hour, when God Himself draws
nigh,
Well pleased his people's voice to hear,
To hush the penitential sigh,
And wipe away the mourner's tear.

4. Blest hour, for where the Lord resorts—
Foretastes of future bliss are given,
And mortals find his earthly courts
The house of God, the gate of Heaven.

147. *Praise for Divine Protection.*

1. WITH all my powers of heart and
tongue,
I'll praise my Maker in my song;
Angels shall hear the notes I raise,
Approve the song, and join the praise.

2. To God I cried, when troubles rose;
He heard me, and subdued my foes;
He did my rising fears control,
And strength diffused through all my
soul.

3. Amid a thousand snares I stand,
Upheld and guarded by thy hand;
Thy words my fainting soul revive,
And keep my dying faith alive.

4. I'll sing thy truth and mercy, Lord;
I'll sing the wonders of thy word;
Not all the works and names below,
So much thy power and glory show.

148. *Christ's Love.*

1. JESUS, thy boundless love to me
No thought can reach, no tongue
declare;
Unite my thankful heart to thee,
And reign without a rival there.

2. Thy love, how cheering is its ray!
All pain before its presence flies:
Care, anguish, sorrow, melt away,
Where'er its healing beams arise.

3. O let thy love my soul inflame,
And to thy service sweetly bind:
Transfuse it through my inmost frame,
And mould me wholly to thy mind.

4. Thy love in sufferings be my peace;
Thy love in weakness make me
strong;
And when the storms of life shall cease,
Thy love shall be my heaven and
song.

149. *Morning.*

1. NEW every morning is the love
Our wakening and uprising prove;
Through sleep and darkness safely
brought,
Restored to life, and power, and thought

2. New mercies each returning day
Hover around us while we pray;
New perils past, new sins forgiven,
New thoughts of God, new hopes of
heaven.

3. If on our daily course our mind
Be set to hallow all we find,
Some softening gleam of love and
prayer
Shall dawn on every cross and care.

4. The trivial round, the common task
Will furnish all we ought to ask;
Room to deny ourselves, a road
To bring us daily nearer God.

5. Seek we no more; content with these,
Let present rapture, comfort, ease,
As heaven shall bid them, come and go;
The secret this of rest below.

6. Only, O Lord, in Thy dear love
Fit us for perfect rest above;
And help us this, and every day,
To live more nearly as we pray.

BOYLSTON. S. M.*

L. MASON.

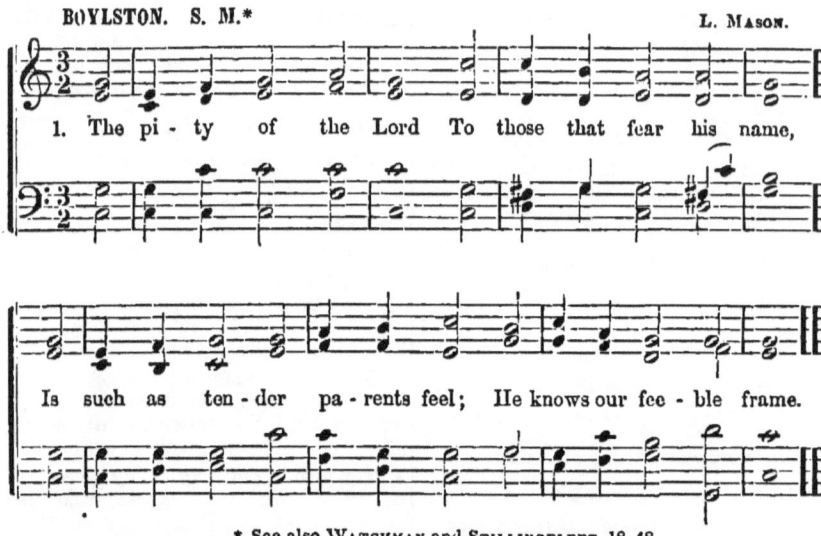

1. The pi - ty of the Lord To those that fear his name,

Is such as ten - der pa - rents feel; He knows our fee - ble frame.

* See also WATCHMAN and STILLINGFLEET 18. 48.

150. *The Pity of God.*

1. THE pity of the Lord
   To those that fear his name,
   Is such as tender parents feel;
   He knows our feeble frame.

2. He knows we are but dust,
   Scattered with every breath:
   His anger, like a rising wind,
   Can send us swift to death.

3. Our days are as the grass,
   Or like the morning flower;
   If one sharp blast sweep o'er the field,
   It withers in an hour.

4. But thy compassions, Lord,
   To endless years endure;
   And children's children ever find
   Thy words of promise sure.

151. *Uncertainty of Life.*

1. TO-MORROW, Lord, is thine!
   Lodged in thy sovereign hand;
   And if its sun arise and shine,
   It shines by thy command.

2. The present moment flies,
   And bears our life away;
   Oh make thy servants truly wise,
   That they may live to-day.

3. Since on this fleeting hour
   Eternity is hung,
   Awaken, by thy mighty power,
   The aged and the young.

4. One thing demands our care—
   Be that one thing pursued;
   Lest, slighted once, the season fair
   Should never be renewed.

5. To Jesus may we fly,
   Swift as the morning light,
   Lest life's young golden beams should
   die
   In sudden, endless night.

152. *God working in the Soul.*

1. 'TIS God the Spirit leads
   In paths before unknown;
   The work to be performed is ours:
   The strength is all His own.

2. Supported by His grace,
   We still pursue our way,
   And hope at last to reach the prize,
   Secure in endless day.

3. 'Tis He that works to will;
   'Tis He that works to do;
   The power by which we act is His,
   And His the glory too.

153. *Prayer for a Revival.*

1. O LORD, thy work revive,
In Zion's gloomy hour,
And let our dying graces live
By thy restoring power.

2. O let thy chosen few
Awake to earnest prayer;
Their covenant again renew,
And walk in filial fear.

3. Thy Spirit then will speak
Through lips of humble clay,
Till hearts of adamant shall break,
Till rebels shall obey.

4. Now lend thy gracious ear;
Now listen to our cry;
O, come and bring salvation near;
Our souls on thee rely.

154. *Thy Way, not Mine.*

1. THY way, not mine, O Lord,
However dark it be!
Lead me by thy own faithful hand,
Choose out the path for me.

2. Smooth let it be or rough,
It will be still the best,
Winding or straight, it matters not,
It leads me to thy rest.

3. I dare not choose my lot:
I would not if I might;
Choose thou for me, my gracious God,
So shall I walk aright.

4. The kingdom that I seek
Is thine; so let the way
That leads to it be truly thine,
Else I must surely stray.

155. *Solicitude for the Conversion of Children.*

1. THOU God of sovereign grace,
In mercy now appear;
We long to see thy smiling face,
And feel that thou art near.

2. Receive these lambs to-day,
O Shepherd of the flock,
And wash the stains of guilt away
Beside the smitten Rock.

3. Thy saving health impart,
O Comforter divine;
Make all these children pure in heart;
Make them entirely thine.

4. To-day in love descend;
O come, this precious hour;
In mercy now their spirits bend
By thy resistless power.

5. Low bending at thy feet,
Our offspring we resign:
Thine arm is strong, thy love is great,
And high thy glories shine.

156. *Prayer for Sanctification of Children.*

1. O GOD of Abra'm, hear
The parents' humble cry;
In cov'nant mercy now appear,
While in the dust we lie.

2. These children of our love,
In mercy thou hast given,
That we thro' grace may faithful prove
In training them for heaven.

3. O, grant thy Spirit, Lord,
Their hearts to sanctify;
Remember now thy gracious word,
Our hopes on thee rely.

4. Draw forth the melting tear,
The penitential sigh;
Inspire their hearts with faith sincere,
And fix their hopes on high.

5. These children now are thine,
We give them back to thee;
O lead them, by thy grace divine,
Along the heavenly way.

157. *The Presence of Christ.*

1. WHILE my Redeemer's near,
My shepherd and my guide,
I bid farewell to every fear;
My wants are all supplied.

2. To ever fragrant meads,
Where rich abundance grows,
His gracious hand indulgent leads,
And guards my sweet repose

3. Dear Shepherd, if I stray,
My wandering feet restore;
And guard me with thy watchful eye,
And let me rove no more.

Doxology.

YE angels round the throne,
And saints that dwell below,
Worship the Father, praise the Son,
And bless the Spirit too.

HEBRON. L. M.

Slow.

L. Mason. 1830.

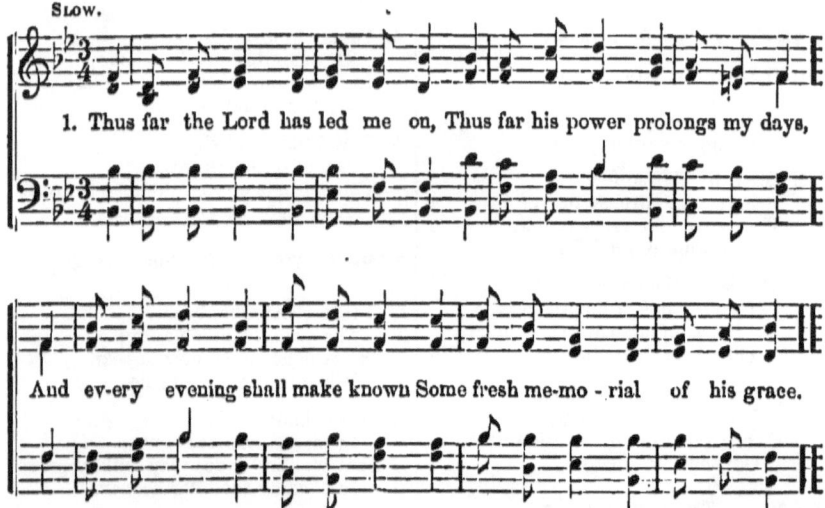

1. Thus far the Lord has led me on, Thus far his power prolongs my days,

And ev-ery evening shall make known Some fresh me-mo - rial of his grace.

158. *An Evening Hymn.*

1. Thus far the Lord has led me on,
Thus far his power prolongs my days,
And every evening shall make known
Some fresh memorial of his grace.

2. Much of my time has run to waste,
And I perhaps am near my home;
But he forgives my follies past,
He gives me strength for days to come.

3. I lay my body down to sleep;
Peace is the pillow for my head;
While well appointed angels keep
Their watchful stations round my bed.

4. Thus when the night of death shall come,
My flesh shall rest beneath the ground,
And wait thy voice to rouse my tomb,
With sweet salvation in the sound.

159. *An Evening Sacrifice.*

1. Great God, to thee my evening song
With humble gratitude I raise;
O, let thy mercy tune my tongue,
And fill my heart with lively praise.

2. My days unclouded, as they pass,
And every gently rolling hour,
Are monuments of wondrous grace,
And witness to thy love and power.

3. Seal my forgiveness in the blood
Of Jesus; his dear name alone
I plead for pardon, gracious God,
And kind acceptance at thy throne.

4. Let this blest hope mine eyelids close,
With sleep refresh my feeble frame;
Safe in thy care may I repose,
And wake with praises to thy name.

160. *Decrees and Submission.*

1. Wait, O my soul, thy Maker's will,
Tumultuous passions all be still!
Nor let a murm'ring thought arise;
His ways are just, his counsels wise.

2. He in the thickest darkness dwells,
Performs his work, the cause conceals;
But, though his methods are unknown,
Judgment and truth support his throne.

3. In heaven, and earth, and air, and seas,
He executes his firm decrees;
By saints and angels still confess'd,
That what he does is ever best.

4. Wait, then, my soul, submissive wait,
Prostrate before his awful seat;
Amid the terrors of his rod,
Still trust a wise and gracious God.

161. *Traveler's Hymn.*

1. To us remains nor place nor time;
Our country is in every clime;
We can be calm and free from care
On any shore, since God is there.

2. While place we seek, or place we shun,
The soul finds happiness in none;
But with our God to guide our way,
'Tis equal joy to go or stay.

3. Could we be cast where Thou art not,
That were indeed a dreadful lot;
But regions none remote we call,
Secure of finding God in all.

162. *The Presence of Christ implored.*

1. WHERE two or three with sweet accord,
Obedient to their sovereign Lord,
Meet to recount his acts of grace,
And offer solemn prayer and praise :

2. There will the gracious Saviour be,
To bless the little company;
There to unveil his smiling face,
And bid his glories fill the place.

3. We meet at thy command, O Lord,
Relying on thy faithful word :
Now send the Spirit from above,
And fill our hearts with heavenly love.

163. *Prayer for the Millennium.*

1. JESUS, we bow before thy throne;
We lift our eyes to seek thy face ;
To bleeding hearts thy love make
known ;
On contrite souls bestow thy grace.

2. See, spread beneath thy gracious eye,
A world o'erwhelmed in guilt and
tears,
Where deathless souls in ruin lie,
And no kind voice dispels their fears.

3. Lord, arm thy truth with power divine,
Its conquests spread from shore to
shore,
Till suns and stars forget to shine,
And earth and skies shall be no more.

4. O rise, ye ransomed captives, rise,
Peal the loud anthem here below;
Let earth reflect it to the skies,
And heaven with new-born rapture
glow

164. *God merciful in Chastisement.*

1. THE Lord, how wondrous are his ways !
How firm his truth ! how large his grace !
He takes his mercy for his throne—
And thence he makes his glories known

2. Not half so high his power hath spread
The starry heavens above our head,
As his rich love exceeds our praise;
Exceeds the highest hopes we raise.

3. Not half so far has nature placed
The rising morning from the west,
As his forgiving grace removes
The daily guilt of those he loves.

4. How slowly doth his wrath arise !
On swifter wings salvation flies;
And if he lets his anger burn,
How soon his frowns to pity turn !

5. Amidst his wrath compassion shines ;
His strokes are lighter than our sins;
And while his rod corrects his saints,
His ear indulges their complaints.

165. *Christ knocking at the Heart of a
Sinner.*

1. BEHOLD a Stranger at the door !
He gently knocks, has knocked before;
Hath waited long—is waiting still ;
You treat no other friend so ill.

2. Oh, lovely attitude ! he stands
With melting heart and bleeding hands !
Oh, matchless kindness ! and he shows,
This matchless kindness to his foes!

3. But will he prove a friend indeed ?
He will; the very friend you need,
The friend of sinners—yes 'tis He,
With garments dyed on Calvary.

4. Rise, touched with gratitude divine,
Turn out his enemy and thine,
That soul-destroying monster, Sin,
And let the heavenly Stranger in.

5. Admit him, ere his anger burn,
His feet departed ne'er return ;
Admit him, or the hour's at hand,
You'll at His door rejected stand.

Doxology.

To God the Father, God the Son,
And God the Spirit—Three in One,
Be honor, praise, and glory given,
By all on earth, and all in heaven.

1. Awake, my soul, to joy-ful lays, And sing thy great Re-deem-er's praise;

He just-ly claims a song from me—His lov-ing kindness, O how free!

166. *Loving-kindness of God.*

1. AWAKE, my soul, to joyful lays,
   And sing the great Redeemer's praise;
   He justly claims a song from me—
   His loving-kindness, Oh, how free!

2. He saw me ruined in the fall,
   Yet loved me, notwithstanding all:
   He saved me from my lost estate—
   His loving-kindness, Oh, how great!

3. Though num'rous hosts of mighty foes,
   Though earth and hell my way oppose,
   He safely leads my soul along—
   His loving-kindness, Oh, how strong!

4. When trouble, like a gloomy cloud,
   Has gather'd thick, and thunder'd loud,
   He near my soul has always stood—
   His loving-kindness, Oh, how good!

5. Often I feel my sinful heart,
   Prone from my Jesus to depart;
   But, though I have him oft forgot,
   His loving-kindness changes not.

6. Soon shall I pass the gloomy vale,
   Soon all my mortal powers must fail;
   Oh, may my last expiring breath
   His loving-kindness sing in death!

7. Then let me mount, and soar away
   To the bright world of endless day,
   And sing, with rapture and surprise,
   His loving-kindness in the skies.

167. *Majesty and Dominion of God.*

1. COME, O my soul, in sacred lays
   Attempt thy great Creator's praise:
   But, O, what tongue can speak his
   fame?
   What verse can reach the lofty theme?

2. Enthroned amid the radiant spheres,
   He glory like a garment wears;
   To form a robe of light divine
   Ten thousand suns around him shine.

3. In all our Maker's grand designs,
   Almighty power, with wisdom, shines;
   His works, through all this wondrous
   frame,
   Declare the glory of his name.

4. Raised on devotion's lofty wing,
   Do thou, my soul, his glories sing;
   And let his praise employ thy tongue
   Till listening worlds shall join the song.

168. *The God of all Grace.*

1. GREAT God, let all my tuneful powers
   Awake, and sing thy mighty name ·
   Thy hand revolves my circling hours—
   Thy hand, from whence my being
   came.

2. Seasons and moons, still rolling round
   In beauteous order, speak thy praise;
   And years, with smiling mercy
   crowned,
   To thee successive honors raise.

3. My life, my health, my friends, I owe
All to thy vast, unbounded love;
Ten thousand precious gifts below,
And hope of nobler joys above.

4. Thus will I sing till nature cease,
Till sense and language are no more,
And after death thy boundless grace,
Through everlasting years, adore.

169. *Jesus the only Saviour.*

1. JESUS, the spring of joys divine,
Whence all our hopes and comforts
flow:
Jesus, no other name, but thine,
Can save us from eternal woe.

2. In vain would boasting reason find
The way to happiness and God;
Her weak directions leave the mind
Bewildered in a dubious road.

3. No other name will Heaven approve;
Thou art the true, the living way,
Ordained by everlasting love
To the bright realms of endless day.

4. Safe lead us through this world of
night,
And bring us to the blissful plains,
The regions of unclouded light,
Where perfect joy for ever reigns.

170. *Thy Kingdom Come.*

1. SOVEREIGN of worlds! display thy
power,
Be this thy Zion's favored hour:
Bid the bright morning star arise,
And point the nations to the skies.

2. Set up thy throne where Satan reigns,
On Afric's shore, in India's plains,
On wilds and continents unknown;
And make the universe thine own.

3. Speak, and the world shall hear thy
voice,
Speak! and the desert shall rejoice:
Scatter the gloom of heathen night,
And bid all nations hail the light.

171. *Triumphant Ascension of Christ.*

1. OUR Lord is risen from the dead,
Our Jesus is gone up on high;
The powers of hell are captive led,
Dragged to the portals of the sky.

2 Lo! his triumphal chariot waits,
And angels chant the solemn lay—
Lift up your heads, ye heavenly gates,
Ye everlasting doors, give way!

3. Loose all your bars of massy light,
And wide unfold th' ethereal scene:
He claims these mansions as his right;
Receive the King of Glory in.

4. "Who is the King of Glory—who?"
The Lord that all his foes o'creame,
The world, sin, death, and hell o'er-
threw;
And Jesus is the conq'ror's name.

5. Lo! his triumphal chariot waits,
And angels chant the solemn lay—
Lift up your heads, ye heavenly gates,
Ye everlasting doors, give way!

6. "Who is the King of Glory—who?"
The Lord of boundless power pos-
sessed,
The King of saints and angels too,
God over all, for ever blest.

172. *Praise to the great Redeemer.*

1. BE thou, O God, exalted high;
And as thy glory fills the sky,
So let it be on earth displayed,
Till thou art here, as there, obeyed.

2. O God, my heart is fixed; 'tis bent,
Its thankful tribute to present;
And, with my heart, my voice I'll raise
To thee, my God, in songs of praise.

3. Thy praises, Lord, I would resound
To all the listening nations round;
Thy mercy, highest heaven transcends;
Thy truth beyond the clouds extends.

4. Be thou, O God, exalted high;
And as thy glory fills the sky,
So let it be on earth displayed,
Till thou art here, as there, obeyed.

173. *Preserving and Restoring Grace.*

1. WITH all my powers of heart and
tongue
I'll praise my Maker in my song;
Angels shall hear the notes I raise,
Approve the song, and join the praise.

2. To God I cried when troubles rose:
He heard me, and subdued my foes:
He did my rising fears control,
And strength diffused thro' all my soul.

3. Amidst a thousand snares I stand,
Upheld and guarded by thy hand;
Thy words my fainting soul revive,
And keep my dying faith alive.

4. Grace will complete what grace begins,
To save from sorrow and from sins;
The work that wisdom undertakes
Eternal mercy no'er forsakes.

OLD HUNDRED. L. M.

NOT TOO SLOW.   GUIL. FRANC.

To God the Father, God the Son, And God the Spi-rit, Three in One,

Be hon-or, praise, and glo-ry given, By all on earth, and all in heaven.

174. *Praise to our Creator.*

1. YE nations round the earth rejoice
   Before the Lord, your sovereign King:
   Serve him with cheerful heart and voice;
   With all your tongues his glory sing.

2. The Lord is good, 'tis he alone
   Doth life and breath and being give:
   We are his work, and not our own,
   The sheep that on his pastures live.

3. Enter his gates with songs of joy;
   With praises to his courts repair;
   And make it your divine employ
   To pay your thanks and honors there.

4. The Lord is good, the Lord is kind;
   Great is his grace, his mercy sure;
   And the whole race of man shall find
   His truth from age to age endure.

175. *A Heavenly Portion.*

1. WHAT sinners value, I resign;
   Lord, 'tis enough that thou art mine:
   I shall behold thy blissful face,
   And stand complete in righteousness.

2. This life's a dream, an empty show;
   But the bright world to which I go
   Hath joys substantial and sincere;
   When shall I wake and find me there?

3. O, glorious hour! O, blest abode!
   I shall be near, and like my God;
   And flesh and sin no more control
   The sacred pleasures of the soul.

4. My flesh shall slumber in the ground
   Till the last trumpet's joyful sound;
   Then burst the chains with sweet surprise,
   And in my Saviour's image rise.

176. *General Praise.*

1. FROM all that dwell below the skies
   Let the Creator's praise arise:
   Let the Redeemer's name be sung
   Through every land, by every tongue.

2. Eternal are thy mercies, Lord,
   Eternal truth attends thy word;
   Thy praise shall sound from shore to shore,
   Till suns shall rise and set no more.

177. *God a King.*

1. JEHOVAH reigns; he dwells in light,
   Girded with majesty and might;
   The world, created by His hands,
   · Still on its firm foundation stands.

2 But ere this spacious world was made,
   Or had its first foundation laid,

Thy throne eternal ages stood,
Thyself the ever-living God.

3. Like floods the angry nations rise,
   And aim their rage against the skies;
   Vain floods, that aim their rage so high;
   At thy rebuke the billows die.

_ For ever shall thy throne endure;
   Thy promise stands for ever sure;
   And everlasting holiness
   Becomes the dwelling of thy grace.

1. Dismiss us with thy blessing, Lord;
   Help us to feed upon thy word;
   All that has been amiss, forgive,
   And let thy truth within us live.

2. Though we are guilty, Thou art good;
   Wash all our works in Jesus' blood;
   Give every burdened soul release,
   And bid us all depart in peace.

OLIVE'S BROW. L. M.   W. B. BRADBURY.

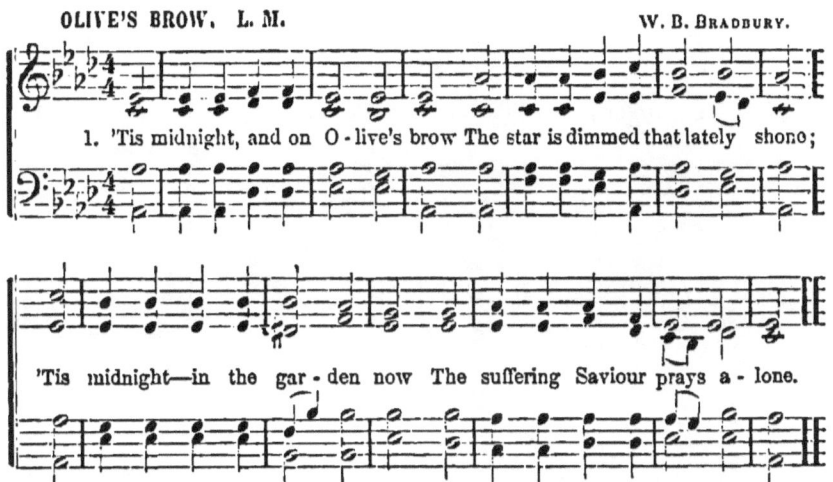

1. 'Tis midnight, and on O-live's brow The star is dimmed that lately shone;

'Tis midnight—in the gar-den now The suffering Saviour prays a-lone.

178.   *Agony in the Garden.*

1. 'TIS midnight—and on Olive's brow
   The star is dimmed that lately shone;
   'Tis midnight—in the garden now
   The suffering Saviour prays alone.

2 'Tis midnight—and from all removed,
   Immanuel wrestles lone with fears;
   E'en the disciple that he loves,
   Heeds not his Master's griefs and tears.

3. 'Tis midnight—and for others' guilt
   The Man of sorrows weeps in blood;
   Yet he that hath in anguish knelt,
   Is not forsaken by his God.

4. 'Tis midnight—from the heavenly plains
   Is borne the song that angels know;
   Unheard by mortals are the strains
   That sweetly soothe the Saviour's woe.

179.   *Christ's Passion.*

1. BROUGHT forth to judgment, Jesus stands,
   Arraigned, condemned at Pilate's bar;
   Here spurned by fierce Prætorian bands,
   There mocked by Herod's men of war.

2. He bears their buffeting and scorn,
   Mock homage of the lip, the knee;
   The purple robe, the crown of thorn,
   The scourge, the nail, th' accursèd tree.

3. No guile within his mouth is found,
   He neither threatens, nor complains;
   Meek as a lamb for slaughter bound,
   Dumb, 'mid his murderers, he remains.

4. But hark, he prays! 'tis for his foes;
   He speaks—'tis comfort to his friends
   Answers—and paradise bestows;
   He bows his head, the conflict ends.

5. Truly this was the Son of God!
   Though as a servant in disguise;
   And bruised beneath the Father's rod,
   Not for himself—for man he dies.

MONMOUTH, L. M.   MARTIN LUTHER.

1. He reigns! the Lord, the Saviour reigns! Praise him in e - van -
gel - ic strains; Let the whole earth in songs re - joice, And
dis - tant islands join their voice, And dis - tant is - lands join their voice.

180. *Christ coming to Judgment.*

1. · HE reigns! the Lord, the Saviour
    reigns!
Praise him in evangelic strains;
Let the whole earth in songs rejoice,
And distant islands join their voice.

2. Deep are his counsels and unknown;
But grace and truth support his throne;
Though gloomy clouds his way surround,
Justice is their eternal ground.

3. In robes of judgment, lo! he comes;
Shakes the wide earth, and cleaves the
    tombs;
Before him burns devouring fire;
The mountains melt, the seas retire.

4. His enemies, with sore dismay,
Fly from the sight, and shun the day:
Then lift your heads, ye saints, on high,
And sing, for your redemption's nigh.

181. *Christ the Supreme God and King.*

1. AROUND the Saviour's lofty throne,
    Ten thousand times ten thousand
        sing;
They worship him as God alone,
    And crown him—everlasting King!

2. Approach, ye saints! this God is yours;
    'Tis Jesus fills the throne above:
Ye can not want, while God endures;
    Ye can not fail, while God is love

3. Jesus, thou everlasting King!
    To Thee the praise of heaven belongs;
Yet, smile on us, who fain would bring
    The tribute of our humble songs.

4. Though sin defile our worship here,
    We hope, ere long, Thy face to view;
And, when our souls in heaven appear,
    We'll praise Thy name as angels do.

BEETHOVEN. L. M.

MAESTOSO.

HAYDN.

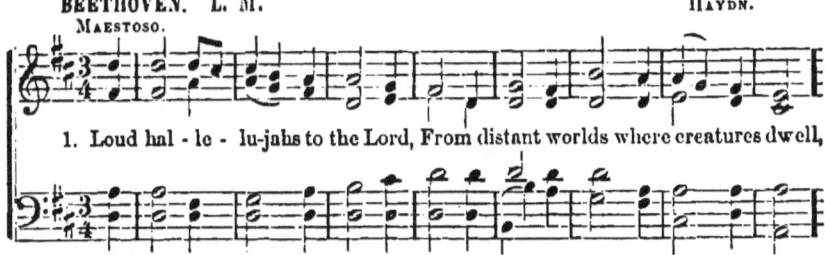

1. Loud hal - le - lu-jahs to the Lord, From distant worlds where creatures dwell,

CHOIR.

CONGREGATION.

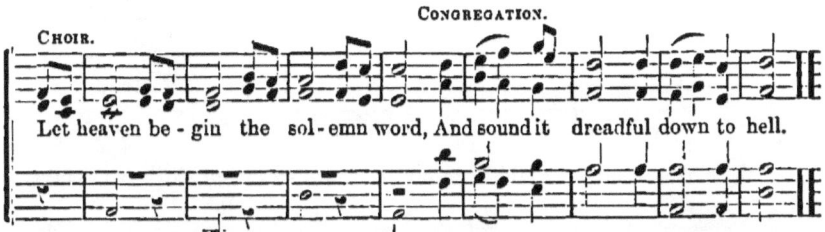

Let heaven be - gin the sol-emn word, And sound it dreadful down to hell.

182. *Universal Praise.*

1. LOUD hallelujahs to the Lord,
   From distant worlds where creatures
     dwell,
   Let heaven begin the solemn word,
   And sound it dreadful down to hell.

2. High on a throne his glories dwell,
   An awful throne of shining bliss:
   Fly through the world, O sun! and tell
   How dark thy beams compared to His.

3. Jehovah—'tis a glorious word!
   O, may it dwell on every tongue!
   But saints, who best have known the Lord
   Are bound to raise the noblest song.

4. Speak of the wonders of that love
   Which Gabriel plays on every chord;
   From all below, and all above,
   Loud hallelujahs to the Lord!

183. *The Eternal and Sovereign God.*

1. JEHOVAH reigns; he dwells in light,
   Girded with majesty and might;
   The world, created by his hands,
   Still on its first foundation stands.

2. But, ere this spacious world was made,
   Or had its first foundations laid,
   Thy throne eternal ages stood—
   Thyself, the ever-living God.

3. Like floods the angry nations rise,
   And aim their rage against the skies:
   Vain floods, that aim their rage so high!
   At thy rebuke the billows die.

4. Forever shall thy throne endure,
   Thy promise stands for ever sure;
   And everlasting holiness
   Becomes the dwellings of thy grace.

184. *Perfection of God combined in his
     Government.*

1. JEHOVAH reigns; his throne is high;
   His robes are light and majesty;
   His glory shines with beams so bright,
   No mortal can sustain the sight.

2. His terrors keep the world in awe;
   His justice guards his holy law;
   His love reveals a smiling face;
   His truth and promise seal the grace.

3. Through all his works his wisdom
     shines,
   And baffles Satan's deep designs;
   His power is sovereign to fulfill
   The noblest counsels of his will.

4. And will this glorious Lord descend
   To be my Father and my Friend?
   Then let my songs with angels join;
   Heaven is secure, if God be mine.

SWEET IS THE LIGHT. L. M.

SLOW AND DELICATE.

BEETHOVEN.

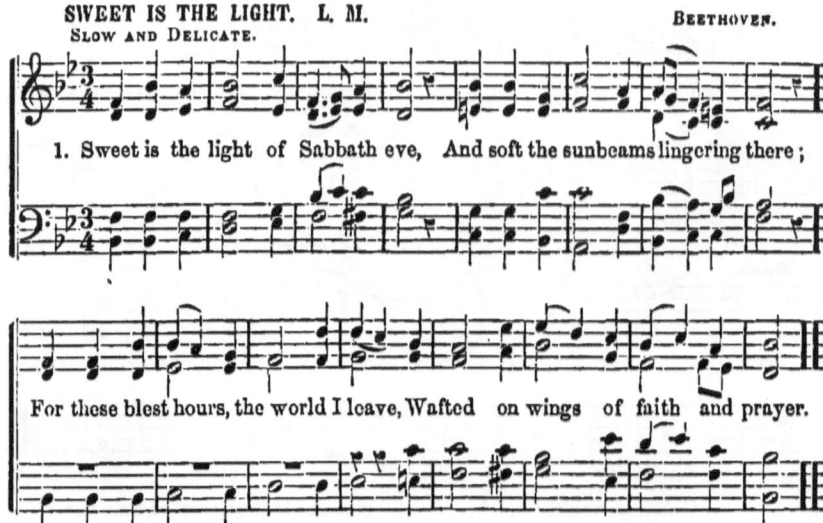

1. Sweet is the light of Sabbath eve, And soft the sunbeams lingering there;

For these blest hours, the world I leave, Wafted on wings of faith and prayer.

185.   *Sabbath Eve.*

1. SWEET is the light of Sabbath eve,
    And soft the sunbeams lingering
    there;
    For these blest hours, the world I leave,
    Wafted on wings of faith and prayer.

2. The time how lovely and how still;
    Peace shines and smiles on all be-
    low—
    The plain, the stream, the wood, the
    hill—
    All fair with evening's setting glow.

3. Season of rest! the tranquil soul
    Feels the sweet calm, and melts to
    love—
    And while these sacred moments roll,
    Faith sees the smiling heaven above

4. Nor will our days of toil be long,
    Our pilgrimage will soon be trod;
    And we shall join the ceaseless song—
    The endless Sabbath of our God.

186.   *Brevity of Life.*

1. ERE mountains reared their forms sub-
    lime,
    Or heaven and earth in order stood,
    Before the birth of ancient time,
    From everlasting Thou art God.

2. A thousand ages, in their flight,
    With Thee are as a fleeting day,

    Past, present, future to Thy sight
    At once their various scenes display.

3. But our brief life's a shadowy dream,
    A passing thought, that soon is o'er,
    That fades with morning's earliest beam,
    And fills the musing mind no more.

4. To us, O Lord, the wisdom give,
    Each passing moment so to spend,
    That we at length with Thee may live
    Where life and bliss shall never end.

187.   *Heaven.*

1. THERE is a region lovelier far
    Than sages tell, or poets sing;
    Brighter than summer beauties are,
    And softer than the tints of spring.

2. It is not fann'd by summer's gale;
    'Tis not refresh'd by vernal showers,
    It never needs the moon-beam pale,
    For there are known no evening
    hours.

3. It is all holy and serene,
    The land of glory and repose;
    No cloud obscures the radiant scene,
    There not a tear of sorrow flows.

4. In vain the philosophic eye
    May seek to view the fair abode,
    Or find it in the curtained sky;
    It is *the dwelling-place of God!*

188. *Safety in the Cross.*

1. WHY droops my soul with grief oppressed?
Whence these wild tumults in my breast?
Is there no balm to heal my wound,
No kind physician to be found?

2. Yes, in the gospel's faithful lines
Jehovah's boundless mercy shines;
There, dressed in love, the Saviour stands,
With pitying heart, and bleeding hands.

3. Raise to the cross thy weeping eyes;
Behold the Prince of glory dies:
He dies, extended on the tree;
Thence sheds a sovereign balm for me.

4. Dear Saviour, at thy feet I lie,
Here to receive a cure or die;
But grace forbids that painful fear,
Infinite grace, which triumphs here.

189. *Public Worship.*

1. BE still! be still! for all around,
On either hand, is holy ground:
Here in his house, the Lord to-day
Will listen while his people pray.

2. Thou, tossed upon the waves of care,
Ready to sink with deep despair,
Here ask relief, with heart sincere,
And thou shalt find that God is here.

3. Thou, who hast laid within the grave
Those whom thou hadst no power to save,
Believe their spirits now are near,
For angels wait while God is here.

4. Thou, who hast dear ones far away,
In foreign lands, 'mid ocean's spray,
Pray for them now, and dry the tear,
And trust the God who listens here.

5. Thou, who art mourning o'er thy sin,
Deploring guilt that reigns within,
The God of peace is ever near;
The troubled spirit meets him here.

OBERLIN. L. M.
QUICK, BUT GENTLE.
BOST.

1. A-while they rest with-in the tomb
In sweet re-pose, till morn-ing come! Then rise with
joy to meet their God, And ev-er dwell in his a-bode.

190. *The Resurrection.*

1. AWHILE they rest within the tomb
In sweet repose, till morning come!
Then rise with joy to meet their God,
And ever dwell in his abode.

2. Celestial dawn! triumphant hour!
How glorious that awak'ning power,
Which bids the sleeping dust arise,
And join the anthems of the skies!

3. This weary life will soon be past,
The ling'ring morn will come at last,
And gloomy mists will roll away
Before that bright, unfading day.

FAYETTEVILLE.   7s & 6s.   Pec,
NOT TOO SLOW.   GERMAN THEME.

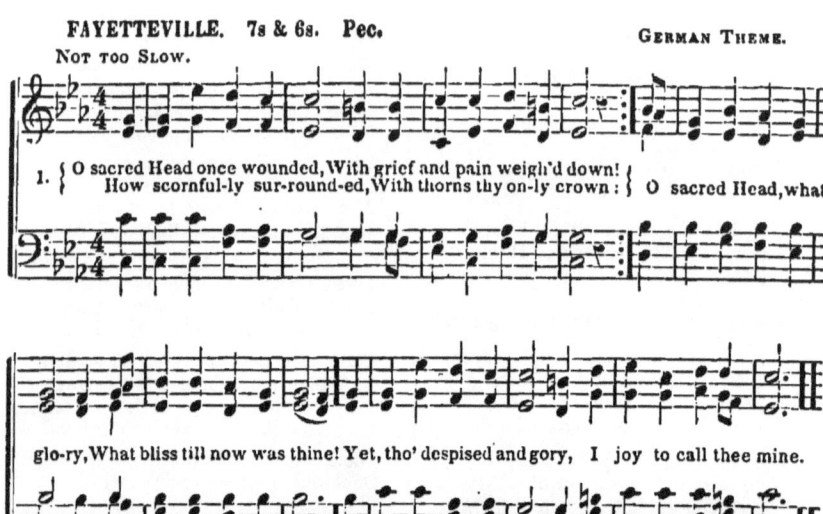

1. { O sacred Head once wounded, With grief and pain weigh'd down! } { O sacred Head, what
    { How scornful-ly sur-round-ed, With thorns thy on-ly crown : }

glo-ry, What bliss till now was thine! Yet, tho' despised and gory, I joy to call thee mine.

191.   *Scene at the Cross.*

1. O SACRED Head once wounded,
    With grief and pain weigh'd down!
How scornfully surrounded,
    With thorns thy only crown :
O sacred Head, what glory,
    What bliss till now was thine!
Yet, though despised and gory,
    I joy to call thee mine.

2. How art thou pale with anguish,
    With sore abuse and scorn!
How does that visage languish,
    Which once was bright as morn!
Thy grief, and thy compassion,
    Were all for sinners' gain;
Mine, mine was the transgression,
    But thine the deadly pain.

3. What language shall I borrow,
    To praise thee, heav'nly Friend :
For this, thy dying sorrow,
    Thy pity without end?
Lord, make me thine for ever,
    Nor let me faithless prove :
O let me never, never,
    Abuse such dying love.

4. Forbid that I should leave thee;
    O Jesus, leave not me;
By faith I would receive thee;
    Thy blood can make me free :
When strength and comfort languish,
    And I must hence depart :
Release me then from anguish,
    By thine own wounded heart.

192.   *Coloss. i. 19*

1. I LAY my sins on Jesus,
    The spotless Lamb of God ;
He bears them all, and frees us
    From the accursèd load.
I bring my guilt to Jesus,
    To wash my crimson stains
White, in his blood most precious,
    Till not a spot remains.

2. I lay my wants on Jesus;
    All fullness dwells in him,
He heals all my diseases,
    He doth my soul redeem.
I lay my griefs on Jesus,
    My burdens and my cares;
He from them all releases,
    He all my sorrow shares.

3. I long to be like Jesus,
 Meek, loving, lovely, mild,
I long to be like Jesus,
 The Father's holy child.
I long to be with Jesus,
 Amid the heavenly throng,
To sing with saints his praises,
 To learn the angels' song.

193.   *In Affliction.*

1. LORD God of my salvation,
 To thee, to thee I cry;
O let my supplication
 Arrest thine ear on high.
Distresses round me thicken,
 My life draws nigh the grave,
Descend, O Lord, to quicken,
 Descend my soul to save.

2. Thy wrath lies hard upon me,
 Thy billows o'er me roll;
My friends all seem to shun me,
 And foes beset my soul.
Where'er on earth I turn me,
 No comforter is near;
Wilt thou, my Father, spurn me,
 Wilt thou refuse to hear?

3 No! banished and heart-broken,
 My soul still clings to thee;
The promise thou hast spoken,
 Still, still my refuge be;
To present ills and terrors,
 May future joy increase,
And scourge me from my errors
 To duty, hope, and peace.

194. *Conviction and Submission.*

1. WHY sinks my soul desponding,
 Why fill my eyes with tears,
When nature all surrounding
 The smile of beauty wears?
Why burdened still with sorrow
 Is every lab'ring thought?
Each vision that I borrow,
 With gloom and sadness fraught?

2. The pleasures that deceived me
 My soul no more can charm;
Of rest they have bereaved me,
 And filled me with alarm:
The objects I have cherished
 Are empty as the wind;
My earthly joys have perished,—
 What comfort shall I find?

3. If inward still inquiring
 I turn my searching eye,
Or upward now aspiring,
 I raise my feeble cry,
No heavenly light is beaming
 To cheer my troubled breast ·
No ray of comfort gleaming
 To give my spirit rest.

4. Oh! from this dreadful anguish
 Is there no refuge nigh?
'Tis guilt that makes me languish,
 And leaves me thus to die:
I will renounce my folly
 Before the throne of grace;
And make the Lord most holy
 My strength and righteousness.

195.   *Repentance.*

1. BEFORE thy cross lamenting,
 My Saviour, I would lie,
Of all my sins repenting,
 That caused my Lord to die.
My soul with tears of anguish
 Her follies would confess;
O! while in pain I languish,
 Restore me by thy grace.

Doxology.

To Father, Son, and Spirit,
 Eternal praise be given,
By all that earth inherit,
 And all that dwell in heaven,
Thou triune God! before thee,
 Our inmost souls adore:
For, thou alone art worthy,
 And shalt be evermore.

WHAT SOFT DELIGHT. 10s 4 lines. ABR. FROM A HEBREW CHANT
WITH VARIED EXPRESSION.

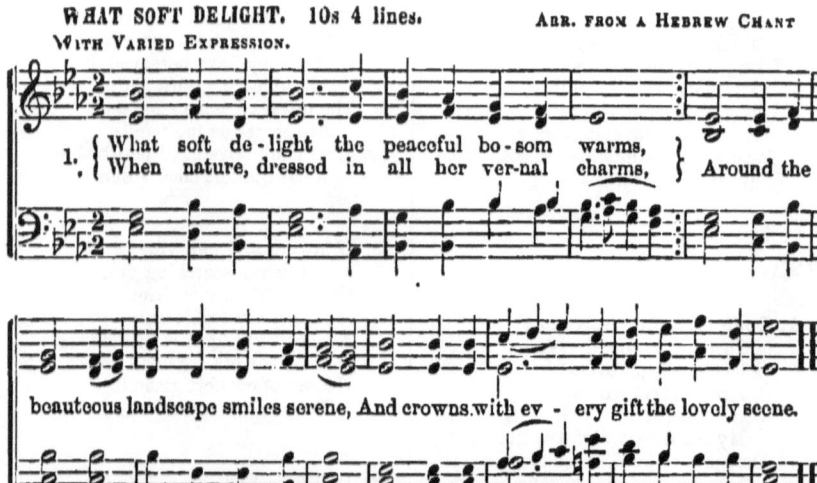

1. What soft de-light the peaceful bo-som warms,
   When nature, dressed in all her ver-nal charms, Around the
beauteous landscape smiles serene, And crowns with ev - ery gift the lovely scene.

196. *Spring. Canticles* ii. 13, 14.

1. WHAT soft delight the peaceful bosom warms,
   When nature, dressed in all her vernal charms,
   Around the beauteous landscape smiles serene,
   And crowns with every gift the lovely scene.

2. But this delightful season must decay,
   The year rolls on, and steals its charms away:—
   Swiftly the gay, the transient pleasure flies,
   Stern winter comes, and every beauty dies.

3. While pensive thought the fleeting bliss deplores,
   The mind in search of nobler pleasure soars;
   And seeks a fairer paradise on high,
   Where beauties rise and bloom, and never die.

197. *This do in Remembrance of Me.*

1. HERE, O my Lord, I see thee face to face;
   Here would I touch and handle things unseen;
   Here grasp with firmer hand th' eternal grace,
   And all my weariness upon thee lean.

2. Here would I feed upon the bread of God;
   Here drink with thee the royal wine of heaven;
   Here would I lay aside each earthly load,
   Here taste afresh the calm of sin forgiven.

3. Too soon we rise, the symbols disappear;
   The feast, though not the love, is passed and gone;
   The bread and wine remove, but thou art here—
   Nearer than ever—still my Shield and Sun.

4. Feast after feast thus comes and passes by ;
   Yet, passing, points to the glad feast above,
   Giving sweet foretaste of the festal joy,
   The Lamb's great bridal feast of bliss and love.

198.   *Night.*

1. THOU hast provided midnight's hour of peace,
   Thou stretchest over us the wing of rest ;
   With more than all a parent's tenderness,
   Foldest us sleeping to thy gentle breast.

2. Grief flies away ; care quits our easy couch,
   Till wakened by thy hand, when breaks the day—
   Like the lone prophet by the angel's touch—
   We rise to tread again our pilgrim-way.

3. God of our life ! God of each day and night !
   Oh, keep us still till life's short race is run !
   Until there dawns the long, long day of light,
   That knows no night, yet needs no star nor sun.

199.   *The Captive Tribes.*

1. ALONG the banks where Babel's current flows,
   The captive bands in deep despondence strayed ;
   While Zion's fall in sad remembrance rose,
   Her friends, her children, mingled with the dead.

2. The tuneful harp that once with joy they strung,
   When praise employed and mirth inspired the lay,
   Was now in silence on the willows hung,
   While growing grief prolonged the tedious day.

3. Their proud oppressors, to increase their woe,
   With taunting smiles a song of Zion claim ;
   Bid sacred praise, in strains melodious flow,
   While they blaspheme the great Jehovah's name.

4. But how, in heathen chains, and lands unknown,
   Shall Israel's bands the sacred anthems raise ?
   " O hapless Salem ! God's terrestrial throne,
   Thou land of glory, sacred mount of praise !

5. " If e'er my mem'ry lose thy lovely name,
   If my cold heart neglect my kindred race,
   Let dire destruction seize this guilty frame,
   My hand shall perish, and my voice shall cease."

200.   *The Sabbath.*

1. AGAIN the day returns of holy rest,
   Which, when he made the world, Jehovah blest
   When, like his own, he bade our labors cease,
   And all be piety, and all be peace.

2. Let us devote this consecrated day
   To learn his will—and all we learn obey ;
   So shall he hear, when fervently we raise
   Our supplications and our songs of praise.

3. Father in heaven, in whom our hopes confide,
   Whose power defends us, and whose precepts guide,
   In life our Guardian, and in death our Friend,
   Glory supreme be thine till time shall end.

SABBATH. L. M.
GENTLY.

"SPIRITUAL SONGS."

CHOIR.

CONGREGATION.

1. Lord of the Sab-bath and its light, I hail thy hal-lowed day of rest; It is my wea-ry soul's de - light, The sol - ace of my care-worn breast, The sol-ace of my care-worn breast.

201. *Sabbath.*

1. LORD of the Sabbath and its light,
 I hail thy hallowed day of rest;
It is my weary soul's delight,
 The solace of my care-worn breast.

2. Its dewy morn, its glowing noon,
 Its tranquil eve, its solemn night,
Pass sweetly; but they pass too soon,
 And leave me saddened at their flight.

3. Yet sweetly as they glide along,
 And hallowed tho' the calm they yield,
Transporting tho' their rapturous song,
 And heavenly visions seem revealed;

4. My soul is desolate and drear,
 My silent harp untuned remains,
Unless, my Saviour, thou art near,
 To heal my wounds and soothe my
      pains

5. O! Jesus, let me ever hail
 Thy presence with the day of rest;

Then will thy servant never fail
 To deem thy Sabbath doubly blest.

202. *The Sacrifice of the Heart.*

1. WHEN, as returns this solemn day,
 Man comes to meet his Maker, God,
What rites, what honors shall he pay?
 How spread his sovereign name
  abroad?

2. From marble domes and gilded spires
 Shall curling clouds of incense rise,
And gems, and gold, and garlands, deck
 The costly pomp of sacrifice?

3. Vain, sinful man! creation's Lord
 Thy golden offerings well may spare;
But give thy heart, and thou shalt find
 Here dwells a God who heareth prayer.

4. O, grant us, in this solemn hour,
 From earth and sin's allurements free,
To feel thy love, to own thy power,
 And raise each raptured tho't to thee!

203. *Holy Enjoyment anticipated.*

1. ANOTHER six days' work is done,
Another Sabbath is begun;
Return, my soul, enjoy thy rest,
Improve the day that God hath blest.

2. O that our thoughts and thanks may rise,
As grateful incense, to the skies,
And draw from heaven that sweet repose
Which none but he that feels it knows!

3 A heavenly calm pervades the breast,
The earnest of that glorious rest
Which for the church of God remains,
The end of cares, the end of pains.

4. With joy, great God, thy works we view,
In various scenes both old and new:
With praise, we think on mercies past;
With hope, we future pleasures taste.

5. In holy duties let the day,
In holy pleasures, pass away;
How sweet, a Sabbath thus to spend,
In hope of one that ne'er shall end!

204. *A Song for the opening Year.*

1. GREAT God, we sing that mighty hand,
By which supported still we stand:
The opening year thy mercy shows;
Let mercy crown it till it close.

2. By day, by night, at home, abroad,
Still we are guarded by our God;
By his continual bounty fed,
By his unerring counsel led.

3. With grateful hearts the past we own;
The future—all to us unknown—
We to thy guardian care commit,
And peaceful leave before thy feet.

4. In scenes exalted or depressed,
Be thou our joy, and thou our rest;
Thy goodness all our hopes shall raise,
Adored through all our changing days.

5. When death shall close our earthly songs,
And seal in silence mortal tongues,
Our Helper, God, in whom we trust,
In brighter worlds our souls shall boast.

205. *The Year crowned with Goodness.*

1. ETERNAL Source of every joy,
Thy praise may well our lips employ,
While in thy temple we appear,
Whose goodness crowns the circling
year.

2. Wide as the wheels of nature roll,
Thy hand supports and guides the
whole;
The sun is taught by thee to rise, •
And darkness when to veil the skies.

3. The flowery spring, at thy command,
Embalms the air and paints the land;
The summer rays with vigor shine,
To raise the corn and cheer the vine.

4. Thy hand in autumn richly pours
Through all our coasts abundant stores;
And winters, softened by thy care,
No more a dreary aspect wear.

5. Still be the cheerful homage paid
With morning light and evening shade;
Seasons, and months, and weeks, and
days,
Demand successive songs of praise.

206. *A Blessing implored.*

1. HERE, in thy name, eternal God,
We build this earthly house for thee;
O, choose it for thy fixed abode,
And guard it long from error free.

2. Here when thy messengers proclaim
The blessèd gospel of thy Son,
Still by the power of his great name
Be mighty signs and wonders done.

3. When children's voices raise the song,
Hosanna! to their heavenly King,
Let heaven with earth the strain pro-
long;
Hosanna! let the angels sing.

4. But will, indeed, Jehovah deign
Here to abide, no transient guest?
Here will our great Redeemer reign,
And here the Holy Spirit rest?

5. Thy glory never hence depart;
Yet choose not, Lord, this house alone;
Thy kingdom come to every heart;
In every bosom fix thy throne.

207. *Christ, our Wisdom and our Righteousness.*

1. BURIED in shadows of the night,
We lie, till Christ restores the light;
Wisdom descends to heal the blind,
And chase the darkness of the mind.

2. Our guilty souls are drowned in tears,
Till his atoning blood appears;
Then we awake from deep distress,
And sing the Lord, our righteousness.

3. Jesus beholds where Satan reigns,
Binding his slaves in heavy chains;
He sets the pris'ners free, and breaks
The iron bondage from our necks.

4. Poor, helpless worms in thee possess
Grace, wisdom, power, and righteousness,
Thou art our mighty All;—and we
Give our whole selves, O Lord! to thee.

MY SHEPHERD. 11s & 9s.   "SPIRITUAL SONGS."

1. The Lord is my Shepherd, he makes me re-pose Where the pas-tures in beau-ty are grow-ing; He leads me a - far from the world and its woes, Where in peace the still wa-ters are flow - ing.

208.   *Psalm xxiii.*

1. THE Lord is my shepherd, he makes me reposo
   Where the pastures in beauty aro growing;
   He leads mo afar from the world and its woes,
   Where in peace tho still waters aro flowing.

2. Ho strengthens my spirit, he shows me the path,
   Where tho arms of his love shall enfold mo;
   And when I walk through tho dark valley of death,
   His rod and his staff will uphold me!

209.   *Return to the Fold.*

1. O TELL me, thou life and delight of my soul,
   Where the flock of thy pasture aro feeding;
   I seek thy protection, I need thy control,
   I would go where my Shepherd is leading.

2. O tell me the place where thy flock are at rest,
   Where the noontide will find them reposing
   The tempest now rages, my soul is distressed,
   And the pathway of peace I am losing.

3. And why should I stray with the flocks of thy foes,
   In the desert where lawless they're roving;
  Where hunger and thirst, where contentions and woes,
   And fierce conflicts their ruin are proving?

4. Ah, when shall my woes and my wandering cease,
   And the follies that fill me with weeping?
  O Shepherd of Israel, restore me that peace
   Thou hast given to the flock thou art keeping!

5. A voice from the Shepherd now bids me return,
   By the way where the foot-prints are lying;
  No longer to wander, no longer to mourn;
   And homeward my spirit is flying.

CHILD OF SIN AND SORROW. Special.　　　　　　HASTINGS

1. { Child of sin and sorrow, Fill'd with dismay, }
  { Wait not for to-morrow, Yield thee to-day ; } Heav'n bids thee come, While yet there's
D. C. Child of sin and sorrow, Hear, and o-bey.　　　　　　　　　[room,

210.　*Gospel Invitation.*

1. CHILD of sin and sorrow,
   Fill'd with dismay,
  Wait not for to-morrow,
   Yield thee to-day:
  Heaven bids thee come,
  While yet there's room;
  Child of sin and sorrow,
   Hear and obey.

2. Child of sin and sorrow,
   Why wilt thou die?
  Come while thou canst borrow
   Help from on high:
  Grieve not that love
  Which from above,
  Child of sin and sorrow,
   Would bring thee nigh.

3. Child of sin and sorrow,
   Thy moments glide,
  Like the flitting arrow,
   Or the rushing tide;
  Ere time is o'er
  Heaven's grace implore,
  Child of sin and sorrow,
   . In Christ confide.

211.　*Gospel Invitation.*

1. WHY that soul's commotion,
   Trembling, oppress'd,
  Like the troubled ocean,
   Heaving its breast?
  Some hidden grief
  Demands relief.
  Why that soul's commotion,
   Panting for rest?

2. Why that soul's commotion?
   Cease from thy sin:
   Choose the better portion;
   Cleanse thee within:
  A fountain flows
  To heal thy woes:
  Why that soul's commotion?
   Wash and be clean.

3. Why that soul's commotion?
   Heaven can forgive:
  With thy heart's devotion
   Firmly believe;
  To-day return,
  And cease to mourn.
  Why that soul's commotion?
   Oh turn and live!

GATHERING CLOUDS. L. M. 6 lines.   M. Sacra. Arranged.

1. When gath'ring clouds a-round I view, And days are dark, and friends are
few, On him I lean, who not in vain Experienced ev-ery hu-man pain:
He feels my griefs, he sees my fears, And counts and treasures up my tears.

212. *Christ a sympathizing Priest.*

1. WHEN gathering clouds around I view,
And days are dark, and friends are few,
On him I lean, who not in vain
Experienced every human pain:
He feels my griefs, he sees my fears,
And counts and treasures up my tears.

2. If aught should tempt my soul to stray
From heavenly wisdom's narrow way,
To fly the good I would pursue,
Or do the ill I would not do;
Still he who felt temptation's power
Shall guard me in that dangerous hour.

3. When vexing thoughts within me rise,
And, sore dismay'd, my spirit dies;
Then he who once vouchsafed to bear
The sick'ning anguish of despair,
Shall sweetly soothe, shall gently dry,
The throbbing heart, the streaming eye.

4. When sorrowing o'er some stone I bend
Which covers all that was a friend,
And from his voice, his hand, his smile
Divides me for a little while;
Thou, Saviour, seest the tears I shed,
For thou didst weep o'er Laz'rus dead.

5. And Oh! when I have safely past
Through every conflict but the last,
Still, still unchanging watch beside
My bed of death; for thou hast died
Then point to realms of endless day,
And wipe the latest tear away.

213. *Panting after God.*

1. As panting in the sultry beam,
The hart desires the cooling stream,
So to thy presence, Lord, I flee,
So longs my soul, O God, for thee
Athirst to taste thy living grace
And see thy glory face to face.

2. High waves of sorrow o'er me roll,
And troubles overwhelm my soul,
For many an evil voice is near,
To chide my woe, and mock my fear;
And silent memory weeps alone,
O'er hours of peace, and gladness flown.

3. For I have walked the happy round,
That circles Zion's holy ground;
And gladly swelled the choral lays,
That hymn'd my great Redeemer's praise,
What time the hallowed arch along,
Responsive swelled the solemn song.

4. Ah, why by passing clouds oppressed,
Should rising thoughts distract my breast;
Turn, turn to him in every pain,
Whom never suppliant sought in vain:
Thy strength in joy's ecstatic day,
Thy hope when joy has passed away.

214. *A sympathizing Saviour.*

1. As oft with worn and weary feet,
We tread earth's rugged valley o'er,
The thought how comforting and sweet,
Christ trod this very path before;
Our wants and weaknesses he knows,
From life's first dawning till its close.

2. Do sickness, feebleness, or pain,
Or sorrow in our path appear;
The recollection will remain,
More deeply did he suffer here,
His life how truly sad and brief,
Fill'd up with suffering and with grief.

3. If Satan tempt our hearts to stray,
And whisper evil things within,
So did he in the desert way,
Assail our Lord with thoughts of sin;
When worn, and in a feeble hour,
The tempter came with all his power.

4. Just such as I, this earth he trod,
With every human ill but sin;
And, tho' indeed the very God,
As I am now, so he has been:
My God, my Saviour, look on me
With pity, love, and sympathy.

215. *Contrition at the Cross.*

[For this hymn repeat the last strain.]

1. Fast flow, my tears! the cause is great;
This tribute claims an injured Friend;

One whom I long pursued with hate,
While he would love me to the end:
When justice frowned above my head,
And death its terrors round me spread,
He interposed the wounds he bore,
And bade me live to die no more.

2. Fast flow, my tears! yet faster flow!
Streams copious as yon purple tide:
Who was't that gave the deadly blow?
Who urged the hand that pierced his side?
My soul! thy victim here behold,
What pangs, what agonies untold,
While justice, armed with power divine,
Pours on his head what's due to thine!

3. Fast and yet faster flow my tears!
Now break this heart, and drown these eyes;—
His visage marred toward heaven he rears,
And, pleading for his murderers, dies!
My grief no measure knows, nor end,
Till he appears, the sinner's Friend,
And gives me, in some happy hour,
To feel the risen Saviour's power.

216. *Omniscience and Omnipresence of God.*
Psalm cxxxix.

1. SEARCHER of hearts, to thee are known
The inmost secrets of my breast;
At home, abroad, in crowds, alone,
My rising hours, my peaceful rest,
My thoughts far off through every maze,—
Thine all-discerning eye surveys.

2. How from thy presence should I go,
Or whither from thy Spirit flee;
Since all above, around, below,
Exist in thine immensity;
If up to heaven I climb my way,
I meet Thee in eternal day.

3. Search me, O God, and know my heart;
Try me, my secret soul survey:
Oh! warn thy servant to depart
From every false and treach'rous way;
And guide me by thy watchful eye
To life and immortality.

PARK STREET. L. M.   VENUA.
BOLD—STACCATO.

1. Hark! how the cho-ral song of heaven Swells full of peace and joy a-bove; Hark! how they strike their gold-en harps, And raise the tune-ful notes of love, And raise the tune-ful notes of love.

217.   *Praises of Heaven.*

1. HARK! how the choral song of heaven
Swells full of peace and joy above;
Hark! how they strike their golden
harps,
And raise the tuneful notes of love.

2. No anxious care nor thrilling grief,
No deep despair, nor gloomy woe
They feel, when high their lofty strains
In noblest, sweetest concord flow.

3. When shall we join the heavenly host,
Who sing Immanuel's praise on high,
And leave behind our doubts and fears,
To swell the chorus of the sky?

4. O! come, thou rapture-bringing morn,
And usher in the joyful day;
We long to see thy rising sun
Drive all these clouds of grief away.

218.   *Star of Bethlehem.*

1. WHEN marshaled on the nightly plain,
The glittering host bestud the sky,
One star alone of all the train
Can fix the sinner's wandering eye.

2. Hark, hark! to God the chorus breaks,
From every host, from every gem;
But one alone the Saviour speaks,
It is the Star of Bethlehem.

3. Once on the raging seas I rode,
The storm was loud—the night was
dark—
The ocean yawn'd—and rudely blow'd
The wind that toss'd my foundering
bark.

4. Deep horror then my vitals froze;
Death-struck, I ceased the tide to
stem;
When suddenly a star arose,
It was the Star of Bethlehem.

5. It was my guide, my light, my all,
It bade my dark foreboding cease;
And thro' the storm and danger's thrall
It led me to the port of peace.

6. Now safely moored—my perils o'er,
I'll sing, first in night's diadem,
For ever and for evermore,
The Star, the Star of Bethlehem!

219. *Temptation; or, Safely in the Storm.*

1. The billows swell, the winds are high,
Clouds overcast my wintry sky;
Out of the depths to thee I call,
My fears are great, my strength is small.

2. O Lord, the pilot's part perform,
And guide and guard me through the storm!
Defend me from each threatening ill,
Control the waves—say, "Peace—be still!"

3. Amidst the roaring of the sea,
My soul still hangs her hopes on thee;
Thy constant love, thy faithful care,
Is all that saves me from despair.

4. Dangers of every shape and name
Attend the followers of the Lamb,
Who leave the world's deceitful shore,
And leave it to return no more.

5. Though tempest-tossed and half a wreck,
My Saviour through the floods I seek,
Let neither winds, nor stormy rain,
Force back my shattered bark again.

220. *Grace and Glory.*

1. Th' Almighty reigns, exalted high
O'er all the earth, o'er all the sky;
Though clouds and darkness vail his feet,
His dwelling is the mercy-seat.

2. O ye that love his holy name,
Hate every work of sin and shame:
He guards the souls of all his friends,
And from the snares of hell defends.

3. Immortal light, and joys unknown,
Are for the saints in darkness sown;
Those glorious seeds shall spring and rise,
And the bright harvest bless our eyes.

4. Rejoice, ye righteous, and record
The sacred honors of the Lord;
None but the soul that feels his grace
Can triumph in his holiness.

221. *The Great Commission.*

1. "Go, preach my gospel," saith the Lord,
"Bid the whole earth my grace receive;
He shall be saved that trusts my word,
And he condemned who'll not believe.

2. "I'll make your great commission known;
And ye shall prove my gospel true,
By all the works that I have done,
By all the wonders ye shall do.

3. "Teach all the nations my commands;
I'm with you till the world shall end;
All power is trusted in my hands;
I can destroy and I defend."

4. He spake, and light shone round his head;
On a bright cloud to heaven he rode:
They to the farthest nations spread
The grace of their ascended God.

222. *Divine Power supplicated.*

1. Arm of the Lord, awake, awake;
Put on thy strength, the nations shake,
Now let the world, adoring, see
Triumphs of mercy wrought by thee.

2. Say to the heathen, from thy throne,
"I am Jehovah, God alone:"
Thy voice their idols shall confound,
And cast their altars to the ground.

3. Almighty God, thy grace proclaim
Through every clime, of every name;
Let adverse powers before thee fall,
And crown the Saviour Lord of all.

223. *Universal Reign of Christ.*

1. Great God, whose universal sway
The known and unknown worlds obey,
Now give the kingdom to thy Son;
Extend his power, exalt his throne.

2. As rain on meadows newly mown,
So shall he send his influence down;
His grace on fainting souls distills,
Like heavenly dew on thirsty hills.

3. The heathen lands that lie beneath
The shades of overspreading death,
Revive at his first dawning light,
And deserts blossom at the sight.

4. The saints shall flourish in his days,
Dressed in the robes of joy and praise
Peace, like a river, from his throne,
Shall flow to nations yet unknown.

LANESBOROUGH. C. P. M.* ENGLISH.

1. There is an hour of peace-ful rest, To mourn-ing wanderers giv'n: There is a joy for souls dis-tressed, A balm for ev-ery wound-ed breast—'Tis found a-bove— in heaven.

* See also ZERED, on the opposite page.

224. *Heaven Anticipated.*

1. THERE is an hour of peaceful rest
   To mourning wand'rers given;
   There is a joy for souls distressed,
   A balm for every wounded breast,
   'Tis found above in heaven.

2. There is a home for weary souls,
   By sin and sorrow driven;
   When tossed on life's tempest'ous shoals,
   Where storms arise and ocean rolls,
   And all is drear but heaven.

3. There faith lifts up her cheerful eye,
   To brighter prospects given;
   And views the tempest passing by,
   The evening shadows quickly fly,
   And all serene in heaven.

4. There fragrant flowers immortal bloom;
   And joys supreme are given;
   There rays divine disperse the gloom;
   Beyond the confines of the tomb
   Appears the dawn of heaven.

225. *Incitements to Praise.*

1. Go, tune thy voice to sacred song,
   Exert thy noblest powers;
   Go, mingle with the choral throng,
   The Saviour's praises to prolong,
   Amid life's fleeting hours.

2. O hast thou felt a Saviour's love,
   That flame of heavenly birth?
   Then let thy strains melodious prove,
   With raptures soaring far above
   The trifling toys of earth.

3. Hast found the pearl of price unknown
   That cost a Saviour's blood?
   Heir of a bright celestial crown
   That sparkles round th' eternal throne,
   O sing the praise of God.

4. Sing of the Lamb that once was slain,
   That man might be forgiven;
   Sing how He broke death's bars in twain,
   Ascending high in bliss to reign,
   The God of earth and heaven!

ZERED. C. P. M.　　　　　　　　　A. J. ABBEY.

1. O say no more there's noth-ing true But the bright scenes of
heaven: There's truth in mer-cy's cheer-ing page, Di-
rect-ing youth, con-sol-ing age, De-clar-ing sin for-given.

5. Begin on earth the notes of praise,
　"Glory to God on high!"
Sing through the remnant of thy days,
At death the song of vict'ry raise,
　And soar beyond the sky.

226.　*Heavenly Joys on Earth.*

1. On! say no more, there's nothing true
　But the bright scenes of heaven!
There's truth in mercy's cheering page;
Directing youth, consoling age,
　Declaring sin forgiven.

2. Oh! say no more there's naught but heav'n
　That's calm, or true, or bright;
Bright are the beams the Saviour sheds,
The radiance that the gospel spreads,
　Amid this realm of night.

3. Tho' loud the blast, tho' dark the day,
　We oft have peace at even:
And if we *here* have such delight,
In objects not unknown to sight,
　How calm, how bright is heaven!

227.　*God is Love.*

1. Tis sweet when cloudless suns arise,
　As through the vale we move,
But O, more sweet to recognize
Through dreary nights and starless skies
　The smiles of heavenly love.

2. I hail the breeze that soft and clear
　Wafts influence from above,
But chief the storm delighted hear,
Which breathes o'er faith's attentive ear
　The whispering voice of love.

3. When health invigorates the frame
　Let joy the bliss improve:
But torturing pain and fever's flame,
With teaching power alike proclaim
　The tender hand of love.

4. Thou canst not weep, frail child of clay,
　Such blessings taught to prove,
Each cloud that dims thy upward way,
Shall more endear the glorious day,
　That gilds the land of love.

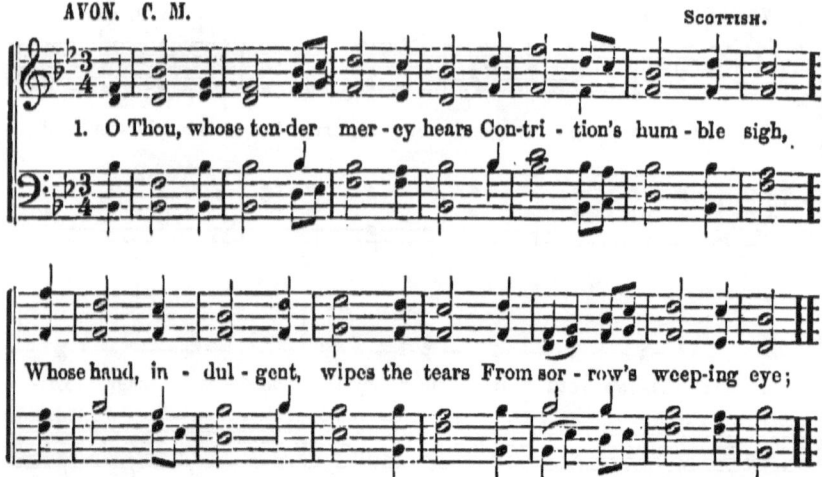

AVON. C. M. SCOTTISH.

1. O Thou, whose ten-der mer-cy hears Con-tri-tion's hum-ble sigh,

Whose hand, in-dul-gent, wipes the tears From sor-row's weep-ing eye;

228. *Contrition.*

1. O Thou, whose tender mercy hears
   Contrition's humble sigh;
   Whose hand, indulgent, wipes the tears
   From sorrow's weeping eye;

2. See low before thy throne of grace
   A wretched wand'rer mourn:
   Hast thou not bid me seek thy face?
   Hast thou not said "Return?"

3. And shall my guilty fears prevail
   To drive me from thy feet?
   Oh let not this dear refuge fail,
   This only safe retreat!

4. Absent from thee, my Guide, my Light,
   Without one cheering ray,
   Thro' dangers, fears, and gloomy night,
   How desolate my way!

5. Oh shine on this benighted heart,
   With beams of mercy shine!
   And let thy healing voice impart
   A taste of joys divine.

229. *Hope in Afflictions.*

1. When musing sorrow weeps the past,
   And mourns the present pain;
   How sweet to think of peace at last,
   And feel that death is gain!

2. 'Tis not that murm'ring thoughts arise,
   And dread a Father's will;
   'Tis not that meek submission flies,
   And would not suffer still.

3. It is that heaven-taught faith surveys
   The path to realms of light;
   And longs her eagle plumes to raise,
   And lose herself in sight.

4. It is that hope with ardor glows,
   To see him face to face,
   Whose dying love no language knows
   Sufficient art to trace.

5. It is that harassed conscience feels
   The pangs of struggling sin;
   Sees, though afar, the hand that heals,
   And ends her war within.

6. Oh! let me wing my hallowed flight
   From earth-born woe and care:
   And soar beyond these realms of night,
   My Saviour's bliss to share.

230. *God All in All.*

1. My God, my portion, and my love,
   My everlasting all,
   I've none but thee in heaven above,
   Or on this earthly ball.

2. How vain a toy is glittering wealth,
   If once compared to thee!
   Or what's my safety, or my health,
   Or all my friends, to me?

3. Were I possessor of the earth,
   And called the stars my own;
   Without thy graces, and thyself,
   I were a wretch undone.

4. Let others stretch their arms like seas,
And grasp in all the shore;
Grant me the visits of thy grace,
And I desire no more.

231. *Trusting God in old Age.*

1. My God, my everlasting hope,
I live upon thy truth;
Thy hands have held my childhood up,
And strengthened all my youth.

2. Still has my life new wonders seen,
Repeated every year;
Behold, my days that yet remain,
I trust them to thy care.

3. Cast me not off when strength declines,
When hoary hairs arise;
And round me let thy glory shine,
Whene'er thy servant dies.

4. Then, in the history of my age,
When men review my days,
They'll read thy love in every page,
In every line thy praise.

232. *Sustaining Grace in old Age implored.*

1. God of my childhood and my youth,
The Guide of all my days,
I have declared thy heavenly truth,
And told thy wondrous ways.

2. Wilt thou forsake my hoary hairs,
And leave my fainting heart?
Who shall sustain my sinking years,
If God, my strength, depart?

3. Let me thy power and truth proclaim
Before the rising age,
And leave a savor of thy name
When I shall quit the stage.

4. The land of silence and of death
Attends my next remove;
O, may these poor remains of breath
Teach all the world thy love.

233. *Adoption.*

1. My God, my Father, blissful name!
O, may I call thee mine?
May I with sweet assurance claim
A portion so divine?

2. This only can my fears control,
And bid my sorrows fly:
What harm can ever reach my soul,
Beneath my Father's eye?

3. Whate'er thy providence denies,
I cheerfully resign;
Lord, thou art good, and just, and **wise**,
I yield my will to thine.

4. Whate'er thy sacred will ordains,
Still give me strength to bear:
Let me but know my Father reigns,
I 'll trust his tender care.

234. *Pardoning Love.*

1. How oft, alas! this wretched heart
Has wandered from the Lord!
How oft my roving thoughts depart,
Forgetful of his word!

2. Yet sovereign mercy calls "Return;"
Dear Lord, and may I come?
My vile ingratitude I mourn;
O, take the wanderer home.

3. And canst thou, wilt thou, yet forgive,
And bid my crimes remove?
And shall a pardoned rebel live
To speak thy wondrous love?

4. Thy pardoning love, so free, so sweet,
Blest Saviour, I adore;
O keep me at thy sacred feet,
And let me rove no more.

235. *Prayer for Direction.*

1. O that the Lord would guide my ways
To keep his statutes still!
O that my God would grant me grace
To know and do his will!

2. O, send thy Spirit down, to write
Thy law upon my heart;
Nor let my tongue indulge deceit,
Nor act the liar's part.

3. From vanity turn off my eyes:
Let no corrupt design,
Nor covetous desire, arise
Within this soul of mine.

4. Direct my footsteps by thy word,
And make my heart sincere;
Let sin have no dominion, Lord,
But keep my conscience clear.

5. Make me to walk in thy commands:
'Tis a delightful road—
Nor let my head, nor heart, nor **hands**
Offend against my God.

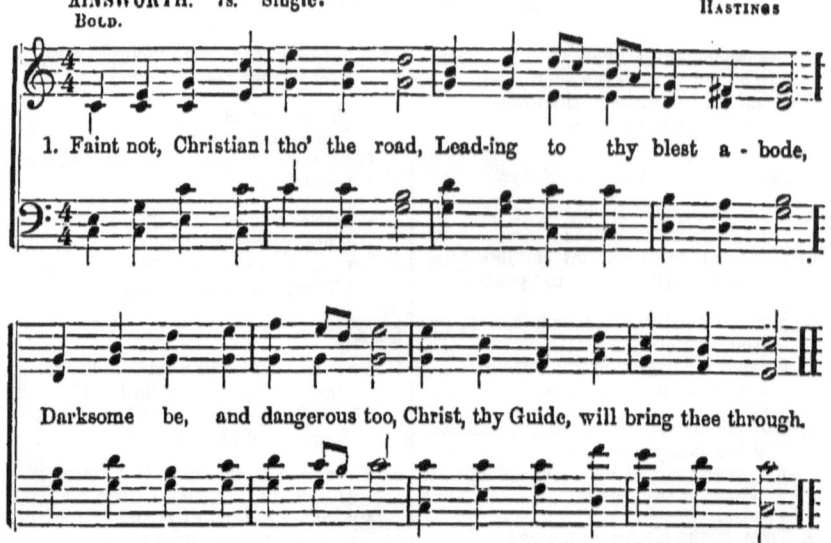

AINSWORTH. 7s. Single.
Bold.
HASTINGS

1. Faint not, Christian! tho' the road, Lead-ing to thy blest a - bode,

Darksome be, and dangerous too, Christ, thy Guide, will bring thee through.

236. *Christian Courage.*

1. Faint not, Christian! though the road,
Leading to thy blest abode,
Darksome be, and dangerous too,
Christ thy Guide will bring thee through.

2. Faint not, Christian! though in rage
Satan would thy soul engage,
Gird on faith's anointed shield,
Bear it to the battle-field.

3. Faint not, Christian! though the world
Has its hostile flag unfurled;
Hold the cross of Jesus fast,
Thou shalt overcome at last.

4. Faint not, Christian! though within,
There's a heart so prone to sin;
Christ the Lord is over all,
He'll not suffer thee to fall.

5. Faint not, Christian! though thy God
Smite thee with his chastening rod;
Smite he must, with father's care,
That he may his love declare.

6. Faint not, Christian! Jesus near,
Soon in glory he'll appear;
And his love will then bestow
Power over every foe.

7. Faint not, Christian! look on high,
See the harpers in the sky;
Patient wait, and thou wilt join—
Chant with them of love divine.

237. *The Reign of Christ.*

1. HASTEN, Lord! the glorious time,
When, beneath Messiah's sway,
Every nation, every clime,
Shall the gospel-call obey.

2. Mightiest kings his power shall own,
Heathen tribes his name adore;
Satan and his host, o'erthrown,
Bound in chains, shall hurt no more.

3. Then shall wars and tumults cease,
Then be banished grief and pain;
Righteousness, and joy, and peace,
Undisturbed shall ever reign.

4. Bless we, then, our gracious Lord;
Ever praise his glorious name;
All his mighty acts record;
All his wondrous love proclaim.

238. *The Fight of Faith.*

1. MUCH in sorrow, oft in woe,
Onward, Christians, onward go,

Fight tho fight, and worn with strife,
Steep with tears tho bread of life.

2. Onward, Christians, onward go,
Join tho war and face the foe,
Faint not, much doth yet remain,
Dreary is the long campaign.

3. Shrink not, Christians, will yo yield?
Will ye quit the painful field?
Onward till your feet shall stand
Firm within tho promised land.

239. *Redeeming Love.*

1. Now begin tho heavenly theme;
Sing aloud in Jesus' name;
Ye who his salvation prove,
Triumph in redeeming love.

2. Ye who see tho Father's grace
Beaming in the Saviour's face,
As to Canaan on ye move,
Praise and bless redeeming love.

3. Mourning souls, dry up your tears;
Banish all your guilty fears;
See your guilt and curse remove,
Cancel'd by redeeming love.

4. Welcome, all by sin oppressed,
Welcome to his sacred rest;
Nothing brought him from above,
Nothing but redeeming love.

5. Hither, then, your music bring;
Strike aloud each cheerful string;
Mortals, join tho host above—
Join to praise redeeming love.

240. *Thanksgiving.*

1. SWELL the anthem, raise the song;
Praises to our God belong;
Saints and angels join to sing
Praises to the heavenly King.

2. Blessings from his liberal hand
Flow around this happy land:
Kept by him no foes annoy,
Peace and freedom wo enjoy.

3. Here, beneath a virtuous sway,
May we cheerfully obey—
Never feel oppression's rod—
Ever own and worship God.

4. Hark! the voice of nature sings
Praises to tho King of kings;
Let us join the choral song,
And the grateful notes prolong.

241. *Ps.* 117.

1. ALL yo nations, praise the Lord,
All ye lands, your voices raise;
Heaven and earth with loud accord,
Praise the Lord, for ever praise.

2. For his truth and mercy stand,
Past, and present, and to be,
Like tho years of his right hand,
Like his own eternity.

3. Praise him, ye who know his love,
Praise him from tho depths beneath;
Praise him in the heights above:
Praise your Maker, all that breathe.

242. *The Messengers of God.*

1. Go, ye messengers of God;
Like the beams of morning, fly;
Take the wonder-working rod;
Wave the banner-cross on high.

2. Go to many a tropic isle,
In the bosom of the deep,
Where the skies for ever smile,
And th' oppressed for ever weep.

3. O'er the pagan's night of care
Pour the living light of heaven;
Chase away his wild despair;
Bid him hope to be forgiven.

4. Where tho golden gates of day
Open on tho palmy east,
There tho Saviour's cross display,
Spread the gospel's richest feast.

243. *Christ coming to save his People.*

1. HARK—that shout of rapturous joy,
Bursting forth from yonder cloud:
Jesus comes, and through tho sky,
Angels tell their joy aloud.

2. Hark! the trumpet's awful voice
Sounds abroad through sea and land:
Let his people now rejoice,
Their redemption is at hand.

3. See! the Lord appears in view;
Heaven and earth before him fly;
Rise, ye saints! he comes for you—
Rise, to meet him in the sky.

4. Go and dwell with him above,
Where no foe can e'er molest;
Happy in tho Saviour's love,
Ever blessing, ever blest.

SEYMOUR. 7s. Single.*   Arr. from Winter.

1. Come, my soul, thy suit pre-pare—Je-sus loves to an - swer prayer;

He him - self has bid thee pray, There-fore will not say thee nay.

* See also the tune on the opposite page.

244. *Encouragement to Prayer.*

1. Come, my soul, thy suit prepare,
Jesus loves to answer prayer;
He himself has bid thee pray,
Therefore will not say thee nay.

2 Thou art coming to a King,
Large petitions with thee bring;
For his grace and power are such,
None can ever ask too much.

3. With my burden I begin,
Lord, remove this load of sin;
Let thy blood, for sinners spilt,
Set my conscience free from guilt

4. Lord! I come to thee for rest,
Take possession of my breast;
There thy blood-bought right maintain,
And without a rival reign.

5. Snow me what I have to do,
Every hour my strength renew;
Let me live a life of faith,
Let me die thy people's death.

245. *A Blessing humbly requested.*

1. Lord, we come before thee now;
At thy feet we humbly bow;
O do not our suit disdain,
Shall we seek thee, Lord, in vain?

2. Lord, on thee our souls depend;
In compassion now descend;

Fill our hearts with thy rich grace;
Tune our lips to sing thy praise.

3. In thine own appointed way,
Now we seek thee; here we stay;
Lord, from hence we would not go,
Till a blessing thou bestow.

4. Comfort those who weep and mourn;
Let the time of joy return;
Those that are cast down lift up;
Make them strong in faith and hope

5. Grant that all may seek and find
Thee a God supremely kind;
Heal the sick; the captive free;
Let us all rejoice in thee.

246. *The Good Shepherd.*

1. To thy pastures fair and large,
Heavenly Shepherd, lead thy charge,
And my couch, with tenderest care,
'Mid the springing grass prepare.

2. When I faint with summer's heat,
Thou shalt guide my weary feet
To the streams that, still and slow,
Through the verdant meadows flow.

3. Safe the dreary vale I tread,
By the shades of death o'erspread,
With thy rod and staff supplied,
This my guard, and that my guide.

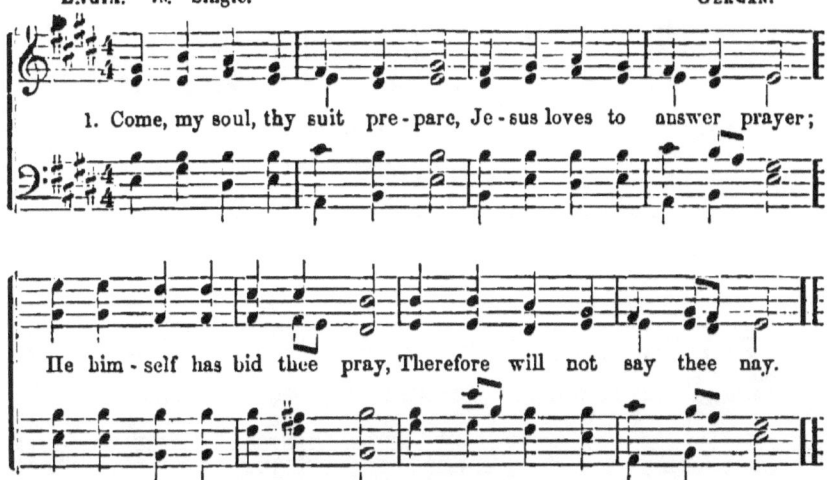

1. Come, my soul, thy suit pre-pare, Je-sus loves to answer prayer;

He him-self has bid thee pray, Therefore will not say thee nay.

4. Constant to my latest end,
Thou my footsteps shalt attend;
And shalt bid thy hallowed dome
Yield me an eternal home.

247. *The Sanctuary.*

1. Soft and holy is the place
Where the light that beams from heaven
Shows the Saviour's smiling face,
With the joy of sin forgiven.

2. There, with one accord we meet,
All the words of life to hear;
Bending low at Jesus' feet,
Worshiping with godly fear.

3. Let the world and all its cares
Now retire from every breast;
Let the tempter and his snares
Cease to hinder or molest.

4. Precious Sabbath of the Lord,
Fairest type of heaven above!
Purest joy thy scenes afford
To the heart that's tuned to love.

248. *Welcoming the Cross.*

1. 'Tis my happiness below,
Not to live without the cross;

But the Saviour's power to know,
Sanctifying every loss.

2. Trials must and will befall;
But, with humble faith to see
Love inscribed upon them all,
This is happiness to me.

3. Trials make the promise sweet,
Trials give new life to prayer;
Trials bring me to his feet,—
Lay me low, and keep me there.

249. *The Three Mountains.*

1. When on Sinai's top I see
God descend in majesty,
To proclaim his holy law,
All my spirit sinks with awe.

2. When in ecstasy sublime,
Tabor's glorious steep I climb,
At the too transporting light
Darkness rushes o'er my sight.

3. When on Calvary I rest—
God, in flesh made manifest,
Shines in my Redeemer's face,
Full of beauty, truth, and grace.

4. Here I would for ever stay,
Weep and gaze my soul away;
Thou art heaven on earth to me,
Lovely, mournful Calvary.

LA MIRA. C. M.

W. B. BRADBURY.

1. Bless ye the Lord in sol-emn rite, With pure de-vo-tion's flame;

Praise ye the Lord with songs by night, By day re-hearse his name.

250. *Constant Devotion.*

1. BLESS ye the Lord in solemn rite,
   With pure devotion's flame;
   Praise ye the Lord with songs by night,
   By day rehearse his name.

2. Lift up your hands amid the place
   ·Where God reveals his love,
   And seals the trophies of his grace
   For brighter realms above.

3. From Zion, from his holy hill,
   The Lord our Maker send
   The saving knowledge of his will,
   To earth's remotest end.

251. *The Gospel Trumpet.*

1. LET every mortal ear attend,
   And every heart rejoice;
   The trumpet of the gospel sounds,
   With an inviting voice.

2. Ho! all ye hungry, starving souls,
   That feed upon the wind,
   And vainly strive with earthly toils
   To fill th' immortal mind,—

3. Eternal wisdom has prepared
   A soul-reviving feast,
   And bids your longing appetites
   The rich provision taste.

4. Ho! ye that pant for living streams,
   And pine away and die—
   Here you may quench your raging thirst,
   With springs that never die.

5. Rivers of love and mercy here,
   In a rich ocean join;
   Salvation in abundance flows,
   Like floods of milk and wine.

6. The happy gates of gospel grace
   Stand open night and day;
   Lord—we are come to seek supplies,
   And drive our wants away.

252. *Saints in the Hands of Christ.*

1. FIRM as the earth thy gospel stands,
   My Lord, my hope, my trust;
   If I am found in Jesus' hands,
   My soul can ne'er be lost.

2. His honor is engaged to save
   The meanest of his sheep;
   All, whom his heavenly Father gave,
   His hands securely keep.

3. Nor death, nor hell shall e'er remove
   His favorites from his breast;
   In the dear bosom of his love
   They must for ever rest.

1. How sweet, how heavenly is the sight, When those that love the Lord

In one an-oth-er's peace de-light, And thus ful-fill his word.

253. *Brotherly Love.*

1. How sweet, how heavenly is the sight,
   When those that love the Lord
   In one another's peace delight,
   And thus fulfill his word!

2. When each can feel his brother's sigh,
   And with him bear a part;
   When sorrow flows from eye to eye,
   And joy from heart to heart!

3. When, free from envy, scorn, and pride,
   Our wishes all above,
   Each can his brother's failings hide,
   And show a brother's love!

4. Love is the golden chain that binds
   The happy souls above;
   And he's an heir of heaven that finds
   His bosom glow with love.

254. *Prayer for the Kingdom of Christ.*

1. FATHER! is not thy promise pledged
   To thine exalted Son,
   That, through the nations of the earth,
   Thy word of life shall run?—

2. "Ask, and I'll give the heathen lands
   For thine inheritance,
   And, to the world's remotest shores,
   Thine empire shall advance."

3. Hast thou not said, the blinded Jews
   Shall their Redeemer own,

While gentiles to his standard crowd,
   And bow before his throne?

4. Are not all kingdoms, tribes, and tongues,
   Beneath th' expanse of heaven,
   To the dominion of thy Son,
   With all their millions given?

5. From east to west, from north to south,
   Then be his name adored;
   The world, through all its nations, shout
   Hosannas to the Lord.

255. *Regeneration by the Spirit.*

1. NOT all the outward forms on earth,
   Nor rites that God has given,
   Nor will of man, nor blood, nor birth,
   Can raise a soul to heaven.

2. The sovereign will of God alone
   Creates us heirs of grace,
   Born in the image of his Son,
   A new, peculiar race.

3. The Spirit, like some heavenly wind,
   Breathes on the sons of flesh;
   Creates anew the carnal mind,
   And forms the man afresh.

4. Our quickened souls awake and rise
   From the long sleep of death:
   On heavenly things we fix our eyes,
   And praise employs our breath.

UXBRIDGE. L. M.

LOWELL MASON.

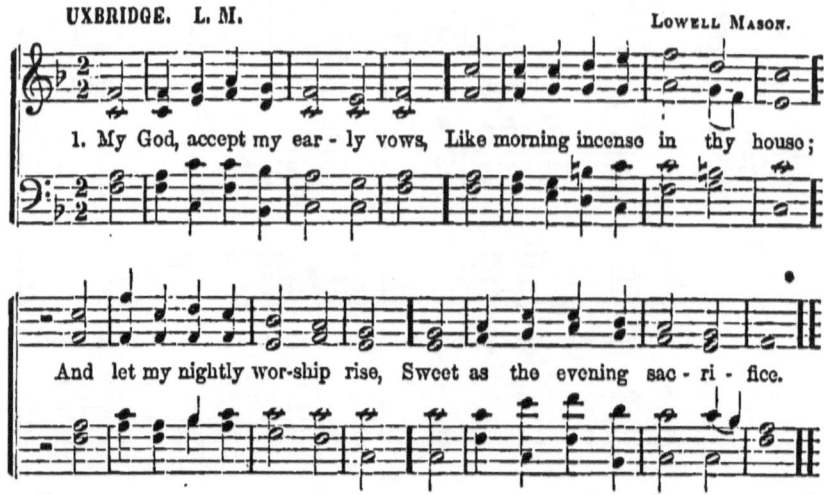

1. My God, accept my ear - ly vows, Like morning incense in thy house;

And let my nightly wor-ship rise, Sweet as the evening sac - ri - fice.

---

256. *Christian Watchfulness.—A Morning Psalm.*

1. My God! accept my early vows,
Like morning incense in thy house;
And let my nightly worship rise,
Sweet as the evening sacrifice.

2. Watch o'er my lips, and guard them,
Lord!
From every rash and heedless word;
Nor let my feet incline to tread
The guilty path where sinners lead.

3. Oh! may the righteous, when I stray,
Smite, and reprove my wandering way;
Their gentle words, like ointment shed,
Shall never bruise, but cheer my head.

4. When I behold them pressed with grief,
I'll cry to heaven for their relief;
And, by my warm petitions, prove
How much I prize their faithful love.

257. *The Striving of the Spirit.*

1. Say, sinner, hath a voice within,
Oft whispered to thy secret soul,
Urged thee to leave the ways of sin,
And yield thy heart to God's control?

2. Hath something met thee in the path
Of worldliness and vanity,

And pointed to the coming wrath,
And warned thee from that wrath to
flee?

3. Sinner, it was a heavenly voice,
It was the Spirit's gracious call,
It bade thee make the better choice,
And haste to seek in Christ thine all.

4. Spurn not the call to life and light;
Regard in time the warning kind;
That call thou may'st not always slight,
And yet the gate of mercy find.

5. God's Spirit will not always strive,
With hardened, self-destroying man;
Ye, who persist his love to grieve,
May never hear his voice again.

6. Sinner—perhaps this very day
Thy last accepted time may be;
Oh, shouldst thou grieve him now away,
Then hope may never beam on thee.

258. *The Church, the Palace of God.*

1. Happy the church, thou sacred place,
The seat of thy Creator's grace!
Thy holy courts are his abode,
Thou earthly palace of our God!

2. Thy walls are strength; and at thy gates
A guard of heavenly warriors waits;
Nor shall thy deep foundation move,
Fixed on his counsels and his love.

3. Thy foes in vain designs engage—
   Against thy throne in vain they rage,
   Like rising waves, with angry roar, .
   That dash and die upon the shore.

4. God is our shield, and God our sun:
   Swift as the fleeting moments run,
   On us he sheds new beams of grace,
   And we reflect his brightest praise.

259. *God, the Portion of the Soul.* *

1. FAR from thy fold, O God! my feet
   Once moved in error's devious maze;
   Nor found religious duties sweet,
   Nor sought thy face, nor loved thy
     ways.

2. With tenderest voice thou bad'st me flee
   The paths, which thou couldst ne'er
     approve ;
   And gently drew my soul to thee,
   With cords of sweet, eternal love.

3. Now to thy footstool, Lord! I fly,
   And low in self-abasement fall ;
   A vile, a helpless worm, am I,
   And thou, my God! art all in all.

4. Dearer—far dearer to my heart,
   Than all the joys that earth can give ;
   From fame, from wealth, from friends I'll
     part,
   Beneath thy countenance to live. '

260. *Not ashamed of Christ.*

1. AT thy command, our dearest Lord!
   Here we attend thy dying feast ;
   Thy blood, like wine, adorns thy board,
   And thine own flesh feeds every guest.

2. Our faith adores thy bleeding love,
   And trusts for life in One who died ;
   We hope for heavenly crowns above,
   From a Redeemer crucified.

3. Let the vain world pronounce it shame,
   And cast their scandals on thy cause ;
   We come to boast our Saviour's name,
   And make our triumphs in his cross.

261. *Original and actual Sin confessed.*

1. LORD, I am vile, conceived in sin,
   And born unholy and unclean ;
   Sprung from the man, whose guilty fall
   Corrupts the race, and taints us all.

2. Soon as we draw our infant breath,
   The seeds of sin grow up for death :
   Thy law demands a perfect heart ;
   But we 're defiled in every part.

3. Behold, I fall before thy face ;
   My only refuge is thy grace :
   No outward forms can make me clean ,
   The leprosy lies deep within.

4. No bleeding bird, nor bleeding beast,
   Nor hyssop branch, nor sprinkling priest,
   Nor running brook, nor flood, nor sea,
   Can wash the dismal stain away.

5. Jesus, my God, thy blood alone
   Hath power sufficient to atone :
   Thy blood can make me white as snow ;
   No Jewish types can cleanse me so.

262. *The Altar and the School.*

1. WHEN driven by oppression's rod,
   Our fathers fled beyond the sea,
   Their care was first to honor God,
   And next to leave their children free.

2. Above the forest's gloomy shade,
   The altar and the school appeared :
   On that the gifts of faith were laid,
   On this their precious hopes were
     reared.

3. The altar and the school still stand,
   The sacred pillars of our trust ;
   And freedom's sons shall fill the land,
   While we are sleeping in the dust.

4. Before thine altar, Lord, we bend,
   With grateful song and fervent prayer ;
   For Thou, who wast our fathers' Friend,
   Wilt make their offspring still thy care.

263. *Meekness.*

1. HAPPY the meek whose gentle breast,
   Clear as the summer's evening ray,
   Calm as the regions of the blest,
   Enjoys on earth celestial day.

2. His heart no broken friendships sting,
   No storms his peaceful tent invade ;
   He rests beneath th'Almighty's wing,
   Hostile to none, of none afraid.

3. Spirit of grace, all meek and mild !
   Inspire our breasts, our souls possess :
   Repel each passion rude and wild,
   And bless us as we aim to bless.

Doxology.

Praise God, from whom all blessings flow ;
Praise him, all creatures here below !
Praise him above, ye heavenly host !
Praise Father, Son, and Holy Ghost.

ROTHWELL. L. M.   ENGLISH.

1. The heavens de-clare thy glo - ry, Lord! In ev - ery star thy
wis - dom shines; But when our eyes be - hold thy word, We read thy
name in fair - er lines, We read thy name in fair - er lines.

264. *God's Glory in Creation.*

1. THE heavens declare thy glory, Lord!
    In every star thy wisdom shines;
    But when our eyes behold thy word,
    We read thy name in fairer lines;

2. The rolling sun, the changing light,
    And night and day thy power confess;
    But the blest volume thou hast writ
    Reveals thy justice and thy grace.

3. Sun, moon, and stars convey thy praise
    Round the whole earth, and never stand;
    So when thy truth began its race,
    It touched and glanced on every land.

4. Nor shall thy spreading gospel rest
    Till thro' the world thy truth has run;
    Till Christ has all the nations blessed
    That see the light, or feel the sun.

5. Great Sun of Righteousness, arise;
    Bless the dark world with heav'nly light;
    Thy gospel makes the simple wise,
    Thy laws are pure, thy judgments right.

6. Thy noblest wonders here we view
    In souls renewed, and sins forgiven;
    Lord, cleanse my sins, my soul renew,
    And make thy word my guide to heaven.

265. *Commission to the Gentiles.*

1. Go—messenger of peace and love!
    To nations plunged in shades of night;
    Like angels sent from fields above,
    Be thine to shed celestial light.

2. Go, to the hungry food impart;
    To paths of peace the wanderer guide,
    And lead the thirsty, panting heart,
    Where streams of living waters glide.

3. Go, bid the bright and morning star,
From Bethlehem's plains, resplendent
shine,
And, piercing through the gloom afar,
Shed heavenly light and love divine.

4. To India's various castes, proclaim
The gospel's soft, but powerful voice;
And, at the blest Redeemer's name,
Let ocean's lonely isles rejoice.

5. From north to south, from east to west,
Messiah yet shall reign supreme;
His name, by every tongue confessed,—
His praise—the universal theme.

266. *Warning against Delay.*

1. COME, let our voices join to raise
A sacred song of solemn praise;
God is a sovereign King;—rehearse
His honors in exalted verse.

2. Come, let our souls address the Lord,
Who framed our natures with his word;
He is our Shepherd;—we the sheep,
His mercy chose, his pastures keep.

3. Come, let us hear his voice to-day;
The counsels of his love obey;
Nor let our hardened hearts renew
The sins and plagues that Israel knew.

4. Look back, my soul, with holy dread,
And view those ancient rebels dead: .
Attend the offered grace to-day,
Nor lose the blessing by delay.

5. Seize the kind promise while it waits,
And march to Zion's heavenly gates;
Believe,—and take the promised rest;
Obey,—and be for ever blest.

267. *The Blessings of the new Covenant.*

1. GOD, in the gospel of his Son,
Makes his eternal counsels known,
Where love in all its glory shines,
And truth is drawn in fairest lines.

2. Here sinners of a humble frame
May taste his grace, and learn his name;
May read, in characters of blood,
The wisdom, power, and grace of God.

3. Here, faith reveals, to mortal eyes,
A brighter world beyond the skies;
Here, shines the light which guides our
way
From earth to realms of endless day.

4. Oh! grant us grace, almighty Lord!
To read and mark thy holy word,
Its truths with meekness to receive,
And by its holy precepts live.

5. May this blest volume ever lie
Close to my heart, and near mine eye,—
Till life's last hour, my soul engage,
And be my chosen heritage.

268. *Salvation through Christ.*

1. Now, to the power of God supreme,
Be everlasting honors given;
He saves from hell,—we bless his name,—
He calls our wandering feet to heaven.

2. Not for our duties, or deserts,
But of his own abounding grace,
He works salvation in our hearts,
And forms a people for his praise.

3. 'Twas his own purpose, that begun
To rescue rebels, doomed to die;
He gave us grace in Christ his Son,
Before he spread the starry sky.

4. Jesus, the Lord, appears at last,
And makes his Father's counsels
known;
Declares the great transaction past,
And brings immortal blessings down.

5. He dies,—and, in that dreadful night,
Did all the powers of hell destroy;
Rising—he brought our heaven to light,
And took possession of the joy.

269. *The Light of Nature.*

1. "THERE is a God"—creation cries,
The earth, the sea, the lofty skies,
All things existing loud proclaim
The power and glory of his name.

2. There is a God of boundless might,
Wisdom and goodness infinite,
A great Creator, by whose power
Worlds are sustained from hour to hour.

3. But man hath sinned against this God,
And felt the terrors of his rod:
And earth, and sea, and star-lit sky,
Proclaim that he deserves to die.

4. How shall the sinner be forgiven?
How shall he make his peace with heaven?
'T is inspiration must declare;
Nature would leave us to despair.

HELENA. C. M.
TENDERLY.
WM. B. BRADBURY.

1. O Thou, who driest the mourner's tear, How dark this world would be.

If, when by sor-rows wound-ed here, We could not fly to thee.

270. *Light in Darkness.*

1. O THOU, who driest the mourner's tear,
   How dark this world would be,
   If, when by sorrows wounded here,
   We could not fly to thee!

2. The friends, who in our sunshine live,
   When winter comes, are flown;
   And he who has but tears to give,
   Must weep those tears alone.

3. But thou wilt heal that broken heart,
   Which, like the plants that throw
   Their fragrance from the wounded part,
   Breathes sweetness out of woe.

4. When joy no longer soothes or cheers,
   And e'en the hope that threw
   A moment's sparkle o'er our tears,
   Is dimmed and vanished, too:

5. Oh! who could bear life's stormy doom,
   Did not thy wing of love
   Come brightly wafting thro' the gloom
   Our peace-branch from above?

6. Then sorrow, touched by thee, grows bright,
   With more than rapture's ray;
   As darkness shows us worlds of light,
   We never saw by day.

271. *Invocation.*

1. O SHEPHERD of thy people, hear
   Thy presence now display:
   Thou that hast given a house of prayer,
   Now give us hearts to pray.

2. Within these walls let holy peace,
   And love, and concord, dwell;
   Here give the troubled conscience ease,
   The wounded spirit heal.

3. May we in faith receive thy word,
   In faith present our prayers;
   And in the presence of the Lord
   Unbosom all our cares.

4. And may the gospel's joyful sound,
   By thy almighty grace,
   Awaken slumbering sinners round
   To come and fill the place.

272. *Self-Righteousness renounced.*

1. How long beneath the law I lay
   In bondage and distress!
   I toiled the precept to obey,
   But toiled without success.

2. Then, all my servile works were done
   A righteousness to raise;
   Now, freely chosen in the Son,
   I freely choose his ways.

3. To see the law by Christ fulfilled,
   And hear his pardoning voice,
   Will change a slave into a child,
   And duty into choice.

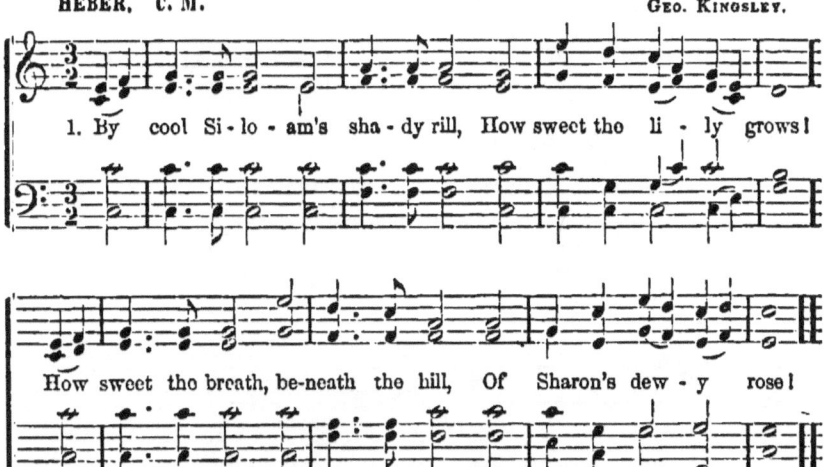

1. By cool Si-lo-am's sha-dy rill, How sweet the li-ly grows!

How sweet tho breath, be-neath the hill, Of Sharon's dew-y rose!

273.   *The sanctified Child.*

1. By cool Siloam's shady rill,
   How sweet the lily grows!
How sweet the breath, beneath tho hill,
   Of Sharon's dewy rose!

2. And such the child whose early feet
   The paths of peace have trod;
Whose secret heart, with influence sweet,
   Is upward drawn to God.

3. O Thou, whose infancy was found
   With heavenly rays to shine,
Whose years, with changeless virtue
   crowned,
Were all alike divine;

4. Dependent on thy bounteous breath,
   We seek thy grace alone,
In childhood, manhood, and in death,
   To keep us still thy own.

274.   *For a Sabbath-School.*

1. There is a glorious world of light
   Above the starry sky,
Where saints departed, clothed in white,
   Adore the Lord most high.

2. And hark! amid the sacred songs
   Those heavenly voices raise,
Ten thousand thousand infant tongues
   Unite in perfect praise.

3. Those are the hymns that we shall know,
   If Jesus we obey;
That is the place where we shall go,
   If found in wisdom's way.

4. This is the joy we ought to seek,
   And make our chief concern;
For this we come, from week to week,
   To read, and hear, and learn.

5. Soon will our earthly race be run,
   Our mortal frame decay,
Children and teachers, one by one,
   Must pass from earth away.

6. Great God, impress the serious thought
   This day on every breast,
That both the teachers and the taught
   May enter to thy rest.

275.   *The Holy Spirit.*

1. Spirit of peace, celestial Dove,
   How excellent thy praise!
How rich the gift of Christian love
   Thy gracious power displays!

2. Sweet as the dew on hill and flower,
   That silently distills,
At evening's soft and balmy hour,
   On Zion's fruitful hills.

3. So, with mild influence from above,
   Shall promised grace descend;
Till universal peace and love
   O'er all the earth extend.

PRATT. C. M.* FROM "SELAH." BY PERMISSION.

1. God moves in a mys - te - rious way, His wonders to per - form;

Cres. *Dim.* *p*

He plants his foot - steps in the sea, And rides up - on the storm.

* See also BYEFIELD 26.

276. *Light shining out of Darkness.*

1. GOD moves in a mysterious way,
His wonders to perform;
He plants his footsteps in the sea,
And rides upon the storm.

2. Deep in unfathomable mines
Of never-failing skill,
He treasures up his bright designs,
And works his sovereign will.

3. Ye fearful saints, fresh courage take;
The clouds ye so much dread,
Are big with mercy, and shall break
With blessings on your head.

4. Judge not the Lord by feeble sense,
But trust him for his grace;
Behind a frowning providence
He hides a smiling face.

5. His purposes will ripen fast,
Unfolding every hour;
The bud may have a bitter taste,
But sweet will be the flower.

6. Blind unbelief is sure to err,
And scan his work in vain;
God is his own interpreter,
And he will make it plain.

277. *Prospect of the Resurrection unto Life.*

1. THROUGH sorrow's night, and danger's path,
Amid the deepening gloom,
We, soldiers of an injured King,
Are marching to the tomb.

2. There, when the turmoil is no more,
And all our powers decay,
Our cold remains in solitude
Shall sleep the years away.

3. Our labors done, securely laid
In this our last retreat,
Unheeded, o'er our silent dust,
The storms of life shall beat.

4. Yet not thus lifeless, thus inane,
The vital spark shall lie;
For o'er life's wreck that spark shall rise
To seek its kindred sky.

5. These ashes too, this little dust,
Our Father's care shall keep,
Till the last angel rise and break
The long and dreary sleep.

6. Then love's soft dew o'er every eye
Shall shed its mildest rays,
And the long silent dust shall burst
With shouts of endless praise.

278. *God a Sovereign.*

1. KEEP silence, all created things,
And wait your Maker's nod:
My soul stands trembling while she sings
The honors of her God.

2. Life, death, and hell, and worlds un-
known,
Hang on his firm decree:
He sits on no precarious throne,
Nor borrows leave to be.

3. His providence unfolds the book,
And makes his counsels shine;
Each opening leaf, and every stroke,
Fulfills some deep design.

4. My God, I would not long to see
My fate with curious eyes;
What gloomy lines are writ for me,
Or what bright scenes may rise.

5. In thy fair book of life and grace,
Oh may I find my name,
Recorded in some humble place,
Beneath my Lord the Lamb.

279. *The general Assembly of Saints.*

1. NOT to the terrors of the Lord,
The tempest, fire, and smoke;
Not to the thunder of that word
Which God on Sinai spoke;—

2. But we are come to Zion's hill,
The city of our God,
Where milder words declare his will,
And spread his love abroad.

3. Behold the great, the glorious host
Of angels clothed in light;
Behold the spirits of the just,
Whose faith is turned to sight.

4. Behold the blest assembly there,
Whose names are writ in heaven,
And God, the Judge, who doth declare
Their every sin forgiven.

5. The saints on earth, and all the dead,
But one communion make;
All join in Christ, their living Head,
And of his grace partake.

6. In such society as this
My weary soul would rest;
The man who dwells where Jesus is
Must be for ever blest.

280. *Conviction of Sin by the Law.*

1. LORD, how secure my conscience was,
And felt no inward dread!
I was alive, without the law,
And thought my sins were dead.

2. My hopes of heaven were firm and bright,
But since the precept came,
With a convincing power and light,
I find how vile I am.

3. My guilt appeared but small before,
Till terribly I saw
How perfect, holy, just, and pure,
Is thine eternal law.

4. Then felt my soul the heavy load,
My sins revived again:
I had provoked a holy God,
And all my hopes were slain.

5. I'm like a helpless captive, sold
Under the power of sin;
I can not do the things I would,
Nor keep my conscience clean.

6. My God, I cry with every breath
For some kind Power to save;
To break the bonds of sin and death,
And thus redeem the slave.

281. *Desiring the Presence of God.*

1. HEAR, gracious God! my humble moan,
To thee I breathe my sighs;
When will the mournful night be gone,
And when my joys arise!

2. My God! Oh! could I make the claim,—
My Father, and my Friend,—
And call thee mine, by every name,
On which thy saints depend;—

3. By every name of power and love,
I would thy grace entreat;
Nor should my humble hopes remove,
Nor leave thy mercy-seat.

4. Yet, though my soul in darkness mourns,
Thy word is all my stay;
Here I would rest till light returns;—
Thy presence makes my day.

5. Speak, Lord! and bid celestial peace
Relieve my aching heart;
Oh! smile, and bid my sorrows cease,
And all the gloom depart.

6. Then shall my drooping spirit rise,
And bless the healing rays,
And change these deep, complaining
sighs
To songs of sacred praise.

HEAVENLY HOME. 11s.   ENGLISH.

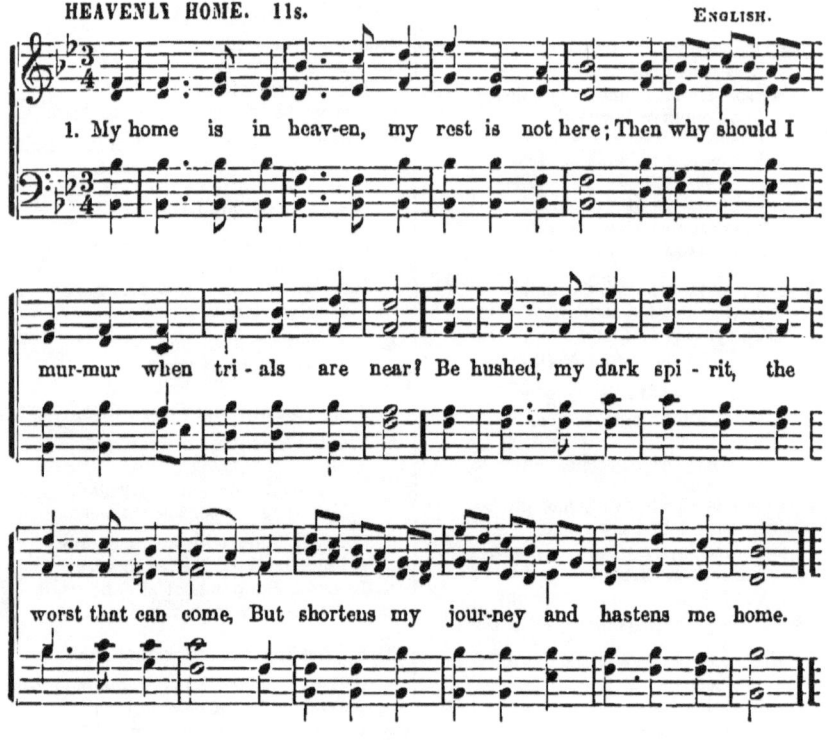

1. My home is in heav-en, my rest is not here; Then why should I mur-mur when tri-als are near? Be hushed, my dark spi-rit, the worst that can come, But shortens my jour-ney and hastens me home.

282.   *Rest in Heaven.*

1. My home is in heaven, my rest is not here,
Then why should I murmur when trials are near?
Be hush'd, my dark spirit, the worst that can come
But shortens my journey, and hastens me home.

2. It is not for me to be seeking my bliss,
And building my hopes in a region like this;
I look for a city which hands have not piled,
I pant for a country by sin undefiled.

3. The thorn and the thistle around me may grow,
I would not recline upon roses below,
I ask not my portion, I seek not my rest,
Till I find them for ever in Jesus's breast.

283.   *Praise for Mercies and Afflictions.*

1. For what shall I praise thee, my God and my King,
For what blessings the tribute of gratitude bring?
Shall I praise thee for pleasure, for health, or for ease,
For the sunshine of youth, for the garden of peace?

2. Shall I praise thee for flowers that bloom on my breast,
For joys in prospective, for pleasures possessed ?
For the spirits that heightened my days of delight,
And the slumbers that fell on my pillow by night?

3. For this I should praise, but if *only* for this,
I should leave half untold the donation of bliss ;
I thank thee for sickness, for sorrow and care,
For the thorns I have gathered, the anguish I bear.

4. For nights of anxiety, watching and tears,
A present of pain, a prospective of fears,
I praise thee, I bless thee, my Lord and my God,
For the good and the evil thy hand hath bestowed.

5. The flowers were sweet, but their fragrance is flown,
They yielded no fruit, they are withered and gone ;
The thorn it was poignant ; but precious to me
Was the message of mercy—it led me to thee.

284. *Longing for Rest.*

1. I AM weary of straying—O I fain would I rest
In the far distant land of the pure and the blest,
Where sin can no more her blandishments spread,
And tears and temptations for ever have fled.

2. I am weary of sighing o'er sorrows of earth,
O'er joy's glowing visions, that fade at their birth ;
O'er the pangs of the loved, which we can not assuage,
O'er the blightings of youth, and the weakness of age.

3. I am weary of loving what passeth away,
The sweetest, the dearest, alas I may not stay ;
I long for that land where these partings are o'er,
And death and the tomb can divide hearts no more.

4. I am weary, my Saviour, of grieving thy love ;
Oh I when shall I rest in thy presence above ?
I am weary—but, O I let me never repine,
While thy word, and thy love, and thy promise are mine.

285. *Longing for Heaven.*

1. O HAD I, my Saviour, the wings of a dove,
How soon would I soar to thy presence above ;
How soon would I flee where the weary have rest,
And hide all my cares in thy sheltering breast.

2. I flutter, I struggle, I long to be free,
I feel me a captive while banished from thee ;
A pilgrim and stranger, the desert I roam,
And look on to heaven, and fain would be home.

3. Ah, there the wild tempest for ever shall cease,
No billow shall ruffle that haven of peace ;
Temptation and trouble alike shall depart,
All tears from the eye, and all sin from the heart.

4. Soon, soon may this Eden of promise be mine ;
Rise, bright sun of glory, no more to decline I
Thy light, yet unrisen, the wilderness cheers—
O I what will it be when the fullness appears.

DEDHAM. C. M.*　　　　　　　　　　　　　　　ENGLISH.

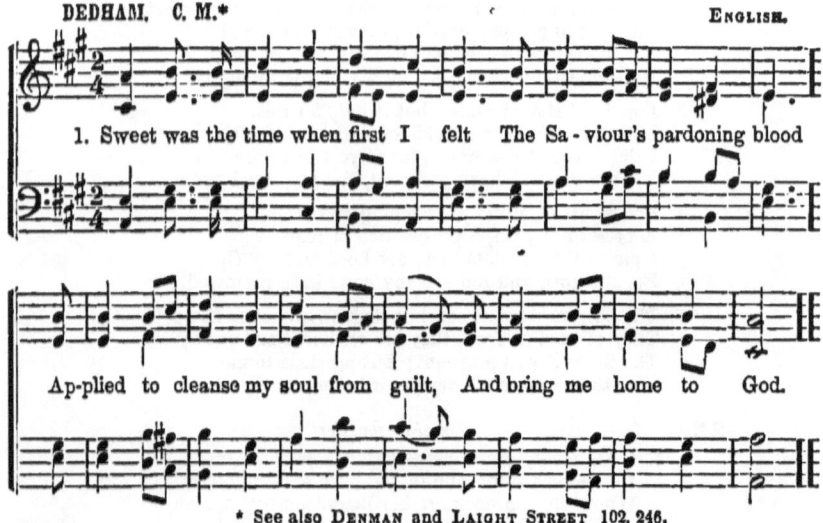

1. Sweet was the time when first I felt The Sa - viour's pardoning blood

Ap-plied to cleanse my soul from guilt, And bring me home to God.

* See also DENMAN and LAIGHT STREET 102, 246.

286. *Mourning over departed Comforts.*

1. SWEET was the time when first I felt
The Saviour's pardoning blood
Applied to cleanse my soul from guilt,
And bring me home to God.

2. Soon as the morn the light revealed,
His praises tuned my tongue;
And when the evening shades prevailed,
His love was all my song.

3. In prayer my soul drew near the Lord,
And saw his glory shine;
And when I read his holy word,
I called each promise mine.

4. But now, when evening shade prevails,
My soul in darkness mourns;
And when the morn the light reveals,
No light to me returns.

5. Rise, Lord, and help me to prevail;
O, make my soul thy care:
I know thy mercy can not fail;
Let me that mercy share.

287. *Prayer and Hope.*

1. SOON as I heard my Father say,—
"Ye children! seek my grace,"
My heart replied without delay,—
"I 'll seek my Father's face."

2. Let not thy face be hid from me,
Nor frown my soul away;

God of my life! I fly to thee,
In a distressing day.

3. Should friends and kindred, near and
dear,
Leave me to want, or die,
My God would make my life his care,
And all my need supply.

4. My fainting flesh had died with grief,
Had not my soul believed,
To see thy grace provide relief;—
Nor was my hope deceived.

5. Wait on the Lord, ye trembling saints!
And keep your courage up;
He 'll raise your spirit when it faints,
And far exceed your hope.

288. *The Young entering into Covenant*

1. COME, let us join our souls to God,
In everlasting bands;
And seize the blessings he bestows,
With eager hearts and hands.

2. Come, let us to his temple haste,
And seek his favor there;
Before his footstool humbly bow,
And pour our fervent prayer.

3. Come, let us seal, without delay,
The covenant of his grace;
Nor shall the years of distant life
Its memory e'er efface.

4. Thus may our young companions haste
  To seek their fathers' God;
Nor e'er forsake the happy path
  Their fathers' feet have trod.

289. *The triumphal Feast.*

1. COME, let us lift our voices high,
  High as our joys arise,
And join the songs above the sky,
  Where pleasure never dies.

2. Jesus, our God, invites us here,
  To this triumphal feast;
And brings immortal blessings down
  For each redeeméd guest.

3. Victorious King! what can we pay
  For favors so divine?
We would devote our hearts away,
  To be for ever thine.

4. We give thee, Lord, our highest praise,
  The tribute of our tongues;
But themes so infinite as these
  Exceed our noblest songs.

290. *Various Success of the Gospel.*

1. CHRIST and his cross is all our theme;
  The mysteries that we speak
Are scandal in the Jews' esteem,
  And folly to the Greek.

2. But souls, enlightened from above,
  With joy receive the word;
They see what wisdom, power, and love,
  Shine in their dying Lord.

3. The vital savor of his name
  Restores their fainting breath;
But unbelief perverts the same
  To guilt, despair, and death.

4. Till God diffuse his graces down,
  Like showers of heavenly rain,
In vain Apollos sows the ground,
  And Paul may plant in vain.

291. *Union of Saints in Heaven and on
Earth.*

1. COME, let us join our friends above,
  Who have obtained the prize,
And, on the eagle wings of love,
  To joy celestial rise.

2. Let saints below in concert sing
  With those to glory gone,
For all the servants of our King
  In heaven and earth are one:—

3. One family,—we dwell in him;
  One church,—above, beneath;
Though now divided by the stream—
  The narrow stream of death.

4. One army of the living God,
  To his command we bow;
Part of the host have crossed the flood,
  And part are crossing now.

5. Ev'n now to their eternal home
  Some happy spirits fly;
And we are to the margin come,
  And soon expect to die!

6. Dear Saviour! be our constant guide;
  Then, when the word is given,
Bid Jordan's narrow stream divide,
  And land us safe in heaven.

292. *Asking the Presence of Christ.*

1. COME, thou desire of all thy saints!
  Our humble strains attend,
While, with our praises and complaints,
  Low at thy feet we bend.

2. How should our songs, like those above,
  With warm devotion rise!
How should our souls, on wings of love,
  Mount upward to the skies!

3. Come, Lord, thy love alone can raise
  In us the heavenly flame;
Then shall our lips resound thy praise, ✳
  Our hearts adore thy name.

4. Dear Saviour! let thy glory shine,
  And fill thy dwellings here,
Till life, and love, and joy divine
  A heaven on earth appear.

5. Then shall our hearts enraptured say,—
  Come, great Redeemer! come,
And bring the bright, the glorious day,
  That calls thy children home.

293. *Daily and nightly Devotion.*

1. YE that obey th' immortal King,
  Attend his holy place;
Bow to the glories of his name,
  And sing his wondrous grace.

2. Lift up your hands by morning light,
  And raise your thanks on high;
Send your admiring thoughts by night
  Above the starry sky.

3. The God of Zion cheer your hearts
  With rays of quick'ning grace:
'Tis he that spreads the heavens abroad
  Whose presence fills the place.

ORTONVILLE. C. M.

HASTINGS.

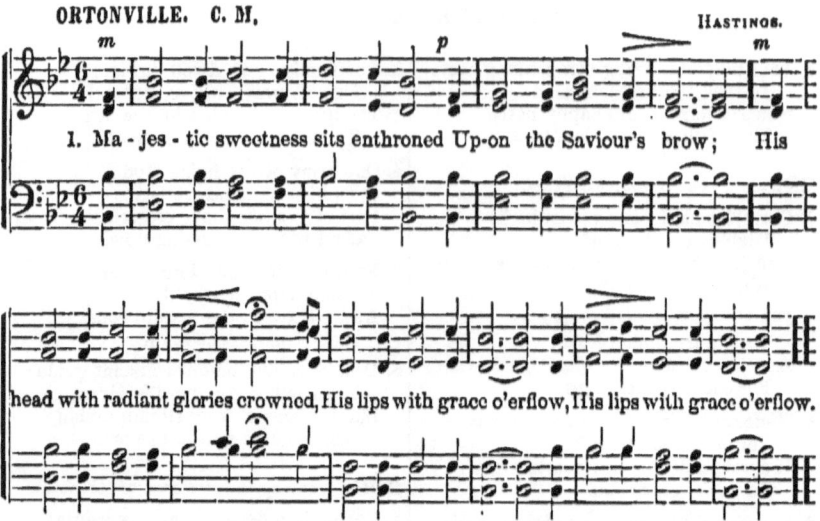

1. Ma-jes-tic sweetness sits enthroned Up-on the Saviour's brow; His
head with radiant glories crowned, His lips with grace o'erflow, His lips with grace o'erflow.

294. *Chief among ten Thousand.*

1. MAJESTIC sweetness sits enthroned
Upon the Saviour's brow;
His head with radiant glories crowned,
His lips with grace o'erflow.

2. No mortal can with him compare,
Among the sons of men;
Fairer is he than all the fair
Who fill the heavenly train.

3. He saw me plunged in deep distress,
And flew to my relief;
For me he bore the shameful cross,
And carried all my grief.

4. To him I owe my life and breath,
And all the joys I have:
He makes me triumph over death,
And saves me from the grave.

5. Since from his bounty I receive
Such proofs of love divine,
Had I a thousand hearts to give,
Lord, they should all be thine.

295. *A blessed Gospel.*

1. BLEST are the souls that hear and know
The gospel's joyful sound;
Peace shall attend the path they go,
And light their steps surround.

2. Their joy shall bear their spirits up,
Through their Redeemer's name;
His righteousness exalts their hope,
And fills their foes with shame.

3. The Lord, our glory and defense,
Strength and salvation gives:
Israel, thy King for ever reigns,
Thy God for ever lives.

296. *Dedication Hymn.*

1. O THOU, whose own vast temple stands
Built over earth and sea,
Accept the walls that human hands
Have raised to worship thee.

2. Lord, from thine inmost glory send,
Within these courts to bide,
The peace that dwelleth, without end,
Serenely by thy side.

3. May erring minds that worship here
Be taught the better way;
And they who mourn, and they who fear,
Be strengthened as they pray.

4. May faith grow firm, and love grow
warm,
And pure devotion rise,
While round these hallowed walls the
swarm
Of earth-born passion dies!

297. *Praise to the Redeemer.*

1. O, FOR a thousand tongues to sing
My dear Redeemer's praise,
The glories of my God and King,
The triumphs of his grace.

2. My gracious Master and my God,
Let saints thy love proclaim,
And spread thro' all the earth abroad
The honors of thy name.

3. Jesus, the name that calms my fears,
That bids my sorrow cease;
'Tis music to my ravished ears;
'Tis life, and health, and peace.

4. It breaks the power of reigning sin,
And sets the prisoner free;
Thy blood can cleanse the foulest stain;
And can avail for me.

298. *Submission in Trials.*

1. MY times of sorrow and of joy,
Great God! are in thy hand;
My choicest comforts come from thee,
And go at thy command.

2. If thou shouldst take them all away,
Yet would I not repine;
Before they were possessed by me,
They were entirely thine.

3. Nor would I drop a murmuring word,
Though the whole world were gone,
But seek enduring happiness,
In thee, and thee alone.

299. *Pious Resolutions.*

1. O THAT thy statutes every hour
Might dwell upon my mind!
Thence I derive a quickening power,
And daily peace I find.

2. To meditate thy precepts, Lord,
Shall be my sweet employ;
My soul shall ne'er forget thy word,
Thy word is all my joy.

3. How would I run in thy commands,
If thou my heart discharge
From sin, and Satan's hateful chains,
And set my feet at large?

4. My lips with courage shall declare
Thy statutes and thy name;
I'll speak thy word, though kings should
hear,
Nor yield to sinful shame.

300. *Faith encouraged by ancient Examples.*

1. RISE, O my soul! pursue the path,
By ancient worthies trod;
Aspiring, view those holy men,
Who lived and walked with God.

2. Though dead, they speak in reason's ear,
And in example live;
Their faith, and hope, and mighty deeds,
Still fresh instruction give.

3. 'Twas through the Lamb's most precious
blood
They conquered every foe;
And to his power and matchless grace
Their crowns of life they owe.

4. Lord! may I ever keep in view
The patterns thou hast given;
And ne'er forsake the blessed road,
That led them safe to heaven.

301. *Desires for Holiness.*

1. O, COULD I find, from day to day,
A nearness to my God,
Then would my hours glide sweet away,
While leaning on his word.

2. Lord, I desire with thee to live
Anew from day to day,
In joys the world can never give,
Nor ever take away.

3. Blest Jesus, come, and rule my heart,
And make me wholly thine,
That I may never more depart,
Nor grieve thy love divine.

4. Thus, till my last, expiring breath,
Thy goodness I'll adore;
And when my frame dissolves in death,
My soul shall love thee more.

302. *Depending on Grace.*

1. AMAZING grace! how sweet the sound!
That saved a wretch like me;
I once was lost, but now am found,
Was blind, but now I see.

2. 'Twas grace that taught my heart to fear
And grace my fears relieved;
How precious did that grace appear,
The hour I first believed.

3. Through many dangers, toils, and snares,
I have already come;
'Tis grace hath brought me safe thus far,
And grace will lead me home.

4. Yea, when this flesh and heart shall fail,
And mortal life shall cease,
I shall possess, within the vail,
A life of joy and peace.

DEARBORN.   C. M.*   W. B. B   "MENDELSSOHN COLL."

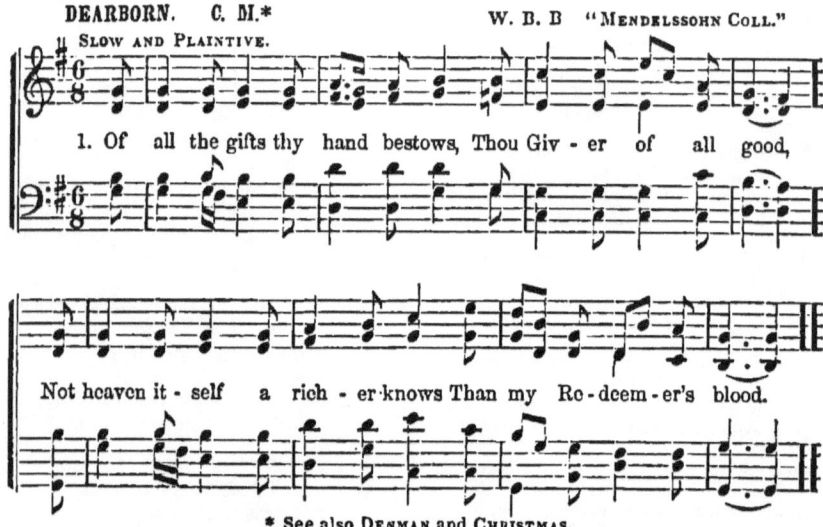

SLOW AND PLAINTIVE.

1. Of all the gifts thy hand bestows, Thou Giv - er   of   all   good,

Not heaven it - self   a   rich - er knows Than my Re - deem - er's blood.

* See also DENMAN and CHRISTMAS.

303.   *Faith the Gift of the Spirit.*

1. OF all the gifts thy hand bestows,
    Thou Giver of all good,
Not heaven itself a richer knows
    Than my Redeemer's blood.

2. Faith too— th' appropriating grace,
    From the same hand we gain;
Else, sweetly as it suits our case,
    That gift had been in vain.

3. We praise thee, and would praise thee
      more;
    To thee our all we owe:—
The precious Saviour,—and the power
    That makes him precious too.

304.   *Saturday Evening.*

1. WHEN the worn spirit wants repose,
    And sighs her God to seek,
How sweet to hail the evening's close
    That ends the weary week!

2. How sweet will be the early dawn
    That opens on the sight,
When first the soul-reviving morn
    Shall shed new rays of light.

3. Blest day! thine hours too soon will
      cease,
    Yet, while they gently roll,
Breathe, heavenly Spirit, source of peace,
    A Sabbath o'er my soul.

4. When will my pilgrimage be done,
    The world's long week be o'er,
That Sabbath dawn which needs no sun,
    That day which fades no more.

305.   *Backslidings and Returns.*

1. WHY is my heart so far from thee,
    My God, my chief delight?
Why are my thoughts no more, by day,
    With thee, no more by night.

2. Why should my foolish passions rove?
    Where can such sweetness be,
As I have tasted in thy love,
    As I have found in thee?

3. When my forgetful soul renews
    The savor of thy grace,
My heart presumes, I can not lose
    The relish all my days.

4. But ere one fleeting hour is past,
    The flattering world employs
Some sensual bait to seize my taste,
    And to pollute my joys.

5. Wretch that I am, to wander thus,
    In chase of false delight!
Let me be fastened to thy cross,
    Rather than lose thy sight.

6. Make haste, my days, to reach the goal,
    And bring my heart to rest
On the dear centre of my soul,
    My God, my Saviour's breast.

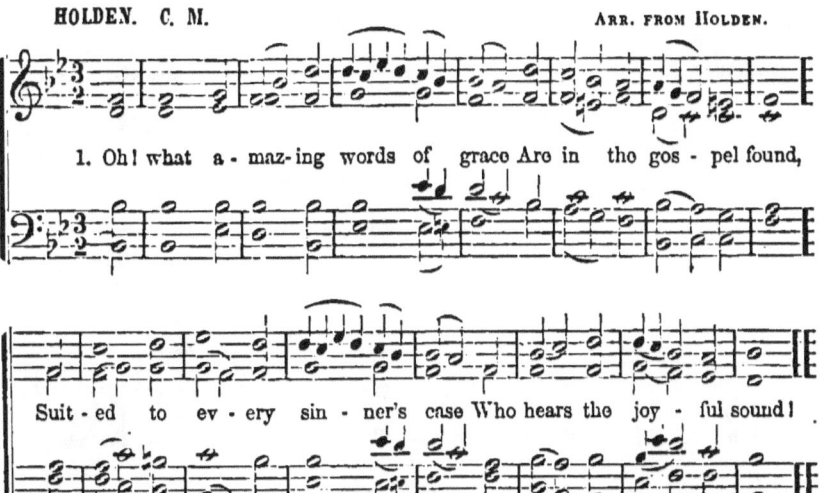

1. Oh! what a-maz-ing words of grace Are in the gos-pel found,

Suit-ed to ev-ery sin-ner's case Who hears the joy-ful sound!

306. *The Fountain of living Waters.*

1. Oh! what amazing words of grace
   Are in the gospel found,
   Suited to every sinner's case
   Who hears the joyful sound.

2. Come, then, with all your wants and
       wounds,
   Your every burden bring;
   Here love, unchanging love, abounds,—
   A deep celestial spring.

3. This spring with living waters flows,
   And heavenly joys imparts;
   Come, thirsty souls, your wants disclose,
   And drink with thankful hearts.

4. Millions of sinners, vile as you,
   Have here found life and peace;
   Come, then, and prove its virtues, too,
   And drink, adore, and bless.

307.   *Confidence in God.*

1. O Lord, I would delight in thee,
   And on thy care depend;
   To thee in every trouble flee,
   My best, my only Friend.

2. When all created streams are dried,
   Thy fullness is the same:
   May I with this be satisfied,
   And glory in thy name.

3. Why should the soul a drop bemoan,
   Who has a fountain near!
   A fountain which will ever run
   With waters sweet and clear.

4. No good in creatures can be found
   But may be found in Thee;
   I must have all things and abound,
   While God is God to me.

5. O Lord, I cast my care on thee,
   I triumph and adore;
   Henceforth my great concern shall be
   To love and praise thee more.

308. ˙   *Pleasures Unseen.*

1. Oh, could our thoughts and wishes fly,
   Above these gloomy shades,
   To those bright worlds beyond the sky,
   Which sorrow ne'er invades!

2. There joys, unseen by mortal eyes,
   Or reason's feeble ray,
   In ever blooming prospects rise,
   Unconscious of decay.

3. Lord, send a beam of light divine,
   To guide our upward aim;
   With one reviving touch of thine,
   Our languid hearts inflame.

4. O then, on faith's sublimest wing,
   Our ardent hope shall rise,
   To those bright scenes where pleasures
   Immortal in the skies.   [spring

DENMAN.　C. M.*　　　　　　　　　　Arranged from De Call.

1. I love the Lord; he heard my cries, And pit - ied ev - ery groan;

Long as I live, when troubles rise, I'll hast-en to his throne.

* See also Christmas 12.

309. *Thanks for restoring Mercy.*

1. I love the Lord; he heard my cries,
　And pitied every groan;
Long as I live, when troubles rise,
　I'll hasten to his throne.

2. I love the Lord: he bowed his ear,
　And chased my griefs away:
O, let my heart no more despair
　While I have breath to pray.

3. My flesh declined, my spirits fell,
　And I drew near the dead,
While inward pangs and fears of hell
　Perplexed my wakeful head.

4. "My God," I cried, "thy servant save,
　Thou ever good and just!
Thy power can rescue from the grave—
　Thy power is all my trust.

5. The Lord beheld me sore distrest,
　He bade my pains remove;
Return, my soul, to God thy rest,
　For thou hast known his love.

6. My God hath saved my soul from death,
　And dried my falling tears;
Now to his praise I'll spend my breath,
　And my remaining years.

310.　　*The Heavenly City.*

1. Jerusalem, my happy home!
　Name ever dear to me;
When shall my labors have an end
　In joy, and peace, and thee?

2. When shall these eyes thy heaven-built
　　walls
And pearly gates behold?
Thy bulwarks with salvation strong,
　And streets of shining gold.

3. O, when, thou city of my God,
　Shall I thy courts ascend?
Where congregations ne'er break up,
　And Sabbaths never end.

4. Why should I shrink at pain or woe,
　Or feel at death dismay?
I've Canaan's goodly land in view,
　And realms of endless day.

5. Redeeméd saints and angels there,
　Around my Saviour stand;
And soon my friends in Christ, below,
　Will join the glorious band.

6. Jerusalem, my happy home!
　My soul still pants for thee;
Then shall my labors have an end,
　When I thy joys shall see.

311. *"Hinder me not."* Gen. xxiv. 56.

1. In all my Lord's appointed ways
    My journey I 'll pursue ;
"Hinder me not," ye much-loved saints,
    For I must go with you.

2. Through floods and flames, if Jesus lead,
    I'll follow where he goes ;
"Hinder me not," shall be my cry,
    Though earth and hell oppose.

3. Through duty, and through trials, too,
    I 'll go at his command :
"Hinder me not," for I am bound
    To my Immanuel's land.

4. And when my Saviour calls me home,
    My joyful cry shall be,
" Hinder me not;" come, welcome death,
    I 'll gladly go with thee.

312. *A joyous Event.*

1. Calm on the listening ear of night
Come heaven's melodious strains,
Where wild Judea stretches far
    Her silver-mantled plains.

2. Celestial choirs, from courts above,
    Shed sacred glories there,
And angels, with their sparkling lyres,
    Make music on the air.

3. The joyous hills of Palestine
    Send back the glad reply,
And greet, from all their holy heights,
    The day-spring from on high.

4. O'er the blue depths of Galilee
    There comes a holier calm,
And Sharon waves, in solemn praise,
    Her silent groves of palm.

5. " Glory to God !" the sounding skies
    Aloud with anthems ring ;
"Peace to the earth, good-will to men,
    From heaven's eternal King !"

313. *Instruction from the Scriptures.*

1. How shall the young secure their hearts,
    And guard their lives from sin ?
Thy word the choicest rules imparts
    To keep the conscience clean.

2. When once it enters to the mind,
    It spreads such light abroad ;
The meanest souls instruction find,
    And raise their thoughts to God.

3. 'Tis like the sun, a heavenly light,
    That guides us all the day ;
And, through the dangers of the night,
    A lamp to lead our way.

4. Thy precepts make me truly wise ;
    I hate the sinner's road ;
I hate my own vain thoughts that rise,
    But love thy law, my God !

5. Thy word is everlasting truth ;
    How pure is every page !
That holy book shall guide our youth,
    And well support our age.

314. *The Hope of Heaven.*

1. When I can read my title clear
    To mansions in the skies,
I bid farewell to every fear,
    And wipe my weeping eyes.

2. Should earth against my soul engage,
    And fiery darts be hurled,
Then I can smile at Satan's rage,
    And face a frowning world.

3. Let cares, like a wild deluge, come,
    And storms of sorrow, fall !
May I but safely reach my home,
    My God, my heaven, my all:

4. There shall I bathe my weary soul
    In seas of heavenly rest,
And not a wave of trouble roll
    Across my peaceful breast.

315. *Prayer for our Country.*

1. Lord, while for all mankind we pray,
    Of every clime and coast,
O, hear us for our native land,—
    The land we love the most.

2. O, guard our shores from every foe,
    With peace our borders bless,
With prosperous times our cities crown,
    Our fields with plenteousness.

3. Unite us in the sacred love
    Of knowledge, truth, and thee ;
And let our hills and valleys shout
    The songs of liberty.

4. Here may religion, pure and mild,
    Smile on our Sabbath hours ;
And piety and virtue bless
    The home of us and ours.

5. Lord of the nations, thus to thee
    Our country we commend ;
Be thou her refuge and her trust,
    Her everlasting friend.

BOYNTON. C. M.*   MALAN. Arranged.

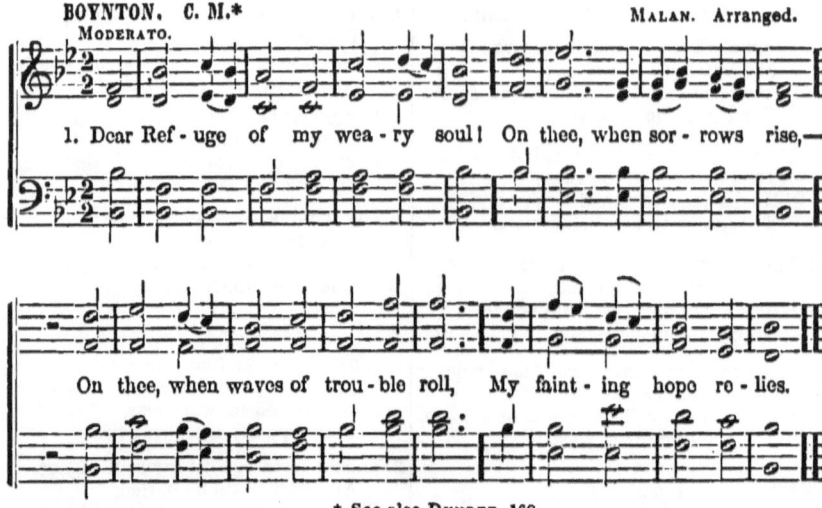

1. Dear Ref - uge of my wea - ry soul! On thee, when sor - rows rise,—

On thee, when waves of trou - ble roll, My faint - ing hope re - lies.

* See also DUNDEE 108.

316.   *God our Refuge.*

1. DEAR Refuge of my weary soul!
   On Thee, when sorrows rise,—
   On Thee, when waves of trouble roll,
   My fainting hope relies.

2. To Thee I tell each rising grief,
   For Thou alone canst heal;
   Thy word can bring a sweet relief,
   For every pain I feel.

3. But Oh! when gloomy doubts prevail,
   I fear to call Thee mine;
   The springs of comfort seem to fail,
   And all my hopes decline.

4. Hast Thou not bid me seek thy face?
   And shall I seek in vain?
   And can the ear of sovereign grace
   Be deaf when I complain?

5. No,—still the ear of sovereign grace
   Attends the mourner's prayer:
   Oh! may I ever find access
   To breathe my sorrows there!

6. Thy mercy-seat is open still:
   Here let my soul retreat;
   With humble hope attend thy will,
   And wait beneath thy feet.

317.   *Old Things passed away.*

1. LET earthly minds the world pursue,
   It has no charms for me;

Once I admired its trifles, too,
But grace hath set me free.

2. Its joys can now no longer please,
   Nor happiness afford:
   Far from my heart be joys like these,
   For I have seen the Lord.

3. As by the light of opening day,
   The stars are all concealed;
   So earthly pleasures fade away,
   When Jesus is revealed.

4. Creatures no more divide my choice,
   I bid them all depart;
   His name, his love, his gracious voice,
   Have fixed my roving heart.

5. But may I hope that thou wilt own
   A worthless worm like me!
   Dear Lord, I would be thine alone,
   And wholly live to thee.

318.   *Evening Devotion.*

1. LORD, thou wilt hear me when I pray ·
   I am for ever thine:
   I fear before thee all the day,
   Nor would I dare to sin.

2. And while I rest my weary head
   From cares and business free,
   'Tis sweet conversing on my bed
   With my own heart and thee.

3 I pay this evening sacrifice ;
  And when my work is done,
Great God, my faith, my hope relies
  Upon thy grace alone.

4. Thus with my thoughts composed to
    peace,
  I 'll give mine eyes to sleep ;
Thy hand in safety keeps my days,
  And will my slumbers keep.

319.   *God every where.*

1. In all my vast concerns with thee,
  In vain my soul would try,
To shun thy presence, Lord ! or flee
  The notice of thine eye.

2. Thine all-surrounding sight surveys
  My rising and my rest,
My public walks, my private ways,
  And secrets of my breast.

3. My thoughts lie open to the Lord,
  Before they 're formed within ;
And, ere my lips pronounce the word,
  He knows the sense I mean.

4. Oh ! wondrous knowledge, deep and high,
  Where can a creature hide ?
Within thy circling arms I lie,
  Enclosed on every side.

5. So let thy grace surround me still,
  And like a bulwark prove,
To guard my soul from every ill,
  Secured by sovereign love.

320.   *Affliction sweetened.*

1. When languor and disease invade
  This trembling house of clay,
'Tis sweet to look beyond my pains,
  And long to fly away.

2. Sweet to look inward, and attend
  The whispers of his love ;
Sweet to look upward to the place
  Where Jesus pleads above.

3. Sweet on his faithfulness to rest,
  Whose love can never end ;
Sweet on his covenant of grace
  For all things to depend.

4. Sweet, in the confidence of faith,
  To trust his firm decrees ;
Sweet to lie passive in his hand,
  And know no will but his.

5. If such the sweetness of the streams,
  What must the fountain be,
Where saints and angels draw their bliss
  Immediately from thee !

321.   *Inquiring the Way to Zion.*

1. Inquire, ye pilgrims, for the way
  That leads to Zion's hill,
And thither set your anxious face
  With a determined will.

2. Oh come, to God's own temple haste ·
  And seek his favor there ;
Before his footstool humbly bow,
  And pour your fervent prayer.

3. Oh come, and join your souls to God
  In everlasting bands ;
Accept the blessings he bestows,
  With thankful hearts and hands.

322.   *The Gospel Feast.*

1. How sweet and awful is the place,
  With Christ within the doors—
While everlasting love displays
  The choicest of her stores.

2. While all our hearts, and all our songs,
  Join to admire the feast ;
Each of us cries, with thankful tongues,
  " Lord, why was I a guest ?

3. " Why was I made to hear thy voice,
  And enter while there 's room—
When thousands make a wretched choice
  And rather starve than come ? "

4. 'T was the same love that spread the feast
  That sweetly forced us in ;
Else we had still refused to taste,
  And perished in our sin.

5. Pity the nations, O our God,
  Constrain the earth to come ;
Send thy victorious word abroad,
  And bring the strangers home.

6. We long to see thy churches full,
  That all the chosen race
May with one voice, and heart, and soul,
  Sing thy redeeming grace.

323.   *Dying in the Lord.*

1. Hear what the voice from heaven pro-
    claims,
  For all the pious dead ;—
" Sweet is the savor of their names,
  And soft their sleeping-bed.

2. " They die in Jesus, and are blessed,—·
  How kind their slumbers are !
From sufferings, and from sins, released,
  And freed from every snare.

3. " Far from this world of toil and strife,
  They 're present with the Lord ;
The labors of their mortal life
  End in a large reward."

BRATTLE STREET. C. M. Double.*   PLEYEL. Arranged.

1. Whilst thee I seek, pro - tect-ing Power! Be my vain wish-es stilled;

And may this con - se - crat-ed hour With bet - ter hopes be filled.
A.S. Thy mer - cy o'er my life has flowed; That mer - cy I a - dore.

Choir.   AL SEG.

Thy love the power of thought bestowed; To thee my thoughts would soar:

* See also HONOLULU 110.

324.   *Devotion.*

1. WHILST thee I seek, protecting Power!
    Be my vain wishes stilled;
    And may this consecrated hour
    With better hopes be filled.

2. Thy love the power of thought bestowed;
    To thee my thoughts would soar:
    Thy mercy o'er my life has flowed;
    That mercy I adore.

3. In each event of life how clear
    Thy ruling hand I see!
    Each blessing to my soul most dear,
    Because conferred by thee.

4. In every joy that crowns my days,
    In every pain I bear,
    My heart shall find delight in praise,
    Or seek relief in prayer.

5. When gladness wings my favored hour,
    Thy love my thoughts shall fill;

Resigned when storms of sorrow lower,
    My soul shall meet thy will.

6. My lifted eye, without a tear,
    The gathering storm shall see;
    My steadfast heart shall know no fear;
    That heart will rest on thee.

325.   *Christ our Hope.*

1. OUR souls, by love together knit,
    Cemented, mixed in one,
    One hope, one heart, one mind, **one**
        voice,
    'Tis heaven on earth begun.

2. Our hearts have often burned within,
    And glowed with sacred fire,
    While Jesus spoke, and fed, and blessed,
    And filled th' enlarged desire.

3. The little cloud increases still,
The heavens are big with rain ;
We haste to catch the teeming shower,
And all its moisture drain.

4. A rill, a stream, a torrent flows!
But pour a mighty flood ;
O sweep the nations, shake the earth,
'Till all proclaim thee, God !

5. And when thou mak'st thy jewels up,
And sett'st thy starry crown;
When all thy sparkling gems shall shine,
Proclaimed by thee thine own;

6. May we, a little band of love,
We sinners, saved by grace,
From glory unto glory changed,
Behold thee face to face.

326. *Presence of God in Affliction.*

1. THY gracious presence, O my God !
Can soothe my inward pains ;
With this, beneath affliction's load,
My heart no more complains.

2. This can·my every care control,
And gild each scene with light;
This is the sunshine of the soul ;
Without it, all is night.

3. My Lord! my Life! Oh! cheer my heart
With thy reviving ray;
Oh! bid these mournful shades depart,
And bring the dawn of day.

4. Oh! happy scenes of pure delight,
Where thy full beams arise;—
Unclouded beauty to the sight,—
Sweet rapture and surprise!

5. Lord! shall those breathings of my heart
Aspire, in vain, to thee?
Confirm my hope, that, where thou art,
I shall for ever be.

6. Then shall my cheerful spirit sing
The darkest hours away,
And rise, on faith's expanding wing,
To everlasting day.

327. *The Change effected by Grace.*

1. WHEN God revealed his gracious name,
And changed my mournful state,
My rapture seemed a pleasing dream,
The grace appeared so great.

2. The world beheld the glorious change,
And did thy hand confess;

My tongue broke out in unknown strains,
And sung surprising grace.

3. "Great is the work!" my neighbors cried,
And owned the power divine ;
"Great is the work!" my heart replied,
"And be the glory thine."

4. The Lord can clear the darkest skies,
Can give us day for night;
Make drops of sacred sorrow rise
To rivers of delight.

5. Let those, who sow in sadness, wait
Till the fair harvest come:
They shall confess their sheaves are great,
And shout the blessings home.

328. *Vows made in Trouble, paid in the Church.*

1. WHAT shall I render to my God,
For all his kindness shown ?
My feet shall visit thine abode,
My songs address thy throne.

2. Among the saints that fill thy house,
My offering shall be paid ;
There shall my zeal perform the vows
My soul in anguish made.

3. How much is mercy thy delight,
Thou ever-blesséd God !
How dear thy servants in thy sight—
How precious is their blood !

4. How happy all thy servants are !
How great thy grace to me !
My life, which thou hast made thy care,
Lord! I devote to thee.

5. Now I am thine—for ever thine;
Nor shall my purpose move;
Thy hand hath loosed my bonds of pain,
And bound me with thy love.

6. Here, in thy courts, I leave my vow,
And thy rich grace record ;
Witness, ye saints ! who hear me now
If I forsake the Lord.

Doxology.

1. THE God of mercy be adored,
Who calls our souls from death ;
Who saves by his redeeming Word
And new-creating Breath.

2. To praise the Father, and the Son,
And Spirit, all divine,
The One in Three, and Three in One,
Let saints and angels join.

Not too Fast.

1. There is a fountain filled with blood, Drawn from Immanuel's veins; And

FINAL. p

sinners plunged beneath that flood, Lose all their guilty stains, Lose all their guilty stains.

* See also CHRISTMAS 12.

329.   *Christ the Living Fountain.*

1. THERE is a fountain filled with blood,
Drawn from Immanuel's veins;
And sinners plunged beneath that flood,
Lose all their guilty stains.

2. The dying thief rejoiced to see
That fountain in his day;
And there may I, though vile as he,
Wash all my sins away.

3. Dear, dying Lamb! thy precious blood
Shall never lose its power,
Till all the ransomed church of God
Be saved, to sin no more.

4. E'er since by faith I saw the stream
Thy flowing wounds supply,
Redeeming love has been my theme,
And shall be till I die.

5. Then in a nobler, sweeter song,
I 'll sing thy power to save,
When this poor lisping, faltering tongue
Lies silent in the grave.

330.   *Access to God by Christ.*

1. COME, let us lift our joyful eyes
Up to the courts above,
And smile to see our Father there,
Upon a throne of love.

2. Rich were the drops of Jesus' blood,
That calmed his frowning face,—
That sprinkled o'er the burning throne,
And turned the wrath to grace.

3. Now we may bow before his feet,
And venture near the Lord;
No fiery cherub guards his seat,
Nor double-flaming sword.

4. The peaceful gates of heavenly bliss
Are opened by the Son;
High let us raise our notes of praise,
And reach th' Almighty throne.

5. To thee ten thousand thanks we bring,
Great Advocate on high!
And glory to th' eternal King,—
He lays his anger by.

331.   *Fear not.*

1. YE trembling souls, dismiss your fears;
Be mercy all your theme;
For mercy like a river flows,
In one perpetual stream.

2. "Fear not" the powers of earth and hell;
God will those powers restrain;
His arm will all their rage repel,
And make their efforts vain.

8. "Fear not" tho want of outward good;
  For his ho will provide,
Grant tnem supplies of daily food,
  And give them heaven beside.

4. " Fear not" that he will e'er forsake,
  Or leave his work undone;
He 's faithful to his promises,
  And faithful to his Son.

5. " Fear not" the terrors of the grave,
  Nor death's relentless sting;
He will from endless wrath preserve,
  To endless glory bring.

332.   *Gospel Invitation.*

1. YE wretched, hungry, starving poor,
  Behold a royal feast!
Where mercy spreads her bounteous
    store
For every humble guest.

2. Here Jesus stands with open arms;
  He calls, he bids you come;
Guilt holds you back, and fear alarms;
  But see, there yet is room.

3. Room in the Saviour's bleeding heart;
  There love and pity meet;
Nor will he bid the soul depart,
  That trembles at his feet.

4. O come, and with his children, taste
  The blessings of his love;
While hope attends the sweet repast
  Of nobler joys above.

5. There, with united heart and voice,
  Before th' eternal throne,
Ten thousand thousand souls rejoice,
  In songs on earth unknown.

333. *Sufferings of Christ for Sinners.*

1. FATHER! I sing thy wondrous grace,
  I bless my Saviour's name;
He brought salvation for the poor,
  And bore the sinner's shame.

2. His deep distress hath raised us high;
  His duty and his zeal
Fulfilled the law, which mortals broke,
  And finished all thy will.

3. Zion is thine, most holy God!
  Thy Son shall bless her gates;
And glory, purchased by his blood,
  For thine own Israel waits.

4. Let heaven, and all that dwell on high,
  To God their voices raise;
While lands and seas assist the sky,
  And join t' advance his praise.

334.   *Gratitude.*

1. PERPETUAL blessings from above
  Encompass me around;
But, Oh! how few returns of love
  Hath my Creator found!

2. What have I done for him, who died
  To save my wretched soul?
How are my follies multiplied,
  Fast as the minutes roll!

3. Lord! with this guilty heart of mine,
  To thy dear cross I flee;
And to thy grace my soul resign,
  To be renewed by thee.

4. Sprinkled afresh with pardoning blood,
  I lay me down to rest,—
As in th' embraces of my God,
  Or on my Saviour's breast.

335. *The Promise to Abraham.*

1. How large the promise—how divine,
  To Abra'm and his seed!
"I'll be a God to thee and thine,
  Supplying all their need."

2. The words of his extensive love
  From age to age endure;
The Angel of the covenant proves,
  And seals the blessings sure.

3. Jesus the ancient faith confirms,
  To our forefathers given;
He takes young children in his arms,
  And calls them heirs of heaven.

4. Our God,—how faithful are his ways!
  His love endures the same;
Nor, from the promise of his grace,
  Blots out the children's name.

336.   *Seeking a Rest.*

1. WE seek a rest beyond the skies,
  In everlasting day;
Through floods and flames the passage
    lies,
But Jesus guards the way.

2. The swelling flood, and raging flame,
  Hear and obey his word;
Then let us triumph in his name,—
  Our Saviour is the Lord.

HONOLULU. C. M. Double.*   H. From the "SHAWM."

1. I heard tho voice of Je-sus say, Come un-to me and rest;

Lay down, thou wea-ry one, lay down Thy head up-on my breast.

Choir.

I came to Je-sus as I was, Wea-ry, and worn, and sad,

Congregation. f

I found in him a rest-ing-place, And ho has made me glad.

* See also BRATTLE STREET 106.

337. *Come unto me.* Matt. xi. 28.

1. I HEARD the voice of Jesus say,
Come unto mo and rest;
Lay down, thou weary one, lay down
Thy head upon my breast.
I came to Jesus as I was,
Weary, and worn, and sad,
I found in him a resting-place,
And ho has made me glad.

2 I heard the voice of Jesus say,
Behold, I freely give
The living water; thirsty one,
Stoop down, and drink, and live.

I came to Jesus, and I drank
Of that life-giving stream;
My thirst was quenched, my soul re-
vived,
And now I live in him.

3. I heard tho voice of Jesus say,
I am this dark world's light;
Look unto me, thy morn shall rise,
And all thy day bo bright.
I looked to Jesus, and I found
In him my Star, my Sun;
And in that light of life I'll walk,
Till traveling days are done.

338. *Rejoice in the Lord.*

1. REJOICE, ye chosen of the Lord,
Your tuneful voices raise ;
Resound his deeds, his love record,
And celebrate his praise.
Rejoice in your Redeemer's name,
Lord of the realms on high :
The riches of his grace proclaim,
Who brings salvation nigh.

2. Rejoice, ye chosen of the Lord,
No more the slaves of sin ;
He, who is faithful to his word,
Will cleanse from every stain ;
Present you faultless at the last
Before his Father's throne,
And there, amid th' assembly vast,
Proclaim you as his own.

3. Rejoice, that he on earth shall reign,
That millions yet unborn
Shall celebrate, o'er hill and plain,
The bright, millennial morn.
E'en now behold the glimmering rays
Of that refulgent day ;
Be hopeful—give to God the praise ;
Be fervent—watch and pray.

339. *Influence of Prayer.*

1. SWEET is the prayer whose holy stream
In earnest pleading flows :
Devotion dwells upon the theme,
And warm and warmer glows.
2. Faith grasps the blessing she desires,
Hope points the upward gaze ;
And love, untrembling love, inspires
The eloquence of praise.

3. But sweeter far the still small voice,
Heard by no human ear,
When God hath made the heart rejoice,
And dried the bitter tear.
4. Nor accents flow, nor words ascend ;
All utterance faileth there ;
But listening spirits comprehend,
And God accepts the prayer.

340. *Funeral.*

1. BENEATH our feet, and o'er our head,
Is equal warning given ;
Beneath us lie the countless dead,—
Above us is the heaven.
2. Death rides on every passing breeze,
And lurks in every flower ;
Each season has its own disease,
Its peril—every hour.

3. Our eyes have seen the rosy light,
Of youth's soft cheek, decay ;
And fate descend, in sudden night,
On manhood's middle day.
4. Our eyes have seen the steps of age
Halt feebly to the tomb ;
And yet shall earth our hearts engage,
And dreams of days to come ?

5. Turn, mortal ! turn, thy danger know ;
Where'er thy foot can tread,
The earth rings hollow from below,
And warns thee of her dead.
6. Turn, Christian ! turn ; thy soul apply
To truths divinely given ;
The forms, which underneath thee lie,
Shall live, for hell, or heaven.

341. *The Church.*

1. CHURCH of the everlasting God,
The Father's gracious choice,
Amid the voices of this earth
How feeble is thy voice !
2. Thy words amid the words of earth,
How noiseless and how low !
Amid the hurrying crowds of time,
Thy steps how calm and slow !

3. But 'mid the wrinkled brows of earth,
Thy brow how free from care ;
'Mid the flushed cheeks of riot here,
Thy cheek how pale and fair !
4. Amid the restless eyes of earth,
How steadfast is thine eye,
Fixed on the silent loveliness
Of the far eastern sky.

342. *Endless Praise.*

1. YES—I will bless thee, O my God !
Through all my mortal days,
And to eternity prolong
Thy vast, thy boundless praise.
2. Nor shall my tongue alone proclaim
The honors of my God ;
My life, with all its active powers,
Shall spread thy praise abroad.

3. Not death itself shall stop my song,
Though death will close my eyes ;
My thoughts shall then to nobler heights,
And sweeter raptures rise.
4. There shall my lips, in endless praise,
Their grateful tribute pay ;
The theme demands an angel's tongue,
And an eternal day.

"COME, LET US RAISE." C. L. M.   HASTINGS.

1. Come, let us raise A song of praise To Him who rules on high; Whose love and power, From hour to hour, Can ev - ery want sup - ply: The good - ness of our God and King Let all with hal - le - lu - jahs sing, with hal - le - lu - jahs sing.

343.   *Joyful Praise.*

1. COME, let us raise
   A song of praise
To Him who rules on high;
   Whose love and power,
   From hour to hour,
Can every want supply:
The goodness of our God and King
Let all with hallelujahs sing.

2. His bounties flow
   Where'er we go,
Abound where'er we stay;

From every snare
His gracious care
Defends by night and day:
The goodness of our God and King
Let all with hallelujahs sing.

3. We're traveling on,
   Yet not alone,
Through life's dark wilderness:
   Close by our side
   A heavenly Guide
Is pledged for our success.
The goodness of our God and King
Let all with hallelujahs sing.

4. Though sorrows, tears,
Though foes and fears,
And dangers crowd our road;
Nought can withstand
The powerful hand
That leads us home to God.
The goodness of our God and King
Let all with hallelujahs sing.

5. Our labors done,
The victory won,
We'll rise to realms above;
To that reward
By grace prepared—
The home of boundless love.
The goodness of our God and King
Till then we joyfully will sing.

HARBOROUGH. C. M.*

MAESTOSO.

SHRUBSOLE.

1. All hail the power of Je - sus' name! Let an - gels prostrate fall; Bring forth the roy - al di - a - dem, And crown him, crown him, crown him, crown him Lord of all.

* See also CORONATION, 263.

344. *Coronation of Christ.*

1. ALL hail the power of Jesus' name!
Let angels prostrate fall;
Bring forth the royal diadem,
And crown him—Lord of all.

2. Crown him, ye morning stars of light,
Who formed this floating ball;
Now hail the strength of Israel's might,
And crown him—Lord of all.

3. Ye chosen seed of Israel's race,
Ye ransomed from the fall,

Hail him who saves you by his grace,
And crown him—Lord of all.

4. Sinners, whose love can ne'er forget
The wormwood and the gall,
Come, spread your trophies at his feet,
And crown him—Lord of all.

5. Let every kindred, every tribe,
On this terrestrial ball,
To him all majesty ascribe,
And crown him—Lord of all.

MOORFIELD. S. M.   WOOD. Arranged.

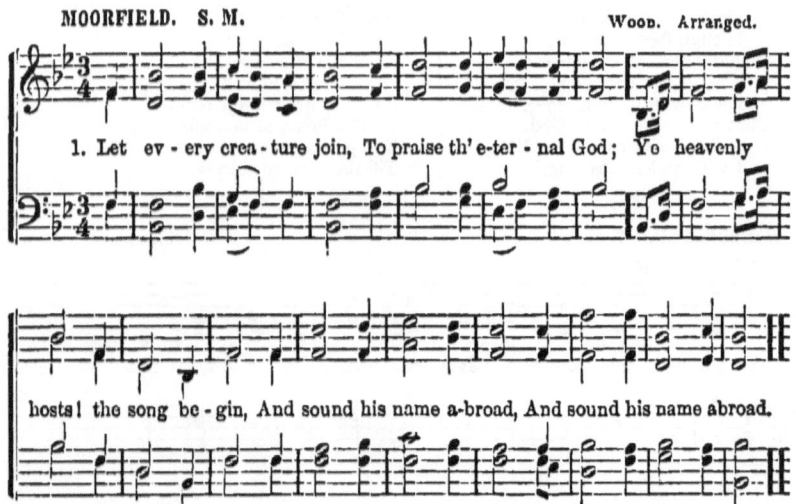

1. Let ev - ery crea - ture join, To praise th' e-ter - nal God; Ye heavenly

hosts! the song be - gin, And sound his name a-broad, And sound his name abroad.

345.   *Exhortation to Praise.*

1. LET every creature join,
     To praise th' eternal God ;
Ye heavenly hosts ! the song begin,
     And sound his name abroad.

2. Thou sun, with golden beams !
     And moon, with paler rays !
Ye starry lights ! ye twinkling flames !
     Shine to your Maker's praise.

3. He built those worlds above,
     And fixed their wondrous frame ;
By his command they stand or move,
     And ever speak his name.

4. Ye vapors ! when ye rise,
     Or fall in showers or snow,—
Ye thunders ! murmuring round the skies,
     His power and glory show.

5. Wind, hail, and flaming fire !
     Agree to praise the Lord,
When ye in dreadful storms conspire
     To execute his word.

6. By all his works above,
     His honors be expressed ;
But saints, who taste his saving love,
     Should sing his praises best.

346.   *The Saviour's Mission.*

1. RAISE your triumphant songs,
     To an immortal tune ;
Let the wide earth resound the deeds
     Celestial grace has done.

2. Sing how eternal Love
     Its chief Belovéd chose,
And bade him raise our wretched race
     From their abyss of woes.

3. His hand no thunder bears ;
     No terrors clothe his brow ;
No bolts to drive our guilty souls
     To fiercer flames below.

4. 'T was mercy filled the throne,
     And wrath stood silent by,
When Christ was sent with pardon down
     To rebels doomed to die.

5. Now sinners, dry your tears ;
     Let hopeless sorrow cease ;
Bow to the sceptre of his love,
     And take the offered peace.

347.   *Christian Joy.*

1. REJOICE in God alway ;
     When earth looks heavenly bright ;
When joy makes glad the livelong day,
     And peace shuts in the night.

2. Rejoice, when care and woe
　　The fainting soul oppress;
When tears at wakeful midnight flow,
　　And morn brings heaviness.

3. Rejoice in hope and fear,
　　Rejoice in life and death;
Rejoice, when threatening storms are near,
　　And comfort languisheth.

4. When should not they rejoice,
　　Whom Christ his brethren calls;
Who hear and know his guiding voice,
　　When on their hearts it falls?

5. So, though our path is steep,
　　And many a tempest lowers,
Shall his own peace our spirit keep,
　　And Christ's dear love be ours.

348.　　*Exhortation to Praise.*

1. STAND up, and bless the Lord,
　　Ye people of his choice !
Stand up, and bless the Lord your God,
　　With heart, and soul, and voice.

2. Though high above all praise,
　　Above all blessing high,
Who would not fear his holy name,
　　And laud, and magnify?

3. Oh! for the living flame
　　From his own altar brought,
To touch our lips, our souls inspire,
　　And wing to heaven our thought!

4. God is our strength and song,
　　And his salvation ours;
Then be his love in Christ proclaimed,
　　With all our ransomed powers.

5. Stand up, and bless the Lord,—
　　The Lord, your God, adore;
Stand up, and bless his glorious name,
　　Henceforth, for evermore.

349.　　*The Nativity of Christ.*

1. BEHOLD the grace appear—
　　The blessing promised long !
Angels announce the Saviour near,
　　In their triumphant song :—

2. "Glory to God on high,
　　　　And heavenly peace on earth;
Good-will to men—to angels joy,
　　At the Redeemer's birth."

3. In worship so divine
　　Let saints employ their tongues;
With the celestial host we join,
　　And loud repeat their songs:—

4. "Glory to God on high,
　　And heavenly peace on earth;
Good-will to men—to angels joy,
　　At our Redeemer's birth."

350.　　*Safety of the Church.*

1. GREAT is the Lord our God,
　　And let his praise be great;
He makes his churches his abode,
　　His most delightful seat.

2. In Zion God is known,—
　　A refuge in distress;
How bright has his salvation shone,
　　Through all her palaces !　　·

3. When kings against her joined,
　　And saw the Lord was there,
In wild confusion of the mind
　　They fled with hasty fear.

4. Oft have our fathers told,
　　Our eyes have often seen,
How well our God secures the fold
　　Where his own sheep have been.

5. In every new distress
　　We 'll to his house repair;
We 'll think upon his wondrous grace,
　　And seek deliverance there.

351.　　*Redemption completed.*

1. "THE Lord is risen indeed;"
　　He lives to die no more;
He lives the sinner's cause to plead,
　　Whose curse and shame he bore.

2. "The Lord is risen indeed;"
　　Then hell has lost his prey;
With him is risen the ransomed seed,
　　To reign in endless day.

3. "The Lord is risen indeed;"
　　Attending angels, hear;
Up to the courts of heaven, with speed,
　　The joyful tidings bear.

4. Then wake your golden lyres,
　　And strike each cheerful chord;
Join, all ye bright, celestial choirs,
　　To sing our risen Lord.

ABODE.　S. M.*　　　　　　　　　　　　　　　　　CARAMENI.

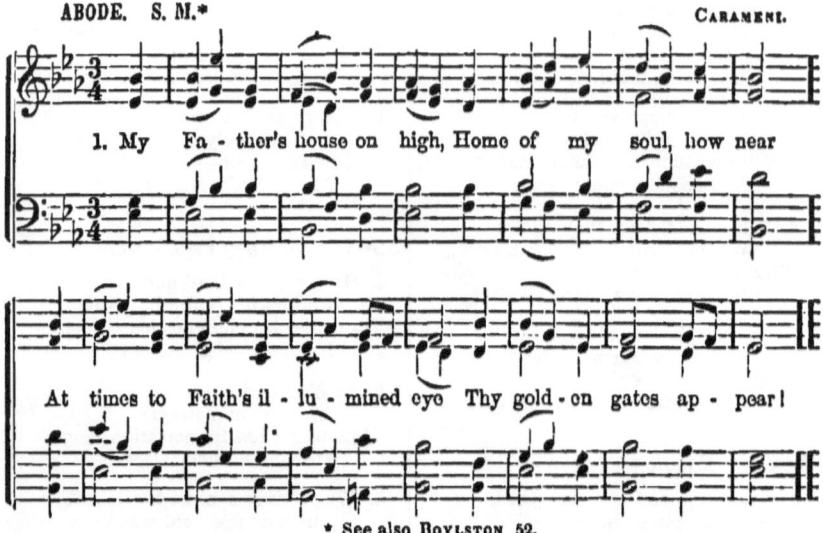

1. My Fa - ther's house on high, Home of my soul, how near

At times to Faith's il - lu - mined eye Thy gold - en gates ap - pear!

* See also BOYLSTON 52.

352. *Heavenly Aspirations.* 1 Thess. iv. 17.

1. MY Father's house on high,
　　Home of my soul, how near
At times to Faith's illumined eye
　　Thy golden gates appear!

2. My thirsty spirit faints
　　To reach the land I love,
The bright inheritance of saints,—
　　Jerusalem above.

3. Yet clouds will intervene,
　　And all my prospect flies;
Like Noah's dove, I flit between
　　Rough seas and stormy skies.

4. Anon the clouds depart,
　　The winds and waters cease,
While sweetly o'er my gladdened heart
　　Expands the bow of peace.

353.　　　*With the Lord.*

1. "FOR ever with the Lord!"
　　So, Jesus! let it be;
Life from the dead is in that word;
　　'Tis immortality.

2. Here, in the body pent,
　　Absent from thee, I roam;
Yet nightly pitch my moving tent
　　A day's march nearer home.

3. "For ever with the Lord!"
　　Saviour, if 'tis thy will,
The promise of that faithful word
　　E'en here to me fulfill.

4. So when my latest breath
　　Shall rend the vail in twain,
By death I shall escape from death,
　　And life eternal gain.

5. Knowing as I am known,
　　How shall I love that word,
And oft repeat before the throne—
　　"For ever with the Lord!"

354. *God, my Creator and Benefactor.*

1. MY Maker and my King!
　　To thee my all I owe;
Thy sovereign bounty is the spring
　　Whence all my blessings flow.

2. The creature of thy hand,—
　　On thee alone I live;
My God! thy benefits demand
　　More praise than life can give

3. Shall I withhold thy due?
　　And shall my passions rove?
Lord! form this wretched heart anew,
　　And fill it with thy love.

4. Oh! let thy grace inspire
　　My soul with strength divine;
Let all my powers to thee aspire,
　　And all my days be thine.

1. To God in whom I trust, I lift my heart and voice;

O, let me not be put to shame, Nor let my foes re - joice.

355.   *Pleading for Mercy.*

1. To God in whom I trust,
  I lift my heart and voice;
O, let me not be put to shame,
  Nor let my foes rejoice.

2. Thy mercies and thy love,
  O Lord, recall to mind;
And graciously continue still,
  As thou wast ever, kind.

3. Let all my youthful crimes
  Be blotted out by thee;
And O, for thy great goodness' sake,
  In mercy think on me.

4. His mercy and his truth
  The righteous Lord displays;
In bringing wandering sinners home,
  And teaching them his ways.

356.   *Daily Devotion.*

1. LET sinners take their course,
  And choose the road to death:
But, in the worship of my God,
  I 'll spend my daily breath.

2. My thoughts address his throne,
  When morning brings the light;
I seek his blessing every noon,
  And pay my vows at night.

3. Thou wilt regard my cries
  O my eternal God!

While sinners perish in surprise,
  Beneath thine angry rod.

4. Because they dwell at ease,
  And no sad changes feel,
They neither fear, nor trust thy name,
  Nor learn to do thy will.

5. But I, with all my cares,
  Will lean upon the Lord;
I 'll cast my burden on his arm,
  And rest upon his word.

6. His arm shall well sustain
  The children of his love:
The ground, on which their safety stands
  No earthly power can move.

357.   *The Spirit in Baptism.*

1. GREAT God! now condescend
  To bless our rising race;
Soon may their willing spirits bend,
  The subjects of thy grace.

2. O! what a pure delight
  Their happiness to see!
Our warmest wishes all unite
  To lead their souls to thee.

3. Now bless, thou God of love!
  This ordinance divine;
Send thy good Spirit from above,
  And make these children thine.

EMMAUS. C. M.*

FROM THE "PSALMODIST."

SLOW, LEGATO

1. Spi - rit Di - vine! at - tend our prayer, And make this house thy home;

De - scend, with all thy gra - cious power, Oh! come, Great Spi - rit, come!

* See also DUNDEE 168.

358. *Invocation of the Spirit.*

1. SPIRIT Divine! attend our prayer,
And make this house thy home;
Descend, with all thy gracious power,
Oh! come, Great Spirit, come!

2. Come as the light; to us reveal
Our emptiness and woe:
And lead us in those paths of life
Where all the righteous go.

3. Come as the fire, and purge our hearts
Like sacrificial flame;
Let our whole souls an offering be
To our Redeemer's name.

4. Come as the dew, and sweetly bless
This consecrated hour;
May barren minds be taught to own
Thy fertilizing power.

5. Come as a dove, and spread thy wings,
The wings of peaceful love;
And let the Church on earth become
Blest as the Church above.

359. *Young Persons entreated.*

1. BESTOW, dear Lord, upon our youth,
The gift of saving grace;
And let the seed of sacred truth
Fall in a fruitful place.

2. Grace is a plant, where'er it grows,
Of pure and heavenly root;
But fairest in the youngest shows,
And yields the sweetest fruit.

3. Ye careless ones, O hear betimes
The voice of sovereign love!
Your youth is stained with many crimes,
But mercy reigns above.

4. For you the public prayer is made—
Oh, join the public prayer!
For you the secret tear is shed—
O shed, yourselves, a tear.

5. We pray that you may early prove
The Spirit's power to teach;
You can not be too young to love
That Jesus whom we preach.

360. *Preservation by Day and Night.*

1. To heaven I lift my waking eyes,
There all my hopes are laid;
The Lord, that built the earth and skies,
Is my perpetual aid.

2. Their steadfast feet shall never fall,
Whom he designs to keep;
His ear attends their humble call,
His eyes can never sleep.

3. Israel, rejoice, and rest secure,
Thy keeper is the Lord;
His watchful eye, his boundless power,
Are thine eternal guard.

4. Nor scorching sun, nor sickly moon,
Shall have his leave to smite;
He shields thy head from burning noon,
From blasting damps at night.

5. He guards thy soul, he keeps thy breath,
Where thickest dangers come;
Go, and return secure from death,
Till God commands thee home.

361. *Salvation by Grace.*

1. Lord! we confess our numerous faults;
How great our guilt has been!
Foolish and vain were all our thoughts,
And all our lives were sin.

2. But, O my soul! for ever praise,
For ever love his name,
Who turns thy feet from dangerous ways
Of folly, sin, and shame.

3. 'Tis not by works of righteousness
Which our own hands have done,
But we are saved by sovereign grace,
Abounding through his Son.

4. 'Tis from the mercy of our God,
That all our hopes begin; •
'Tis by the water, and the blood,
Our souls are washed from sin.

5. 'Tis through the purchase of his death
Who hung upon the tree,
The Spirit is sent down, to breathe
On such dry bones as we.

6. Raised from the dead, we live anew;
And, justified by grace,
We shall appear in glory, too,
And see our Father's face.

362. *Shortness of Time.*

1. Behold, my soul, the narrow bound
Of the revolving year: [round,
How swift the weeks complete their
How short the months appear.

2. So fast eternity comes on,
And that important day,
When all that mortal life has done
God's judgment shall survey.

3. Yet, like an idle tale, we spend
The swift-advancing year;
And study artful ways to mend
The speed of its career.

4. Waken, O God! my trifling heart,
Its great concern to see;
That I may act the Christian part,
And give the year to thee.

5. So shall their course more grateful roll,
If future years arise;
Or this shall bear my happy soul
To joy that never dies.

363. *For a Public Fast.*

1. See, gracious God, before thy throne,
Thy mourning people bend !
'Tis on thy sovereign grace alone
Our humble hopes depend.

2. Tremendous judgments from thy hand
Thy dreadful power display;
Yet mercy spares this guilty land,
And yet we live to pray.

3. Great God, why is this nation spared,
Ungrateful as we are !
Oh, be thy voice of warning heard,
While mercy cries, forbear.

4. What sins, what crimes, increasing rise
This nation to defile !
What land so favored of the skies;
And yet what land so vile !

5. Oh! bid us turn, Almighty Lord,
By thy resistless grace:
Then shall our hearts obey thy word,
And humbly seek thy face.

364. *Sabbath.*

1. Frequent the day of God returns,
To shed its quickening beams;
And yet how slow devotion burns!
How languid are its flames!

2. Accept our faint attempts to love,
Our frailties, Lord, forgive;
We would be like thy saints above,
And praise thee while we live.

3. Increase, O Lord, our faith and hope,
And fit us to ascend
Where the assembly ne'er breaks up,
The Sabbath ne'er shall end.

4. Where we shall breathe in heavenly air,
With heavenly lustre shine;
Before the throne of God appear,
And feast on love divine;

5. Where we in high, seraphic strains
Shall all our powers employ;
Delighted range th' ethereal plains,
And take our fill of joy.

ABERDEEN. 8s & 7s. Double.

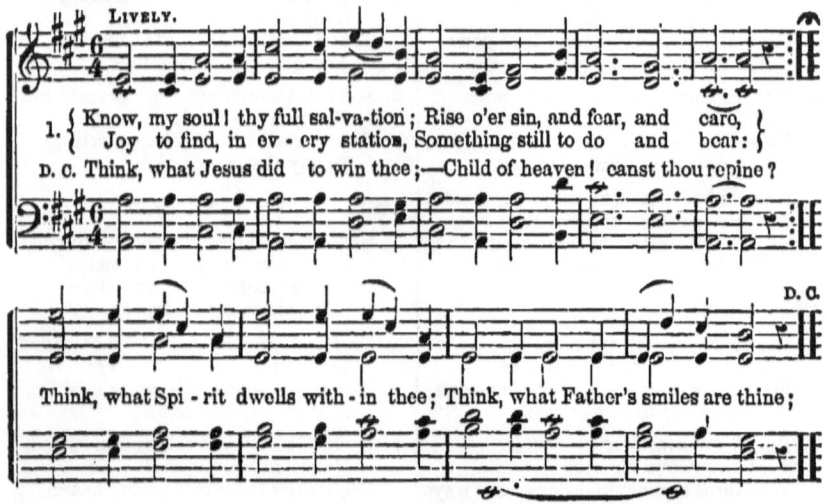

1. { Know, my soul! thy full sal-va-tion; Rise o'er sin, and fear, and care,
     Joy to find, in ev-ery station, Something still to do and bear: }

D. C. Think, what Jesus did to win thee;—Child of heaven! canst thou repine?

Think, what Spi-rit dwells with-in thee; Think, what Father's smiles are thine;

---

365. *Joyful Hope.*

1. KNOW, my soul! thy full salvation;
    Rise o'er sin, and fear, and care,
Joy to find, in every station,
    Something still to do and bear:
Think, what Spirit dwells within thee;
    Think, what Father's smiles are thine;
Think, what Jesus did to win thee;—
    Child of heaven! canst thou repine?

2. Haste thee on from grace to glory,
    Armed with faith, and winged with
        prayer;
Heaven's eternal day 's before thee,
    God's own hand shall guide thee there:
Soon shall close thine earthly mission,
    Soon shall pass thy pilgrim days;
Hope shall change to glad fruition,—
    Faith to sight, and prayer to praise.

366. *Desiring Sanctification.*

1. LOVE divine, all love excelling,
    Joy of heaven, to earth come down;
Fix in us thy humble dwelling;
    All thy faithful mercies crown:
Jesus, thou art all compassion;
    Pure, unbounded love thou art;
Visit us with thy salvation;
    Enter every trembling heart.

2. Breathe, O breathe thy loving Spirit
    Into every troubled breast;

Let us all thy grace inherit;
    Let us find thy promised rest:
Take away the love of sinning;
    Take our load of guilt away;
End the work of thy beginning;
    Bring us to eternal day.

3. Carry on thy new creation;
    Pure and holy may we be;
Let us see our whole salvation
    Perfectly secured by thee;
Changed from glory unto glory,
    Till in heaven we take our place,
Till we cast our crowns before thee,
    Lost in wonder, love, and praise.

367. *The Divine Protection.*

1. CALL Jehovah thy salvation,
    Rest beneath th' Almighty's shade,
In his secret habitation,
    Dwell, and never be dismayed:
There no tumult can alarm thee,
    Thou shalt dread no hidden snare;
Guile nor violence can harm thee,
    In eternal safeguard there.

2. From the sword, at noonday wasting,
    From the noisome pestilence,
In the depth of midnight, blasting,
    God shall be thy sure defense:
Fear not thou the deadly quiver,
    When a thousand feel the blow;
Mercy shall thy soul deliver,
    Though ten thousand be laid low.

3. Since, with pure and firm affection,
   Thou on God hast set thy love,
With the wings of his protection,
   He will shield thee from above;
Thou shalt call on him in trouble,—
   He will hearken, he will save;
Here, for grief, reward thee double,
   Crown with life beyond the grave.

868. *The Light of the World.*

1. LIGHT of those whose dreary dwelling
   Borders on the shades of death !
Come, and, by thy love revealing,
   Dissipate the clouds beneath :
The new heaven and earth's Creator,
   In our deepest darkness rise,—
Scattering all the night of nature,
   Pouring eye-sight on our eyes.

2. Still we wait for thine appearing;
   Life and joy thy beams impart,
Chasing all our fears, and cheering
   Every poor, benighted heart :
Come, and manifest thy favor
   To the ransomed, helpless race;
Come, thou glorious God and Saviour !
   Come, and bring the gospel grace.

3. Save us, in thy great compassion,
   O thou mild, pacific Prince !
Give the knowledge of salvation,
   Give the pardon of our sins;
By thine all-sufficient merit,
   Every burdened soul release;
Every weary, wandering spirit,
   Guide into thy perfect peace.

369. *Glory of the Church.*

1. GLORIOUS things of thee are spoken,
   Zion, city of our God !
He, whose word can not be broken,
   Formed thee for his own abode:
On the Rock of ages founded,
   What can shake thy sure repose ?
With salvation's walls surrounded,
   Thou mayst smile at all thy foes.

2. See the streams of living waters,
   Springing from eternal love,
To supply thy sons and daughters,
   And all fear of want remove !
Who can faint, while such a river
   Ever flows his thirst t' assuage;
Grace, which, like the Lord, the giver,
   Never fails from age to age.

3. Round each habitation, hovering,
   See the cloud and fire appear,
For a glory and a covering,
   Showing that the Lord is near !
Glorious things of thee are spoken,
   Zion, city of our God !
He, whose word can not be broken,
   Formed thee for his own abode.

370. *Songs in the Night.*

1. SONGS of joy Jehovah giveth,
   In the night of sorrows drear,
To the pilgrim who believeth,
   Meekly bowed in filial fear ;
While the heart is inly mourning,
   Still the heaven-directed eye,
Straight beholds sweet bliss returning,
   From the treasures of the sky.

2. Songs of joy Jehovah giveth,
   In the night of toil and pain,
When the eye of faith perceiveth
   All that toil is heavenly gain :
Then the burden groweth lighter,
   And the anguish will remove ;
While the thoughts of heaven are
   brighter,
And the heart is filled with love.

3. Songs of joy Jehovah giveth,
   When *temptation's* night appears;
He that in the conflict liveth
   Still the precious promise hears—
"Though the tempter oft may grieve
   thee
In a dark and trying hour,
Grace Divine shall never leave thee,
   Heaven shall all thy peace restore !"

4. Songs of joy Jehovah giveth,
   When the night of death has come ,
When the hand that ne'er reprieveth,
   Leads the pilgrim to the tomb:
Angels then are hovering o'er him,
   And the soul within hath peace ;
Heaven is opening wide before him,
   And its joys will never cease.

371. *Benediction.*

MAY the grace of Christ, our Saviour,
   And the Father's boundless love,
With the Holy Spirit's favor,
   Rest upon us from above.
Thus may we abide in union
   With each other and the Lord,
And possess, in sweet communion,
   Joys which earth can not afford.

MISSIONARY HYMN.   7s & 6s, Peculiar.   L. MASON.

1. From Greenland's i - cy mountains, From India's coral strand, Where Afric's sunny fountains Roll down their golden sand: From many an an - cient riv - er, From many a palm-y plain, They call us to de - liv - er Their land from error's chain.

372.   *Claims of the Heathen.*

1. From Greenland's icy mountains,
    From India's coral strand,
  Where Afric's sunny fountains
    Roll down their golden sand,—
  From many an ancient river,
    From many a palmy plain,—
  They call us to deliver
    Their land from error's chain.

2. What though the spicy breezes
    Blow soft o'er Ceylon's isle,
  Though every prospect pleases,
    And only man is vile;
  In vain, with lavish kindness,
    The gifts of God are strown:
  The heathen, in his blindness,
    Bows down to wood and stone.

3. Shall we, whose souls are lighted
    By wisdom from on high,
  Shall we to man benighted
    The lamp of life deny?
  Salvation! O, salvation!
    The joyful sound proclaim,
  Till earth's remotest nation
    Has learned Messiah's name.

4. Waft, waft, ye winds, his story,
    And you, ye waters, roll,
  Till, like a sea of glory,
    It spreads from pole to pole;
  Till o'er our ransomed nature
    The Lamb, for sinners slain,
  Redeemer, King, Creator,
    In bliss returns to reign.

373. *Times of Revival.*

1. THE morning light is breaking,
The darkness disappears,
The sons of earth are waking
To penitential tears:
Each breeze that sweeps the ocean
Brings tidings from afar,
Of nations in commotion,
Prepared for Zion's war.

2. Rich dews of grace come o'er us,
In many a gentle shower,
And brighter scenes before us
Are opening every hour:
Each cry to Heaven going,
Abundant answers brings,
And heavenly gales are blowing,
With peace upon their wings.

3. See heathen nations bending
Before the God we love,
And thousand hearts ascending
In gratitude above;
While sinners, now confessing,
The gospel call obey,
And seek the Saviour's blessing,
A nation in a day.

4. Blest river of salvation,
Pursue thy onward way,
Flow thou to every nation,
Nor in thy richness stay;
Stay not till all the lowly,
Triumphant reach their home,
Stay not till all the holy
Proclaim, the Lord is come.

374. *Human Frailty.*

1. O, WHAT is earthly pleasure
Compared with thy rich grace?
Lord, teach us how to measure
The remnant of our days.
How brief is our existence!
How frail a thing is man!
O, grant us thine assistance
Eternal things to scan.

2. How soon the hours of gladness,
That cheer us on our way,
Are changed to gloom and sadness,
Or filled with deep dismay!
Man, in his best condition,
Is vanity and dust;
Soon past the fleeting vision;
He then gives up the ghost!

3. Earth's treasures quickly leave us,
Its honors ne'er endure;
Its pleasures but deceive us,
Its hopes are insecure:
But, Lord, while time is flying,
And filled with many a snare,
My soul, on thee relying,
Would seek thy guardian care.

375. *Desire for Heaven.*

1. FROM every earthly pleasure,
From every transient joy,
From every mortal treasure,
That soon will fade and die;—
No longer these desiring,
Upward our wishes tend,
To nobler bliss aspiring,
And joys that never end.

2. From every piercing sorrow
That heaves our breast to-day,
Or threatens us to-morrow,
Hope turns our eyes away;
On wings of faith ascending,
We see the land of light,
And feel our sorrows ending,
In infinite delight.

3. 'Tis true we are but strangers,
And pilgrims here below,
And countless snares and dangers
Surround the path we go:
Though painful and distressing,
Yet there's a rest above;
And onward still we're pressing,
To reach that land of love.

376. *The Salvation of Israel.*

1. OH, that the Lord's Salvation
Were out of Zion come,
To heal his ancient nation,
To lead his outcasts home.
How long the holy city
Shall heathen feet profane?
Return, O Lord, in pity:
Rebuild her walls again.

2. Let fall thy rod of terror.
Thy saving grace impart;
Roll back the vail of error;
Release the fettered heart.
Let Israel, home returning,
Their lost Messiah see;
Give oil of joy for mourning,
And bind thy church to thee.

ROCK OF AGES. 7s. 6 lines.*   HASTINGS.

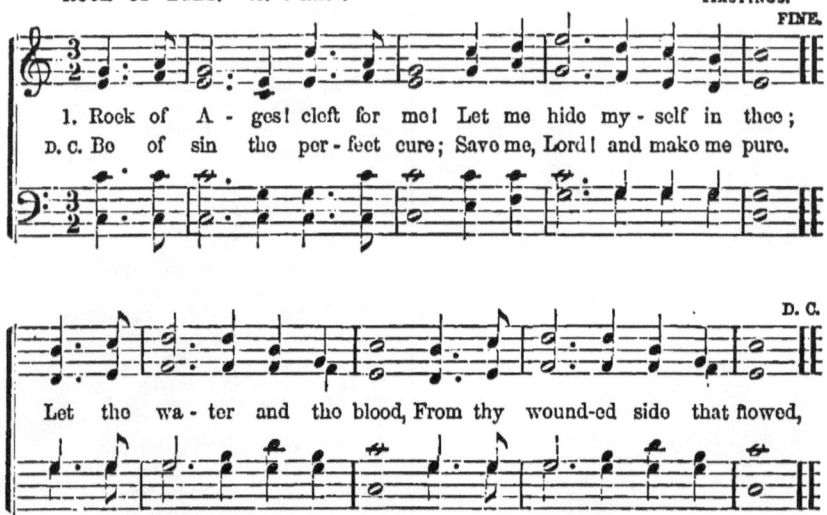

1. Rock of A - ges! cleft for me! Let me hide my - self in thee;
D. C. Be of sin the per - fect cure; Save me, Lord! and make me pure.

Let the wa - ter and the blood, From thy wound-ed side that flowed,

* See also SIDMOUTH and ZADOC 164, 125.

377.   *The Rock of Ages.*

1. ROCK of Ages, cleft for me!
Let me hide myself in thee;
Let the water and the blood,
From thy wounded side that flowed,
Be of sin the perfect cure ;
Save me, Lord ! and make me pure.

2. Should my tears for ever flow,
Should my zeal no languor know,
This for sin could not atone,
Thou must save, and thou alone:
In my hand no price I bring;
Simply to thy cross I cling.

3. While I draw this fleeting breath,
When mine eyelids close in death,
When I rise to worlds unknown,
And behold thee on thy throne,
Rock of Ages, cleft for me!
Let me hide myself in thee.

378.   *The Lord's Supper.*

1. BREAD of heaven! on thee I feed,
For thy flesh is meat indeed,
Ever may my soul be fed,
With this true and living bread :
Day by day with strength supplied,
Through the life of him who died.

2. Vine of heaven! thy blood supplies
This blest cup of sacrifice,
'Tis thy wounds, my healing give,
To thy cross I look, and live.
Thou my life! O let me be
Rooted, grounded, built on thee.

379.   *At the Communion.*

1. SAVIOUR of our ruined race,
Fountain of redeeming grace,
Let us now thy fullness see,
While we here converse with thee ;
Hearken to our ardent prayer—
Let us all thy blessing share.

2. While we thus, with glad accord
Meet around thy table, Lord,
Bid us feast with joy divine,
On th' appointed bread and wine :
Emblems may they truly prove
Of the Saviour's bleeding love.

3. Weak, unworthy, sinful, vile,
Yet we seek thy heavenly smile:
Canst thou all our sins forgive ?
Dost thou bid us look and live ?
Lord, we wonder and adore !
O, for grace to love thee more !

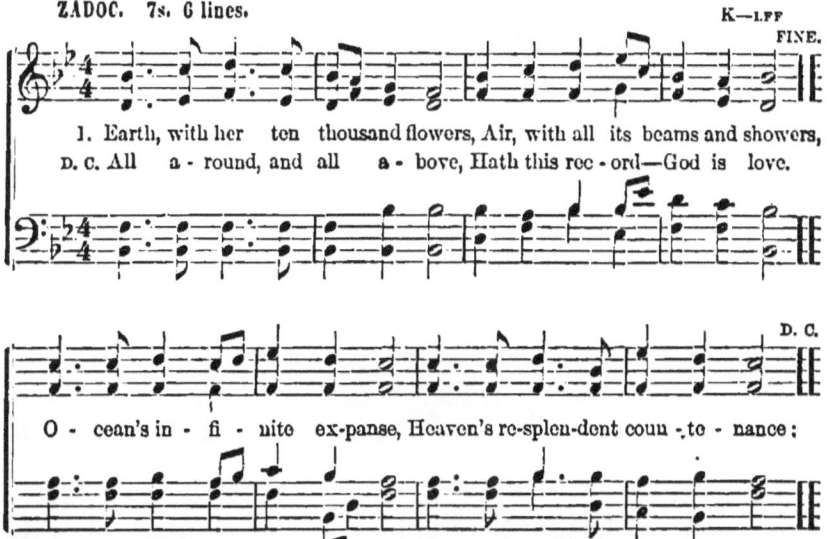

1. Earth, with her ten thousand flowers, Air, with all its beams and showers,
D. C. All a - round, and all a - bove, Hath this rec - ord—God is love.

O - cean's in - fi - nite ex-panse, Heaven's re-splen-dent coun - te - nance:

380.   *God is Love.*

1. EARTH, with her ten thousand flowers,
Air, with all its beams and showers,
Ocean's infinite expanse,
Heaven's resplendent countenance ;
All around, and all above,
Hath this record—God is love.

2. Sounds among the vales and hills,
In the woods, and by the rills,
Of the breeze and of the bird,
By the gentle murmur stirred ;
All these songs, beneath, above,
Have one burden—God is love.

3. All the hopes and fears that start
From the fountain of the heart ;
All the quiet bliss that lies
In our human sympathies ;
These are voices from above,
Sweetly whispering—God is love.

381.   *Sinners urged to accept the Invitation.*

1. YE, who in his courts are found,
Listening to the joyful sound,
Lost and helpless as ye are,
Sons of sorrow, sin, and care—

Glorify the King of kings,
Take the peace the gospel brings.

2. Turn to Christ your longing eyes,
View this bleeding sacrifice ;
See, in him, your sins forgiven,
Pardon, holiness, and heaven ;
Glorify the King of kings,
Take the peace the gospel brings.

382.   *Sun of Righteousness.*

1. CHRIST, whose glory fills the skies,—
Christ, the true, the only light,
Sun of Righteousness ! arise,
Triumph o'er the shades of night :
Day-spring from on high ! be near ;
Day-star ! in my heart appear.

2. Dark and cheerless is the morn,
If thy light is hid from me ;
Joyless is the day's return,
Till thy mercy's beam I see—
Till they inward light impart—
Peace and gladness to my heart.

3. Visit, then, this soul of mine,
Pierce the gloom of sin and **grief**;
Fill me, Radiancy divine !
Scatter all my unbelief ;
More and more thyself display,
Shining to the perfect day.

CULLODEN. H. M.*   ENGLISH MELODY.

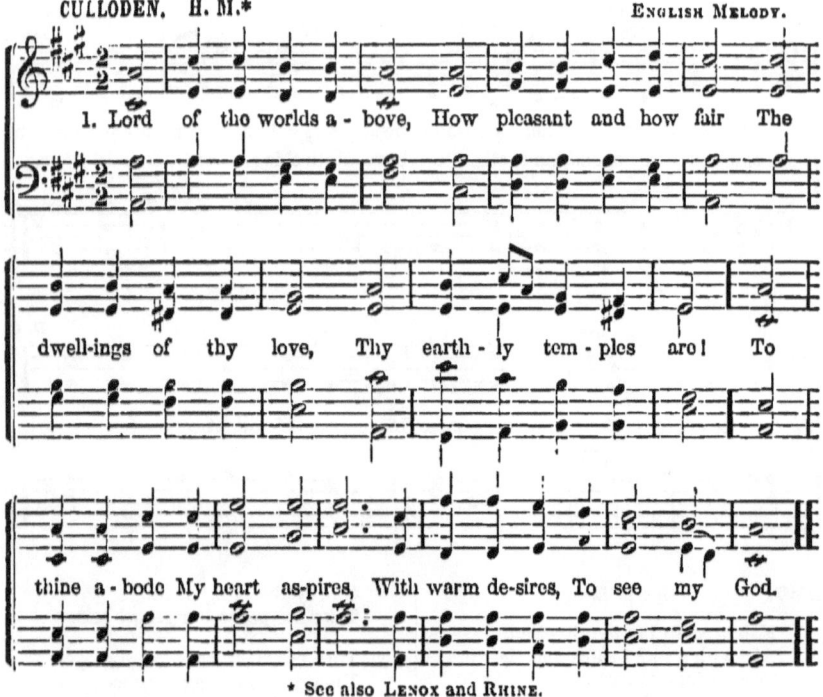

1. Lord of the worlds a - bove, How pleasant and how fair The dwell-ings of thy love, Thy earth - ly tem - ples are! To thine a - bode My heart as-pires, With warm de-sires, To see my God.

* See also LENOX and RHINE.

383. *Longing for the House of God.*

1. LORD of the worlds above,
    How pleasant, and how fair,
   The dwellings of thy love,
    Thy earthly temples are!
      To thine abode
      My heart aspires,
      With warm desires,
    To see my God.

2. [The sparrow for her young
    With pleasure seeks a nest;
   And wandering swallows long
    To find their wonted rest!
      My spirit faints,
      With equal zeal,
      To rise and dwell
    Among thy saints.]

3. O happy souls, who pray
    Where God appoints to hear!
   O happy men, who pay
    Their constant service there!
      They praise thee still;
      And happy they,
      Who love the way
    To Zion's hill.

4. They go from strength to strength,
    Through this dark vale of tears;
   Till each arrives at length,
    Till each in heaven appears.
      O glorious seat,
      When God our King
      Shall thither bring
    Our willing feet!

384. *Prophet, Priest, and King.*

1. JOIN all the glorious names
    Of wisdom, love, and power,
   That ever mortals knew,
    That angels ever bore :—
   All are too mean to speak his worth,
   Too mean to set my Saviour forth.

2. Great Prophet of our God!
    Our tongues would bless thy name;
   By thee the joyful news
    Of our salvation came ;—
   The joyful news of sins forgiven,
   Of hell subdued, and peace with heaven.

3. Jesus, our great High-Priest,
    Hath shed his blood and died;

My guilty conscience needs
No sacrifice beside:
His precious blood did once atone,
And now it pleads before the throne.

4. O thou almighty Lord,
  Our Conqueror and our King!
Thy sceptre and thy sword,
  Thy reigning grace, we sing;
Thine is the power; Oh! make us sit,
In willing bonds, beneath thy feet.

385.   *Divine Blessing implored.*

1. WELCOME, delightful morn,
  Thou day of sacred rest;
I hail thy kind return;
  Lord, make these moments blessed.
From the low train of mortal toys,
I soar to reach immortal joys.

2. Now may the King descend,
  And fill his throne of grace;
Thy sceptre, Lord, extend,
  While saints address thy face:
Let sinners feel thy quickening word,
And learn to know and fear the Lord.

3. Descend, celestial Dove,
  With all thy quickening powers;
Disclose a Saviour's love,
  And bless these sacred hours:
Then shall my soul new life obtain,
Nor Sabbaths be bestowed in vain.

386.   *God our Preserver.*

1. UPWARD I lift mine eyes,
  From God is all mine aid—
The God that built the skies,
  And earth and nature made:
  God is the tower
    To which I fly;
    His grace is nigh
  In every hour.

2. My feet shall never slide,
  Nor fall in fatal snares;
Since God, my guard and guide,
  Defends me from my fears:
  Those wakeful eyes
    That never sleep,
    Shall Israel keep
  When dangers rise.

3. No burning heats by day,
  Nor blasts of evening air,
Shall take my health away,
  If God be with me there:
  Thou art my sun,
    And thou my shade,
    To guard my head
  By night or noon.

4. Hast thou not given thy word
  To save my soul from death?
And I can trust my Lord
  To keep my mortal breath·
  I 'll go and come,
    Nor fear to die,
    Till from on high
  Thou call me home.

387.   *The Name of Christ a sweet savor.*

1. PRAISE to the Lord on high,
  Who spreads his triumphs wide!
While Jesus' fragrant name
  Is breathed on every side;
Balmy and rich the odors rise,
And fill the earth, and reach the skies.

2. Ten thousand dying souls
  Its influence feel, and live;
Sweeter than vital air
  The incense they receive:
They breathe anew, and rise and sing—
Jesus, the Lord, their conquering King.

3. But they, who scorn the grace
  That brings salvation nigh,
And turn away their face,
  Must faint, and fall, and die:
So sad a doom, ye saints! deplore,
For Oh! they fall to rise no more.

388.   *The Sabbath.*

1. To spend one sacred day
  Where God and saints abide,
Affords diviner joy
  Than thousand days beside;
  Where God resorts,
    I love it more,
    To keep the door
  Than shine in courts

2. God is our sun and shield,
  Our light and our defense;
With gifts his hands are filled,
  We draw our blessings thence;
  He shall bestow
    On Jacob's race,
    Peculiar grace,
  And glory, too.

3. The Lord his people loves;
  His hand no good withholds
From those his heart approves,
  From pure and pious souls:
  Thrice happy he,
    O God of hosts,
    Whose spirit trusts
  Alone in thee.

WOODSTOCK.   C. M.*

D. DUTTON, JR.

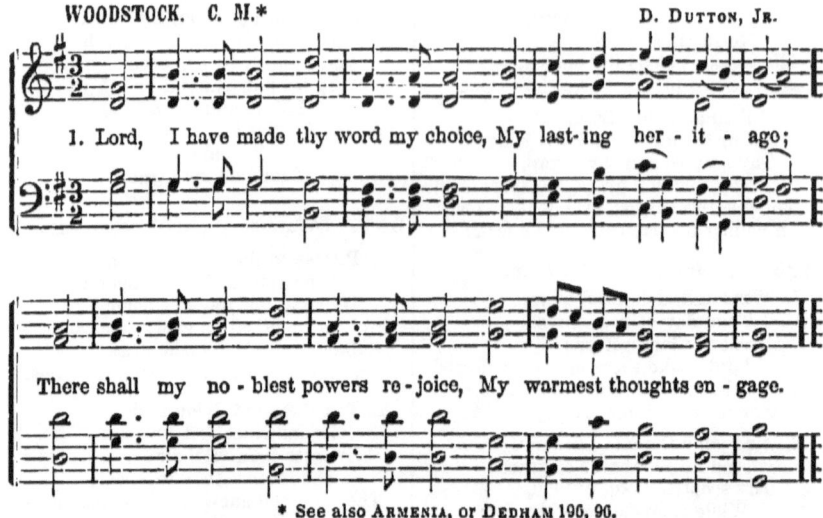

1. Lord, I have made thy word my choice, My last-ing her - it - ago;

There shall my no - blest powers re - joice, My warmest thoughts en - gage.

* See also ARMENIA, or DEDHAM 195, 96.

389.   *Comfort from the Bible.*

1. LORD, I have made thy word my choice,
    My lasting heritage ;
There shall my noblest powers rejoice,
    My warmest thoughts engage.

2. I 'll read the histories of thy love,
    And keep thy laws in sight,
While through the promises I rove,
    With ever-fresh delight.

3. 'Tis a broad land, of wealth unknown,
    Where springs of life arise,
Seeds of immortal bliss are sown,
    And hidden glory lies.

4. The best relief that mourners have,
    It makes our sorrows blest ;
Our fairest hope beyond the grave,
    And our eternal rest.

390.   *Blessedness of Saints.*

1. BLEST are the undefiled in heart,
    Whose ways are right and clean ;
Who never from thy law depart,
    But fly from every sin.

2. Blest are the men who keep thy word,
    And practice thy commands ;
With their whole heart they seek the
       Lord,
And serve thee with their hands.

3. Great is their peace who love thy law,
    How firm their souls abide !
Nor can a bold temptation draw
    Their steady feet aside.

4. Then shall my heart have inward joy,
    And keep my face from shame,
When all thy statutes I obey,
    And honor all thy name.

391.   *The Heavenly Guest.*

1. AND will the Lord thus condescend
    To visit sinful worms ?
Thus at the door shall mercy stand,
    In all her winning forms ?

2. Shall Jesus for admittance plead,
    His charming voice unheard ?
And this vile heart, for which he bled,
    Remain for ever barred ?

3. 'Tis sin, alas ! with tyrant power,
    The lodging has possessed ;
And crowds of traitors bar the door,
    Against the heavenly Guest.

4. Lord ! rise in thine all-conquering grace,
    Thy mighty power display ;
One beam of glory from thy face
    Can drive my foes away.

MONSON. C. M.

MODERATO AFFETTUOSO.

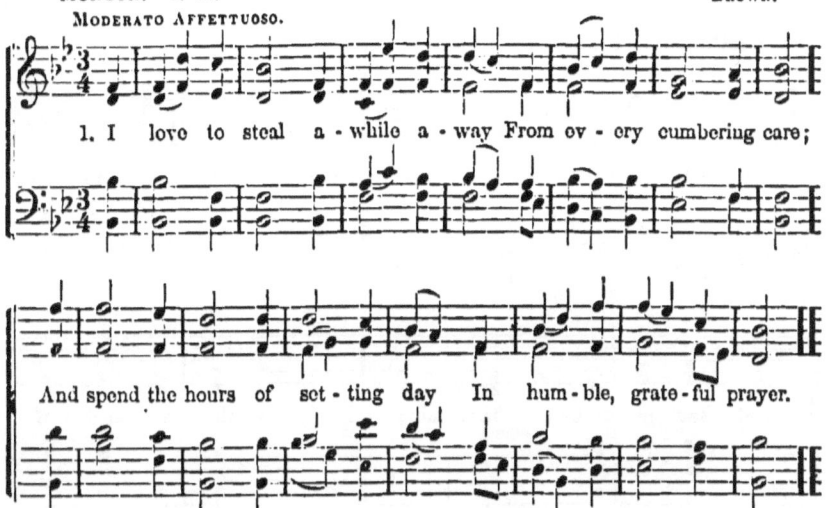

1. I love to steal a - while a - way From ov - ery cumbering care;

And spend the hours of set - ting day In hum - ble, grate - ful prayer.

392. *Twilight Meditation.*

1. I LOVE to steal awhile away
   From every cumbering care;
   And spend the hours of setting day
   In humble, grateful prayer.

2. I love in solitude to shed
   The penitential tear,
   And all his promises to plead,
   Where none but God can hear.

3. I love to think on mercies past,
   And future good implore,
   My cares and sorrows all to cast
   On him whom I adore.

4. I love by faith to take a view
   Of brighter scenes in heaven;
   The prospect doth my strength renew,
   While here by tempests driven.

5. And, when life's toilsome day is o'er,
   May its departing ray
   Be calm as this impressive hour,
   And lead to endless day.

393. *Confidence in God's Government.*

1. SINCE all the varying scenes of time
   God's watchful eye surveys,
   Oh! who so wise to choose our lot,
   Or to appoint our ways?

2. Good, when he gives—supremely good;
   Nor less, when he denies;
   E'en crosses, from his sovereign hand,
   Are blessings in disguise.

3. Why should we doubt a Father's love,
   So constant and so kind?
   To his unerring, gracious will,
   Be every wish resigned.

4. In thy fair book of life divine,
   My God! inscribe my name;
   There let it fill some humble place,
   Beneath my Lord, the Lamb!

394. *Sincerity and Hypocrisy.*

1. GOD is a Spirit, just and wise;
   He sees our inmost mind:
   In vain to heaven we raise our cries,
   And leave our souls behind.

2. Nothing but truth, before his throne,
   With honor can appear:
   The painted hypocrites are known,
   Through the disguise they wear.

3. Their lifted eyes salute the skies,
   Their bending knees the ground,
   But God abhors the sacrifice,
   Where not the heart is found.

4. Lord, search my thoughts, and try my
   And make my soul sincere;   [ways,
   Then shall I stand before thy face,
   And find acceptance there.

"HAIL TO THE BRIGHTNESS." 11s & 10s.*   L. MASON.

1. Hail to the brightness of Zi - on's glad morning! Joy to the
lands that in dark-ness have lain; Hushed be the ac - cents of
sor-row and mourning, Zi - on in tri-umph be-gins her mild reign.

* See also SAMOS 131.

395.   *The latter Day.*

1. HAIL to the brightness of Zion's glad morning!
   Joy to the lands that in darkness have lain;
   Hushed be the accents of sorrow and mourning,
   Zion in triumph begins her mild reign.

2. Hail to the brightness of Zion's glad morning,
   Long by the prophets of Israel foretold;
   Hail to the millions from bondage returning,
   Gentiles and Jews the blest vision behold.

3. Lo! in the desert rich flowers are springing,
   Streams ever copious are gliding along;
   Loud from the mountain-tops echoes are ringing,
   Wastes rise in verdure, and mingle in song.

4. See, from all lands—from the isles of the ocean,
   Praise to Jehovah ascending on high;
   Fallen are the engines of war and commotion,
   Shouts of salvation are rending the sky.

SAMOS. 11s & 10s.*   Melody by Bosr.

1. Daughter of Zi - on! a - wake from thy sad - ness; A-
-wake,—for thy foes shall op - press thee no more;   Bright o'er thy
hills dawns the day - star of glad - ness; A - rise, for the night of thy
sor - row is o'er, A - rise,—for the night of thy sor - row is o'er.

* See also "HAIL TO THE BRIGHTNESS." 130.

396.   *Zion encouraged.*

1. DAUGHTER of Zion! awake from thy sadness;
Awake,—for thy foes shall oppress thee no more;
Bright o'er thy hills dawns the day star of gladness,
Arise,—for the night of thy sorrow is o'er.

2. Strong were thy foes; but the arm that subdued them,
And scattered their legions, was mightier far;
They fled, like the chaff, from the scourge that pursued them,
Vain were their steeds and their chariots of war.

3. Daughter of Zion! the power that hath saved thee,
Extolled with the harp and the timbrel should be:
Shout,—for the foe is destroyed that enslaved thee,
Th' oppressor is vanquished, and Zion is free.

SOLNEY, 8s & 7s. Single.*　　　　　　SHL
MODERATO.

1. Pilgrims in this vale of sor-row, Pressing on-ward t'ward the prize;

Strength and comfort here we bor-row From the Hand that rules the skies.

* See also SICILIAN 249.

397. *Pilgrimage.*

1. PILGRIMS in this vale of sorrow,
   Pressing onward t'ward the prize,
   Strength and comfort here we borrow
   From the Hand that rules the skies.

2. 'Mid these scenes of self-denial,
   We are called the race to run;
   We must meet full many a trial
   Ere the victor's crown is won.

3. Love shall every conflict lighten,
   Hope shall urge us swifter on,
   Faith shall every prospect brighten,
   Till the light of heaven shall dawn.

4. On th' Eternal arm reclining,
   We at length shall win the day:
   All the powers of earth combining,
   Shall not snatch our crown away.

398. *Prayer for comforting Influences.*

1. HOLY GHOST! dispel our sadness,
   Pierce the clouds of nature's night;
   Come, thou Source of joy and gladness!
   Breathe thy life, and spread thy light.

2. Author of our new creation!
   Bid us all thine influence prove;
   Make our souls thy habitation,
   Shed abroad the Saviour's love.

399. *"Am I my brother's keeper?"*
　　　　GEN. iv. 9.

1. BLESSÉD angels, high in heaven
   O'er the penitent rejoice;
   Hast thou for thy brother striven
   With an importuning voice?

2. Art thou not thy brother's keeper?
   Canst thou not his soul obtain?
   He that wakes his brother sleeper
   Double light himself shall gain.

3. Ah! how many may be given
   To that during, fiery lake,
   Who had found a place in heaven
   Had'st thou toiled for Jesus' sake.

4. Think how words in season spoken,
   In the sinful heart sink deep,
   And the first link may have broken
   Of the chains that round him creep.

5. Think of *that* day when each brother
   To his brother shall be known:
   If thy prayers have saved another,
   God will then thy service own.

6. Then, when ends this life's short fever,
   They, who many turn to God,
   Like the stars shall shine for ever,
   A bright, eternal brotherhood!

400. *Call from the Heathen.*

1. HARK! that voice among the nations—
Is it war in deadly strife?
'Tis a brother's lamentations,
Calling for the bread of life.

2. Mark ye not what millions languish,
Sink into a hopeless grave;
Every bosom torn with anguish,
None to pity, none to save.

3. From the land with bounty flowing,
Where the streams of knowledge rise,
Where the trees of life are growing,
Filled with fragrance for the skies:

4. Thence send forth to every nation,
By the messengers of peace,
Tidings of the great salvation,
Till the reign of ruin cease.

5. Wait not till that voice shall slumber
In the silence of the tomb;
Wait not till the grave shall number
Millions to a hopeless doom.

6. Hasten on the heavenly mission,
Answer to that wailing voice;
Heaven will smile on your decision,
Listening angels will rejoice.

OBION. 8s & 7s. Single. From a Theme by MOZART.

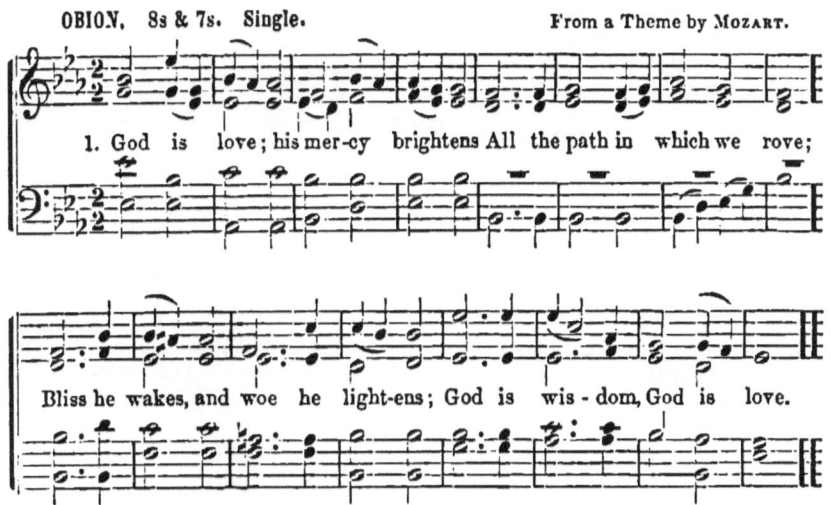

1. God is love; his mer-cy brightens All the path in which we rove;
Bliss he wakes, and woe he light-ens; God is wis - dom, God is love.

401. *Divine Wisdom and Goodness.*

1. GOD is love; his mercy brightens
All the path in which we rove;
Bliss he wakes, and woe he lightens;
God is wisdom, God is love.

2. Chance and change are busy ever;
Man decays, and ages move;
But his mercy waneth never;
God is wisdom, God is love.

3. E'en the hour that darkest seemeth
Will his changeless goodness prove;
From the gloom his brightness streameth,
God is wisdom, God is love.

4. He with earthly cares entwineth
Hope and comfort from above;
Every where his glory shineth;
God is wisdom, God is love

Doxology.

1. PRAISE the God of all creation;
Praise the Father's boundless love;
Praise the Lamb, our expiation;
Praise the Spirit from above:

2. Praise the Fountain of salvation,
Him by whom our spirits live;
Undivided adoration
To the one Jehovah give.

HUTTON. S. M.* HASTINGS

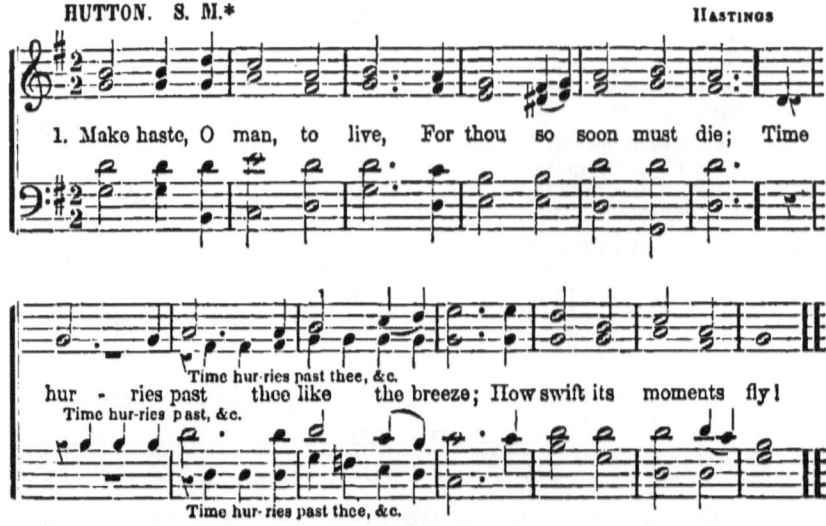

1. Make haste, O man, to live, For thou so soon must die; Time

Time hur-ries past thee, &c.

hur - ries past thee like the breeze; How swift its moments fly!

Time hur-ries past, &c.

Time hur-ries past thee, &c.

* See also LUTHER 194.

402. *Live.*

1. MAKE haste, O man, to live,
   For thou so soon must die;
Time hurries past thee like the breeze;
   How swift its moments fly!

2. To breathe, and wake, and sleep,
   To smile, to sigh, to grieve,
To move in idleness through earth—
   This, this is not to live.

3. Make haste, O man, to do
   Whatever must be done;
Thou hast no time to lose in sloth,
   Thy day will soon be gone.

4. Up, then, with speed, and work;
   Fling ease and self away—
This is no time for thee to sleep—
   Up, watch, and work and pray!

403. *Rejoicing.*

1. Now let our voices join
   To raise the sacred song;
Ye pilgrims! in Jehovah's ways,
   With music pass along.

2. See—flowers of paradise,
   In rich profusion, spring;
The sun of glory gilds the path,
   And dear companions sing.

3. See—Salem's golden spires,
   In beauteous prospect, rise;
And brighter crowns than mortals wear,
   Which sparkle through the skies.

4. All honor to his name,
   Who marks the shining way—
To him who leads the pilgrims on
   To realms of endless day.

404. *Salvation by Grace.*

1. GRACE!—'tis a charming sound—
   Harmonious to the ear;
Heaven with the echo shall resound,
   And all the earth shall hear.

2. Grace first contrived the way
   To save rebellious man;
And all the steps that grace display,
   Which drew the wondrous plan.

3. Grace led my roving feet
   To tread the heavenly road;
And new supplies each hour I meet,
   While pressing on to God.

4. Grace all the work shall crown,
   Through everlasting days;
It lays in heaven the topmost stone,
   And well deserves the praise.

ST. THOMAS. S. M. HANDEL.

1. How beauteous are their feet Who stand on Zi - on's hill!

Who bring sal - va - tion on their tongues, And words of peace re - veal.

405. *Ministers the Bearers of good Tidings.*

1. How beauteous are their feet
Who stand on Zion's hill!
Who bring salvation on their tongues,
And words of peace reveal.

2. How charming is their voice!
How sweet their tidings are!
" Zion, behold thy Saviour King ;
He reigns and triumphs here."

3. How happy are our ears,
That hear this joyful sound!
Which kings and prophets waited for,
And sought, but never found.

4. How blessèd are our eyes,
That see this heavenly light!
Prophets and kings desired it long,
But died without the sight.

5. The watchmen join their voice,
And tuneful notes employ ;
Jerusalem breaks forth in songs,
And deserts learn the joy.

6. The Lord makes bare his arm
Through all the earth abroad ;
Let every nation now behold
Their Saviour and their God.

406. *Christian Watchfulness.*

1. A CHARGE to keep I have,
A God to glorify ;
A never-dying soul to save,
And fit it for the sky :—

2. To serve the present age,
My calling to fulfill—
Oh! may it all my powers engage—
To do my Master's will.

3. Arm me with jealous care,
As in thy sight to live ;
And oh! thy servant, Lord! prepare
A strict account to give.

4. Help me to watch and pray,
And on thyself rely—
Assured, if I my trust betray,
I shall for ever die.

407. *And when they had sung a hymn
they went out.*—Matth. xxvi. 30

1. A PARTING hymn we sing,
Around thy table, Lord,
Again our grateful tribute bring,
Our solemn vows record.

2. Here have we seen thy face,
And felt thy presence here,
So may the savor of thy grace
In word and life appear.

3. The purchase of thy blood—
By sin no longer led—
The path our dear Redeemer trod
May we rejoicing tread.

4. In self-forgetting love
Be Christian union shown,
Until we join the church above,
And know as we are known.

LAEL. S. M.   From the ' SHAWM."

1. Blest be the tie that binds Our hearts in Chris-tian love;

Ritard.

The fel-low-ship of kin-dred minds Is like to that a-bove.

* See also the opposite page.

408.   *Christian Fellowship.*

1. BLEST be the tie that binds
    Our hearts in Christian love;
The fellowship of kindred minds
    Is like to that above.

2. Before our Father's throne
    We pour our ardent prayers;
Our fears, our hopes, our aims are one,
    Our comforts and our cares.

3. We share our mutual woes;
    Our mutual burdens bear;
And often for each other flows
    The sympathizing tear.

4. When we asunder part,
    It gives us inward pain;
But we shall still be joined in heart,
    And hope to meet again.

5. This glorious hope revives
    Our courage by the way;
While each in expectation lives,
    And longs to see the day.

6. From sorrow, toil, and pain,
    And sin, we shall be free;
And perfect love and friendship reign
    Through all eternity.

409.   *Vital Union to Christ.*

1. DEAR Saviour! we are thine
    By everlasting bands;
Our names, our hearts, we would resign,
    Our souls are in thy hands.

2. To thee we still would cleave,
    With ever-growing zeal;
If millions tempt us Christ to leave,
    Oh! let them ne'er prevail.

3. Thy Spirit shall unite
    Our souls to thee, our Head;
Shall form us to thine image bright,
    That we thy paths may tread.

4. Death may our souls divide
    From these abodes of clay;
But love shall keep us near thy side,
    Through all the gloomy way.

5. Since Christ and we are one,
    Why should we doubt and fear?
If he in heaven hath fixed his throne,
    He 'll fix his members there.

Doxology.

YE angels round the throne,
    And saints that dwell below,
Worship the Father—love the Son,
    And bless the Spirit, too.

SHIRLAND. S. M.   STANLEY,

1. The man is ev - er blest, Who shuns the sin - ner's ways; A-

- mong their coun - cils nev - er stands, Nor takes the scorner's place.

410. *The Saint happy, the Sinner miserable.*

1. THE man is ever blest,
   Who shuns the sinner's ways;
Among their councils never stands,
   Nor takes the scorner's place:

2. But makes the law of God,
   His study and delight,
Amidst the labors of the day,
   And watches of the night.

3. He like a tree shall thrive,
   With waters near the root:
Fresh as the leaf his name shall live,
   His works are heavenly fruit.

4. Not so th' ungodly race;
   They no such blessings find:
Their hopes shall flee like empty chaff
   Before the driving wind.

5. How will they bear to stand
   Before that judgment seat,
Where all the saints, at Christ's right hand,
   In full assembly meet.

411.   *Preserving Grace.*

1. To God, the only-wise,
   Our Saviour and our King,
Let all the saints, below the skies,
   Their humble praises bring.

2. 'Tis his almighty love,
   His counsel and his care,
Preserves us safe from sin and death,
   And every hurtful snare.

3. He will present our souls,
   Unblemished and complete,
Before the glory of his face,
   With joys divinely great.

4. Then all the chosen seed
   Shall meet around the throne;
Shall bless the conduct of his grace,
   And make his wonders known.

5. To our Redeemer-God,
   Wisdom, with power, belongs;
Immortal crowns of majesty,
   And everlasting songs.

412.   *Exhortation to Prayer for the Unconverted.*

1. AWAKE, awake to prayer,
   For souls condemned to die,
That through forgiveness they may share
   God's blessing from on high.

2. Awake, awake to prayer!
   The promises are plain:
Wrestling in faith and filial fear,
   Ye will not plead in vain.

AZMON. C. M.   Theme from GLAZER.

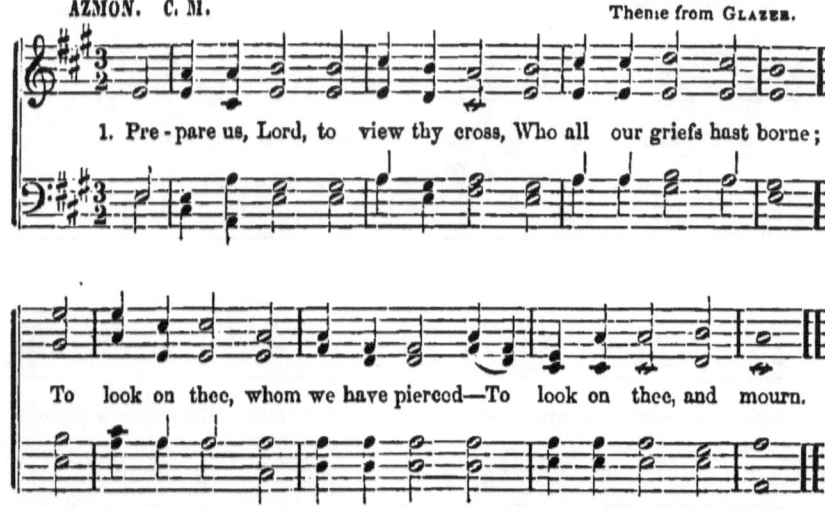

1. Pre-pare us, Lord, to view thy cross, Who all our griefs hast borne;

To look on thee, whom we have pierced—To look on thee, and mourn.

413. *Before Communion.*

1. PREPARE us, Lord, to view thy cross,
Who all our griefs hast borne;
To look on thee, whom we have pierced,
To look on thee, and mourn.

2. While thus we mourn, we would rejoice;
And, as thy cross we see,
Let each exclaim, in faith and hope,
"The Saviour died for me!"

414. *The pure Heart.*

1. WHATEVER dims thy sense of truth,
Or stains thy purity,
Though light as breath of summer air,
Count it as sin to thee.

2. Preserve the tablet of thy thoughts
From every blemish free,
While the Redeemer's lovely faith
Its temple makes with thee.

3. And pray of God, that grace be given
To tread time's narrow way:—
How dark soever it may be,
It leads to cloudless day.

415. *Faith, Hope, and Charity.*

1. FAITH, hope, and love, now dwell on earth,
And earth by them is blest;

But faith and hope must yield to love,
Of all the graces best.

2. Hope shall to full fruition rise,
And faith be sight above;
These are the means, but this the end,
For saints for ever love.

416.   Heb. xiii. 3.

1. FOR those in bonds as bound with them
To Thee, O God! we pray,
That some celestial, radiant beam
May bring a brighter day.

2. Pity, O Lord! that injured race,
And thy deliverance send;
Grant them the treasures of thy grace,
And bid their bondage end.

3. They sit in darkness, slow to learn
The blessings that they need;
Nor can our anxious thought discern,
How best their cause to plead.

4. All helpless, and without a plan,
We come before thy throne;
We put no confidence in man,
But trust in Thee alone.

5. The means of rescue, and the hour,
Thy mercy will reveal:
Thine is the wisdom, Thine the power
Teach us to do thy will.

ARCADIA. C. M.
From the "Psalmodist."

1. In time of fear, When trouble's near, I look to thine a-
- bode; Though help - ers fail, And foes pre - vail, I'll
put my trust in God, I'll put my trust.... in God.

417. *Trust in God amid Perils.*

1. In time of fear,
   When trouble's near,
I look to thine abode;
   Though helpers fail,
   And foes prevail,
I'll put my trust in God.

2. And what is life,
   But toil and strife?
What terror has the grave?
   Thine arm of power,
   In peril's hour,
The trembling soul will save.

3. In darkest skies,
   Though storms arise,
I will not be dismayed:
   O God of light,
   And boundless might,
My soul on thee is stayed!

418. *God in the Storm.*

1. GREAT Ruler of all nature's frame,
   We own thy power divine;
   We hear thy breath in every storm,
   For all the winds are thine.

2. Wide as they sweep their sounding way,
   They work thy sovereign will;
   And, awed by thy majestic voice,
   Confusion shall be still.

3. Thy mercy tempers every blast
   To them that seek thy face,
   And mingles with the tempest's roar
   The whispers of thy grace.

4. Those gentle whispers let me hear,
   Till all the tumult cease;
   And gales of paradise shall lull
   My weary soul to peace.

1. Lord, let my prayer like in-cense rise: And when I lift my hands to thee,

As in the eveuing sa - cri - fice, Look down from heaven, well pleased, on me.

* See also UXBRIDGE 86.

419. *Christian Watchfulness and Reproof.*

LORD, let my prayer like incense rise:
And when I lift my hands to thee,
As in the evening sacrifice,
Look down from heaven, well pleased,
  on me.

2. Qut thou a watch to keep my tongue,
Let not my heart to sin incline;
Save me from men who practice wrong:
Let me not share their mirth and wine.

3. But let the righteous, when I stray,
Smite me in love; his strokes are kind:
His mild reproofs, like oil, allay
The wounds they make, and heal the
  mind.

4. But O, redeem me from the snares
With which the world surrounds my
  feet,
Its riches, vanities, and cares,
Its love, its hatred, and deceit.

420. *For a Temperance Anniversary.*

1. WE praise thee, if one rescued soul,
While the past year prolonged its
  flight,
Turned, shuddering, from the poisonous
  bowl,
To health, and liberty, and light.

2. We praise thee, if one clouded home,
Where broken hearts despairing pined,

Behold the sire and husband come
Erect and in his perfect mind;

3. No more a weeping wife to mock,
Till all her hopes in anguish end;
No more the trembling child to shock,
And sink the father in the fiend.

4. Still give us grace, almighty King!
Unwavering at our posts to stand,
Till grateful to thy shrine we bring
The tribute of a ransomed land.

421. *"Ye are complete in Him."*—Col. ii
               10.

1. COMPLETE in Thee, no work of mine
May take, dear Lord, the place of thine
Thy blood has pardon bought for me,
And I am now complete in Thee.

2. Complete in Thee—no more shall sin
Thy grace has conquered, reign within;
Thy voice will bid the tempter flee,
And I shall stand complete in Thee.

3. Complete in Thee—each want supplied,
And no good thing to me denied,
Since thou my portion, Lord, wilt be,
I ask no more—complete in Thee.

4. Dear Saviour, when, before thy bar
All tribes and tongues assembled are,
Among thy chosen may I be
At thy right hand—complete in Thee.

5. Complete in Thee, for ever blest,
Of all thy fullness, Lord, possessed,
Thy praise throughout eternity—
Thy love I 'll sing, complete in Thee.

422. *Who on Earth are blessed.*

1. BLEST are the humble souls that see
Their emptiness and poverty ;
Treasures of grace to them are given,
And crowns of joy laid up in heaven.

2. Blest are the men of broken heart,
Who mourn for sin with inward smart ;
The blood of Christ divinely flows—
A healing balm for all their woes.

3. Blest are the meek, who stand afar
From rage and passion, noise and war ;
God will secure their happy state,
And plead their cause against the great.

4. Blest are the souls that thirst for grace—
Hunger and long for righteousness ;
They shall be well supplied, and fed,
With living streams and living bread.

423. *Retirement and Devotion.*

1. My God, permit me not to be
A stranger to myself and thee ;
Amidst a thousand thoughts I rove,
Forgetful of my highest love.

2. Why should my passions mix with earth,
And thus debase my heavenly birth ?
Why should I cleave to things below,
And let my God, my Saviour go ?

3. Call me away from flesh and sense ;
One sovereign word can draw me thence ;
I would obey the voice divine,
And all inferior joys resign.

4. Be earth with all her scenes withdrawn ;
Let noise and vanity be gone ;
In secret silence of the mind,
My heaven, and there my God, I find.

424. *God acknowledged in National Blessings.*

1. GREAT God of nations ! now to thee
Our hymn of gratitude we raise ;
With humble heart, and bending knee,
We offer thee our song of praise.

2. Thy name we bless, Almighty God !
For all the kindness thou hast shown,
To this fair land the pilgrims trod—
This land we fondly call our own.

3. Here freedom spreads her banner wide,
And casts her soft and hallowed ray—
Here, thou our fathers' steps didst guide
In safety, through their dangerous way.

4. We praise thee, that the gospel's light,
Through all our land its radiance sheds ;
Dispels the shades of error's night,
And heavenly blessings round us
spreads.

5. Great God ! preserve us in thy fear ;
In dangers still our guardian be ;
Oh ! spread thy truth's bright precepts
here—
Let all the people worship thee.

425. *For the Blessing of Schools.*

1. O THOU, at whose dread name we bend,
To whom our purest vows we pay,
God over all, in love descend,
And bless the labors of this day.

2. Our fathers here, a pilgrim oand,
Fixed the proud empire of the free ;
Art moved in gladness o'er the land,
And faith her altars reared to thee.

3. Here, too, to guard, through every age,
The sacred rites their valor won,
They bade instruction spread her page,
And send down truth from sire to son.

4. Here still, through all succeeding time,
Their stores may truth and learning
bring,
And still the anthem-note sublime
To thee from children's children sing.

426. *Clinging to God.*

1. O LORD, thy heavenly grace impart,
And fix my frail, inconstant heart :
Henceforth my chief desire shall be
To dedicate myself to thee.

2. Whate'er pursuits my time employ,
One thought shall fill my soul with joy :
That silent, secret thought shall be
That all my hopes are fixed on thee.

3. Thy glorious eye pervadeth space ;
Thy presence, Lord, fills every place ;
And wheresoe'er my lot may be,
Still shall my spirit cleave to thee.

4. Renouncing every earthly thing,
And safe beneath thy spreading wing,
My sweetest thought henceforth shall be
That all I want I find in thee.

LAVATER. L. M.*

W. B. BRADBURY

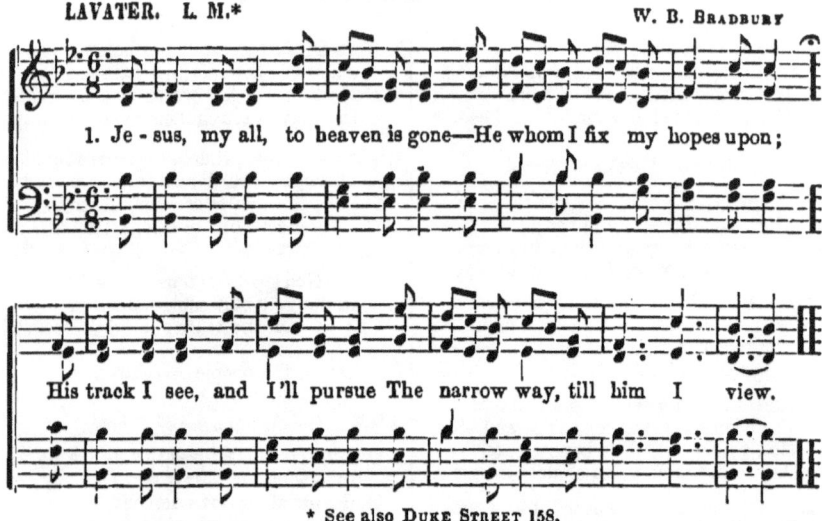

1. Je-sus, my all, to heaven is gone—He whom I fix my hopes upon;

His track I see, and I'll pursue The narrow way, till him I view.

*See also DUKE STREET 158.

427. *The Way to Heaven.*

1. JESUS, my all, to heaven is gone,—
He whom I fix my hopes upon;
His track I see, and I'll pursue
The narrow way, till him I view.

2. This is the way I long have sought,
And mourned because I found it not;
Till late I heard my Saviour say,—
"Come hither, soul! I am the way."

3. Lo! glad I come, and thou, blest Lamb!
Shalt take me to thee as I am;
Nothing but sin to Thee I give—
Nothing but love shall I receive.

4. Then will I tell to sinners round,
What a dear Saviour I have found;
I'll point to thy redeeming blood,
And say,—"Behold the way to God!"

428. *Grateful Recollections.*

1. I LOVE the Lord;—his gracious ear
Was opened to my mournful prayer;
He heard my supplicating voice,
And bade my fainting heart rejoice.

2. Return, my soul, and sweetly rest
On thy almighty Father's breast;
The riches of his grace adore,
And tell his wondrous mercies o'er.

3. What shall I render to the Lord?
Or how his matchless grace record?
To him my grateful voice I'll raise,
And pour libations to his praise.

4. His crowded courts shall see me pay
The vows of my distressful day;
In life and death, the saints shall find
Their guardian God for ever kind.

429. *Christ's Invitation to Sinners.*

1. "COME hither, all ye weary souls!
Ye heavy-laden sinners! come;
I'll give you rest from all your toils,
And raise you to my heavenly home.

2. "They shall find rest, who learn of me,—
I'm of a meek and lowly mind;
But passion rages like the sea,
And pride is restless as the wind.

3. "Blessed is the man, whose shoulders take
My yoke, and bear it with delight;
My yoke is easy to his neck,
My grace shall make the burden light."

4. Jesus! we come at thy command;
With faith, and hope, and humble zeal,
Resign our spirits, to thy hand.
To mould and guide us at thy will.

430. *A Welcome to Christian Fellowship.*

1. COME in, thou blesséd of the Lord!
   Oh! come in Jesus' precious name;
   We welcome thee, with one accord,
   And trust the Saviour does the same.

2. Those joys which earth can not afford,
   We'll seek in fellowship to prove,
   Joined in one spirit to our Lord,
   Together bound by mutual love.

3. And, while we pass this vale of tears,
   We'll make our joys and sorrows known;
   We'll share each other's hopes and fears,
   And count a brother's cares our own.

4. Once more, our welcome we repeat;
   Receive assurance of our love;
   Oh! may we all together meet
   Around the throne of God above.

431. *Blessing and Honor to the Lamb.*

1. WHAT equal honors shall we bring
   To thee, O Lord, our God, the Lamb!
   When all the notes that angels sing,
   Are far inferior to thy name?

2. Worthy is he who once was slain,—
   The Prince of peace, who groaned and died,
   Worthy to rise, and live, and reign,
   At his almighty Father's side.

3. Honor immortal must be paid,
   Instead of scandal and of scorn;
   While glory shines around his head,
   And a bright crown without a thorn.

4. Blessings for ever on the Lamb,
   Who bore the curse for wretched men!
   Let angels sound his sacred name,
   And every creature say,—Amen.

432. *Hosannas to Christ.*

1. WHAT are those soul-reviving strains
   That echo thus from Salem's plains?
   What anthems loud, and louder still,
   Sweetly resound from Zion's hill?

2. Lo! 'tis an infant chorus sings
   Hosanna to the King of kings:
   The Saviour comes, and babes proclaim
   Salvation sent in Jesus' name.

3. Nor these alone their voice shall raise,
   For we will join this song of praise:
   Still Israel's children forward press
   To hail the Lord, their righteousness.

4. Proclaim hosannas loud and clear:
   See David's Son and Lord appear!
   Glory and praise on earth be given,—
   Hosanna in the highest heaven.

433. *Glory and Grace in Christ.*

1. NOW to the Lord a noble song!
   Awake, my soul! awake, my tongue!
   Hosanna to th' eternal name,
   And all his boundless love proclaim.

2. See where it shines in Jesus' face,—
   The brightest image of his grace!
   God, in the person of his Son,
   Has all his mightiest works outdone.

3. Grace!—'tis a sweet, a charming theme;
   My thoughts rejoice at Jesus' name:
   Ye angels! dwell upon the sound:
   Ye heavens! reflect it to the ground.

4. Oh! may I reach that happy place,
   Where he unvails his lovely face,
   Where all his beauties you behold,
   And sing his name to harps of gold.

434. *A Pastor welcomed.*

1. We bid thee welcome in the name
   Of Jesus, our exalted Head:
   Come as a servant: so he came;
   And we receive thee in his stead.

2. Come as a shepherd: guard and keep
   This fold from Satan and from sin;
   Nourish the lambs, and feed the sheep;
   The wounded heal, the lost bring in.

3. Come as a teacher sent from God,
   Charged his whole counsel to declare;
   Lift o'er our ranks the prophet's rod,
   While we uphold thy hands with prayer.

4. Come as a messenger of peace,
   Filled with the Spirit, fired with love;
   Live to behold our large increase,
   And die to meet us all above.

435. *Dismission.*

1. DISMISS us with thy blessing, Lord;
   Help us to feed upon thy word;
   All that has been amiss, forgive,
   And let thy truth within us live.

2. Though we are guilty, Thou art good;
   Wash all our works in Jesus' blood;
   Give every burdened soul release,
   And bid us all depart in peace.

WESLEY. 7s. Double.*   HASTINGS.

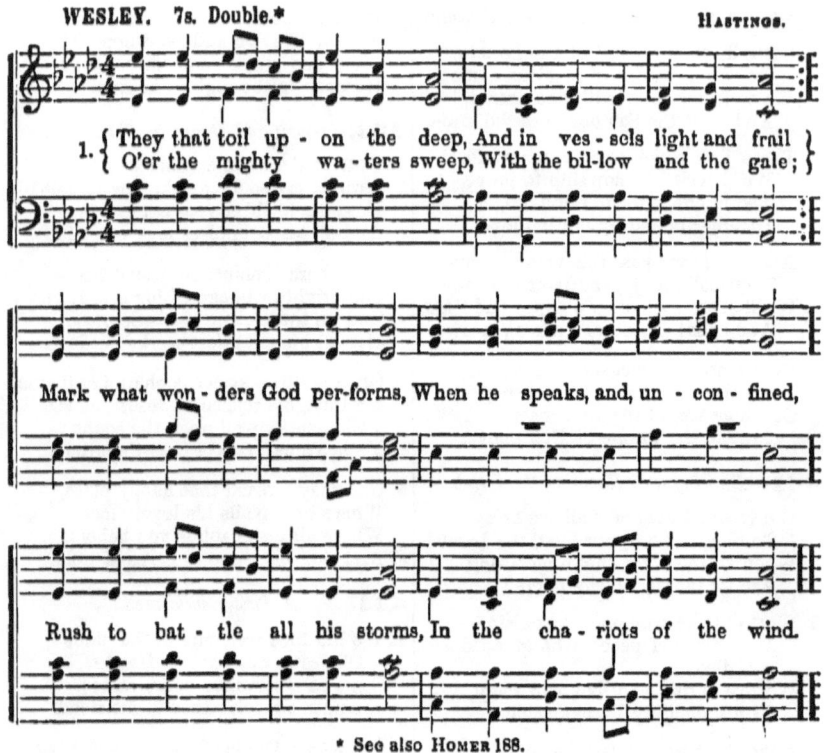

1. They that toil up - on the deep, And in ves - sels light and frail
O'er the mighty wa - ters sweep, With the bil-low and the gale;

Mark what won - ders God per-forms, When he speaks, and, un - con - fined,

Rush to bat - tle all his storms, In the cha - riots of the wind.

* See also HOMER 188.

436.   *Seamen.*

1. THEY that toil upon the deep,
   And in vessels light and frail
O'er the mighty waters sweep,—
   With the billow and the gale,—
Mark what wonders God performs,
   When he speaks, and, unconfined,
Rush to battle all his storms,
   In the chariots of the wind.

2. Up to heaven their bark is whirled
   On the mountain of the wave
Downward suddenly 'tis hurled
   To th' abysses of the grave:
'Mid the tempest now they roll,
   As intoxicate with wine:
Terrors paralyze their soul
   Helm they quit, and hope resign.

3. Then unto the Lord they cry:
   He inclines his gracious ear;
Sends deliverance from on high,
   Rescues them from all their fear

Oh that men would praise the Lord
   For his goodness to their race;
For the wonders of his word,
   And the riches of his grace.

437.   *Christ's Ascension.*

1. "WIDE, ye heavenly gates, unfold,
   Closed no more by death and sin:
Now the conquering Lord behold,
   Let the King of glory in."
Hark, th' angelic host inquire,
   "Who is he, th' almighty King?"
Hark again, the answering choir
   Thus in strains of triumph sing:—

2. "He whose powerful arm, alone,
   On his foes destruction hurled;
He who hath the victory won,
   He who saved a ruined world;
He who God's pure law fulfilled,
   Jesus the Incarnate Word;
He whose truth with blood was sealed—
   He is heaven's all-glorious Lord."

5. " Who shall to this blest abode
Follow in the Saviour's train?"
" They who in his cleansing blood
Wash away each guilty stain;
They whose daily actions prove
Steadfast faith, and holy fear,
Fervent zeal, and grateful love,
They shall dwell for ever here."

438. *Tell us of the Night.*

1. WATCHMAN! tell us of the night,
What its signs of promise are.
Traveler! o'er yon mountain height
See the glory beaming star!
Watchman! does its beauteous ray
Aught of hope or joy foretell?
Traveler! yes, it brings the day,
Promised day of Israel.

2. Watchman! tell us of the night;
Higher yet that star ascends!
Traveler! blessedness and light,
Peace and truth, its course portends!
Watchman! will its beams alone
Gild the spot that gave them birth?
Traveler! ages are its own;
See, it bursts o'er all the earth.

3. Watchman! tell us of the night,
For the morning seems to dawn:
Traveler ! darkness takes its flight;
Doubt and terror are withdrawn!
Watchman! let thy wandering cease,
Hie thee to thy quiet home;
Traveler! lo! the Prince of peace,
Lo! the Son of God is come!

439. *The Messengers of God.*

1. Go—ye messengers of God!
Like the beams of morning, fly;
Take the wonder-working rod.
Wave the Banner-Cross on high.
2. Where the towering minaret
Gleams along the morning skies,
Wave it till the crescent set,
And the "Star of Jacob" rise.

3. Go to many a tropic isle,
In the bosom of the deep,
Where the skies for ever smile,
And th.' oppressed for ever weep.
4. Where the golden gates of day
Open on the palmy east,
Wide the bleeding cross display—
Spread the gospel's richest feast.

440. *Millennial Glory.*

1. HARK, the song of Jubilee,
Loud as mighty thunders roar;
Or the fullness of the sea,
When it breaks upon the shore!
Hallelujah, for the Lord
God Omnipotent shall reign!
Hallelujah! let the word
Echo through the earth and main.

2. Hallelujah! hark, the sound,
From the depths unto the skies,
Wakes above, beneath, around,
All creation's harmonies!
See Jehovah's banners furled,
Sheathed his sword, he speaks—'tis
done;
And the kingdoms of this world
Are the kingdoms of his Son.

3. He shall reign from pole to pole,
With illimitable sway;
He shall reign, when like a scroll
Yonder heavens are passed away;
Then the end: beneath his rod
Man's last enemy shall fall:
Hallelujah! Christ is God!
God in Christ is all in all.

441. *Songs of the Angels.*

1. HARK ! the herald-angels sing—
"Glory to the new-born King;
Peace on earth, and mercy mild—
God and sinners reconciled."
2. Joyful, all ye nations! rise,
Join the triumph of the skies;
With th' angelic host proclaim—
"Christ is born in Bethlehem."

3. Mild he lays his glory by,
Born that man no more may die,
Born to raise the sons of earth;
Born to give them second birth.
4. Hail! the heaven-born Prince of peace!
Hail! the Sun of righteousness!
Light and life to all he brings,
Risen with healing in his wings.

5. Let us then with angels sing—
"Glory to the new-born King;
Peace on earth, and mercy mild—
God and sinners reconciled."

For 5th stanza repeat from 2d strain.

LUCERNE. C. M. Double.   Melody by the late Rev. CHAS. HALL, D.D.

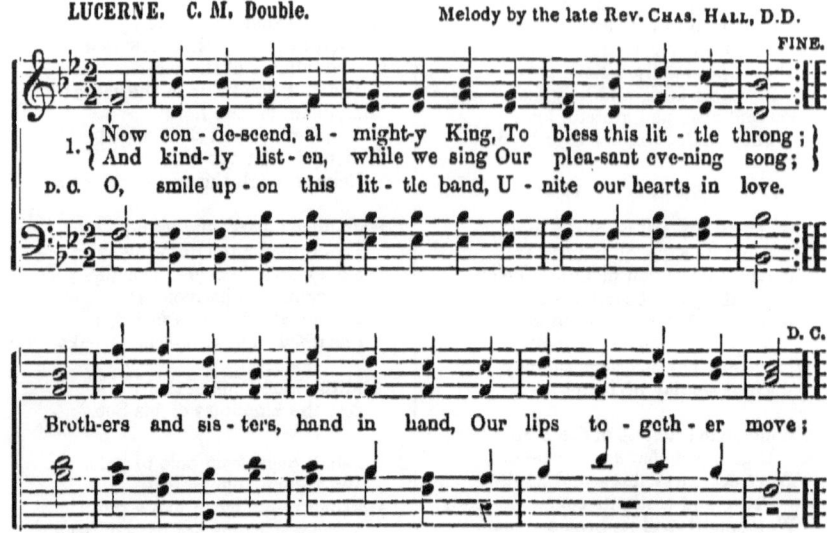

1. Now con-de-scend, al-might-y King, To bless this lit-tle throng;
   And kind-ly list-en, while we sing Our plea-sant eve-ning song;
D. C. O, smile up-on this lit-tle band, U-nite our hearts in love.

Broth-ers and sis-ters, hand in hand, Our lips to-geth-er move;

442. *Children's Evening Hymn.*

1. Now condescend, almighty King,
   To bless this little throng;
   And kindly listen while we sing
   Our pleasant evening song.

2. Brothers and sisters, hand in hand,
   Our lips together move:
   Oh, smile upon this little band,
   Unite our hearts in love.

3. We come to own the Power divine
   That watches o'er our days:
   For this our feeble voices join;
   To God we give the praise.

4. May we in safety sleep to-night,
   From every danger free;
   For, Lord, the darkness and the light
   Are both alike to thee.

5. And when the rising sun displays
   His cheering beams abroad,
   Then may our grateful morning lays
   Declare the love of God.

   (For verse 5, begin at the double bar.)

443. *Christ's Presence with the Aged.*

1. ABIDE with us, for day declines,
   And night is drawing near;

The sun of life now dimly shines,
   And soon will disappear:
But if thou wilt with us abide,
   Earth's shadows well may come,
We shall have light at eventide,
   To dissipate the gloom.

2. Abide with us, that we may know
   More of thy wondrous love,
   Ere thou shalt call us hence to go,
   And dwell with thee above:
   We would be wholly cleansed within,
   Be searched and purified,
   From every secret stain of sin,
   While yet we here reside.

3. Abide with us, that we may learn
   To love thee more and more;
   That we fresh wonders may discern
   From thine exhaustless store:
   We would begin heaven's visions here
   In holy, pure delight,
   Before we reach that higher sphere
   Where faith is lost in sight.

444. *The Sabbath of the Soul.*

1. O FATHER! though the anxious fear
   May cloud to-morrow's way,
   No fear nor doubt shall enter here,—
   All shall be thine to-day.

2. We will not bring divided hearts,
To worship at thy shrine;
But each unworthy thought departs,
And leaves this temple thine.

3 Then sleep to-day, tormenting cares,
Of earth and folly born ;
Ye shall not dim the light that streams
From this celestial morn.

4. To-morrow will be time enough
To feel your harsh control ;
Ye shall not violate this day,
The Sabbath of the soul.

445. *Encouragement to Christian Effort.*

1. SCORN not the slightest word or deed,
Nor deem it void of power;
There 's fruit in each wind-wafted seed,
Waiting its natal hour.

2. A whispered word may touch the heart,
And call it back to life ;
A look of love bid sin depart,
And still unholy strife.

3. No act falls fruitless; none can tell
How vast its power may be;
Nor what results enfolded dwell
Within it silently.

4. Work, and despair not: bring thy mite,
Nor care how small it be ;
God is with all that serve the right,
The holy, true, and free.

446. *Gratitude.*

1. WHEN all thy mercies, O my God,
My rising soul surveys,
Transported with the view, I 'm lost
In wonder, love, and praise.

2. Unnumbered comforts on my soul
Thy tender care bestowed,
Before my infant heart conceived
From whom those comforts flowed.

3. When in the slippery paths of youth
With heedless steps I ran,
Thine arm, unseen, conveyed me safe,
And led me up to man.

4. Ten thousand thousand precious gifts
My daily thanks employ;
Nor is the least a cheerful heart,
That tastes those gifts with joy.

5. Through every period of my life,
Thy goodness I 'll pursue ;
And after death, in distant worlds,
The glorious theme renew.

6. Through all eternity, to thee
A grateful song I 'll raise :
But, Oh ! eternity 's too short
To utter all thy praise.

447. *For a charitable Occasion.*

1. WHO is thy neighbor? he whom thou
Hast power to aid or bless;
Whose aching heart or burning brow
Thy soothing hand may press.

2. Thy neighbor? 'tis the fainting poor,
Whose eye with want is dim ;
O, enter thou his humble door,
With aid and peace for him.

3. Thy neighbor? he who drinks the cup
When sorrow drowns the brim ;
With words of high sustaining hope,
Go thou, and comfort him.

4. Thy neighbor? 'tis the weary slave,
Fettered in mind and limb;
He hath no hope this side the grave,
Go thou, and ransom him.

5. Thy neighbor? pass no mourner by;
Perhaps thou canst redeem
A breaking heart from misery;
Go, share thy lot with him.

448. *Prayer for strong Faith.*

1. O, FOR a faith that will not shrink
Though pressed by every foe,
That will not tremble on the brink
Of any earthly woe!—

2. That will not murmur nor complain
Beneath the chastening rod,
But, in the hour of grief or pain,
Will lean upon its God;—

3. A faith that shines more bright and clear
When tempests rage without ;
That, when in danger, knows no fear,
In darkness, feels no doubt;—

4. Lord, give us such a faith as this,
And then, whate'er may come,
We 'll taste, e'en here, the hallowed bliss
Of an eternal home.

HABOR.   C. M.*

QUICK AND BOLD.

1. O, speed thee, Chris-tian, on thy way, And to thy ar - mor cling; With gird - ed loins the call o - bey That o - - bey,.......... grace and mer - cy bring, That grace and mer - cy bring.

* See also CHRISTMAS 12.

449.   *The whole Armor.*

1. O, SPEED thee, Christian, on thy way,
    And to thy armor cling;
  With girded loins the call obey
    That grace and mercy bring.

2. There is a battle to be fought,
    An upward race to run,
  A crown of glory to be sought,
    A victory to be won.

3. The shield of faith repels the dart
    That Satan's hand may throw;
  His arrow can not reach thy heart,
    If Christ control the bow.

4. The glowing lamp of prayer will light
    Thee on thy anxious road;
  'T will keep the goal of heaven in sight,
    And guide thee to thy God.

5. O, faint not, Christian, for thy sighs
    Are heard before his throne;
  The race must come before the prize,
    The cross before the crown.

450.   *The Ascension and Reign of Christ.*

1. OH! for a shout of sacred joy
    To God, the sovereign King;
  Let every land their tongues employ,
    And hymns of triumph sing.

2. Jesus, our God, ascends on high;
    His heavenly guards around
  Attend him rising through the sky,
    With trumpets' joyful sound.

3. While angels shout, and praise their King.
    Let mortals learn their strains;
  Let all the earth his honor sing;—
    O er all the earth he reigns.

4. Rehearse his praise with awe profound;
Let knowledge lead the song ;
Nor mock him with a solemn sound
Upon a thoughtless tongue.

5. In Israel stood his ancient throne :—
He loved that ancient race ;
But now he calls the world his own;
The heathen taste his grace.

451. *Returning to Zion.*

1. SING, all ye ransomed of the Lord !
Your great Deliverer sing:
Ye pilgrims ! now, for Zion bound,
Be joyful in your King.

2. See the fair way his hand hath made;
How peaceful and how plain !
The simplest traveler need not err,
Nor seek the path in vain.

3. A hand divine shall lead you on,
Through all the blissful road ;
Till to the sacred mount you rise,
And see your smiling God.

4. Bright garlands of immortal joy
Shall bloom on every head ;
While sorrow, sighing, and distress,
Like shadows, all are fled.

5. March on, in your Redeemer's strength;
Pursue his footsteps still ;
With joyful hope, still fix your eye
On Zion's heavenly hill.

452. *Returning to Zion.*

1. DAUGHTER of Zion, from the dust
Exalt thy fallen head ;
Again in thy Redeemer trust ;
He calls thee from the dead.

2. Awake, awake ; put on thy strength,
Thy beautiful array ;
The day of freedom dawns at length,
The Lord's appointed day.

3. Rebuild thy walls, thy bounds enlarge,
And send thy heralds forth ;
Say to the south, "Give up thy charge,"
And, " Keep not back, O north."

4. They come ! they come ! thine exiled
bands,
Where'er they rest or roam,
Have heard thy voice in distant lands,
And hasten to their home.

5 Thus, though the universe shall burn,
And God his works destroy,
With songs thy ransomed shall return,
And everlasting joy.

453. *Promised Aid.*

1. Go, and the Saviour's grace proclaim,
Ye favored men of God !
Go, publish, through Immanuel's name,
Salvation bought with blood.

2. What, though your arduous pathway lie
Through regions dark as death ?
What, though, your faith and zeal to try,
Perils beset your path ?

3. Yet, with determined courage, go,
And armed with power divine;
Your God will needful strength bestow,
And on your labors shine.

4. Shrink not, though earth and hell oppose,
But plead your Master's cause ;
Assured that e'en your mightiest foes
Shall bow before his cross.

454. *The joyful Reign of Christ.*

1. JOY to the world—the Lord is come !—
Let earth receive her King;
Let every heart prepare him room,
And heaven and nature sing.

2. Joy to the world—the Saviour reigns,
Let men their songs employ;
While fields and floods—rocks, hills and
plains
Repeat the sounding joy.

3. No more let sin and sorrow grow,
Nor thorns infest the ground ;
He comes to make his blessings flow
Far as the curse is found.

4. He rules the world with truth and grace
And makes the nations prove
The glories of his righteousness,
And wonders of his love.

455. *The Saints' Safety.*

1. UNSHAKEN as the sacred hill,
And firm as mountains stand,
Firm as a rock the soul shall rest,
That trusts th' Almighty Hand.

2. Not walls nor hills could guard so well
Old Salem's happy ground,
As those eternal arms of love,
That every saint surround.

3. Deal gently, Lord, with souls sincere,
And lead them safely on
To the bright gates of paradise,
Where Christ, their Lord, is gone.

ZIPHRON. L. M.

MODERATO AFFETTUOSO.

Arranged from BEETHOVEN.

1. The God of love will sure indulge The flow-ing tear, the heaving sigh,
When his own chil-dren fall a-round, When tender friends and kin-dred die.

+ See also ROCKINGHAM 238.

456. *Mourning with Submission.*

1. THE God of love will sure indulge
  The flowing tear, the heaving sigh,
  When his own children fall around—
  When tender friends and kindred die.

2. Yet not one anxious, murm'ring thought,
  Should with our mourning passions blend;
  Nor would our bleeding hearts forget
  Th' almighty, ever-living Friend.

3. Beneath a numerous train of ills,
  Our feeble flesh and heart may fail;
  Yet shall our hope in thee, our God,
  O'er every gloomy fear prevail.

4. Our Father God! to thee we look,
  Our Rock, our Portion, and our Friend;
  And on thy covenant love and truth
  Our sinking souls shall still depend.

457. *Inconstant Heart lamented.*

1. Ah! wretched, vile, ungrateful heart!
  That can from Jesus thus depart;
  Thus, fond of trifles, vainly rove,
  Forgetful of a Saviour's love.

2. In vain I charge my thoughts to stay,
  And chide earth's vanities away;
  There's nought beneath a power divine
  That can this roving heart confine.

3. Jesus! to thee I would return,
  And, at thy feet repenting, mourn,
  There let me view thy pardoning love,
  And never from thy sight remove.

4. Oh! let thy love, with sweet control,
  Bind all the passions of my soul;
  Bid every earthly charm depart,
  And dwell for ever in my heart.

458. *Divinity of Christ proved by his Miracles.*

1. BEHOLD! the blind their sight receive;
  Behold! the dead awake and live;
  The dumb speak wonders, and the lame
  Leap like the hart, and bless his name.

2. Thus doth th' eternal Spirit own
  And seal the mission of his Son:
  The Father vindicates his cause,
  While he hangs bleeding on the cross.

3. He dies—the heavens in mourning stood!
  He rises, and appears a God;
  Behold the Lord, ascending high—
  No more to bleed—no more to die!

4. Hence, and for ever, from my heart
  I bid those doubts and fears depart;
  And to thy hands my soul resign,
  Which bear credentials so divine.

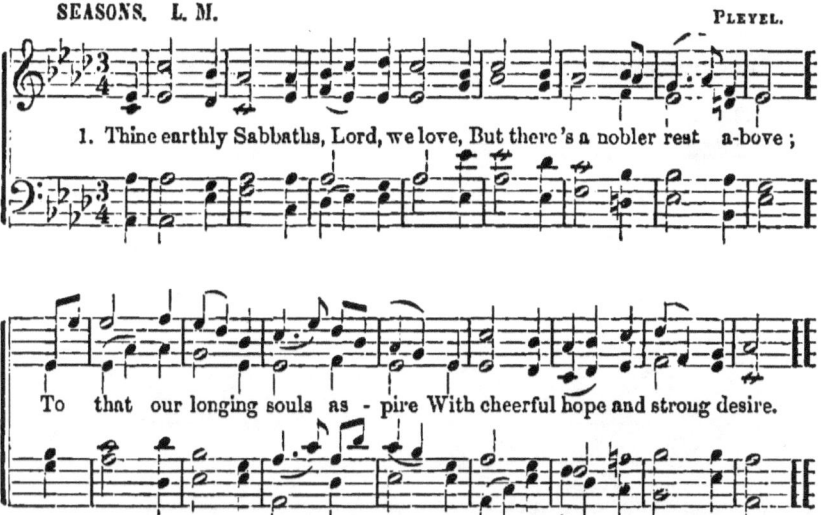

1. Thine earthly Sabbaths, Lord, we love, But there's a nobler rest a-bove;

To that our longing souls as - pire With cheerful hope and strong desire.

459. *The eternal Sabbath.*

1. THINE earthly Sabbaths, Lord, we love,
But there's a nobler rest above;
To that our longing souls aspire
With cheerful hope, and strong desire.

2. No more fatigue—no more distress,
Nor sin, nor death shall reach the place;
No groans shall mingle with the songs
Which warble from immortal tongues.

3. No rude alarms of raging foes,
No cares to break the long repose;
No midnight shade, no clouded sun,
But sacred, high, eternal noon.

4. Thine earthly Sabbaths, Lord, we love,
But there's a nobler rest above;
To that our longing souls aspire
With cheerful hope, and strong desire.

460. *The Goodness of God.*

1. THE Lord is gracious to forgive,
And slow to let his anger move;
The Lord is good to all that live,
And all his tender mercy prove.

2. Glorious in majesty art thou;
Thy throne for ever shall endure;
And angels at thy footstool bow;
Yet dost thou not despise the poor.

3. The Lord upholdeth them that fall;
He raiseth men of low degree:
O God, our health, the eyes of all—
Of all the living, wait on thee.

4. Thou openest thine exhaustless store,
And rainest food on every land;
The dumb creation thee adore,
And eat their portion from thy hand.

5. Man, most indebted, most ingrate,
Man only is a rebel here:
Teach him to know thee, ere too late;—
Teach him to love thee, and to fear

461. *Uniting with the Church.*

1. OH happy day that fixed my choice
On thee, my Saviour and my God;
Well may this glowing heart rejoice,
And tell its raptures all abroad.

2. 'Tis done, the great transaction's done,
I am my Lord's, and he is mine;
He drew me, and I followed on,
Rejoiced to own the call divine.

3. Now rest, my long divided heart,
Fixed on this blissful centre, rest;
Here have I found a nobler part,
Here, heavenly pleasures fill my breast.

EVENING HYMN. L. M.   TH. TALLIS. 1650.

1. Glo-ry to thee, my God! this night, For all the blessings of the light;

Keep me, Oh! keep me, King of kings! Beneath the sha-dow of thy wings.

462.   *Evening Song.*

1. GLORY to thee, my God, this night,
For all the blessings of the light;
Keep me, oh! keep me, King of kings!
Beneath the shadow of thy wings.

2. Forgive me, Lord! for thy dear Son,
The ill that I this day have done;
That with the world, myself, and thee,
My soul, this night, at peace may be.

3. Teach me to live, that I may dread
The grave as little as my bed;
Teach me to die, that so I may
Rise glorious, at the judgment-day.

4. Oh! may my faith on thee repose;
May gentle sleep my eyelids close,
That shall my frame more vigorous make,
To serve my God when I awake.

5. Lord! let my soul for ever share
The bliss of thy parental care;
'Tis heaven on earth, 'tis heaven above,
To see thy face, and sing thy love.

463. *Religion nothing without Love.*—1
Cor. xiii. 1, 3.

1. HAD I the tongues of Greeks and Jews,
And nobler speech than angels use,
If love be absent, I am found
Like tinkling brass, an empty sound.

2. Were I inspired to preach and tell
All that is done in heaven and hell—
Or could my faith the world remove,
Still I am nothing without love.

3. Should I distribute all my store
To feed the hungry, clothe the poor
Or give my body to the flame,
To gain a martyr's glorious name:

4. If love to God and love to men
Be absent, all my hopes are vain;
Nor tongues, nor gifts, nor fiery zeal,
The work of love can e'er fulfill.

464. *Public Worship; or, Grace and
Glory.*

1. GREAT God! attend, while Zion sings
The joy that from thy presence springs;
To spend one day with thee on earth
Exceeds a thousand days of mirth.

2. Might I enjoy the meanest place
Within thy house, O God of grace!
Not tents of ease, nor thrones of power,
Should tempt my feet to leave thy door

3. God is our sun, he makes our day;
God is our shield, he guards our way
From all th' assaults of hell and sin,
From foes without, and foes within.

4. All needful grace will God bestow,
And crown that grace with glory, too;
He gives us all things, and withholds
No real good from upright souls.

465. *Restraining Influence of the Gospel.*

1. How beautiful those rays appear,
Reflections of the gospel light,
Which make the path of virtue clear
To the bewildered wanderer's sight!

2. They warn the guilty, check the proud,
Arrest the thoughtless and the gay:
Disperse the midnight, boisterous crowd,
And take the maddening bowl away.

3. To temperance, industry, and peace,
To comfort, and to health they lead;
They bid earth's crimes and sorrows cease,
And love and happiness succeed.

4. Then let the beams resplendent shine,
Its brightest rays the gospel pour,
Till, by an influence so divine,
The reign of vice shall be no more.

466. *Chief end of Man.*—1 Cor. vi. 19–30.

1. Thou Maker of our mortal frame—
Of all thy works the noblest far,
We bow before thy righteous claim
To all we have, and all we are.

2. Our tongues were fashioned for thy word,
Our hands—to do thy will divine;
Our bodies are thy temple, Lord,
The mind's immortal powers are thine.

3. Its highest thought—to trace thy skill,
Its purest love on thee to rest,
Its noblest action of the will,
To choose thy service, and be blest.

4. Our ransomed spirits rise to thee—
Unfailing source of light and joy!
Thy love has made thy children free,
Thy praise shall life and strength employ.

5. Give grace and mercy to the end—
For we are thine and not our own:
So shall we to thy courts ascend,
And cast our crowns before thy throne.

467. *The Refuge and Defense of the Saints.*

1. God is our refuge and defense,
In trouble our unfailing aid;
Secure in his Omnipotence,
What foe can make our souls afraid?

2. Yea, though the earth's foundations rock,
And mountains down the gulf be hurled,
His people smile amid the shock—
They look beyond this transient world.

3. There is a river, pure and bright,
Whose streams make glad the heaven-ly plains,
Where, in eternity of light,
The city of our God remains.

4. Built by the word of his command,
With his unclouded presence blest,
Firm as his throne the bulwarks stand—
There is our home, our hope, our rest.

5. Thither let fervent faith aspire;
Our treasure, and our heart be there:
O for a seraph's wing of fire!
No:—for the mightier wings of prayer.

6. We reach at once that last retreat,
And range around the ransomed throng,
Fall with the elders at his feet,
Whose name alone inspires their song.

468. *Missionary Meeting.*

1. Assembled at thy great command,
Before thy face, dread King! we stand;
The voice that marshaled every star,
Has called thy people from afar.

2. We meet, through distant lands, to spread
The truth for which the martyrs bled;
Along the line, to either pole,
The thunder of thy praise to roll.

3. Our prayers assist, accept our praise,
Our hopes revive, our courage raise;
Our counsels aid, to each impart
The single eye, the faithful heart.

4. Forth with thy chosen heralds come,
Recall the wandering spirits home;
From Zion's mount send forth the sound,
To spread the spacious earth around.

Doxology.

Praise God, from whom all blessings flow;
Praise him, all creatures here below!
Praise him above, ye heavenly host!
Praise Father, Son, and Holy Ghost.

FARLAND, 8s, 7s & 4s.   KL—FF.

1. Hark! the voice of love and mercy Sounds a - loud from Cal - va - ry;

See !—it rends the rocks a - sunder—Shakes the earth—and veils the sky :

"It is fin-ished! It is fin-ished !" Hear the dy - ing Sa - viour cry.

469. *The expiring Saviour.*

1. HARK! the voice of love and mercy
Sounds aloud from Calvary;
See!—it rends the rocks asunder—
Shakes the earth—and veils the sky :
 " It is finished !"—
Hear the dying Saviour cry.

2. "It is finished !"—Oh! what pleasure
Do these charming words afford!
Heavenly blessings, without measure,
Flow to us, through Christ, the Lord:
 " It is finished !"—
Saints! the dying words record.

3. Tune your harps anew, ye seraphs!
Join to sing the pleasing theme :
All in earth and heaven, uniting,
Join to praise Immanuel's name :
 Hallelujah !—
Glory to the bleeding Lamb !

470. *Hope encouraged.*

1. O MY soul! what means this sadness?
Wherefore art thou thus cast down?
Let thy grief be turned to gladness,
 Bid thy restless fear begone;
 Look to Jesus,
And rejoice in his dear name.

2. Though ten thousand ills beset thee,
 Though thy heart is stained with sin.
Jesus lives, he 'll ne'er forget thee,
 He will make thee pure within;
 He is faithful
To perform his gracious word.

3. Though distresses now attend thee,
 And thou tread'st the thorny road;
His right hand shall still defend thee;
 Soon he 'll bring thee home to God;
 Therefore praise him,—
Praise the great Redeemer's name.

4. Oh! that I could now adore him,
 Like the heavenly host above,
Who for ever bow before him,
 And unceasing sing his love!
 Happy spirits !
When shall I your chorus join ?

GREENVILLE. 8s, 7s & 4s. ROUSSEAU.

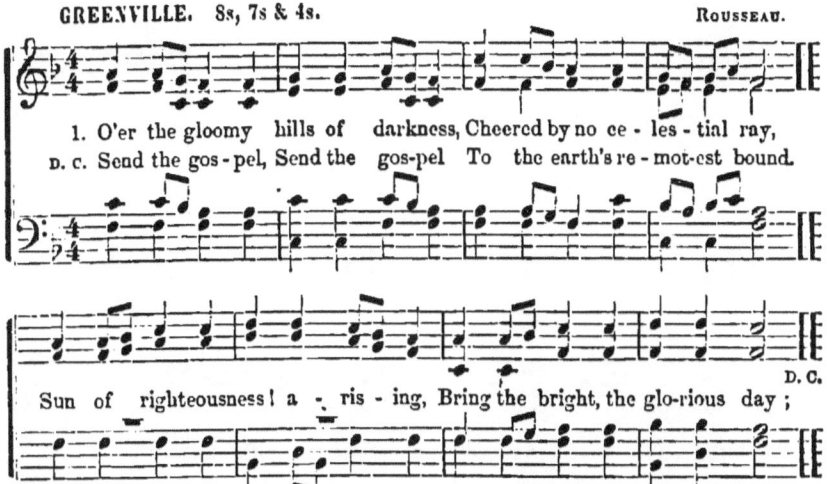

1. O'er the gloomy hills of darkness, Cheered by no ce - les - tial ray,

D. C. Send the gos - pel, Send the gos-pel To the earth's re - mot-est bound.

Sun of righteousness! a - ris - ing, Bring the bright, the glo-rious day ;

D. C.

471. *Success of the Gospel among the Heathen.*

1. O'ER the gloomy hills of darkness,
Cheered by no celestial ray,
Sun of righteousness! arising,
Bring the bright, the glorious day;
Send the gospel
To the earth's remotest bound.

2. Kingdoms wide that sit in darkness,—
Grant them, Lord! the glorious light;
And, from eastern coast to western,
May the morning chase the night;
And redemption,
Freely purchased, win the day.

3. Fly abroad, thou mighty gospel!
Win and conquer, never cease;
May thy lasting, wide dominions,
Multiply, and still increase;
Sway thy sceptre,
Saviour! all the world around.

472.

1. SINNERS, will you scorn the message,
Coming from the courts above?
Mercy beams in every passage;
Every line is full of love;
O, believe it,
Every line is full of love.

2. Now, the heralds of salvation,
Joyful news from Heaven proclaim:
Sinners freed from condemnation,
Through the all-atoning Lamb!
Life receiving
Through the all-atoning Lamb.

3. Who hath their report believéd?
Who hath heard the solemn word?
Who embraced the news of pardon,
Freely offered by the Lord?
Life immortal,
Freely offered by the Lord.

4. O ye angels, hovering round us,
Waiting spirits, speed your way,
Hasten to the court of heaven,
Tidings bear without delay:
Rebel sinners
Glad the message will obey.

473. *Dismission.*

1. LORD, dismiss us with thy blessing,
Fill our hearts with joy and peace,
Let us each, thy love possessing,
Triumph in redeeming grace:
O, refresh us,
Traveling through this wilderness.

2. Thanks we give, and adoration,
For thy gospel's joyful sound;
May the fruits of thy salvation
In our hearts and lives abound;
May thy presence
With us evermore be found.

3. Then, whene'er the signal 's given
Us from earth to call away,
Borne, on angels' wings to heaven—
Glad the summons to obey—
May we ever
Reign with Christ in endless day.

GERMAN HYMN. 7s. Single. PLEYEL.

1. An-gels! roll the rock a - way; Death! yield up thy might-y prey;

See! the Sa - viour leaves the tomb, Glow - ing with im - mor - tal bloom.

474. *Resurrection and Ascension of Christ.*

1. ANGELS! roll the rock away;
Death! yield up thy mighty prey;
See! the Saviour leaves the tomb,
Glowing with immortal bloom.

2. Hark! the wondering angels raise
Louder notes of joyful praise;
Let the earth's remotest bound
Echo with the blissful sound.

3. Now, ye saints, lift up your eyes,
See him high in glory rise!
Hosts of angels, on the road,
Hail him—the incarnate God.

4. Heaven unfolds its portals wide,
See the Conqueror through them ride!
King of glory! mount thy throne—
Boundless empire is thine own.

5. Praise him, ye celestial choirs!
Tune, and sweep your golden lyres;
Raise, O earth! your noblest songs,
From ten thousand thousand tongues.

475. *The House of Prayer and Praise.*

1. LORD of hosts, to thee we raise
Here a house of prayer and praise;
Thou thy people's hearts prepare
Here to meet for praise and prayer.

2. Let the living here be fed
With thy word, the heavenly bread;
Here, in hope of glory blest,
May the dead be laid to rest.

3. Here to thee a temple stand,
While the sea shall gird the land;
Here reveal thy mercy sure,
While the sun and moon endure.

4. Hallelujah!—earth and sky
To the joyful sound reply;
Hallelujah!—hence ascend
Prayer and praise till time shall end.

476. *Early Piety.*

1. YOUNG and happy as thou art
Not a furrow on thy brow:
Not a sorrow in thy heart,
Seek the Lord thy Maker now.

2. In its freshness bring the flower
While the dew upon it lies—
In the cool and cloudless hour
Of the morning sacrifice.

3. As the first fruits of the year
Should be offered to the Lord,
So the first fruits of the heart
On his altar should be poured.

4. Thus the blessing from above
On life's harvest shall be given;
Sown in tears, perhaps on earth,
Reaped in joyfulness in heaven.

ESHTAMOA. 7s. Single.*　　　　　　　　　　T. B. MASON.

1. Thou, from whom we nev - er part, Thou, whose love is ev - ery-where,

Thou, who see - est ev - ery heart, Lis - ten to our eve - ning prayer.

* See also the tune on the opposite page.

477.　　*Evening Hymn.*

1. THOU, from whom we never part,
　　Thou, whose love is every where,
　　Thou, who seest every heart,
　　Listen to our evening prayer.

2. Father, fill our hearts with love,
　　Love unfailing, full and free;
　　Love no injury can move,
　　Love that ever rests on thee.

3. Heavenly Father! through the night
　　Keep us safe from every ill,
　　Cheerful as the morning light
　　May we wake to do thy will.

478.　*Communion with the Triune God.*

1. IN thy presence we appear;
　　Lord! we love to worship here,
　　When, within the veil, we meet
　　Thee upon thy mercy-seat.

2. While thy glorious name is sung,
　　Touch our lips, and loose our tongue;
　　Then our joyful souls shall bless
　　Thee, the Lord, our righteousness.

3. While to thee our prayers ascend,
　　Let thine ear in love attend;
　　Hear us, for thy Spirit pleads;
　　Hear, for Jesus intercedes.

4. While thy word is heard with awe,
　　And we tremble at thy law,

Let the gospel's wondrous love
Every doubt and fear remove.

5. While thy ministers proclaim
　　Peace and pardon through thy name,
　　In their voices, let us own
　　Jesus, speaking from the throne.

6. From thy house when we return,
　　Let our hearts within us burn;
　　That at evening, we may say—
　　"We have walked with God to-day!"

479.　　*Evening Contemplation.*

1. SOFTLY, now, the light of day
　　Fades upon my sight away;
　　Free from care, from labor free,
　　Lord! I would commune with thee.

2. Soon, for me, the light of day
　　Shall for ever pass away;
　　Then, from sin and sorrow free,
　　Take me, Lord, to dwell with thee

480.　　*The good Shepherd.*

1. SHEPHERD of thy little flock,
　　Lead me to the shadowing rock,
　　Where the richest pasture grows,
　　Where the living water flows.

2. By that pure and silent stream,
　　Sheltered from the scorching beam,
　　Shepherd, Saviour, Guardian, Guide,
　　Keep me ever near thy side.

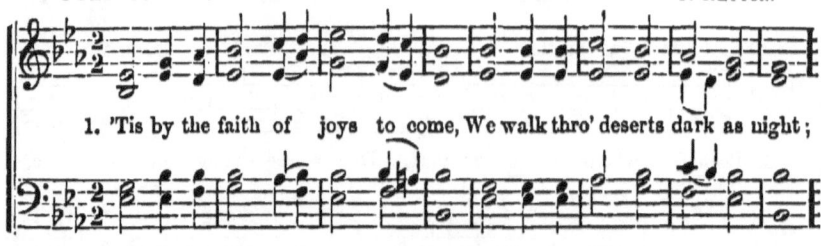

1. 'Tis by the faith of joys to come, We walk thro' deserts dark as night;

Till we ar-rive at heaven our home, Faith is our guide, and faith our light.

481. *Faith our Guide.*

1. 'Tis by the faith of joys to come,
   We walk through deserts dark as night;
   Till we arrive at heaven our home,
   Faith is our guide, and faith our light.

2. The want of sight she well supplies;
   She makes the pearly gates appear;
   Far into distant worlds she pries,
   And brings eternal glories near.

3. Cheerful we tread the desert through,
   While faith inspires a heavenly ray,
   Though lions roar, and tempests blow,
   And rocks and dangers fill the way.

4. So Abr'am, by divine command,
   Left his own house to walk with God;
   His faith beheld the promised land,
   And fired his zeal along the road.

482. *Christ's Ascension.*

1. Lord! when thou didst ascend on high,
   Ten thousand angels filled the sky;
   Those heavenly guards around thee wait,
   Like chariots that attend thy state.

2. Not Sinai's mountain could appear
   More glorious, when the Lord was there;
   While he pronounced his dreadful law,
   And struck the chosen tribes with awe.

3. How bright the triumph none can tell,
   When the rebellious powers of hell,
   That thousand souls had captive made,
   Were all in chains, like captives, led.

4. Raised by his Father to the throne,
   He sent the promised Spirit down,
   With gifts and grace for rebel men,
   That God might dwell on earth again.

483. *Christ's Kingdom among the Gentiles.*

1. Jesus shall reign where'er the sun
   Does his successive journeys run;
   His kingdom stretch from shore to shore,
   Till moons shall wax and wane no more.

2. For him shall endless prayer be made,
   And endless praises crown his head;
   His name, like sweet perfume, shall rise
   With every morning sacrifice.

3. People and realms of every tongue
   Dwell on his love with sweetest song;
   And infant voices shall proclaim
   Their early blessings on his name.

4. Blessings abound where'er he reigns,
   The prisoner leaps to loose his chains;
   The weary find eternal rest,
   And all the sons of want are blest.

5. Let every creature rise and bring
 Peculiar honors to our King;
 Angels descend with songs again,
 And earth repeat the loud amen.

484. *Creation and Redemption.*

1. NATURE, with open volume stands,
 To spread her Maker's praise abroad;
 And every labor of his hands
 Shows something worthy of a God.

2. But in the grace that rescued man,
 His brightest form of glory shines;
 Here, on the cross, 'tis fairest drawn,
 In precious blood and crimson lines.

3. O, the sweet wonders of the cross,
 Where Christ the Saviour loved and
 died;
 Her noblest life my spirit draws,
 From the dear Saviour's bleeding side.

4. I would for ever speak his name,
 In sounds to mortal ears unknown;
 With angels join to praise the Lamb,
 And worship at his Father's throne.

485. *Perfections and Providence of God.*

1. HIGH in the heavens, eternal God!
 Thy goodness in full glory shines;
 Thy truth shall break through every cloud
 That veils or darkens thy designs.

2. For ever firm thy justice stands,
 As mountains their foundations keep;
 Wise are the wonders of thy hands,
 Thy judgments are a mighty deep.

3. My God! how excellent thy grace,
 Whence all our hope, our comfort
 springs!
 The sons of Adam, in distress,
 Fly to the shadow of thy wings.

4. From the provisions of thy house,
 We shall be fed with sweet repast:
 There mercy like a river flows,
 And brings salvation to our taste.

5. Life, like a fountain, rich and free,
 Springs from the presence of my Lord;
 And, in thy light, our souls shall see
 The glories promised in thy word.

486. *The Sight of God and Christ in Heaven.*

1. DESCEND from heaven, immortal Dove,
 Stoop down, and take us on thy
 wings,—

And mount, and bear us far above
 The reach of these inferior things;

2. Beyond, beyond this lower sky,
 Up where eternal ages roll,—
 Where solid pleasures never die,
 And fruits immortal feast the soul.

3. O, for a sight, a blissful sight
 Of our almighty Father's throne!
 There sits the Saviour crowned with light,
 Clothed in a body like our own.

4. Adoring saints around him stand,
 While thrones and powers before him
 fall;
 The God shines gracious through the man,
 And sheds sweet glories on them all.

5. O what amazing joys they feel,
 While to their golden harps they sing,
 And sit on every heavenly hill,
 And spread the triumphs of their King!

487. *Conscience.*

1. MY God, I thank thee for the guide,
 Thou hast implanted in my soul,
 O'er passion's stormy waves to ride,
 And bring self-love to its control.

2. Whene'er the tempter lingers near,
 In sinful paths my soul to lure,
 Teach me that warning voice to hear;
 And in obeying keep me pure.

3. Oh, let no gilded sin deceive,
 To blind my eyes, my soul betray,
 The steadfast truth may I believe,
 And follow where it leads the way.

4. The single eye shall thus be mine,
 And light improved new light convey,
 And brighter still my path shall shine
 To portals of eternal day.

488. *Holiness and Grace.*

1. So let our lips and lives express
 The holy gospel we profess;
 So let our works and virtues shine,
 To prove the doctrine all divine.

2. Thus shall we best proclaim abroad
 The honors of our Saviour God;
 When his salvation reigns within,
 And grace subdues the power of sin.

3. Religion bears our spirits up,
 While we expect that blessèd hope,—
 The bright appearance of the Lord;—
 And faith stands leaning on his word.

REST. L. M.*
W. B. BRADBURY.

TENDERLY.

1. Asleep in Jesus! blessed sleep! From which none ev-er wakes to weep;

A calm and un-dis-turbed re-pose, Unbroken by the last of foes!

* See also ARMSTRONG 291.

489. *Sleeping in Jesus.*

1. ASLEEP in Jesus! blessed sleep!
From which none ever wakes to weep;
A calm and undisturbed repose,
Unbroken by the last of foes.

2. Asleep in Jesus! O how sweet
To be for such a slumber meet!
With holy confidence to sing
That death hath lost its venomed sting!

3. Asleep in Jesus! peaceful rest!
Whose waking is supremely blest;
No fear—no woe, shall dim that hour
That manifests the Saviour's power.

4. Asleep in Jesus! O for me
May such a blissful refuge be:
Securely shall my ashes lie,
Waiting the summons from on high.

5. Asleep in Jesus! time nor space
Debars this precious " hiding-place:"
On Indian plains, or Lapland snows,
Believers find the same repose.

6. Asleep in Jesus! far from thee
Thy kindred and their graves may be:
But there is still a blessed sleep
From which none ever wakes to weep.

490. *The Christian's parting Hour.*

1. How sweet the hour of closing day,
When all is peaceful and serene;

And the broad sun's retiring ray
Sheds a mild lustre o'er the scene !

2. Such is the Christian's parting hour—
So peacefully he sinks to rest;
When faith, endued from heaven with
power,
Strengthens and cheers his languid
breast.

3. Mark but that radiance of his eye,
That smile upon his wasted cheek
They tell us of his glory nigh,
In language which no tongue can
speak.

4. A beam from heaven is sent to cheer
The pilgrim on his gloomy road;
And angels are attending near,
To bear him to their bright abode.

5. Who would not wish to die, like those
Whom God's own Spirit deigns to
bless;
To sink into that soft repose,
Then wake to perfect happiness?

491. *Hope in Times of Darkness.*

1. WHILE I to grief my soul gave way,
To see the work of God decline,
Methought I heard the Saviour say—
" Dismiss thy fears, the ark is mine.

2. " Though for a time I hid my face,
Rely upon my love and power;

Still wrestle at the throne of grace,
And wait for a reviving hour.

3. "Take down thy long neglected harp,
I've seen thy tears, and heard thy
prayer ;
The winter season has been sharp,
But spring shall all its wastes repair."

4. Lord, I obey—my hopes revive,
Come, join with me, ye saints, and sing;
Our foes in vain against us strive,
For God will help and triumph bring.

492. *Asking divine Consolation.*

1. SWEET peace of conscience, heavenly
guest !
Come, fix thy mansion in my breast,
Dispel my doubts, my fears control,
And heal the anguish of my soul.

2. Come, smiling hope! and joy sincere !
Come, make your constant dwelling here;
Still let your presence cheer my heart,
Nor sin compel you to depart.

3. Thou God of hope and peace divine !
Oh! make these sacred pleasures mine;
Forgive my sins, my fears remove,
And send the tokens of thy love.

4. Then should mine eyes, without a tear,
See death, with all its terrors, near,
My heart should then in death rejoice,
And raptures tune my faltering voice.

493. *A Penitent pleading for Pardon.*

1. SHOW pity, Lord, O Lord, forgive ;
Let a repenting rebel live :
Are not thy mercies large and free ?
May not a sinner trust in thee ?

2. O wash my soul from every sin,
And make my guilty conscience clean;
Here on my heart the burden lies,
And past offences pain my eyes.

3. My lips with shame my sins confess,
Against thy law, against thy grace:
Lord, should thy judgment grow severe,
I am condemned, but thou art clear.

4. Should sudden vengeance seize my
breath,
I must pronounce thee just in death;
And if my soul were sent to hell,
Thy righteous law approves it well.

5. Yet save a trembling sinner, Lord,
Whose hope, still hovering round thy
word,

Would light on some sweet promise there,
Some sure support against despair.

494. *Prayer for spiritual Enjoyment.*

1. COME, holy Spirit ! calm my mind,
And fit me to approach my God ;
Remove each vain, each worldly thought,
And lead me to thy blest abode.

2. Hast thou imparted to my soul
A living spark of holy fire ?
Oh ! kindle now the sacred flame ;
Make me to burn with pure desire.

3. A brighter faith and hope impart,
And let me now my Saviour see ;
Oh ! soothe and cheer my burdened heart,
And bid my spirit rest in thee.

495. *Triumph over the Grave.*

1. WHEN I the holy grave survey,
Where once my Saviour deigned to lie,
I see fulfilled what prophets say,
And all the power of death defy.

2. This empty tomb shall now proclaim
How weak the bands of conquered
death ;
Sweet pledge that all who trust his name
Shall rise and draw immortal breath.

3. Though in the dust I lay my head,
Yet, gracious God ! thou wilt not leave
My flesh for ever with the dead,
Nor lose thy children in the grave.

496. *Not ashamed of Christ*

1. JESUS ! and shall it ever be—
A mortal man ashamed of thee ?—
Ashamed of thee, whom angels praise,
Whose glories shine thro' endless days ?

2. Ashamed of Jesus ! sooner far
Let evening blush to own a star ;
He sheds the beams of light divine
O'er this benighted soul of mine.

3. Ashamed of Jesus—that dear friend
On whom my hopes of heaven depend ?
No ;—when I blush, be this my shame—
That I no more revere his name.

4. Ashamed of Jesus ?—yes, I may,
When I've no guilt to wash away—
No tear to wipe—no good to crave—
No fears to quell—no soul to save.

5. Till then—nor is my boasting vain—
Till then, I boast a Saviour slain !
And oh ! may this my glory be—
That Christ is not ashamed of me.

THE PASSION. C. M.

FROM THE "SELAH."

WITH VARIED EXPRESSION.

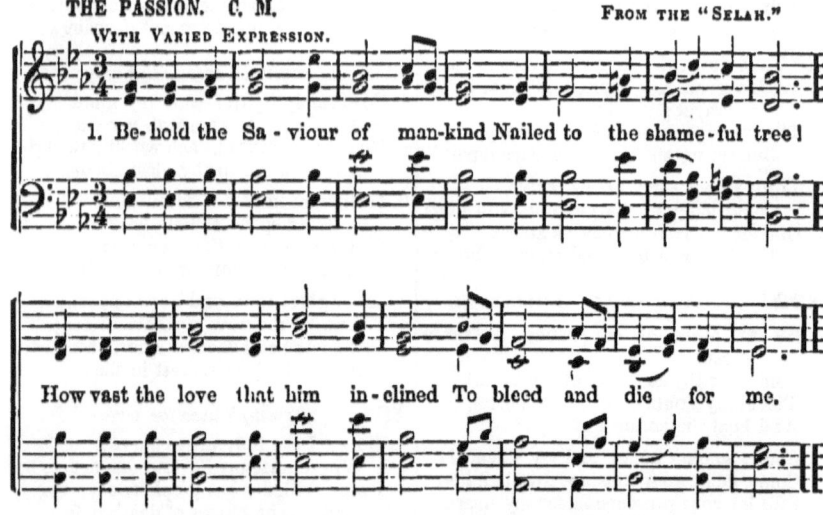

1. Be-hold the Sa - viour of man-kind Nailed to the shame-ful tree!

How vast the love that him in-clined To bleed and die for me.

497. *Crucifixion.*

1. BEHOLD the Saviour of mankind
Nailed to the shameful tree!
How vast the love that him inclined
To bleed and die for me!

2. Hark! how he groans, while nature shakes,
And earth's strong pillars bend!
The temple's vail asunder breaks,
The solid marbles rend.

3. 'Tis finished! now the ransom 's paid,
"Receive my soul!" he cries:
See—how he bows his sacred head!
He bows his head and dies!

4. But soon he 'll break death's iron chain,
And in full glory shine;
O Lamb of God! was ever pain—
Was ever love like thine?

498. *Christ at the Door.*

1. BEHOLD he standeth at the door
Of thy reluctant heart,
He who thy guilt in anguish bore;
And must he now depart?

2. It is the Lord of boundless might
Descended from above;
It is the Son of God's delight
Who seeks to win thy love.

3. It is the blest incarnate God;
Open to him and live!
Too long hast thou his love withstood—
Why still his Spirit grieve?

4. Open to him; with thee he'll dwell,
Thy spirit to control,
The joy of heaven to thee reveal,
And feed thy famished soul.

5. Open to him, nor longer wait:
Sinner, why still delay?
A moment hence may be too late—
Grieve not thy God away!

499. *Watchfulness.*

1. O FOR a principle within
Of jealous, godly fear;
A sensibility to sin,
A pain to feel it near.

2. O for the first approach to feel
Of pride, or fond desire;
To catch the wandering of my will,
And quench the kindling fire.

3. From thee that I no more may part,
No more thy goodness grieve,
The filial awe, the fleshly heart,
The tender conscience, give.

4. Quick as the apple of an eye,
O God, my conscience make!
Awake my soul when sin is nigh,
And keep it still awake.

500. *Benefit of Affliction.*

1. CONSIDER all my sorrows, Lord!
And thy deliverance send;
My soul for thy salvation faints;
When will my troubles end?

2. Yet I have found, 'tis good for me
To bear my Father's rod;
Afflictions make me learn thy law,
And live upon my God.

3. Had not thy word been my delight,
When earthly joys were fled,
My soul, oppressed with sorrow's weight,
Had sunk among the dead.

4. I know thy judgments, Lord! are right,
Though they may seem severe;
The sharpest sufferings I endure
Flow from thy faithful care.

5. Before I knew thy chastening rod,
My feet were apt to stray;
But now I learn to keep thy word,
Nor wander from thy way.

501. *New Year. Prayer for a Blessing.*

1. Now, gracious Lord, thy arm reveal,
And make thy glory known;
Now let us all thy presence feel,
And soften hearts of stone.

2. From all the guilt of former sin
May mercy set us free;
And let the year we now begin,
Begin and end with thee.

3. Send down thy Spirit from above,
That saints may love thee more;
And sinners now may learn to love,
Who never loved before.

4. And when before thee we appear,
In our eternal home,
May growing numbers worship here,
And praise thee in our room.

502. *Goodness of Providence.*

1. LET every tongue thy goodness speak,
Thou sovereign Lord of all!
Thy strengthening hands uphold the weak,
And raise the poor who fall.

2. When sorrow bows the spirit down,
Or virtue lies distressed
Beneath some proud oppressor's frown,
Thou givest the mourners rest.

3. The Lord supports our tottering days,
And guides our giddy youth:
Holy and just are all his ways,
And all his words are truth.

4. He knows the pain his servants feel,
He hears his children cry;
And, their best wishes to fulfill,
His grace is ever nigh.

5. His mercy never shall remove
From men of heart sincere;
He saves the souls, whose humble love
Is joined with holy fear.

6. My lips shall dwell upon his praise,
And spread his fame abroad;
Let all the sons of Adam raise
The honors of their God.

503. *The Mercies of God.*

1. LORD! when I count thy mercies o'er,
They strike me with surprise;
Not all the sands, that spread the shore,
To equal numbers rise.

2. My flesh, with fear and wonder, stands,
The product of thy skill;
And hourly blessings, from thy hands,
Thy thoughts of love reveal.

3. These on my heart by night I keep;
How kind, how dear to me!
Oh! may the hour that ends my sleep
Still find my thoughts with thee.

504. *Presence of the Spirit.*

1. THE Holy Comforter has come—
We feel his presence here—
Our hearts would now no longer roam,
But bow in filial fear.

2. This breathing tenderness of love,
This hush of solemn power;
'Tis heaven descending from above,
To fill this favored hour.

3. Earth's cares and darkness all have fled,
Heaven's light serenely shines,
And every heart, divinely led,
To earnest thought inclines.

4. How excellent the truth appears,
How sweet the song we raise!
Ee'n grief sits smiling in her tears,
And lifts her soul in praise.

5. No more let sin our hearts deceive,
Nor earthly cares betray,
Oh let us never, never grieve
The Comforter away.

SIDMOUTH. 7s. 6 lines.　　　　　　　　Rev. Dr. Malan.

TENDERLY.

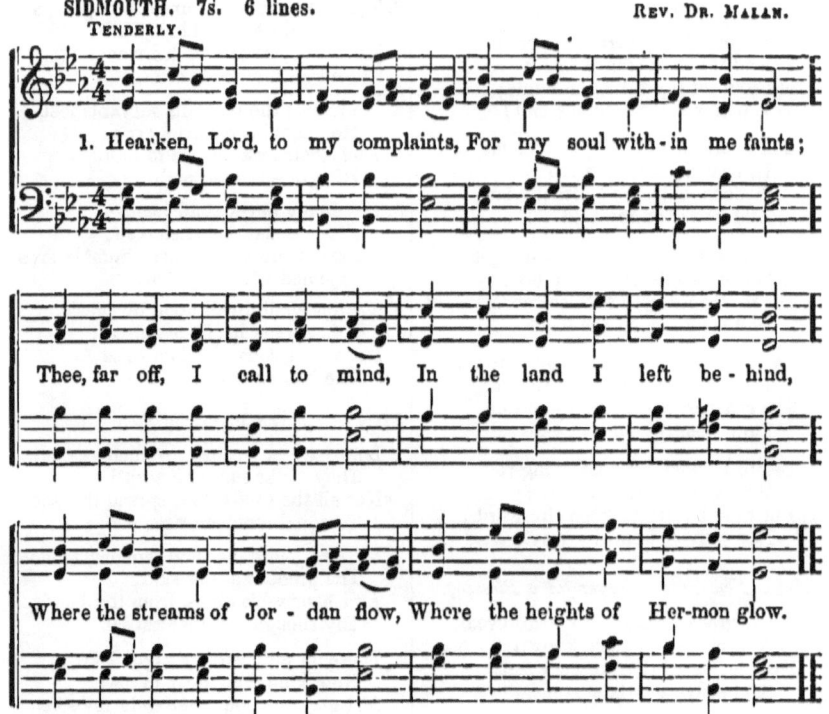

1. Hearken, Lord, to my complaints, For my soul with-in me faints;

Thee, far off, I call to mind, In the land I left be - hind,

Where the streams of Jor - dan flow, Where the heights of Her-mon glow.

505. *Prayer and Hope in Affliction.*

1. HEARKEN, Lord! to my complaints,
For my soul within me faints;
Thee, far off, I call to mind,
In the land I left behind,
Where the streams of Jordan flow,
Where the heights of Hermon glow.

2. Tempest-tossed, my failing bark
Founders on the ocean dark;
Deep to deep around me calls,
With the rush of waterfalls;
While I plunge to lower caves,
Overwhelmed by all thy waves.

3. Once the morning's earliest light
Brought thy mercy to my sight,
And my wakeful song was heard
Later than the evening bird;
Hast thou all my prayers forgot?
Dost thou scorn, or hear them not?

4. Why, my soul! art thou perplexed?
Why with faithless troubles vexed?
Hope in God, whose saving name

Thou shalt joyfully proclaim,
When his countenance shall shine
Through the clouds that darken thine.

506.　　*The Child-like Temper.*

1. QUIET, Lord! my froward heart;
Make me teachable and mild,
Upright, simple, free from art;
Make me as a weaned child;
From distrust and envy free,
Pleased with all that pleases thee.

2. What thou shalt to-day provide,
Let me as a child receive;
What to-morrow may betide,
Calmly to thy wisdom leave:
'Tis enough that thou wilt care;
Why should I the burden bear?

3. As a little child relies
On a care beyond its own,
Knows he's neither strong nor wise,
Fears to move one step alone—
Let me thus with thee abide,
As my Father, Guard, and Guide.

4. Thus preserved from Satan's wiles,
Safe from dangers, free from fears;
May I live upon thy smiles,
Till the promised hour appears,
When the sons of God shall prove
All their Father's boundless love.

507. *Repentance at the Cross of Christ.*

1. HEARTS of stone! relent, relent,
Break, by Jesus' cross subdued;
See his body, mangled, rent,
Covered with a gore of blood!
Sinful soul! what hast thou done!
Crucified God's only Son!

2. Yes, thy sins have done the deed,
Driven the nails that fixed him there,
Crowned with thorns his sacred head,
Pierced him with the bloody spear,
Made his soul a sacrifice—
While for sinful man he dies.

3. Wilt thou let him bleed in vain—
Still to death thy Lord pursue?
Open all his wounds again—
And the shameful cross renew?
No;—with all my sins I'll part,
Break, oh! break, my bleeding heart!

508. *Privileges of Adoption.*

1. BLESSÉD are the sons of God;
They are bought with Jesus' blood;
They are ransomed from the grave—
Life eternal they shall have:
With them numbered may we be,
Here, and in eternity.

2. They are justified by grace,
They enjoy the Saviour's peace;
All their sins are washed away;
They shall stand in God's great day:
With them numbered may we be,
Here, and in eternity.

3. They produce the fruits of grace,
In the works of righteousness;
They are harmless, meek, and mild,
Holy, blameless, undefiled:
With them numbered may we be,
Here, and in eternity.

4. They are lights upon the earth,
Children of a heavenly birth;
One with God, with Jesus one;
Glory is in them begun:
With them numbered may we be,
Here, and in eternity.

509. *Prayer.*

1. WHEN the heart, oppressed with grief,
Feels its light and strength decay,
When the night is vexed with sighs,
When sad tears obscure the day,
Turn, O turn thy soul to prayer,
Trust thee in thy Saviour's care.

2. Pray not as the heathen pray,
Speaking many a heartless word,
God, thy Father, sees each tear,
Every sigh by him is heard;
Pray with heart, and soul, and thought,
As the Lord, our Saviour, taught.

3. Father, hallowed be thy name,
Let thy glorious kingdom come—
Rule in heaven and earth the same,
Let thy holy will be done;
Daily bread to us impart,
Give an humble, grateful heart.

4. Pardon all our trespasses,
As we injuries forgive;
Lead us from temptation's paths,
Far from evil may we live;
Thine the kingdom, thine the power,
Thine the glory, evermore.

510. *"Return unto thy rest, O my soul."*

1. WEARY, Lord, of struggling here
With this constant doubt and fear,
Burdened by the pains I bear,
And the trials I must share—
Help me, Lord, again to flee
To the rest that's found in thee.

2. Weakened by the wayward will
Which controls, yet cheats me still;
Seeking something undefined
With an earnest, darkened mind—
Help me, Lord, again to flee
To the light that breaks from thee.

3. Fettered by this earthly scope
In the reach and aim of hope,
Fixing thought in narrow bound
Where no living truth is found—
Help me, Lord, again to flee
To the hope that's fixed in thee.

4. Fettered, burdened, wearied, weak,
Lord, once more thy grace I seek;
Turn, O turn me not away,
Help me, Lord, to watch and pray—
That I never more may flee
From the rest that's found in thee.

ESSEX. S. M.   Arr. from "SELAH."

1. Let those ce-les-tial themes In sweet-est num-bers flow,

And let no fad-ing, earth-born dreams Their spell a-round you throw.

511. *Characteristics of Praise.*

1. LET those celestial themes
    In sweetest numbers flow,
And let no fading, earth-born dreams
    Their spell around you throw.

2. In gentlest accents tell
    Of mysteries unseen;
While waves of music softly swell,
    Impressive and serene.

3. Let sweet affection rise
    Upon the wings of song;
Ascending far above the skies,
    Where noblest strains belong.

4. Let no ambitious thought,
    Or purpose of display,
Or envious wish be hither brought,
    To lead the heart astray.

5. While ye are called to stand
    On consecrated ground,
The holy service may command
    Rich harmony of sound.

6. But let no thoughtless strain
    Employ the trembling lyre,
For all the chords are swept in vain,
    Where burns no hallowed fire.

512. *Prayer for Spiritual Light.*

1. WE lift our hearts to thee,
    Thou Day Star from on high!
The sun itself is but thy shade,
    Yet cheers both earth and sky.

2. Oh! let thy rising beams
    Dispel the shades of night;
And let the glories of thy love
    Come, like the morning light.

3. How beauteous nature now!
    How dark and sad before!—
With joy we view the pleasing change,
    And nature's God adore.

4. May we this life improve,
    To mourn for errors past;
And live, this short, revolving day,
    As if it were our last.

513.   *Saturday Evening.*

1. THE hours of evening close;
    Its lengthened shadows, drawn
O'er scenes of earth, invite repose,
    And wait the Sabbath dawn.

2. So let its calm prevail
    O'er forms of outward care;
Nor thought for " many things" assail
    The still retreat of prayer.

3. Our guardian Shepherd near
    His watchful eye will keep;
And, safe from violence and fear,
    Will fold his flock to sleep.

4. So may a holier light
    Than earth's our spirits rouse,
And call us, strengthened by his might,
    To pay the Lord our vows.

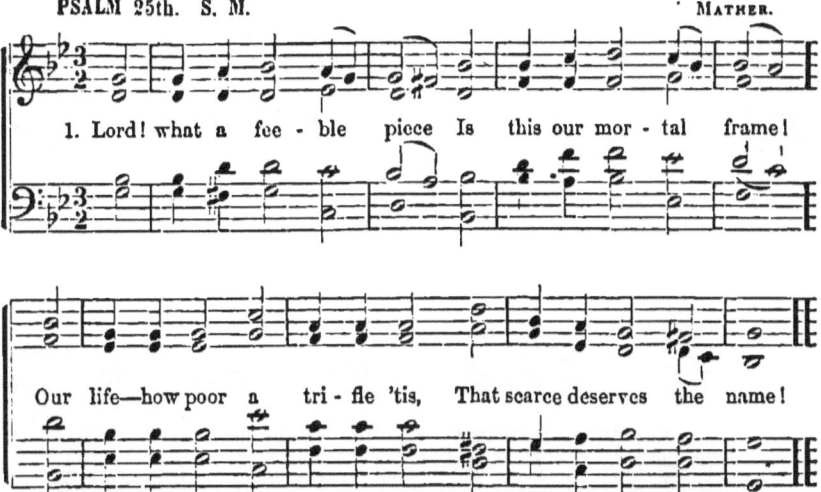

1. Lord! what a fee - ble piece Is this our mor - tal frame!

Our life—how poor a tri - fle 'tis, That scarce deserves the name!

514. *The Frailty and Shortness of Life.*

1. LORD! what a feeble piece
    Is this our mortal frame!
Our life—how poor a trifle 'tis,
    That scarce deserves the name!

2. Alas the brittle clay,
    That built our body first!
And, every month, and every day,
    'Tis mouldering back to dust.

3. Our moments fly apace,
    Nor will our minutes stay;
Just like a flood, our hasty days
    Are sweeping us away.

4. Well, if our days must fly,
    We'll keep their end in sight;
We'll spend them all in wisdom's way,
    And let them speed their flight.

5. They'll waft us sooner o'er
    This life's tempestuous sea:
Soon shall we reach the peaceful shore
    Of blest eternity.

515.   *Safety in God.*

1. WHEN overwhelmed with grief,
    My heart within me dies;
Helpless, and far from all relief,
    To heaven I lift mine eyes.

2. O lead me to the Rock,
    That's high above my head;
And make the covert of thy wings
    My shelter and my shade.

3. Within thy presence, Lord,
    For ever I'll abide;
Thou art the tower of my defense,
    The refuge where I hide.

4. Thou givest me the lot
    Of those that fear thy name;
If endless life be their reward,
    I shall possess the same.

516. *Waiting for Pardon and Direction.*

1. I LIFT my soul to God,
    My trust is in his name;
Let not my foes that seek my blood
    Still triumph in my shame.

2. From the first dawning light
    Till the dark evening rise,
For thy salvation, Lord! I wait
    With ever-longing eyes.

3. Remember all thy grace,
    And lead me in thy truth;
Forgive the sins of riper days,
    And follies of my youth.

4. The Lord is just and kind,
    The meek shall learn his ways;
And every humble sinner find
    The methods of his grace.

5. For his own goodness' sake
    He saves my soul from shame;
He pardons, though my guilt be great,
    Through my Redeemer's name.

DUNDEE. C. M.*

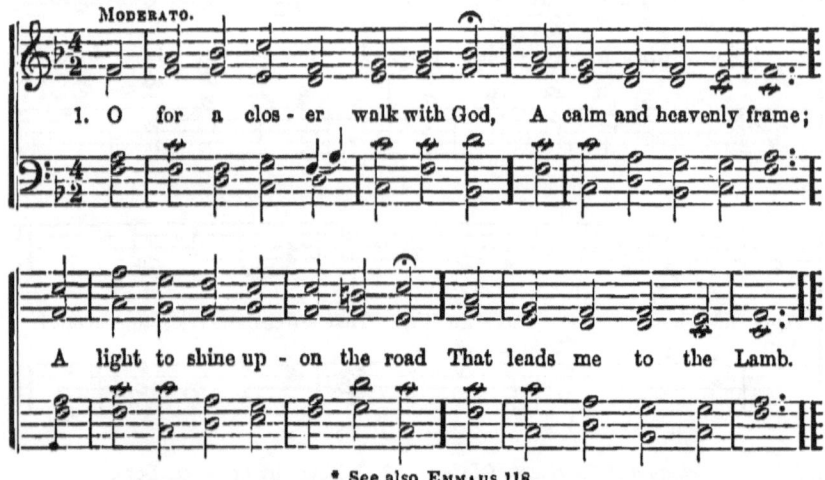

* See also EMMAUS 118.

517. *Sin and Darkness deplored.*

1. O FOR a closer walk with God,
A calm and heavenly frame;
A light to shine upon the road
That leads me to the Lamb.

2. Where is the blessedness I knew
When first I saw the Lord?
Where is the soul-refreshing view
Of Jesus and his word?

3. What peaceful hours I once enjoyed;
How sweet their memory still!
But they have left an aching void
The world can never fill.

4. Return, O holy Dove, return,
Sweet messenger of rest!
I hate the sins that made thee mourn,
And drove thee from my breast.

5. The dearest idol I have known—
Whate'er that idol be—
Help me to tear it from thy throne,
And worship only thee.

6. So shall my walk be close with God—
Calm and serene my frame;
So purer light shall mark the road
That leads me to the Lamb.

518. *Breathing after the Holy Spirit.*

1. COME, Holy Spirit, heavenly Dove!
With all thy quickening powers;

Kindle a flame of sacred love
In these cold hearts of ours.

2. Look— how we grovel here below,
Fond of these trifling toys!
Our souls can neither fly nor go,
To reach eternal joys.

3. In vain we tune our formal songs,
In vain we strive to rise;
Hosannas languish on our tongues,
And our devotion dies.

4. Dear Lord! and shall we ever live,
At this poor dying rate,
Our love so faint, so cold to thee,
And thine to us so great?

5. Come, Holy Spirit, heavenly Dove!
With all thy quickening powers;
Come, shed abroad a Saviour's love,
And that shall kindle ours.

519. *Remembrance of Christ.*

1. JESUS! thy love shall we forget,
And never bring to mind
The grace that paid our hopeless debt,
And bade us pardon find.

2. Shall we thy life of grief forget,
Thy fasting and thy prayer?
Thy locks with mountain vapors wet,
To save us from despair?

3. Gethsemane can we forget—
Thy struggling agony—
When night lay dark on Olivet,
And none to watch with thee ?

4. Our sorrows and our sins were laid
On thee, alone on thee :
Thy precious blood our ransom paid—
Thine all the glory be !

5. Life's brightest joys we may forget—
Our kindred cease to love ;
But he who paid our hopeless debt,
Our constancy shall prove.

520. *Light and Glory of the Word.*

1. THE Spirit breathes upon the word,
And brings the truth to sight ;
Precepts and promises afford
A sanctifying light.

2. A glory gilds the sacred page,
Majestic, like the sun ;
It gives a light to every age,
It gives—but borrows none.

3. The Hand that gave it still supplies
The gracious light and heat ;
His truths upon the nations rise,—
They rise, but never set.

4. Let everlasting thanks be thine,
For such a bright display,
As makes a world of darkness shine
With beams of heavenly day.

5. My soul rejoices to pursue
The steps of him I love,
Till glory breaks upon my view,
In brighter worlds above.

521. *Lord's Supper.*

1. IF human kindness meets return,
And owns the grateful tie ;
If tender thoughts within us burn,
To feel a friend is nigh.

2. Oh ! shall not warmer accents tell
The gratitude we owe
To Him, who died our fears to quell,
Our more than orphan's woe ?

3. While yet his anguished soul surveyed
Those pangs he would not flee,
What love his latest words displayed !
"Meet and remember me."

4. Remember thee ! thy death, thy shame,
Our sinful hearts to share !
Oh, memory ! leave no other name
But His recorded there.

522. *Christ's Compassion to the Weak.*

1. WITH joy we meditate the grace
Of our High Priest above ;
His heart is made of tenderness,
His bowels melt with love.

2. Touched with a sympathy within,
He knows our feeble frame ;
He knows what sore temptations mean,
For he has felt the same.

3. But spotless, innocent, and pure,
The great Redeemer stood ;
While Satan's fiery darts he bore,
And did resist to blood.

4. He, in the days of feeble flesh,
Poured out his cries and tears ;
And, in his measure, feels afresh
What every member bears.

5. Then let our humble faith address
His mercy and his power ;
We shall obtain delivering grace
In the distressing hour.

523. *Prayer for Missions.*

1. GREAT God ! the nations of the earth
Are by creation thine ;
And in thy works, from nature's birth,
Thy radiant glories shine.

2. But, Lord ! thy greater love hath sent
Thy gospel to our race ;
Unveiling thy divine intent
Of rich, redeeming grace.

3. Soon may these gracious tidings roll
The spacious earth around,
Till every tribe and every soul
Shall hear the joyful sound.

4. Then, to her sable sons conveyed,
Shall Afric learn thy word ;
And vassals, long-enslaved, become
The freemen of the Lord.

5. When shall the scattered wanderers
meet,
That now in darkness rove,
And, gathered round Immanuel's feet,
Sing of his saving love ?

6. O Lord ! each faithful effort own,
To spread the gospel rays ;
And rear, on sins's demolished throne,
The temples of thy praise.

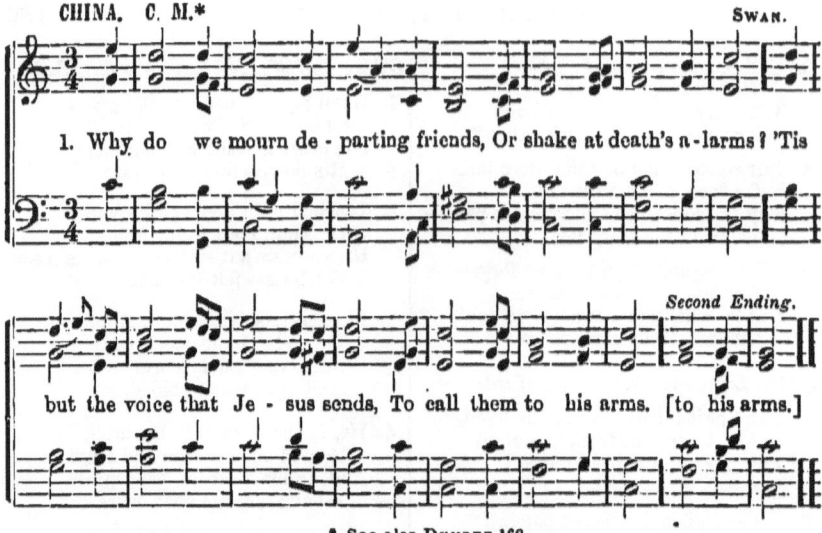

CHINA. C. M.*

SWAN.

1. Why do we mourn de-parting friends, Or shake at death's a-larms? 'Tis but the voice that Je-sus sends, To call them to his arms. [to his arms.]

Second Ending.

* See also DUNDEE 168.

524. *Comfort in the Death of Friends.*

1. Why do we mourn departing friends,
Or shake at death's alarms?
'Tis but the voice that Jesus sends,
To call them to his arms.

2. Are we not tending upward, too,
As fast as time can move?
Nor should we wish the hours more slow,
To keep us from our love.

3. Why should we tremble, to convey
Their bodies to the tomb?
There the dear flesh of Jesus lay,
And left a long perfume.

4. The graves of all the saints he blessed,
And softened every bed:
Where should the dying members rest,
But with their dying Head?

5. Thence he arose, ascended high,
And showed our feet the way;
Up to the Lord his saints shall fly,
At the great rising day.

6. Then let the last loud trumpet sound,
And bid our kindred rise;
Awake, ye nations underground!
Ye saints! ascend the skies.

525. *Everlasting Absence of God intolerable.*

1. That awful day will surely come,
Th' appointed hour makes haste—

When I must stand before my Judge,
And pass the solemn test.

2. Thou lovely Chief of all my joys!
Thou Sovereign of my heart!
How could I bear to hear thy voice
Pronounce the sound—Depart!

3. Oh! wretched state of deep despair—
To see my God remove,
And fix my doleful station, where
I must not taste his love!

4. Jesus! I throw my arms around,
And hang upon thy breast;
Without one gracious smile from thee,
My spirit can not rest.

526. *The Grave peaceful.*

1. How still and peaceful is the grave,
Where—life's vain tumults past—
Th' appointed house, by heaven's decree,
Receives us all at last!

2. The wicked there from troubling cease,
Their passions rage no more;
And there the weary pilgrim rests
From all the toils he bore.

3. All, leveled by the hand of death,
Lie sleeping in the tomb,
Till God, in judgment, call them forth
To meet their final doom.

ANGELLO. C. M.
MODERATO AFFETTUOSO.

GERMAN COLL.

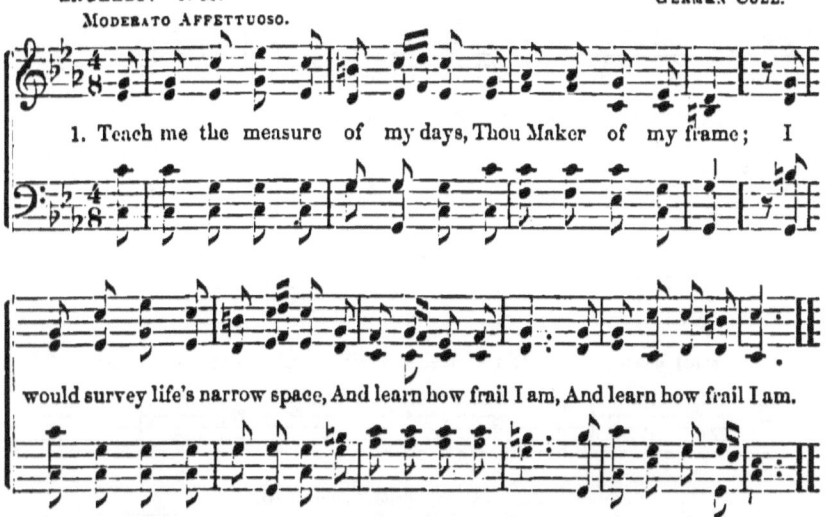

1. Teach me the measure of my days, Thou Maker of my frame; I would survey life's narrow space, And learn how frail I am, And learn how frail I am.

527. *The Vanity of Man.*

1. TEACH me the measure of my days,
Thou Maker of my frame;
I would survey life's narrow space,
And learn how frail I am.

2. A span is all that we can boast,
An inch or two of time;
Man is but vanity and dust,
In all his flower and prime.

3. What should I wish, or wait for then,
From creatures, earth, and dust?
They make our expectations vain,
And disappoint our trust.

4. Now I forbid my carnal hope,
My fond desires recall;
I give my mortal interest up,
And make my God my all.

528. *The Death of a young Person.*

1. WHEN blooming youth is snatched away
By death's resistless hand,
Our hearts the mournful tribute pay,
Which pity must demand.

2. While pity prompts the rising sigh,
O, may this truth, impressed
With awful power, "I, too, must die,"
Sink deep in every breast.

3. Let this vain world engage no more;
Behold the opening tomb;

It bids us seize the present hour:
To-morrow death may come.

4. O, let us fly—to Jesus fly,
Whose powerful arm can save;
Then shall our hopes ascend on high,
And triumph o'er the grave.

529. *Human Frailty ; or, the closing Year.*

1. THEE we adore, eternal Name,
And humbly own to thee,
How feeble is our mortal frame,
What dying worms are we.

2. The year rolls round, and steals away
The breath at first it gave;
Whate'er we do, where'er we be,
We're traveling to the grave.

3. Great God! on what a slender thread
Hang everlasting things—
Th' eternal state of all the dead,
Upon life's feeble strings.

4. Infinite joy or endless woe
Attends on every breath!
And yet how unconcerned we go,
Upon the brink of death!

5. Waken, O Lord, our drowsy sense,
To walk this dangerous road:
And if our souls be hurried hence,
May they be found with God.

1. Earth's storm-y night will soon be o'er, The rag-ing wind shall cease; The Chris-tian's bark will reach the shore Of heaven's e-ter-nal peace. [And ter-rors take their flight.]

Coda for last verse.

* See also ROMBERG 216.

530.   *Earth receding.*

1. EARTH'S stormy night will soon be o'er,
  The raging wind shall cease—
The Christian's bark will reach the shore
  Of heaven's eternal peace.

2. E'en now, the distant rays appear
  To chase the gloom of night;
The Sun of Righteousness is near,
  And terrors take their flight.

531.   *A Look from the Cross.*

1. I SAW One hanging on a tree,
  In agony and blood,
Who fixed his languid eyes on me,
  As near the cross I stood.

2. Sure, never to my latest breath
  Can I forget that look;
It seemed to charge me with his death,
  Though not a word he spoke.

3. Alas, I knew not what I did,
  But all my tears were vain;
Where could my trembling soul be hid,
  For I the Lord had slain.

4. A second look he gave, which said,
  "I freely all forgive;
This blood is for thy ransom paid;
  I die, that thou may'st live."

5. "Thus while my death thy sin displays
  In all its blackest hue;
Such is the mystery of grace,
  It seals thy pardon, too!"

532.   *Seeking God.*

1. AUTHOR of good! to thee we turn;
  Thine ever-wakeful eye
Alone can all our wants discern,
  Thy hand alone supply.

2. Oh! let thy love within us dwell,
  Thy fear our footsteps guide;
That love shall vainer loves expel—
  That fear, all fears beside.

3. Not what we wish—but what we want,
  Let mercy still supply;
The good we ask not, Father! grant;
  The ill we ask—deny.

533. *The Moment after Death.*

1. In vain the fancy strives to paint
 The moment after death,
 The glories that surround a saint
 When yielding up his breath.

2. One gentle sigh the bondage breaks;
 We scarce can say he's gone,
 Before the willing spirit takes
 Its mansion near the throne.

3. Faith strives, but all its efforts fail
 To trace the spirit's flight;
 No eye can pierce within the veil
 Which hides the world of light.

4. Thus much, and 'tis enough to know,
 Saints are completely blest;
 Have done with sin, and care, and woe,
 And with their Saviour rest.

5. On harps of gold they praise his name,
 And see him face to face;
 Oh let us catch the heavenly flame,
 And live in his embrace!

534. *Penitence.*

1. Prostrate, dear Jesus, at thy feet,
 A guilty rebel lies;
 And upwards to thy mercy-seat
 Presumes to lift his eyes.

2. Let not thy justice frown me hence:
 Oh! stay the vengeful storm:
 Forbid it, that Omnipotence
 Should crush a feeble worm.

3. If tears of sorrow could suffice
 To pay the debt I owe,
 Tears should from both my weeping eyes
 In ceaseless currents flow.

4. But no such sacrifice I plead
 To expiate my guilt;
 No tears, but those which thou hast shed,
 No blood, but thou hast spilt.

5. Think of thy sorrows, dearest Lord,
 And all my sins forgive;
 Then Justice will approve the word
 That bids the sinner live.

535. *Pardon and Sanctification in Christ.*

1. How sad our state by nature is!
 Our sin—how deep it stains!
 And Satan binds our captive minds
 Fast in his slavish chains.

2. But there's a voice of sovereign grace,
 Sounds from the sacred word;—

"Ho! ye despairing sinners! come,
 And trust upon the Lord."

3. My soul obeys th' Almighty call,
 And runs to this relief;
 I would believe thy promise, Lord!
 Oh! help my unbelief.

4. To the dear fountain of thy blood,
 Incarnate God! I fly;
 Here let me wash my spotted soul
 From stains of deepest dye.

5. A guilty, weak, and helpless worm,
 On thy kind arms I fall;
 Be thou my strength and righteousness,
 My Jesus, and my all.

536. *Penitence and Hope.*

1. Dear Saviour! when my thoughts re-
 The wonders of thy grace, [call
 Low at thy feet ashamed I fall,
 And hide this wretched face.

2. Oh! while I breathe to thee, my Lord!
 The penitential sigh,
 Confirm the kind, forgiving word,
 With pity in thine eye.

3. Then shall the mourner, at thy feet,
 Rejoice to seek thy face;
 And grateful own—how kind, how
 sweet,
 Thy condescending grace.

537. *The Necessity of renewing Grace.*

1. How helpless guilty nature lies,
 Unconscious of its load!
 The heart, unchanged, can never rise
 To happiness and God.

2. Can aught, beneath a power divine,
 The stubborn will subdue?
 'Tis thine, eternal Spirit! thine,
 To form the heart anew.

3. 'Tis thine, the passions to recall,
 And upward bid them rise;
 To make the scales of error fall
 From reason's darkened eyes;—

4. To chase the shades of death away,
 And bid the sinner live;
 A beam of heaven—a vital ray,
 'Tis thine alone to give.

5. Oh! change these wretched hearts of
 And give them life divine; [ours,
 Then shall our passions and our powers,
 Almighty Lord! be thine.

MAESTOSO.

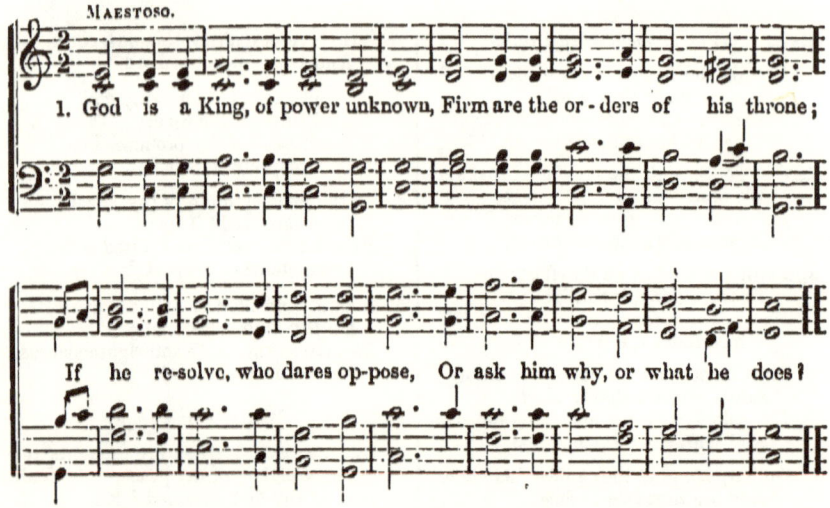

1. God is a King, of power unknown, Firm are the or-ders of his throne;

If he re-solve, who dares op-pose, Or ask him why, or what he does?

538. *God the Sovereign Ruler.*

1. GOD is a King of power unknown,
Firm are the orders of his throne,
If he resolve, who dares oppose,
Or ask him why, or what he does!

2. He wounds the heart, or makes it whole,
He calms the tempest of the soul;
When he shuts up in long despair,
Who can remove the heavy bar?

3. He frowns, and darkness veils the moon,
The fainting sun grows dim at noon,
The pillars of heaven's starry roof
Tremble and start at his reproof.

4. He gave the vaulted heaven its form,
His voice can raise the angry storm,
He swells the billows with his breath,
And whelms the sons of pride in death!

5. These are a portion of his ways;
But who shall dare describe his face?
Who can endure his light, or stand
Beneath the thunders of his hand?

539. *The Operations of the Holy Spirit.*

1. ETERNAL Spirit! we confess,
And sing, the wonders of thy grace:
Thy power conveys our blessings down,
From God the Father, and the Son.

2. Enlightened by thy heavenly ray,
Our shades and darkness turn to day;
Thine inward teachings make us know
Our danger, and our refuge, too.

3. Thy power and glory work within,
And break the chains of reigning sin,
Do our imperious lusts subdue,
And form our wretched hearts anew.

4. The troubled conscience knows thy voice,
Thy cheering words awake our joys:
Thy words allay the stormy wind,
And calm the surges of the mind.

540. *The Sovereign Jehovah.*

1. BEFORE Jehovah's awful throne,
Ye nations, bow with sacred joy;
Know that the Lord is God alone;
He can create, and he destroy.

2. His sovereign power, without our aid,
Made us of clay, and formed us men;
And when, like wandering sheep, we
strayed,
He brought us to his fold again.

3. We are his people; we his care;
Our souls, and all our mortal frame:
What lasting honors shall we rear,
Almighty Maker, to thy name?

4. We'll crowd thy gates, with thankful
songs,
High as the heaven our voices raise;
And earth, with her ten thousand tongues,
Shall fill thy courts with sounding
praise.

5. Wide as the world is thy command;
Vast as eternity thy love;
Firm as a rock thy truth shall stand,
When rolling years shall cease to
move.

541. *The Value of Christ and his Righteousness.*

1. No more—my God! I boast no more
Of all the duties I have done;
I quit the hopes I held before,
To trust the merits of thy Son.

2. Now, for the love I bear his name,
What was my gain, I count my loss;
My former pride I call my shame,
And nail my glory to his cross.

3. Yes,—and I must, and will, esteem
All things but loss for Jesus' sake;
Oh! may my soul be found in him,
And of his righteousness partake.

4. The best obedience of my hands
Dares not appear before thy throne;
But faith can answer thy demands,
By pleading what my Lord has done.

542. *Prayer for the World's Conversion.*

1. O SPIRIT of the living God!
In all thy plenitude of grace,
Where'er the foot of man hath trod,
Descend on our apostate race.

2. Give tongues of fire, and hearts of love,
To preach the reconciling word;
Give power and unction from above,
Where'er the joyful sound is heard.

3. O Spirit of the Lord! prepare
A sinful world their God to meet:
Breathe thou abroad, like morning air,
Till hearts of stone begin to beat.

4. Baptize the nations; far and nigh
The triumphs of the cross record;
The name of Jesus glorify,
Till every kindred call him—Lord.

543. *Day of Judgment.*

1. That day of wrath! that dreadful day,
When heaven and earth shall pass away!
What power shall be the sinner's stay?
How shall he meet that dreadful day?

2. When, shriveling like a parchéd scroll,
The flaming heavens together roll;
And, louder yet, and yet more dread,
Swells the high trump that wakes the
dead.

3. Oh! on that day, that wrathful day,
When man to judgment wakes from clay,
Be thou, O God, the sinner's stay,
Though heaven and earth shall pass away.

544. *Praise to God for his Greatness and
Mercy.*

1. To God, the great, the ever-blessed,
Let songs of honor be addressed;
His mercy firm for ever stands;
Give him the thanks his love demands.

2. Who knows the wonders of thy ways?
Who shall fulfill thy boundless praise?
Blest are the souls that fear thee still,
And pay their duty to thy will.

3. Remember what thy mercy did
For Jacob's race, thy chosen seed;
And, with the same salvation, bless
The meanest suppliant of thy grace.

4. Oh! may I see thy tribes rejoice,
And aid their triumphs with my voice:
This is my glory, Lord! to be
Joined to thy saints, and near to thee.

545. *Entire Consecration.*

1. Now I resolve, with all my heart,
With all my powers, to serve the Lord;
Nor from his ways will I depart,
Whose service is a rich reward.

2. O, be this service all my joy!
Around let my example shine;
Till others love the blest employ,
And join in labors so divine.

3. Be this the purpose of my soul,
My solemn, my determined choice,
To yield to his supreme control,
And in his kind commands rejoice.

4. O may I never faint or tire,
Nor wandering leave his sacred ways;
Great God! accept my soul's desire,
And give me strength to live thy praise.

Doxology.

To God the Father, God the Son,
And God the Spirit, Three in One,
Be honor, praise, and glory given,
By all on earth, and all in heaven.

WATERVILLE. L. M. 6 lines.*

MOD. AFFET.

MOZART Arranged.

1. Where Bab-y-lon's broad waters roll, In ex-ile we sat down to weep,
For thoughts of Zi-on o'er our soul Came, like de-part-ed joys, in sleep,

Whose forms to sad remembrance rise, Tho' fled for ev - er from our eyes.

* See also "GATHERING CLOUDS." 72.

546.   *Zion in Captivity.*

1. WHERE Babylon's broad rivers roll,
In exile we sat down to weep,
For thoughts of Zion o'er our soul
Came, like departed joys, in sleep,
Whose forms to sad remembrance rise,
Though fled for ever from our eyes.

2. Our harps upon the willows hung,
Where, worn with toil, our limbs re-
clined;
The chords, untuned, and trembling, rung
With mournful music on the wind,
While foes, insulting o'er our wrongs,
Cried,—"Sing us one of Zion's songs."

3. How can we sing the songs we love,
Far from our own delightful land?—
If I prefer thee not above
My chiefest joy, may this right hand,
Jerusalem!—forget its skill,
My tongue be dumb, my pulse be still.

547.   *Strength equal to the Day.*

1. WHEN adverse winds and waves arise,
And in my heart despondence sighs;
When life her throng of cares reveals,
And weakness o'er my spirit steals,
Grateful I hear the kind decree,
That "as my day, my strength shall be."

2. When, with sad footsteps, memory roves
'Mid smitten joys and buried loves,

When sleep my tearful pillow flies,
And dewy morning drinks my sighs,
Still to thy promise, Lord! I flee,
That "as my day, my strength shall be."

3. One trial more must yet be past,
One pang—the keenest and the last;
And when, with brow convulsed and pale,
My feeble, quivering heart-strings fail,
Redeemer! grant my soul to see
That "as her day, her strength shall be."

548.   *The Christian's Shepherd.*

1. THE Lord my pasture shall prepare,
And feed me with a shepherd's care;
His presence shall my wants supply,
And guard me with a watchful eye;
My noonday walks he shall attend,
And all my midnight hours defend.

2. When in the sultry glebe I faint,
Or on the thirsty mountain pant,
To fertile vales and dewy meads,
My weary, wandering steps he leads,
Where peaceful rivers, soft and slow,
Amid the verdant landscapes flow.

3. Though in the paths of death I tread,
With gloomy horrors overspread,
My steadfast heart shall fear no ill,
For thou, O Lord, art with me still;
Thy friendly crook shall give me aid,
And guide me through the dismal shade

1. Lord! what a heaven of saving grace Shines thro' the beauties of thy face,

And lights our pas-sions to a flame! Lord, how we love thy charm-ing name!

* L. M. 6 lines, by repeating the first strain.

549. *The Presence of the Saviour.*

1. LORD! what a heaven of saving grace
Shines through the beauties of thy face,
And lights our passions to a flame!
Lord! how we love thy charming name.

2. When I can say,—my God is mine,—
When I can feel thy glories shine,
I tread the world beneath my feet,
And all that earth calls good or great.

3. While such a scene of sacred joys
Our raptured eyes and souls employs,
Here we could sit and gaze away
A long, and everlasting day.

4. Well, we shall quickly pass the night,
To the fair coasts of perfect light;
Then shall our joyful senses rove
O'er the dear object of our love.

5. Send comforts down from thy right hand,
While we pass through this barren land,
And in thy temple let us see
A glimpse of love—a glimpse of thee.

550. *Rest for the weary Penitent.*

1. COME, weary souls! with sin distressed,
Come, and accept the promised rest;
The Saviour's gracious call obey,
And cast your gloomy fears away.

2. Here mercy's boundless ocean flows,
To cleanse your guilt and heal your woes;
Pardon and life, and endless peace,—
How rich the gift, how free the grace!

3. Lord! we accept, with thankful heart,
The hope thy gracious words impart;
We come, with trembling; yet rejoice,
And bless the kind inviting voice.

4. Dear Saviour! let thy powerful love
Confirm our faith,—our fears remove;
Oh! sweetly reign in every breast,
And guide us to eternal rest.

551. *Missionaries encouraged.*

1. YE Christian heralds, go, proclaim
Salvation in Immanuel's name;
To distant climes the tidings bear,
And plant the rose of Sharon there.

2. He'll shield you with a wall of fire,
With holy zeal your hearts inspire,
Bid raging winds their fury cease,
And hush the tempest into peace.

3. And when our labors all are o'er,
Then shall we meet to part no more—
Meet, with the blood-bought throng to fall,
And crown the Saviour Lord of all.

Doxology.

To God the Father, God the Son,
And God the Spirit, Three in One,
Be honor, praise, and glory given,
By all on earth, and all in heaven.

BALERMA. C. M. SCOTTISH.

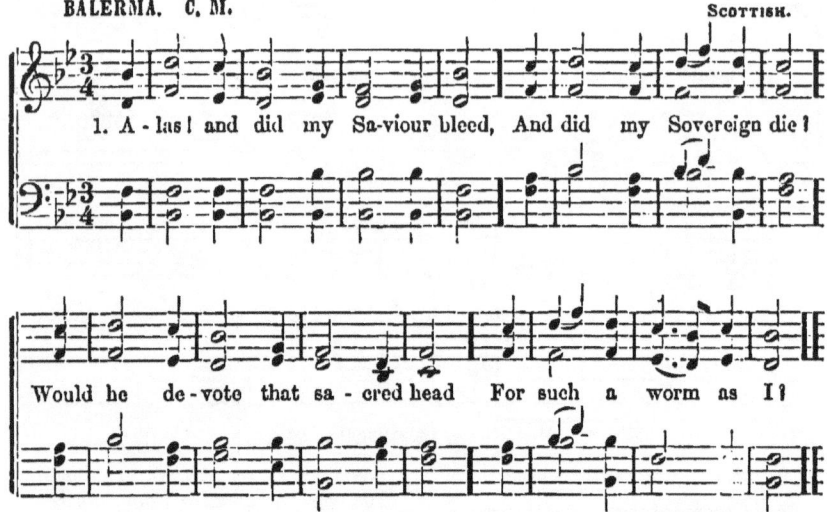

1. A - las! and did my Sa-viour bleed, And did my Sovereign die!

Would he de-vote that sa - cred head For such a worm as I!

552. *Godly Sorrow at the Cross.*

1. ALAS! and did my Saviour bleed,
   And did my Sovereign die?
   Would he devote that sacred head
   For such a worm as I?

2. Was it for crimes that I had done,
   He groaned upon the tree?
   Amazing pity!—grace unknown!—
   And love beyond degree!

3. Well might the sun in darkness hide,
   And shut his glories in,
   When Christ, the mighty Maker, died
   For man the creatures's sin.

4. Thus might I hide my blushing face,
   While his dear cross appears;
   Dissolve my heart in thankfulness,
   And melt mine eyes to tears.

5. But floods of tears can ne'er repay
   The debt of love I owe;
   Here, Lord! I give myself away;—
   'Tis all that I can do.

553. *Repentance and Faith in Christ.*

1. O GOD of mercy! hear my call,
   My load of guilt remove;
   Break down this separating wall,
   That bars me from thy love.

2. Give me the presence of thy grace;
   Then my rejoicing tongue
   Shall speak aloud thy righteousness,
   And make thy praise my song.

3. No blood of goats, nor heifer slain,
   For sin could e'er atone:
   The death of Christ shall still remain
   Sufficient and alone.

4. A soul, oppressed with sin's desert,
   My God will ne'er despise;
   An humble groan, a broken heart,
   Is our best sacrifice.

554. *Watchfulness and Prayer.*

1. ALAS! what hourly dangers rise,
   What snares beset my way!
   To heaven, Oh! let me lift mine eyes,
   And, hourly, watch and pray.

2. How oft my mournful thoughts complain,
   And melt in flowing tears!
   I strive against my foes in vain,—
   I sink amid my fears.

3. O Lord! increase my faith and hope,
   When foes and fears prevail;
   And bear my fainting spirit up,
   Or soon my strength will fail.

4. Oh! keep me in thy heavenly way,
   And bid the tempter flee;
   And never, never let me stray
   From happiness and thee.

555. *God, the Help of the Saints.*

1. O GOD! our help in ages past,
Our hope for years to come,
Our shelter from the stormy blast,
And our eternal home,—

2. Beneath the shadow of thy throne
Thy saints have dwelt secure;
Sufficient is thine arm alone,
And our defense is sure.

3. Before the hills in order stood,
Or earth received her frame;
From everlasting thou art God,—
To endless years the same.

4. Thy word commands our flesh to dust—
"Return, ye sons of men!"
All nations rose from earth at first,
And turn to earth again.

5. O God! our help in ages past,
Our hope for years to come,
Be thou our guard while troubles last,
And our eternal home.

556. *The last Resolve.*

1. COME, trembling sinner, in whose breast
A thousand thoughts revolve,
Come, with your guilt and fear oppressed,
And make this last resolve:

2. "I'll go to Jesus, though my sin
High like a mountain rose;
I know his courts, I'll enter in
Whatever may oppose.

3. "Prostrate I'll bow before his throne,
And there my guilt confess,
I'll tell him I'm a wretch undone
Without his sovereign grace.

4. "I can but perish if I go,
I am resolved to try,
For if I stay away, I know,
I must for ever die."

557. *Submission.*

1. O LORD, my best desires fulfill,
And help me to resign
Life, health, and comfort to thy will,
And make thy pleasure mine.

2. Why should I shrink at thy command?
Thy love forbids my fears;
Why tremble at the gracious hand
That wipes away my tears?

3. No—let me rather freely yield
What most I prize, to thee:
Thou never hast a good withheld,
Or wilt withhold from me.

4. Thy favor, all my journey through,
Shall be my rich supply;
What more I want, or think I do,
Let wisdom still deny.

558. *God, our Portion, here and hereafter.*

1. GOD! my supporter and my hope,
My help for ever near,
Thine arm of mercy held me up,
When sinking in despair.

2. Thy counsels, Lord! shall guide my feet
Through this dark wilderness:
Thy hand conduct me near thy seat,
To dwell before thy face.

3. Were I in heaven without my God,
'T would be no joy to me;
And, while this earth is my abode,
I long for none but thee.

4. What if the springs of life were broke,
And flesh and heart should faint?
God is my soul's eternal rock,
The strength of every saint.

5. But to draw near to thee, my God!
Shall be my sweet employ;
My tongue shall sound thy works abroad,
And tell the world my joy.

559. *Time and Eternity.*

1. LIFE is a span—a fleeting hour:
How soon the vapor flies!
Man is a tender, transient flower,
That e'en in blooming dies.

2. The once-loved form, now cold and dead,
Each mournful thought employs;
And Nature weeps her comforts fled,
And withered all her joys.

3. Hope looks beyond the bounds of time,
When what we now deplore
Shall rise in full, immortal prime,
And bloom to fade no more.

4. Cease, then, fond Nature, cease thy tears;
The Saviour dwells on high;
There everlasting spring appears;
There joys shall never die.

WIRTH. C. M.

W. B. BRADBURY.

1. Ye men and angels, witness now— Be - fore the Lord we speak;

To Him we make our sol - emn vow— A vow we dare not break—

560. *The Pledge of Fidelity.*

1. YE men and angels, witness now—
Before the Lord we speak;
To Him we make our solemn vow—
A vow we dare not break—

2. That, long as life itself shall last,
Ourselves to Christ we yield;
Nor from his cause will we depart,
Or ever quit the field.

3. We trust not in our native strength,
But on his grace rely;
May he, with our returning wants
All needful grace supply.

4. O, guide our doubtful feet aright,
And keep us in thy ways;
And while we turn our vows to prayers,
Turn thou our prayers to praise.

561. *Reigning with Christ.*

1. THE head that once was crowned with thorns,
Is crowned with glory now:
A royal diadem adorns
The mighty Victor's brow.

2. The highest place that heaven affords
Is his by sovereign right;
The King of kings, and Lord of lords,
He reigns in glory bright.

3. The joy of all who dwell above,
The joy of all below,
To whom he manifests his love,
And grants his name to know.

4. To them the cross, with all its shame,
With all its grace, is given;
Their name, an everlasting name,
Their joy, the joy of heaven.

5. They suffer with their Lord below,
They reign with him above;
Their profit and their joy to know
The mystery of his love.

6. The cross he bore is life and health,
Though shame and death to him;
His people's hope, his people's wealth,
Their everlasting theme.

562. *The End of the Righteous and the Wicked.*

1. BLEST is the man, who shuns the place
Where sinners love to meet;
Who fears to tread their wicked ways,
And hates the scoffer's seat:

2. But in the statutes of the Lord
Has placed his chief delight;
By day he reads or hears the word,
And meditates by night.

3. He, like a plant of generous kind,
    By living waters set,
Safe from the storms and blasting wind,
    Enjoys a peaceful state.

4. Not so the impious and unjust;
    What vain designs they form!
Their hopes are blown away like dust,
    Or chaff, before the storm.

5. Sinners, in judgment, shall not stand,
    Among the sons of grace,
When Christ, the Judge, at his right hand
    Appoints his saints a place.

563.   *Sickness and Recovery.*

1. My God! thy service well demands
    The remnant of my days;
Why was this fleeting breath renewed,
    But to renew thy praise?

2. Thine arms of everlasting love
    Did this weak frame sustain,
When life was hovering o'er the grave,
    And nature sunk with pain.

3. Calmly I bowed my fainting head,
    On thy dear, faithful breast;
Pleased to obey my Father's call
    To his eternal rest.

4. Into thy hands, my Saviour God!
    Did I my soul resign,
In firm reliance on that truth
    Which made salvation mine.

5. Back from the borders of the grave,
    At thy command I come;
Nor will I ask a speedier flight
    To my celestial home.

6. Where thou appointest mine abode,
    There would I choose to be;
For in thy presence death is life,
    And earth is heaven with thee.

564.   *Unfruitfulness.*

1. Long have I sat beneath the sound
    Of thy salvation, Lord;
But still how weak my faith is found—
    And knowledge of thy word!

2. Oft I frequent thy holy place,
    And hear almost in vain;
How small a portion of thy grace
    My mem'ry can retain!

3. How cold and feeble is my love!
    How negligent my fear!
How low my hopes of joys above!
    How few affections there!

4. Great God, thy sovereign power impart,
    To give thy word success;
Write thy salvation on my heart,
    And make me learn thy grace.

5. Show my forgetful feet the way
    That leads to joys on high;
There knowledge grows without decay,
    And love shall never die.

565.   *Earthly Pleasures dangerous.*

1. How vain are all things here below!
    How false, and yet how fair!
Each pleasure hath its poison, too,
    And every sweet a snare.

2. The brightest things below the sky
    Shine with deceiving light;
We should suspect some danger nigh,
    Where we possess delight.

3. Our dearest joys, our nearest friends,
    The partners of our blood—
How their divide our wavering minds,
    And leave but half for God!

4. The fondness of a creature's love,
    How strong it strikes the sense!
'Tis there the warm affections move,
    Nor can we call them thence.

5. Dear Saviour, let thy beauties be
    My soul's eternal food,
And grace command my heart away
    From all created good.

566.   *Prayer for quickening Grace.*

1. My soul lies cleaving to the dust;
    Lord! give me life divine;
From vain desires, and every lust,
    Turn off these eyes of mine.

2. I need the influence of thy grace
    To speed me in thy way,
Lest I should loiter in my race,
    Or turn my feet astray.

3. Are not thy mercies sovereign still,
    And thou a faithful God?
Wilt thou not grant me warmer zeal
    To run the heavenly road?

4. Does not my heart thy precepts love,
    And long to see thy face?
And yet how slow my spirits move
    Without enlivening grace!

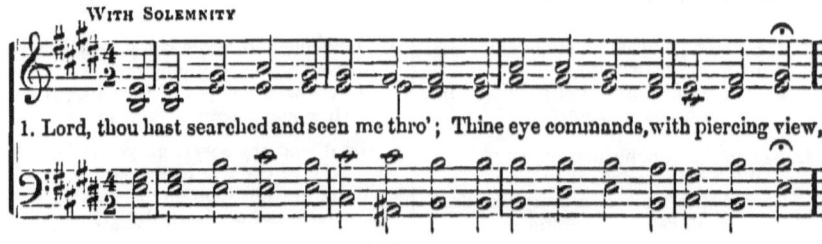

1. Lord, thou hast searched and seen me thro'; Thine eye commands, with piercing view,

Ritard.

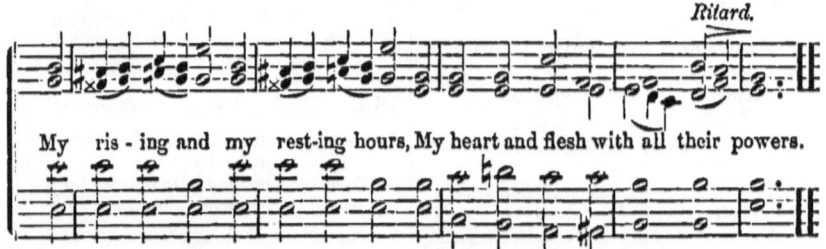

My ris - ing and my rest-ing hours, My heart and flesh with all their powers.

567. *Omniscience of God.*

1. LORD, thou hast searched and seen me
through,
Thine eye commands, with piercing view
My rising and my resting hours,
My heart and flesh, with all their powers.

2. My thoughts, before they are my own,
Are to my God distinctly known;
He knows the words I mean to speak
Ere from my opening lips they break.

3. Within thy circling power I stand,
On every side I find thy hand:
Awake, asleep, at home, abroad,
I am surrounded still with God.

4. Amazing knowledge, vast and great!
What large extent! what lofty height!
My soul, with all the powers I boast,
Is in the boundless prospect lost.

5. O, may these thoughts possess my breast,
Where'er I rove, where'er I rest;
Nor let my weaker passions dare
Consent to sin, for God is there.

568. *Coming to Christ.*

1. BEFORE thy high and holy throne
I stand convicted and undone;
Yet in thy plenitude of grace
Thou bid'st me come and seek thy face.

2. And come I will to Jesus' feet,
And low before the mercy-seat
Acknowledge all my guilt and shame,
And trust for ever in his name.

3. Enough for me that Christ hath died:
Justice Divine is satisfied;
This, this is now my only plea,
That Jesus shed his blood for me.

4. And dost thou, Lord, my sins forgive,
Bid the returning ingrate live?
Never from thee will I depart:
Take full possession of my heart.

569. *God Incomprehensible.*

1. WHAT is our God, or what his name,
Nor men can learn, nor angels teach;
He dwells concealed in radiant flame,
Where neither eye nor thought can
reach.

2. The spacious worlds of heavenly light,
Compared with him, how short they
fall!
They are too dark, and he too bright;
Nothing are they, and God is all.

Doxology.

PRAISE God, from whom all blessings flow;
Praise him, all creatures here below;
Praise him above, ye heavenly host,
Praise Father, Son, and Holy Ghost.

WELLS. L. M.   HOLDRAYD.

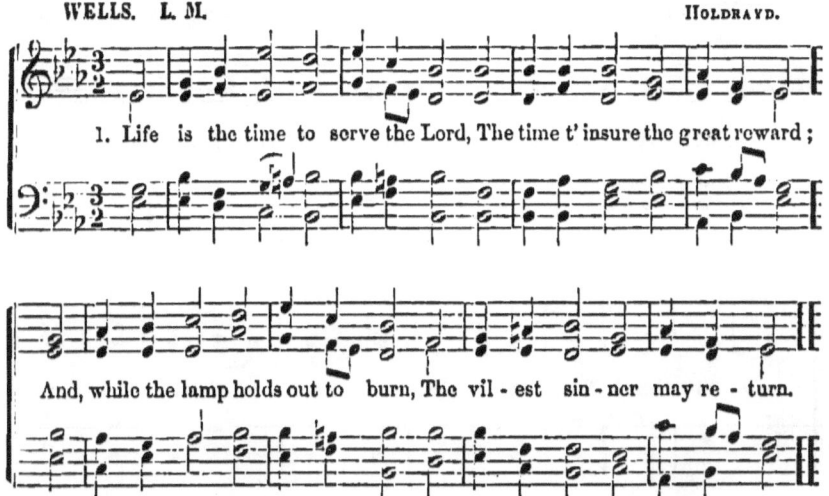

1. Life is the time to serve the Lord, The time t' insure the great reward;

And, while the lamp holds out to burn, The vil - est sin - ner may re - turn.

570. *Life, the Day of Grace and Hope.*

1. LIFE is the time to serve the Lord,
The time t' insure the great reward;
And, while the lamp holds out to burn,
The vilest sinner may return.

2. Life is the hour that God hath given,
To 'scape from hell and fly to heaven;
The day of grace—and mortals may
Secure the blessings of the day.

3. The living know that they must die,
But all the dead forgotten lie;
Their mem'ry and their sense are gone,
Alike unknowing and unknown.

4. Then, what my thoughts design to do,
My hands, with all your might pursue;
Since no device, nor work is found,
Nor faith, nor hope, beneath the ground.

5. There are no acts of pardon passed
In the cold grave to which we haste;
But darkness, death, and long despair,
Reign in eternal silence there.

571. *Who on Earth are blessed.*

1. BLEST are the men, whose hearts do move
And melt with sympathy and love;
From Christ, the Lord, shall they obtain
Like sympathy and love again.

2. Blest are the pure, whose hearts are clean
From the defiling power of sin;

With endless pleasure, they shall see
A God of spotless purity.

3. Blest are the men of peaceful life,
Who quench the coals of growing strife;
They shall be called the heirs of bliss—
The sons of God—the God of peace.

4. Blest are the sufferers, who partake
Of pain and shame, for Jesus' sake;—
Their souls shall triumph in the Lord—
Glory and joy are their reward.

572. *Care of Widows and Orphans.*

1. THOU God of hope, to thee we bow;
Thou art our refuge in distress;
The Husband of the widow thou,
The Father of the fatherless.

2. The poor are thy peculiar care;
To them thy promises are sure:
Thy gifts the poor in spirit share;
O, may we always thus be poor

3. May we thy law of love fulfill,
To bear each other's burdens here,
Endure and do thy righteous will,
And walk in all thy faith and fear.

4. Thou God of hope, to thee we bow;
Thou art our refuge in distress;
The Husband of the widow thou,
The Father of the fatherless.

REMEMBRANCE.　C. M.　With a Coda.　"N. Y. Choralist."　By Permission.

SLOW AND SOLEMN.

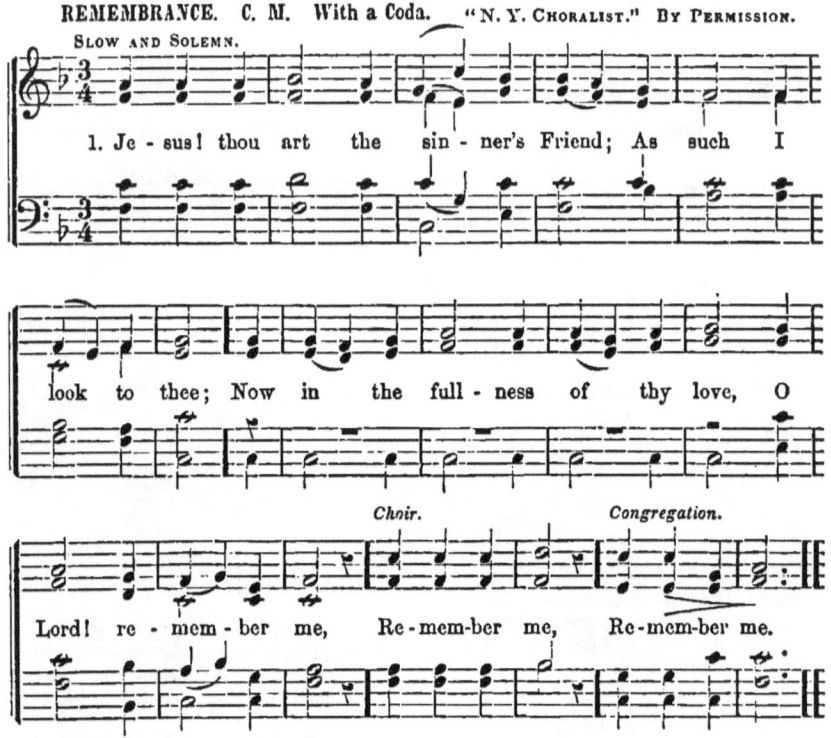

1. Je - sus! thou art the sin - ner's Friend; As such I look to thee; Now in the full - ness of thy love, O Lord! re - mem - ber me, Re - mem-ber me, Re - mem-ber me.

Choir. Congregation.

573.　　*Remember Me.*

1. Jesus! thou art the sinner's Friend;
   As such I look to thee;
   Now, in the fullness of thy love,
   O Lord! remember me.

2. Remember thy pure word of grace—
   Remember Calvary;
   Remember all thy dying groans,
   And, then, remember me.

3. Thou wondrous Advocate with God!
   I yield myself to thee;
   While thou art sitting on thy throne,
   Dear Lord! remember me.

4. Lord! I am guilty—I am vile,
   But thy salvation 's free;
   Then, in thine all-abounding grace,
   Dear Lord! remember me.

5. And, when I close my eyes in death,
   When creature helps all flee,
   Then, O my dear Redeemer-God!
   I pray, remember me.

574.　　*Nearness to God.*

1. Along the mountain track of life,
   Along the weary lea,
   In rocks, in storms, in joy, in strife,
   Let this my heart-cry be—
   "Nearer to thee! Nearer to thee!"

2. This pilgrim-path by thee was trod,
   Jesus! my King! by thee—
   Traced by thy feet,—thy tears,—thy blood,
   In love, in death, for me—
   O! bring my soul—nearer to thee!

3. Let every step, let every thought,
   Sweet memories bear of thee!
   And hear the soul thy love hath bought,
   Whose every cry shall be
   "Nearer to thee! Nearer to thee!"

4. Thou wilt! thou dost!—a still small voice
   Whispers of faith in thee,
   Of hope that might in grief rejoice,
   If still the way-cry be—
   "Nearer to thee! Nearer to thee!"

"WHAT IS LIFE?" 8s & 7s. 6 lines. "Mus. Sacra." Arr.

575. *Heavenly Aspirations.*

1. WHAT is life? 'tis but a vapor,
Soon it vanishes away.
Life is but a dying taper—
O, my soul, why wish to stay!
Why not spread thy wings and fly
Straight to yonder world of joy?

2. See that glory, how resplendent!
Brighter far than fancy paints;
There, in majesty transcendent,
Jesus reigns the King of saints.
Why not spread, etc.

3 Joyful crowds, his throne surround
ing,
Sing with rapture of his love;
Through the heavens his praise re
sounding,
Filling all the courts above.
Why not spread, etc.

4. Go, and share his people's glory,
'Mid the ransomed crowd appear;

Thine a joyful, wondrous story—
One that angels love to hear.
Why not spread, etc.

576. *A Fountain set open.*

1. COME to Calv'ry's holy mountain,
Sinners, ruined by the fall!
Here a pure and healing fountain
Flows to you—to me—to all,
In a full, perpetual tide,
Opened when the Saviour died.

2. Come, in sorrow and contrition,
Wounded, impotent, and blind;
Here the guilty, free remission—
Here the troubled, peace may find,
Health this fountain will restore;
He that drinks shall thirst no more·—

3. He that drinks shall live for ever—
'Tis a soul-reviving flood:
God is faithful—God will never
Break his covenant in blood;—
Signed, when our Redeemer died,
Sealed, when he was glorified.

CONFIDENCE. 8s. Double.   S. B. Pond.

1. In - spir-er and Hearer of prayer, Thou Shepherd and Guardian of mine ;

My all to thy cov - e - nant care, I, sleeping or wak-ing, re - sign.
A. s. And fast as my min-utes roll on, They bring me, but near-er to thee.

If thou art my shield and my sun, The night is no darkness to me ;

577.   *Evening.*

1. INSPIRER and Hearer of prayer,
    Thou Shepherd and Guardian of mine,
My all to thy covenant care,
    I, sleeping or waking, resign.
If thou art my shield and my sun,
    The night is no darkness to me ;   •
And fast as my moments roll on,
    They bring me but nearer to thee.

2. Thy ministering spirits descend,
    To watch while thy saints are asleep:
By day and by night they attend,
    The heirs of salvation to keep:
Bright seraphs, despatched from the
      throne,
    Repair to their stations assigned ;
And angels elect are sent down,
    To guard the redeemed of mankind.

3. Thy worship no interval knows ;
    Their fervor is still on the wing ;
And, while they protect my repose,
    They chant to the praise of my King.

I, too, at the season ordained,
    Their chorus for ever shall join ;
And love and adore without end,
    Their faithful Creator and mine.

578.   *In Darkness.*

1. How tedious and tasteless the hours,
    When Jesus no longer I see !
The woodlands, the fields, and the flowers
    Have lost all their sweetness to me.
His name yields the richest perfume,
    And softer than music his voice ;
His presence can banish my gloom,
    And bid all within me rejoice.

2. Dear Lord ! if indeed thou art mine,
    And thou art my light and my song ;
Say, why do I languish and pine,
    And why are my winters so long ?
O drive these dark clouds from the sky,
    Thy soul cheering presence restore ;
Or bid me soar upward on high,
    Where winter and storms are no more.

579. *Backsliders invited to Return.*

1. RETURN to the Guide of thy youth,
   Thy Maker, thy Father, thy Friend!
   Behold him prepared to receive
   The child who has dared to offend:
   Return, the Redeemer invites;
   Full oft he has sought thee before:
   But lo! with unspeakable grace,
   He deigns to entreat thee once more.

2. Return, and enjoyments are thine,
   Too vast for the heart to conceive:
   Enjoyments which only belong
   To those who repent and believe:

A love which for ever expands;
   Unceasing composure of heart;
A crown of unfading delight,
   A kingdom which can not depart.

580. *Praise to Christ.*

THIS God is the God we adore,
   Our faithful, unchangeable Friend;
Whose love is as large as his power,
   And knows neither measure nor end;
'Tis Jesus, the first and the last,
   Whose Spirit shall guide us safe home,
We'll praise him for all that is past,
   And trust him for all that's to come.

MANEPY. 8s. Single.   From "SELAH."

1. To Je-sus, the crown of my hope, My soul is in haste to be gone,
O, bear me, ye che-ru-bim up, And waft me a-way to his throne.

581. *Longing to be with Christ.*

1. To Jesus, the crown of my hope,
   My soul is in haste to be gone,
   Oh, bear me, ye cherubim up,
   And waft me away to his throne.

2. My Saviour, whom absent I love,
   Whom not having seen I adore,
   Whose name is exalted above
   All glory, dominion, and power:

3. Dissolve thou these bonds that detain
   My soul from her portion in thee:
   O, strike off this adamant chain,
   And make me eternally free.

4. When that happy era begins,
   When arrayed in thy glories I shine,
   Nor grieve any more by my sins
   The bosom on which I recline:

5. O, then shall the veil be removed,
   And round me thy brightness be
   poured,

I shall meet him whom absent I loved,
   Whom not having seen I adored

582. *A Missionary's Death.*

1. WEEP not for the saint that ascends
   To partake of the joys of the sky,
   Weep not for the seraph that bends
   With the worshiping chorus on high.

2. Weep not for the spirit now crowned
   With the garland to martyrdom given,
   O weep not for him, he has found
   His reward and his refuge in heaven.

3. But weep for their sorrows, who stand
   And lament o'er the dead by his grave;
   Who sigh when they muse on the land
   Of their home, far away o'er the wave—

4. And weep for the nations that dwell
   Where the light of the truth never
   shone:
   Where anthems of peace never swell,
   And the love of the Lamb is unknown.

HOMER. 7s. Double. Or 6 lines. GERMAN.

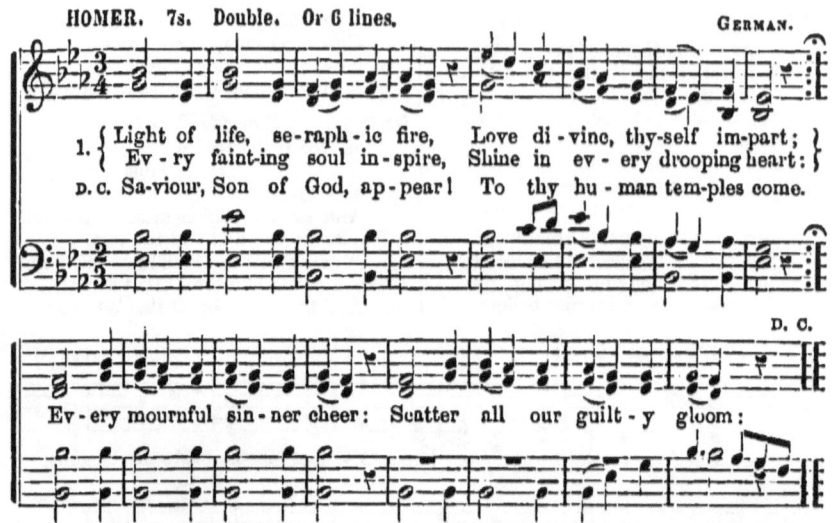

1. Light of life, se-raph-ic fire, Love di-vine, thy-self im-part;
Ev-ry faint-ing soul in-spire, Shine in ev-ery drooping heart:
D. C. Sa-viour, Son of God, ap-pear! To thy hu-man tem-ples come.

Ev-ery mournful sin-ner cheer: Scatter all our guilt-y gloom:

583. *Invocation of the Spirit.*

1. LIGHT of life, seraphic fire,
Love divine, thyself impart;
Every fainting soul inspire:
Shine in every drooping heart:
Every mournful sinner cheer,
Scatter all our guilty gloom:
Saviour, Son of God, appear!
To thy human temples come.

2. Come in this accepted hour;
Bring thy heavenly kingdom in:
Fill us with thy glorious power,
Take away the love of sin:
Nothing more can we require,
We will covet nothing less:
Be thou all our hearts desire,
All our joy, and all our peace.

584. *Divine Love.*

1. WHO can sound the depths of love?
'Tis an ocean unconfined,
Flowing on where'er we rove,
Vast as the Eternal mind!
'Tis the glory of our God,
Filling all his high abode:
'Tis a holy, quenchless flame,
From eternity the same.

2. See from love creation rise,
See in love a Saviour given,
Now, exalted in the skies,
Reconciling earth to heaven:
See, in love, the Spirit come,
All our darkness to illume:

See, through love, a Father's smile,
Every trembling fear beguile.

3. See, through love, the blessings flow,
That encircle all our days;
See, through love, a heaven below
In the mysteries of grace.
Love can smooth affliction's frown,
Love with joy our life can crown;
Love can gild the opening tomb
With the bliss of joys to come.

4. Who can sound the depths of love?
'Tis an ocean unconfined,
Flowing on where'er we rove,
Vast as the Eternal mind!
Let me bathe my weary soul
Where those living waters roll:
And my sins for ever hide
Deep within the swelling tide.

585. *Leaning upon the Saviour.*

1. JESUS, merciful and mild,
Lead me as a helpless child;
On no other arm but thine
Would my weary soul recline;
Thou art ready to forgive,
Thou canst bid the sinner live—
Guide the wanderer, day by day,
In the strait and narrow way.

2. I am weakness, thou art might;
I am darkness, thou art light;
I am all defiled with sin,
Thou canst make me pure within:

Foes that threaten to devour,
In thy presence have no power;
Thou canst bid their rage be still,
And my heart with comfort fill.

3. Thou canst fit me by thy grace
For the heavenly dwelling-place;
All thy promises are sure,
Ever shall thy love endure;
Then what more could I desire,
How to greater bliss aspire?

All I need, in thee I see,
Thou art all in all to me.

4. Jesus, Saviour all divine,
Hast thou made me truly thine?
Hast thou bought me by thy blood?
Reconciled my heart to God?
Hearken to my tender prayer,
Let me thy own image bear;
Let me love thee more and more,
Till I reach heaven's blissful shore.

MARTYN. 7s. Double.*   S. B. MARSH.

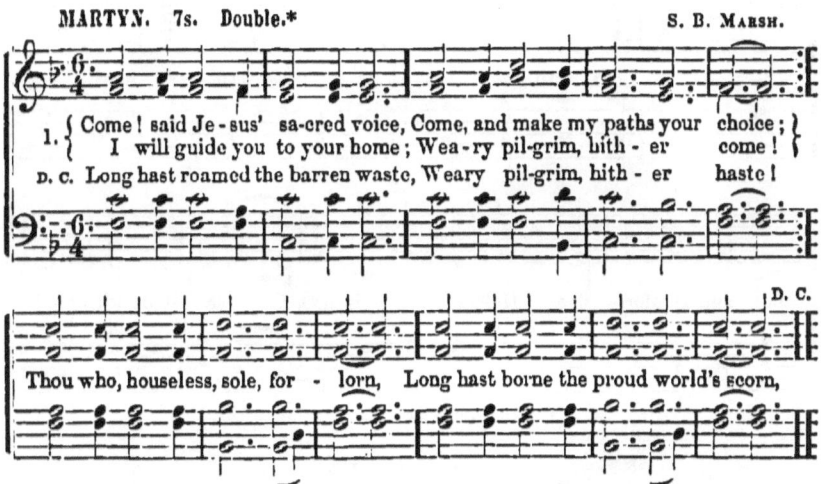

1. { Come! said Je-sus' sa-cred voice, Come, and make my paths your choice; }
   { I will guide you to your home; Wea-ry pil-grim, hith-er come! }
D. C. Long hast roamed the barren waste, Weary pil-grim, hith-er haste!

Thou who, houseless, sole, for - lorn, Long hast borne the proud world's scorn,

586. *The Weary, Sick, and Guilty, invited.*

1. COME! said Jesus' sacred voice,
   Come, and make my paths your choice;
   I will guide you to your home;
   Weary pilgrim, hither come!
2. Thou who, houseless, sole, forlorn,
   Long hast borne the proud world's scorn,
   Long hast roamed the barren waste,
   Weary pilgrim, hither haste!
3. Ye who, tossed on beds of pain,
   Seek for ease, but seek in vain:
   Ye, whose swollen and sleepless eyes
   Watch to see the morning rise;
4. Ye, by fiercer anguish torn,
   In remorse for guilt who mourn,
   Here repose your heavy care:
   Who the sting of guilt can bear?
5. Sinner, come! for here is found
   Balm that flows for every wound;
   Peace that ever shall endure,
   Rest eternal, sacred, sure.

587.   *Rejoicing in Hope.*

1. CHILDREN of the heavenly King!
   As ye journey, sweetly sing;
   Sing your Saviour's worthy praise,
   Glorious in his works and ways.
2. Ye are traveling home to God,
   In the way the fathers trod;
   They are happy now, and ye
   Soon their happiness shall see.
3. Shout, ye little flock! and blest,
   You on Jesus' throne shall rest;
   There your seat is now prepared—
   There, your kingdom and reward.
4. Fear not, brethren! joyful stand
   On the borders of your land;
   Jesus Christ, your Father's Son,
   Bids you, undismayed, go on.
5. Lord! submissive make us go,
   Gladly leaving all below;
   Only thou our Leader be,
   And we still will follow thee.

* *For the fifth stanza, repeat from second strain.*

ABIDING.   10s. 4 lines.*

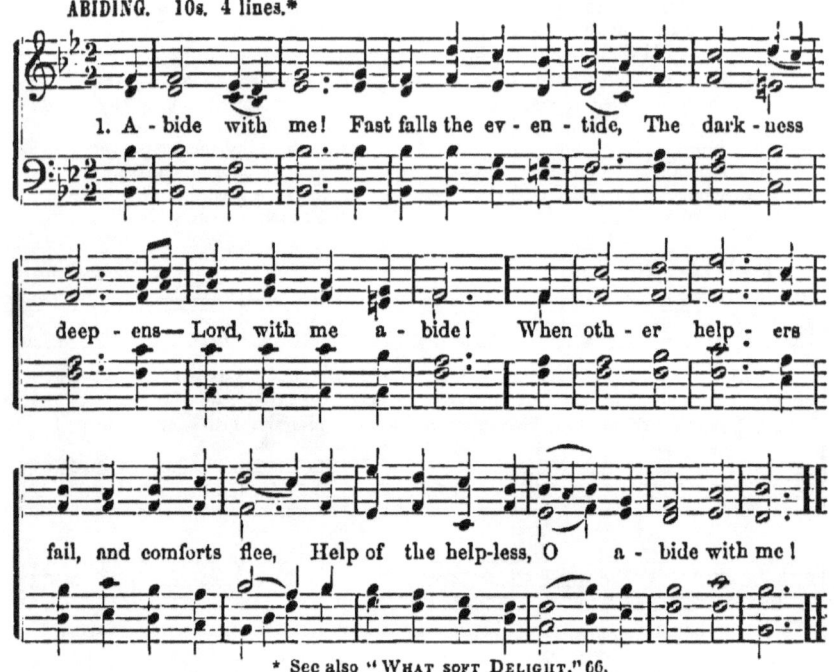

1. A - bide with me! Fast falls the ev - en - tide, The dark - ness

deep - ens—Lord, with me a - bide! When oth - er help - ers

fail, and comforts flee, Help of the help-less, O a - bide with me!

* See also "WHAT SOFT DELIGHT." 66.

588.   *"Abide with me."*

1. ABIDE with me!   Fast falls the eventide,
   The darkness deepens—Lord, with me abide!
   When other helpers fail, and comforts flee,
   Help of the helpless, O abide with me!

2. Swift to its close ebbs out life's little day;
   Earth's joys grow dim, its glories pass away;
   Change and decay in all around I see;
   O Thou, who changest not, abide with me!

3. I need thy presence every passing hour:
   What but thy grace can foil the tempter's power?
   Who, like thyself, my guide and stay can be?
   Through cloud and sunshine, O abide with me!

4. Not a brief glance I long, a passing word,
   But as thou dwell'st with thy disciples, Lord,
   Familiar, condescending, patient, free,
   Come, not to sojourn, but t' abide with me.

589.   John xii. 21.

1. WE would see Jesus—for the shadows lengthen
   Across this little landscape of our life;
   We would see Jesus our weak faith to strengthen,
   For the last weariness—the final strife

2. We would see Jesus—the great Rock Foundation,
    Whereon our feet were set by sovereign grace;
Not life, nor death, with all their agitation,
    Can thence remove us, if we see his face.

3. We would see Jesus—other lights are fading,
    Which for long years we have rejoiced to see;
The blessings of our pilgrimage are failing,
    We would not mourn them, for we go to thee.

4. We would see Jesus—this is all we're needing,
    Strength, joy and willingness come with the sight;
We would see Jesus, dying, risen, pleading,
    Then welcome day, and farewell mortal night.

590. *"Abide in me."*

1. THAT mystic word of thine, O sovereign Lord,
    Is all too pure, too high, too deep for me;
Weary with striving, and with longing faint,
    I breathe it back again in prayer to thee.

2. Abide in me—o'ershadow by thy love
    Each half-formed purpose, and dark thought of sin,
Quench, ere it rise, each selfish, low desire,
    And keep my soul, as thine, calm and divine.

3. As some rare perfume in a vase of clay
    Pervades it with a fragrance not its own—
So, when thou dwellest in a mortal soul,
    All heaven's own sweetness seems around it thrown.

4. The soul alone, like a neglected harp,
    Grows out of tune, and needs that Hand divine;
Dwell thou within it, tune and touch the chords,
    Till every note and string shall answer thine.

5. Abide in me: there have been moments pure,
    When I have seen thy face and felt thy power;
Then evil lost its grasp, and, passion hushed,
    Owned the divine enchantment of the hour.

6. These were but seasons beautiful and rare;
    Abide in me—and they shall ever be;
I pray thee now fulfill my earnest prayer,
    Come and abide in me; and I in thee.

591. *Help my Unbelief.*

1. YES, I do feel, my God, that I am thine!
    Thou art my joy—myself mine only grief;
Hear my complaint, low bending at thy shrine,
    Lord, I believe; help thou mine unbelief.

2. Unworthy even to approach so near,
    My soul lies trembling like a summer's leaf,
Yet, oh, forgive! I doubt not, though I fear,
    Lord, I believe; help thou mine unbelief.

3. O draw me nearer, for, too far away,
    The beamings of thy brightness are too brief;
While faith, though fainting, still hath strength to say,
    Lord, I believe; help thou mine unbelief.

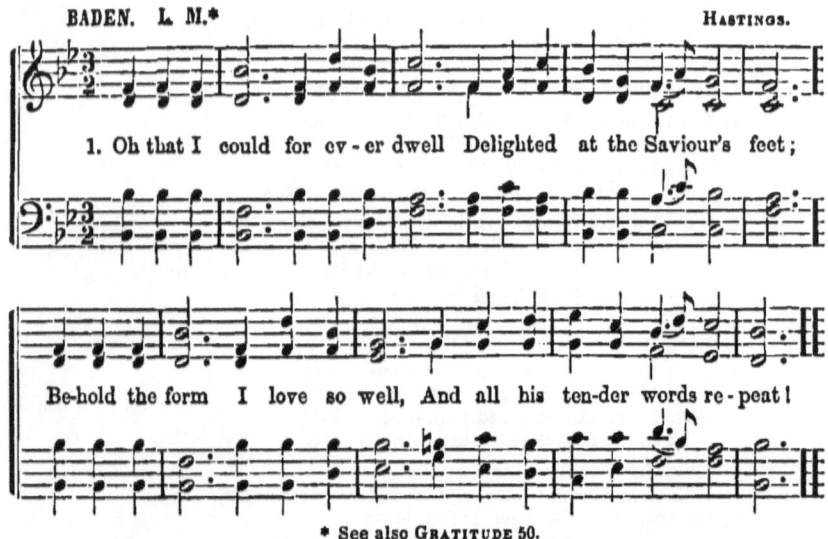

BADEN. L. M.* HASTINGS.

1. Oh that I could for ev-er dwell Delighted at the Saviour's feet;

Be-hold the form I love so well, And all his ten-der words re-peat!

* See also GRATITUDE 50.

592. *Communion with God.*

1. OH that I could for ever dwell
   Delighted at the Saviour's feet;
   Behold the form I love so well,
   And all his tender words repeat!

2. The world shut out from all my soul,
   And heaven brought in with all its
       bliss;
   O, is there aught from pole to pole,
   One moment to compare with this?

3. This is the hidden life I prize,
   A life of penitential love,—
   When most my follies I despise,
   And raise the highest thoughts above.

4. When all I am I clearly see,
   And freely own my deepest shame;
   When the Redeemer's love to me,
   Kindles within a deathless flame:

5. Thus would I live, till nature fail,
   And all my former sins forsake;
   Then rise to God within the vail,
   And of eternal joys partake.

593. *Increasing Light*

1. UPON the Gospel's sacred page
   The gathered beams of ages shine;
   And, as it hastens, every age
   But makes its brightness more divine.

2. On mightier wing, in loftier flight,
   From year to year does knowledge
       soar;
   And, as it soars, the Gospel light
   Adds to its influence more and more.

3. More glorious still as centuries roll,
   New regions blessed, new powers un-
       furled,
   Expanding with th 'expanding soul,
   Its waters shall o'erflow the world—

4. Flow to restore, but not destroy;
   As when the cloudless lamp of day
   Pours out its floods of light and joy,
   And sweeps the lingering mist away.

594. *Christ's Coming to reign.*

1. JESUS! thy church with longing eyes
   For thine expected coming waits:
   When will the promised light arise,
   And glory beam on Zion's gates?

2. E'en now, when tempests round us fall,
   And wintry clouds o'ercast the sky,
   Thy words with pleasure we recall,
   And deem that our redemption 's nigh.

3. Oh! come and reign o'er every land;
   Let Satan from his throne be hurled,—
   All nations bow to thy command,
   And grace revive a dying world

4. Teach us, in watchfulness and prayer,
To wait for thine appointed hour;
And fit us, by thy grace, to share
The triumphs of thy conquering power.

595. *Death and the Resurrection.*

1. WHEN God is nigh, my faith is strong,
His arm is my almighty prop ;
Be glad, my heart ! rejoice, my tongue !
My dying flesh shall rest in hope.

2. Though in the dust I lay my head,
Yet, gracious God ! thou wilt not leave
My soul for ever with the dead,
Nor lose thy children in the grave.

3. My flesh shall thy first call obey,
Shake off the dust, and rise on high ;
Then shalt thou lead the wondrous way,
Up to thy throne above the sky.

4. There streams of endless pleasure flow ;
And full discoveries of thy grace,
Which we but tasted here below,
Spread heavenly joys through all the
place.

596. *The Sun of Righteousness.*

1. O SUN of righteousness, arise,
With gentle beams on Zion shine ;
Dispel the darkness from our eyes,
And souls awake to life divine.

2. On all around, let grace descend,
Like heavenly dew, or copious showers;
That we may call our God our Friend;
That we may hail salvation ours.

597. *Spread of the Gospel.*

1. THY people, Lord, who trust thy word,
And wait the smilings of thy face,
Assemble round thy mercy seat,
And plead the promise of thy grace.

2. Hast thou not said thine only Son
Shall be a light to gentile lands,
To open the benighted eyes,
And loose the wretched prisoners'
bands ?

3. From land to land, from sea to sea,
That his dominion shall extend ?
That every tongue shall call him Lord,
And every knee before him bend ?

4. Now let the happy time appear,
The time to favor Zion come ;
Send forth thy heralds far and near,
And call the wandering exiles home.

598. *The Memorials of Grace.*

1. JESUS is gone above the skies,
Where our weak senses reach him not ;
And carnal objects court our eyes,
To thrust our Saviour from our thought.

2. He knows what wandering hearts we
have,
Apt to forget his lovely face ;
And, to refresh our minds, he gave
These kind memorials of his grace.

3. Let sinful sweets be all forgot,
And earth grow less in our esteem ;
Christ and his love fill every thought,
And faith and hope be fixed on him.

4. Whilst he is absent from our sight,
'Tis to prepare our souls a place,
That we may dwell in heavenly light,
And live for ever near his face.

599. *Parting with carnal Joys.*

1. I SEND the joys of earth away—
Away, ye tempters of the mind !
False as the smooth, deceitful sea,
And empty as the whistling wind

2. Your streams were floating me along,
Down to the gulf of black despair ;
And, while I listened to your song,
Your streams had e'en conveyed me
there.

3. Lord ! I adore thy matchless grace,
That warned me of that dark abyss ;
That drew me from those treacherous
seas,
And bade me seek superior bliss.

4. Now, to the shining realms above,
I stretch my hands, and glance my
eyes;
Oh ! for the pinions of a dove,
To bear me to the upper skies.

5. There, from the bosom of my God,
Oceans of endless pleasure roll ;
There would I fix my last abode,
And drown the sorrows of my soul.

Doxology.

To God the Father, God the Son,
And God the Spirit, Three in One,
Be honor, praise, and glory given,
By all on earth, and all in heaven.

LUTHER. S. M.*
BOLD.
HASTINGS.

1. Give to the winds thy fears, Hope, and be un-dis-mayed;

God hears thy sighs, and counts thy tears, God

shall lift up thy head, God shall lift up thy head.

* See also St. Thomas 135.

600. *Christian Courage.*—Isaiah xxvi. 4.

1. Give to the winds thy fears,
   Hope, and be undismayed;
   God hears thy sighs, and counts thy tears,
   God shall lift up thy head.

2. Through waves, and clouds, and storms,
   He gently clears the way;
   Wait thou his time; so shall this night
   Soon end in joyous day.

3. Still heavy is thy heart?
   Still sink thy spirits down?
   Cast off the weight, let fear depart,
   And every care be gone.

4. What though thou rulest not?
   Yet heaven, and earth, and hell
   Proclaim God sitteth on the throne,
   And ruleth all things well.

5. Leave to his sovereign sway,
   To choose and to command;
   So shalt thou, wondering, own his way
   How wise, how good his hand!

601. *Song of Moses and the Lamb.*
Rev. xiv. 3.

1. Awake, and sing the song
   Of Moses and the Lamb;
   Wake, every heart and every tongue,
   To praise the Saviour's name.

2. Sing of his dying love;
   Sing of his rising power;
   Sing how he intercedes above
   For those whose sins he bore.

3. Sing on your heavenly way,
   Ye ransomed sinners, sing;
   Sing on, rejoicing every day,
   In Christ, th' eternal King.

4. Soon shall we hear him say,
   "Ye blessèd children, come;"
   Soon will he call us hence away,
   And take his wanderers home.

5. Soon shall our raptured tongue
   His endless praise proclaim,
   And sweeter voices tune the song
   Of Moses and the Lamb.

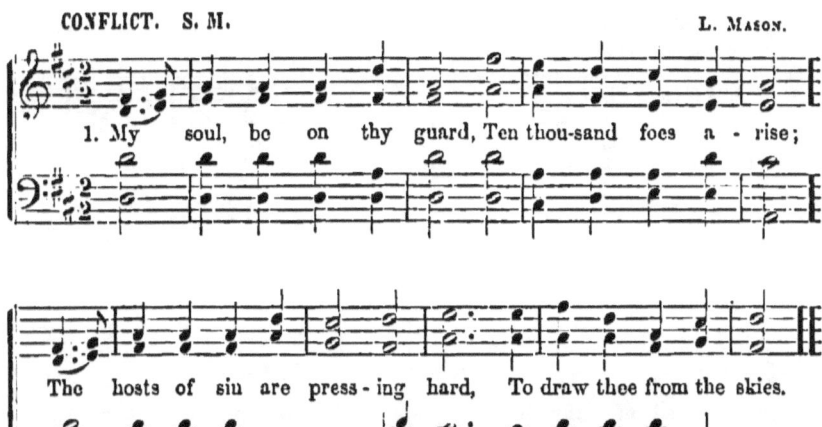

1. My soul, be on thy guard, Ten thou-sand foes a - rise;

The hosts of sin are press-ing hard, To draw thee from the skies.

602. *Vigilance and Warfare.*

1. My soul, be on thy guard,
   Ten thousand foes arise:
The hosts of sin are pressing hard,
To draw thee from the skies.

2. Go, watch, and fight, and pray,
   The battle ne'er give o'er;
Renew it boldly day by day,
And help divine implore.

3. Ne'er think the victory won,
   Nor lay thy armor down;
Thy arduous work will not be done,
Till thou obtain thy crown.

603. *The Saint's Safety in Trial.*

1. FIRM and unmoved are they,
   Who rest their souls on God;
Firm as the mount where David dwelt,
Or where the ark abode.

2. As mountains stood to guard
   The city's sacred ground,
So God, and his almighty love,
Embrace his saints around.

3. What though the Father's rod
   Drop a chastising stroke?
Yet, lest it wound their souls too deep,
Its fury shall be broke.

4. Deal gently, Lord! with those,
   Whose faith and pious fear,—

Whose hope and love, and every grace,
Proclaim their hearts sincere.

604. *God's Word most excellent, or holy Fear.*

1. BEHOLD, the morning sun
   Begins his glorious way;
His beams through all the nations run,
And life and light convey.

2. But where the gospel comes,
   It spreads diviner light;
It calls dead sinners from their tombs,
And gives the blind their sight.

3. How perfect is thy word,
   And all thy judgments just!
For ever sure thy promise, Lord,
And men securely trust.

4. My gracious God, how plain
   Are thy directions given!
Oh may I never read in vain,
But find the path to heaven.

605.   Psalm cxvii.

1. THY name, almighty Lord,
   Shall sound through distant lands;
Great is thy grace, and sure thy word,
Thy truth for ever stands.

2. Far be thine honor spread,
   And long thy praise endure,
Till morning light and evening shade
Shall be exchanged no more.

ARMENIA. C. M.*

DOLCE. LEGATO.

S. B. POND. ARR.

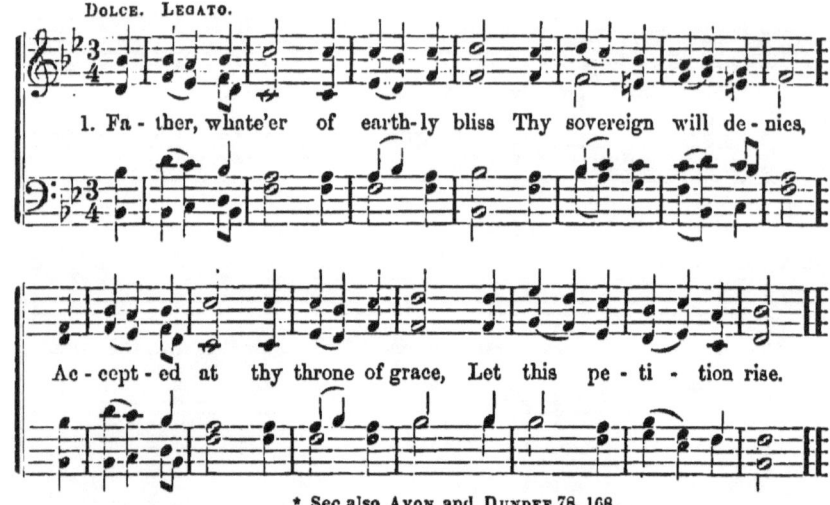

1. Fa - ther, whate'er of earth-ly bliss Thy sovereign will de - nies,

Ac - cept - ed at thy throne of grace, Let this pe - ti - tion rise.

* See also AVON and DUNDEE 78, 168.

606. *Prayer for Submission.*

1. FATHER, whate'er of earthly bliss
Thy sovereign will denies,
Accepted at thy throne of grace,
Let this petition rise:—

2. Give me a calm, a thankful heart,
From every murmur free;
The blessings of thy grace impart,
And make me live to thee.

3. Let the sweet hope that thou art mine
My life and death attend;
Thy presence through my journey shine,
And crown my journey's end.

607. *Filial Submission.*

1. AND can my heart aspire so high,
To say—" My Father, God ?"
Lord! at thy feet I fain would lie,
And learn to kiss the rod.

2. I would submit to all thy will,
For thou art good and wise;
Let each rebellious thought be still,
Nor one faint murmur rise.

3. Thy love can cheer the darkest gloom,
And bid me wait serene;
Till hopes and joys immortal bloom,
And brighten all the scene.

4. " My Father, God !" permit my heart
To plead her humble claim,
And ask the bliss those words impart,
In my Redeemer's name.

608. *Evening Worship in the Family.*

1. O, LORD ! another day has flown,
And we, a lonely band,
Are met once more before thy throne,
To bless thy fostering hand.

2. And wilt thou bend a listening ear
To praises low as ours ?
Thou wilt !—for thou dost love to hear
The song which meekness pours.

3. And, Jesus ! thou thy smiles wilt deign,
As we before thee pray ;
For thou didst bless the infant train,
And are we less than they ?

4. Thy heavenly grace to each impart;
All evil far remove ;
And shed abroad in every heart
Thine everlasting love.

5. Thus, cleansed from sin, and wholly thine,
A flock by Jesus led,
The Sun of righteousness shall shine
In glory on our head.

6. Oh ! still restore our wandering feet,
And still direct our way ;
Till worlds shall fail, and faith shall greet
The dawn of endless day.

609. *Goodness of God.*

1. SWEET is the memory of thy grace,
My God, my heavenly King!
Let age to age thy righteousness
In sounds of glory sing.

2. God reigns on high, but ne'er confines
His goodness to the skies;
Through the whole earth thy bounty shines,
And every want supplies.

3. With longing eyes thy creatures wait
On thee for daily food:
Thy liberal hand provides their meat,
And fills their mouth with good.

4. How kind and gracious is the Lord,
How slow his anger moves!
But soon he sends his pardoning word
To cheer the soul he loves!

5. Creatures with all their endless race,
Thy power and praise proclaim;
But saints that taste thy richer grace
Delight to bless thy name.

610. *The new Covenant sealed.*

1. THE promise of my Father's love
Shall stand for ever good:
He said—and gave his soul to death,
And sealed the grace with blood.

2. To this dear covenant of thy word,
I set my worthless name;
I seal th' engagement to my Lord,
And make my humble claim.

3. I call that legacy my own,
Which Jesus did bequeath;
'T was purchased with a dying groan,
And ratified in death.

4. The light and strength, the pardoning grace,
And glory shall be mine:
My life and soul, my heart and flesh,
And all my powers are thine.

611. *God reconciled in Christ.*

1. DEAREST of all the names above,
My Jesus and my God!
Who can resist thy heavenly love,
Or trifle with thy blood?

2. 'Tis by the merits of thy death,
The Father smiles again;
'Tis by thine interceding breath
The Spirit dwells with men.

3. Till God in human flesh I see,
My thoughts no comfort find;
The holy, just, and sacred Three
Are terrors to my mind.

4. But, if Immanuel's face appear,
My hope, my joy begins;
His name forbids my slavish fear,
His grace removes my sins.

5. While Jews on their own law rely,
And Greeks of wisdom boast;—
I love th' incarnate mystery,
And there I fix my trust.

612. *The Greatness of God.*

1. LONG as I live, I'll bless thy name,
My King, my God of love;
My work and joy shall be the same
In the bright world above.

2. Great is the Lord; his power unknown;
And let his praise be great;
I'll sing the honors of thy throne,
Thy works of grace repeat.

3. Thy grace shall dwell upon my tongue;
And while my lips rejoice,
The men who hear my sacred song,
Shall join their cheerful voice.

4. Fathers to sons shall teach thy name,
And children learn thy ways;
Ages to come thy truth proclaim,
And nations sound thy praise.

5. The world is managed by thy hands;
Thy saints are ruled by love;
And thine eternal kingdom stands—
Though rocks and hills remove.

613. *Mourning with Hope.*

1. WHY should our tears in sorrow flow,
When God recalls his own;
And bids them leave a world of woe,
For an immortal crown?

2. Is not e'en death a gain to those
Whose life to God was given?
Gladly to earth their eyes they close
To open them in heaven.

3. Their toils are past—their work is done,
And they are fully blest;
They fought the fight, the victory won,
And entered into rest.

4. Then let our sorrows cease to flow—
God has recalled his own;
But let our hearts, in every woe,
Still say—"Thy will be done!"

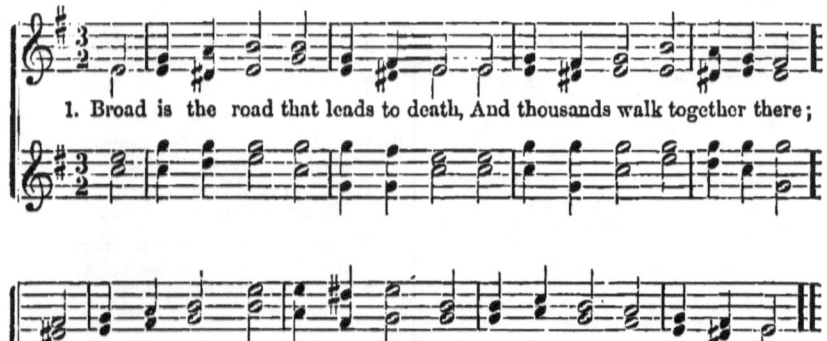

1. Broad is the road that leads to death, And thousands walk together there;

But wis-dom shows a nar-row path, With here and there a trav-el-er.

* See also ZEPHYR 38.

614. *The Road to Life and to Death.*

1. BROAD is the road that leads to death,
And thousands walk together there;
But wisdom shows a narrow path,
With here and there a traveler.

2. "Deny thyself and take thy cross"—
Is the Redeemer's great command:
Nature must count her gold but dross,
If she would gain this heavenly land.

3. The fearful soul that tires and faints,
And walks the ways of God no more,
Is but esteemed almost a saint,
And makes his own destruction sure.

4. Lord, let not all my hopes be vain;
Create my heart entirely new—
Which hypocrites could ne'er attain,
Which false apostates never know.

615. *A dying Saviour.*

1. STRETCHED on the cross the Saviour dies!
Hark! his expiring groans arise:
See—from his hands, his feet, his side;
Fast flows the sacred, crimson tide!

2. But life attends the deathful sound,
And flows from every bleeding wound:
The vital stream,—how free it flows,
To save and cleanse his rebel-foes.

3. Can I survey this scene of woe,
Where mingling grief and wonder flow,
And yet my heart unmoved remain,
Insensible to love or pain?

4. Come, dearest Lord! thy grace impart
To warm this cold, this stupid heart;
Till all its powers and passions move
In melting grief, and ardent love

616. *The Vision of dry Bones.*

1. LOOK down, O Lord, with pitying eye,
See Adam's race in ruin lie;
Sin spreads its trophies o'er the ground,
And scatters slaughtered heaps around

2. And can these dead awake and live?
And can these perished bones revive?
That, mighty God, to thee is known;
That wondrous work is all thy own

3. Thy ministers are sent in vain
To prophesy upon the slain;
In vain they call, in vain they cry,
Till thine Almighty aid is nigh.

4. But if thy Spirit deign to breathe,
Life spreads through all the realms of death:
Dry bones obey thy powerful voice;
They move, they waken, they rejoice.

5. So, when thy trumpet's awful sound
Shall shake the heavens and rend the
ground,
Dead saints shall from their tombs arise,
And spring to life beyond the skies.

617.   *Returning to God.*

1. A BROKEN heart, my God! my King!
Is all the sacrifice I bring;
The God of grace will ne'er despise
A broken heart for sacrifice.

2. My soul lies humbled in the dust,
And owns thy dreadful sentence just;
Look down, O Lord! with pitying eye,
And save the soul condemned to die.

3. Then will I teach the world thy ways;
Sinners shall learn thy sovereign grace;
I'll lead them to my Saviour's blood,
And they shall praise the pardoning God.

4. Oh! may thy love inspire my tongue;
Salvation shall be all my song;
And all my powers shall join to bless
The Lord, my strength, my righteous-
ness.

618. *The Backslider's Supplication.*

1. O THOU, that hearest when sinner's cry!
Though all my crimes before thee lie,
Behold them not with angry look,
But blot their memory from thy book.

2. Create my nature pure within,
And form my soul averse to sin;
Let thy good Spirit ne'er depart,
Nor hide thy presence from my heart.

3. I can not live without thy light,
Cast out and banished from thy sight;
Thy holy joys, my God! restore,
And guard me, that I fall no more.

4. Though I have grieved thy Spirit, Lord!
His help and comfort still afford;
And let a wretch come near thy throne,
To plead the merits of thy Son.

619. *The Hidings of the Father's Face.*

1. FROM Calvary a cry was heard—
A bitter and heart-rending cry;
My Saviour! every mournful word
Bespeaks thy soul's deep agony.

2. A horror of great darkness fell
On Thee, thou spotless, holy One!
And all the swarming hosts of hell
Conspired to tempt God's only Son.

3. The scourge, the thorns, the deep dis-
grace,—
These thou could'st bear, nor once
repine;
But, when Jehovah veiled his face,
Unutterable pangs were thine.

4. Let the dumb world its silence break!
Let pealing anthems rend the sky!
Awake, my sluggish soul! awake!
He died, that we might never die.

5. Lord! on thy cross I fix mine eye;
If e'er I lose its strong control,
Oh! let that dying, piercing cry,
Melt and reclaim my wandering soul.

620. *Meditation on Death.*

1. BEHOLD the path which mortals tread,
Down to the regions of the dead!
Nor will the fleeting moments stay,
Nor can we measure back our day.

2. Our kindred and our friends are gone;
Know, O my soul! this doom thy own;
Feeble as theirs my mortal frame,
The same my way, my home the same.

3. Awake, my soul, thy way prepare,
And lose in this each mortal care;
With steady feet that path they trod,
Which, through the grave, conducts to
God.

4. Father! to thee my all I trust;
And if thou call me down to dust,
I know thy voice, I bless thy hand,
And die in peace at thy command.

621. *The Interment of a Saint.*

1. UNVEIL thy bosom, faithful tomb;
Take this new treasure to thy trust,
And give these sacred relics room
To slumber in the silent dust.

2. Nor pain, nor grief, nor anxious fear
Invade thy bounds; no mortal woes
Can reach the peaceful sleeper here,
While angels watch the soft repose.

3. So Jesus slept; God's dying Son
Passed through the grave, and blessed
the bed:
Rest here, blest saint, till from his throne
The morning break, and pierce the
shade.

4. Break from his throne, illustrious morn!
Attend, O earth, his sovereign word!
Restore thy trust: a glorious form
Shall then arise to meet the Lord.

MENDON. L. M.

GENTLY.

ITALIAN.

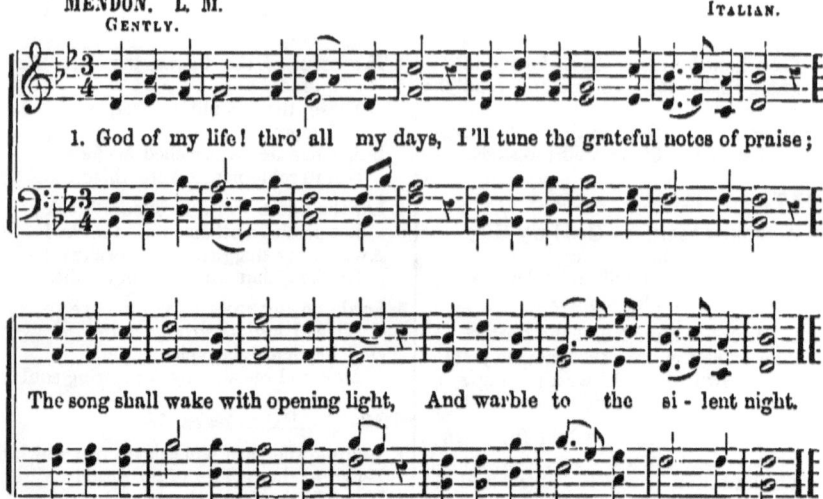

1. God of my life! thro' all my days, I'll tune the grateful notes of praise;

The song shall wake with opening light, And warble to the si - lent night.

622. *Song of Gratitude and Praise.*

1. GOD of my life! through all my days,
I'll tune the grateful notes of praise;
The song shall wake with opening light,
And warble to the silent night.

2. When anxious cares would break my rest,
And griefs would tear my throbbing breast,
The notes of praise, ascending high,
Shall check the murmur and the sigh.

3. When death o'er nature shall prevail,
And all the powers of language fail,
Joy through my swimming eyes shall break,
And mean the thanks I can not speak.

4. But O! when that last conflict's o'er,
And I am chained to earth no more—
With what glad accents shall I rise
To join the music of the skies!

5. Ther shall I learn th' exalted strains,
That echo through the heavenly plains,
And emulate, with joy unknown,
The glowing seraphs round thy throne.

623. *Praise for divine Goodness and Truth.*

1. PRAISE ye the Lord!—my heart shall join
In work so pleasant, so divine:

My days of praise shall ne'er be past,
While life, and thought, and being last.

2. Happy the man, whose hopes rely
On Israel's God ;—he made the sky,
And earth, and seas, with all their train;
And none shall find his promise vain.

3. His truth for ever stands secure; '
He saves th' oppressed, he feeds the poor;
He helps the stranger in distress,
The widow and the fatherless.

4. He loves his saints—he knows them well,
But turns the wicked down to hell:
Thy God, O Zion! ever reigns ;
Praise him in everlasting strains.

624. *The Church, the Garden of God.*

1. LORD! 'tis a pleasant thing to stand
In gardens planted by thy hand ;
Let me within thy courts be seen,
Like a young cedar, fresh and green.

2. There grow thy saints in faith and love,
Blest with thine influence from above;
Not Lebanon, with all its trees,
Yields such a comely sight as these.

3. Laden with fruits of age, they show,
The Lord is holy, just, and true:
None who attend his gates shall find
A God unfaithful or unkind.

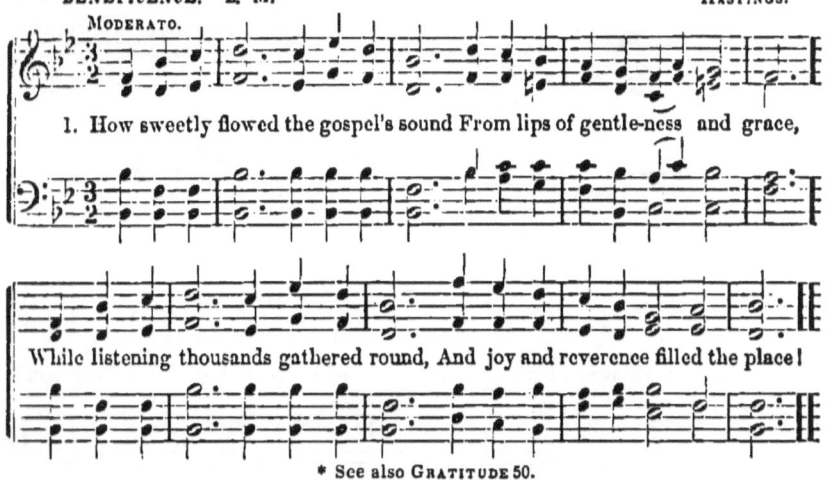

MODERATO.

1. How sweetly flowed the gospel's sound From lips of gentle-ness and grace,

While listening thousands gathered round, And joy and reverence filled the place!

* See also GRATITUDE 50.

625. *The Teaching of Jesus.*

1. How sweetly flowed the gospel's sound
From lips of gentleness and grace,
While listening thousands gathered
round,
And joy and reverence filled the place!

2 From heaven he came, of heaven he
spoke,
To heaven he led his followers' way;
Dark clouds of gloomy night he broke,
Unveiling an immortal day.

3 Come, wanderers! to my Father's home,
Come, all ye weary ones! and rest!—
Yes, sacred Teacher! we will come,
Obey, and be for ever blest.

626. *Morning of the Lord's Day.*

1. HAIL! morning known among the blest—
Morning of hope, and joy, and love—
Of heavenly peace, and holy rest,
Pledge of the endless rest above!

2. Blest be the Father of our Lord,
Who, from the dead, hath brought his
Son;
Hope to the lost was then restored,
And everlasting glory won.

3. Mercy looked down, with smiling eye,
When our Immanuel left the dead;
Faith marked his bright ascent on high,
And hope, with gladness, raised her
head.

4. Descend, O Spirit of the Lord!
Thy fire to every bosom bring;
Then shall our ardent hearts accord,
And teach our lips God's praise to sing.

627. *The Sabbath.*

1. O SACRED day of peace and joy!
Thy hours are ever dear to me;
Ne'er may a single thought destroy,
The holy calm I feel in thee.

2. Thy hours are ever dear to me,
For God has given them in his love,
To tell how calm, how blest shall be
The endless day of heaven above.

628. *Love of Christ in the Heart.*

1. COME, dearest Lord! descend and dwell,
By faith and love, in every breast;
Then shall we know, and taste, and feel,
The joys that can not be expressed.

2. Come, fill our hearts with inward
strength;
Make our enlargéd souls possess,
And learn the height, and breadth, and
length
Of thine eternal love and grace.

3. Now to the God, whose power can do
More than our thoughts and wishes
know,
Be everlasting honors done,
By all the church, through Chirst, the
Son.

WATTS. L. M.* From a Passage in BEETHOVEN.

1. He dies! the Friend of sin-ners dies! Lo! Salem's daughters weep around!

A solemn dark-ness veils the skies! A sud-den trembling shakes the ground!

* See also HAMBURG 28.

629. *Christ's Dying, Rising, and Reigning.*

1. HE dies!—the Friend of sinners dies!
  Lo! Salem's daughters weep around!
  A solemn darkness veils the skies!
  A sudden trembling shakes the ground!

2. Here's love and grief beyond degree—
  The Lord of glory dies for men!
  But, lo! what sudden joys we see!
  Jesus the dead—revives again!

3. The rising God forsakes the tomb!
  Up to his Father's court he flies!
  Cherubic legions guard him home,
  And shout him welcome to the skies!

4. Break off your tears, ye saints, and tell
  How high our great Deliverer reigns;
  Sing how he spoiled the hosts of hell,
  And led the tyrant Death—in chains.

5. Say, "Live for ever, glorious King,
  "Born to redeem, and strong to save!"
  Then ask—"O death, where is thy sting?
  "And where thy victory, boasting
  grave?"

630. *Self-Dedication to God.*

1. LORD, I am thine, entirely thine,
  Purchased and saved by blood divine;
  With full consent thine I would be,
  And own thy sovereign right in me.

2. Grant me, in mercy, now a place
  Among the children of thy grace;
  A wretched sinner, lost to God,
  But ransomed by Immanuel's blood.

3. Thee, my new Master, now I call,
  And consecrate to thee my all;
  Lord, let me live and die to thee,
  Be thine through all eternity.

631. *Peace and Hope through Christ's
  Intercession.*

1. HE lives—the great Redeemer lives!
  What joy the blest assurance gives!
  And now, before his Father-God,
  Pleads the full merits of his blood.

2. Repeated crimes awake our fears,
  And justice, armed with frowns, appears;
  But in the Saviour's lovely face,
  Sweet mercy smiles—and all is peace.

3. In every dark, distressful hour,
  When sin and Satan join their power,
  Let this dear hope repel the dart—
  That Jesus bears us on His heart.

4. Great Advocate, almighty Friend!
  On thee our humble hopes depend:
  Our cause can never, never fail,
  For Jesus pleads, and must prevail.

632. *Teachings of the Spirit.*

1. Come, blessed Spirit! source of light,
    Whose power and grace are unconfined,
    Dispel the gloomy shades of night,—
    The thicker darkness of the mind.

2. To mine illumined eyes display
    The glorious truth thy word reveals;
    Cause me to run the heavenly way,
    Thy book unfold and loose the seals.

3. Thine inward teachings make me know
    The mysteries of redeeming love,
    The vanity of things below,
    And excellence of things above.

4. While through this dubious maze I stray,
    Spread, like the sun, thy beams abroad,
    To show the dangers of the way,
    And guide my feeble steps to God.

MUNICH. L. M.*   OLD GERMAN.

SLOW AND EXPRESSIVE.

1. 'Tis fin - ished! 'Tis fin - ished!— so the Sa - viour cried, And meek-ly bowed his head, and died; 'Tis finished!—yes, the race is run, The bat - tle fought, the vic - to - ry won.

* See also the opposite page.

633. *Christ on the Cross.*

1. 'Tis finished!—so the Saviour cried,
    And meekly bowed his head, and died;
    'Tis finished!—yes, the race is run,
    The battle fought, the victory won.

2. 'Tis finished!—this his dying groan
    Shall sins of every kind atone;
    Millions shall be redeemed from death,
    By this his last expiring breath.

3. 'Tis finished!—Heaven is reconciled,
    And all the powers of darkness spoiled:
    Peace, love, and happiness, again
    Return, and dwell with sinful men.

4. 'Tis finished!—let the joyful sound
    Be heard through all the nations round
    'Tis finished!—let the echo fly
    Through heaven and hell, through earth
    and sky.

"NEARER TO THEE." 6s & 4s. Special. HASTINGS.

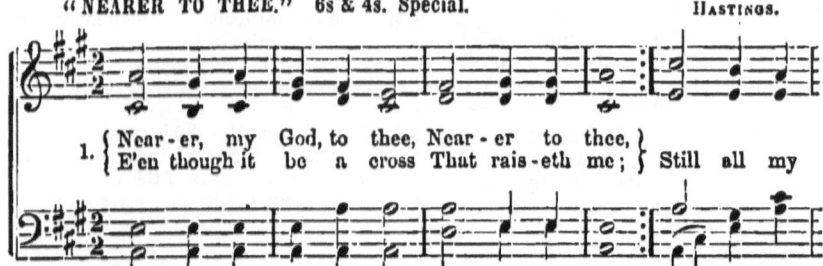

1. { Near-er, my God, to thee, Near-er to thee, }
{ E'en though it be a cross That rais-eth me; } Still all my

song shall be, Near-er, my God, to thee— Near-er to thee.

---

634. *"Nearer to Thee."*

1. NEARER, my God, to thee,
Nearer to thee,
E'en though it be a cross
That raiseth me;
Still all my song shall be,
Nearer, my God, to thee—
Nearer to thee!

2. Though, like the wanderer,
The sun gone down,
Darkness be over me,
My rest a stone;
Yet in my dreams I'd be
Nearer, my God, to thee—
Nearer to thee!

3. There let the way appear,
Steps unto heaven;
All that thou sendest me,
In mercy given;
Angels to beckon me
Nearer, my God, to thee—
Nearer to thee.

4. Then, with my waking thoughts,
Bright with thy praise,

Out of my stony griefs,
Bethel I'll raise;
So by my woes to be
Nearer, my God, to thee—
Nearer to thee!

5. Or if, on joyful wing,
Cleaving the sky,
Sun, moon, and stars forgot,
Upward I fly,
Still all my song shall be,
Nearer, my God, to thee,
Nearer to thee.

[*For the following hymn repeat the first two measures of the second strain.*]

635. *Heaven is my Home.* •

1. I'M but a stranger here,
Heaven is my home;
Earth is a desert drear,
Heaven is my home;
Danger and sorrow stand
Round me on every hand,
Heaven is my Father-land,
Heaven is my home

2. What though the tempests rage,
  Heaven is my home;
 Short is my pilgrimage,
  Heaven is my home;
 And time's wild, wintry blast,
 Soon will be overpast,
 I shall reach home at last,
  Heaven is my home

3. Therefore I murmur not,
  Heaven is my home;
 Whate'er my earthly lot,
  Heaven is my home;
 And I shall surely stand,
 There, at my Lord's right hand,
 Heaven is my Father-land,
  Heaven is my home.

LANSINGBURGH. 6s & 5s. Alternate. GERMAN.

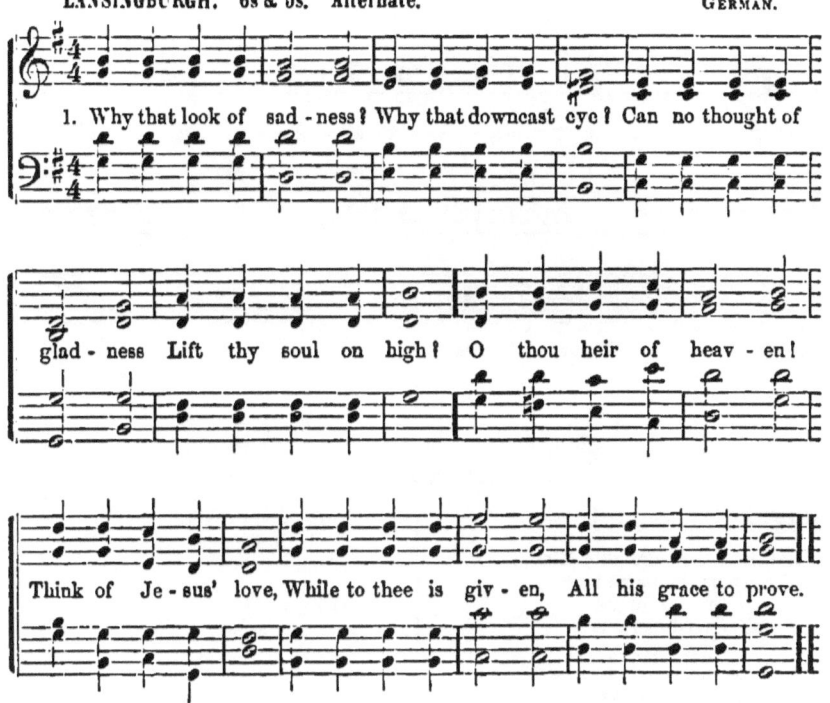

1. Why that look of sad - ness? Why that downcast eye? Can no thought of
glad - ness Lift thy soul on high? O thou heir of heav - en!
Think of Je - sus' love, While to thee is giv - en, All his grace to prove.

636. *Consolation.*

1. Why that look of sadness?
  Why that downcast eye?
 Can no thought of gladness
  Lift thy soul on high?
 O, thou heir of heaven!
  Think of Jesus' love,
 While to thee is given,
  All his grace to prove.

2. Is thy burdened spirit
  Agonized for sin?
 Think of Jesus' merit,
  He can make thee clean:

Think of Calv'ry's mountain,
  Where his blood was spilt;
 In that healing fountain
  Wash away thy guilt.

3. Is thy spirit drooping,
  Is the tempter near?
 Still in Jesus hoping,
  What hast thou to fear?
 Set the prize before thee,
  Gird thy armor on:
 Heir of grace and glory,
  Struggle for thy crown!

ITALIAN HYMN. 6s & 4s.*

GIARDINI.

1. Come, thou al-might-y King, Help us thy name to sing, Help us to praise: Fa-ther! all glo-ri-ous, O'er all vic-to-ri-ous, Come, and reign o-ver us, An-cient of Days!

* See also NEW HAVEN 44.

637. *Invocation.*

1. COME, thou almighty King,
Help us thy name to sing,
Help us to praise:
Father! all-glorious,
O'er all victorious,
Come, and reign over us,
Ancient of Days!

2. Come, thou incarnate Word!
Gird on thy mighty sword;
Our prayer attend:
Come, and thy people bless,
And give thy word success;
Spirit of holiness!
On us descend.

3. Come, holy Comforter!
Thy sacred witness bear,
In this glad hour:
Thou, who almighty art,
Now rule in every heart,
And ne'er from us depart,
Spirit of power!

4. To the great One in Three,
The highest praises be,
Hence evermore!
His sovereign majesty
May we in glory see,
And to eternity
Love and adore.

638. *National Blessings.*

1. GOD bless our native land,
Firm may she ever stand,
Through storm and night;
Where the wild tempests rave,
Ruler of wind and wave,
Do thou our country save,
By thy great might.

2. For her our prayers shall rise,
To God, above the skies,
On him we wait.
Thou, who hast heard each sigh,
Watching each weeping eye,
Be thou for ever nigh,
God save the state.

HEMANS. 6s & 4s.*

STACCATO.

HASTINGS.

1. Glory to God on high : Let heaven and earth reply—Praise ye his name! His love and

grace adore, Who all our sorrows bore, And sing for ev - ermore, Worthy the Lamb.

* See also NEW HAVEN 44.

639. *Worthy the Lamb.*

1. GLORY to God on high :
Let heaven and earth reply—
Praise ye his name!
His love and grace adore, ·
Who all our sorrows bore;
And sing for ever more,
Worthy the Lamb.

2. Ye, who surround the throne,
Cheerfully join in one,
Praising his name :
Ye, who have felt his blood
Scaling your peace with God,
Sound his dear name abroad,
Worthy the Lamb.

3. Join, all ye ransomed race,
Our Lord and God to bless ;
Praise ye his name:
In him we will rejoice,
And make a joyful noise,
Shouting, with heart and voice,
Worthy the Lamb.

4. Soon must we change our place,
Yet will we never cease
Praising his name :
To him our songs we 'll bring,
Hail him our gracious King,
And through all ages sing
Worthy the Lamb.

640. *Evening Devotion.*

1. WHILE at the even-tide,
Gently the breezes glide,
Fragrant the air ;
While noise and tumult cease,
And all is hushed in peace,
Let holy thoughts increase,
Rising in prayer.

2. God of beneficence,
Kind is thy influence
On all around ;
While favors oft renewed
Fill me with gratitude,
Let sin no more intrude
My peace to wound.

3. When life's declining day
Hastens my soul away,
Jesus be near ;
When the last hour shall come,
When through the opening tomb,
Thou shalt command me home,
Save me from fear.

4. Then shall a sweeter song
Rise from this tuneful tongue,
Than earth has known ;
While angels sound thy praise,
And saints their anthems raise,
Shouting redeeming grace,
Round thy bright throne!

GENEVA. 7s & 6s.* Pec.　　　　　　L. MASON "S. SONGS."

1. Time is winging us a - way To our e - ter - nal home;
   Life is but a win - ter's day, A jour - ney to the tomb;

Youth and vi - gor soon will flee, Bloom - ing beau - ty lose its charms;

All that's mor - tal soon will be En - closed in death's cold arms.

* See also AMSTERDAM 47.

641.　　*Flight of Time.*

1. TIME is winging us away
   To our eternal home :
   Life is but a winter's day,
   A journey to the tomb ;
   Youth and vigor soon will flee,
   Blooming beauty lose its charms ;
   All that's mortal soon will be
   Enclosed in death's cold arms.

2. Time is winging us away
   To our eternal home :
   Life is but a winter's day,
   A journey to the tomb :
   But the Christian shall enjoy
   Health and beauty soon above ;
   Far beyond the world's alloy,
   Secure in Jesus' love.

642.　　*Heavenly Aspirations.*

1. TELL me not of earthly toys
   The worldling may admire,

   Tell me not of transient joys
   That sparkle and expire ;
   For there is a heavenly store,
   Earthly riches can not buy,
   Bliss supreme for evermore—
   A glorious home on high.

2. Tell me of my sin forgiven,
   Through Christ's atoning blood,
   Point me to the rest of heaven,
   And bid me hope in God :
   Tell me of the mansions blest
   By the Lord of life prepared,
   Where the weary are at rest,
   No more by sin ensnared.

3. Tell me not of earthly toys
   The worldling may admire,
   Tell me not of transient joys
   That sparkle and expire ;
   Themes celestial fill the soul
   With delights that never die ;
   Waves of transport soon to roll
   Above the starry sky.

GETHSEMANE. 7s. 6 lines.*   Arr. from "Spir. Songs."

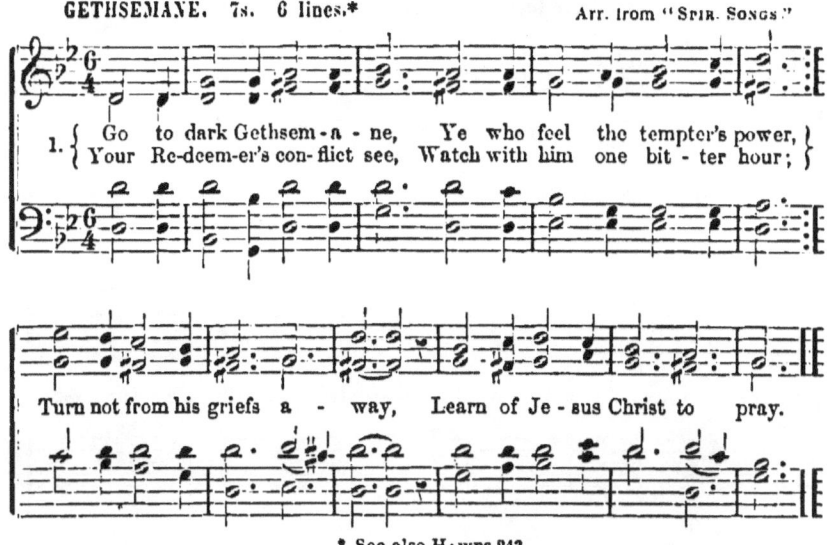

1. { Go to dark Gethsem-a-ne, Ye who feel the tempter's power, }
   { Your Re-deem-er's con-flict see, Watch with him one bit-ter hour; }

Turn not from his griefs a - way, Learn of Je-sus Christ to pray.

* See also HAWES 243.

643. *Christ an Example in Suffering.*

1. Go to dark Gethsemane,
   Ye who feel the tempter's power,
 Your Redeemer's conflict see,
   Watch with him one bitter hour;
 Turn not from his griefs away,
 Learn of Jesus Christ to pray.

2. Follow to the judgment hall,
   View the Lord of life arraigned:
 O, the wormwood and the gall,
   O, the pangs his soul sustained!
 Shun not suffering, shame, or loss,
 Learn of him to bear the cross.

3. Calvary's mournful mountain climb;
   There, adoring at his feet,
 Mark that miracle of time—
   God's own sacrifice complete:
 "It is finished"—hear him cry,
 Learn of Jesus Christ to die.

4. Early hasten to the tomb,
   Where they laid his lifeless clay;
 All is solitude and gloom—
   Who hath taken him away?
 Christ hath risen—he meets our eyes,
 Saviour, teach us so to rise.

644.   *Scene in Golgotha.*

1. Go to Golgotha and weep
   With the suffering Son of God,

And behold, with anguish deep,
   Where the sacred Victim stood,
 Like a lamb to slaughter led,—
 Every friend and helper fled.

2. Go to Golgotha and see
   All the heavens in sackcloth hung,
 While rebuke and blasphemy
   Issue there from every tongue!
 Hear that agonizing cry,
 Hear the rending rocks reply!

4. Go to Golgotha and learn
   All the bitterness of sin,
 In those scenes of woe discern
   What thy portion would have been.
 Thine the shame, reproach and guilt,
 'Twas for thee that blood was spilt!

4. Go to Golgotha and pray
   That thy sins may be forgiven:
 He on whom thy burden lay,
   Now is Advocate in heaven·
 Lift thine eyes to his abode,
 Trusting in the Son of God.

Doxology.

PRAISE the name of God most high,
Praise him, all below the sky,
Praise him, all the heavenly host,
Father, Son, and Holy Ghost;
As through countless ages past,
Evermore his praise shall last.

NUREMBURGH.   7s. 6 lines.   Or 4 lines.   GERMAN.

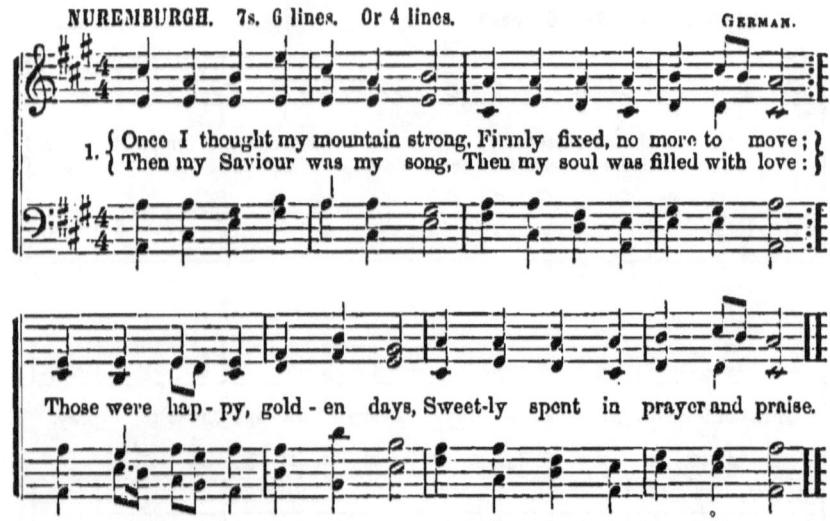

1. { Once I thought my mountain strong, Firmly fixed, no more to move; }
{ Then my Saviour was my song, Then my soul was filled with love : }

Those were hap-py, gold-en days, Sweet-ly spent in prayer and praise.

645.   *In Darkness.*

1. ONCE I thought my mountain strong,
    Firmly fixed, no more to move;
Then my Saviour was my song,
    Then my soul was filled with love :
Those were happy, golden days,
Sweetly spent in prayer and praise.

2. Little, then, myself I knew,
    Little thought of Satan's power;
Now I feel my sins renew,
    Now I feel the stormy hour;
Sin has put my joys to flight,—
Sin has turned my day to night.

3. Saviour! shine, and cheer my soul,
    Bid my dying hopes revive,
Make my wounded spirit whole,
    Far away, the tempter drive;
Speak the word and set me free,—
Let me live alone to thee.

646.   Ps. xliii.

1. WHY art thou cast down, my soul?
God, thy God shall make thee whole!
Why art thou disquieted?
God shall lift thy drooping head;
And his countenance benign
Be the saving health of thine.

2. Once the morning's earliest light
Brought his mercy to my sight;
Once my wakeful song was heard
Later than the evening bird;

Still his countenance shall shine
Through the clouds that darken thine.

3. Why, my soul, art thou perplexed?
Why with faithless trouble vexed?
Hope in God, whose saving name
Thou shalt joyfully proclaim,
When his countenance divine
Sheds the light of heaven on thine.

[For the following omit the repeat.]

647.   *Christ's Ascension.*

1. HAIL the day, which sees him rise
Glorious to his native skies!
Christ, awhile to mortals given,
Enters now the gates of heaven.

2. There the glorious triumph waits:—
Lift your head, eternal gates!
Christ hath vanquished death and sin :—
Take the King of glory in.

3. See,—high heaven its Lord receives ;—
Yet he loves the earth he leaves:
Though returning to his throne,
Still he calls mankind his own

4. Still for us he intercedes,
His prevailing death he pleads,
Near himself prepares our place,
Great Forerunner of our race.

5. What though parted from our sight,
Far above yon starry height?
May our warm affections rise,
Following him beyond the skies.

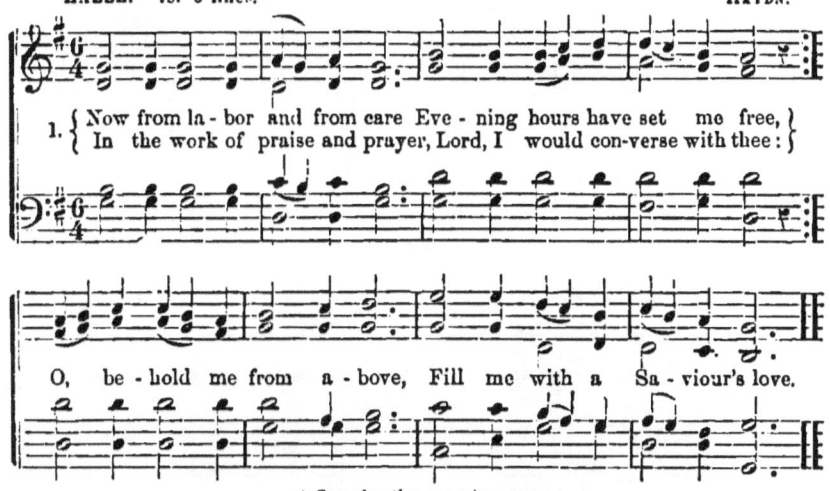

1. {Now from la - bor and from care Eve - ning hours have set me free,
In the work of praise and prayer, Lord, I would con-verse with thee: }

O, be - hold me from a - bove, Fill me with a Sa - viour's love.

* See also the opposite page.

648. *Evening Hymn.*

1. Now from labor and from care
   Evening hours have set me free,
   In the work of praise and prayer,
   Lord, I would converse with thee:
   O behold me from above,
   Fill me with a Saviour's love.

2. Sin and sorrow, guilt and woe
   Wither all my earthly joys;
   Nought can charm me here below,
   But my Saviour's melting voice:
   Lord, forgive, thy grace restore,
   Make me thine for evermore.

3. For the blessings of this day,
   For the mercies of this hour,
   For the gospel's cheering ray,
   For the Spirit's quickening power,
   Grateful notes to thee I raise,
   O, accept the song of praise.

649. *Christ our Refuge in Trouble.*

1. Quiet, Lord, this trembling frame,
   Tranquilize this beating heart,
   Let the savor of thy name
   Sweetest influence now impart,
   Till the thought that thou art near
   Shall dispel each rising fear.

2. Let me find a hallowed rest
   Never more in sin to rove,
   Gently leaning on thy breast
   In humility and love;

Like a simple-hearted child,
With affections undefiled.

3. Then, though earthly cares assail,
   Though afflictions mark my way,
   No temptation shall prevail,
   To dishearten or betray:
   While I thus in thee confide,
   Every want is satisfied.

650. *Teacher's Prayer.*

1. Shepherd of the fold of God,
   Who hast bought us by thy blood,
   Make these little ones thy care,
   Keep their hearts from every snare;
   Bid them see thy heavenly charms,
   Fold them in thy gracious arms.

2. Shepherd of the fold of God,
   Who the vale of sorrows trod,
   Once thyself a little child,
   Holy, harmless, undefiled,
   Now these waiting children see,
   Cause them to resemble thee.

3. Shepherd of the fold of God,
   Hear us from thy high abode;
   For these lambs to thee we cry:
   Let them on thy grace rely;
   Let their follies be forgiven,
   Fit them for the gate of heaven.

1. Gracious Spi - rit! Love di - vine! Let thy light with-in me shine;

All my guilt - y fears re-move, Fill me with thy heavenly love.

* See also GERMAN HYMN 156.

651. *Influences of the Spirit.*

1. GRACIOUS Spirit! Love divine!
Let thy light within me shine;
All my guilty fears remove,
Fill me with thy heavenly love.

2. Speak thy pardoning grace to me;
Set the burdened sinner free:
Lead me to the Lamb of God,
Wash me in his precious blood.

3. Life and peace to me impart,
Seal salvation on my heart;
Breathe thyself into my breast,
Earnest of immortal rest.

4. Let me never from thee stray,
Keep me in the narrow way;
Fill my soul with joy divine;
Keep me, Lord, for ever thine.

652. *Strength equal to the Day.*—Deut.
xxxiii. 25.

1. WAIT, my soul upon the Lord,
To his gracious promise flee,
Laying hold upon his word,
"As thy days thy strength shall be."

2. If the sorrows of thy case
Seem peculiar still to thee,
God has promised needful grace,
"As thy days thy strength shall be."

3. Days of trial, days of grief,
In succession thou may'st see;

This is still thy sweet relief,
"As thy days thy strength shall be."

4. Rock of Ages, I'm secure,
With thy promise full and free;
Faithful, positive, and sure—
"As thy days thy strength shall be."

653. *Parting of Christians.*

1. FOR a season called to part,
Let us now ourselves commend,
To the gracious eye and heart
Of our ever-present Friend.

2. Jesus! hear our humble prayer;
Tender Shepherd of thy sheep!
Let thy mercy and thy care
All our souls in safety keep.

3. In thy strength may we be strong;
Sweeten every cross and pain;
Grant, that, if we live, ere long
We may meet in peace again.

4. Then, if thou thy help afford,
Joyful songs to thee shall rise,
And our souls shall praise the Lord,
Who regards our humble cries.

654. *The Sinner meeting God.*

1. SINNER! art thou still secure?
Wilt thou still refuse to pray?
Can thy heart or hand endure,
In the Lord's avenging day?

2. See—his mighty arm is bared ;
   Awful terrors clothe his brow!
For his judgments stand prepared ;—
   Thou must either break or bow.

3. At his presence nature shakes,
   Earth, affrighted, hastes to flee,
Solid mountains melt like wax,
   What will then become of thee?

4. Who his coming may abide?
   You that glory in your shame!—
Can you find a place to hide,
   When the world is wrapt in flame?

655.   *The Resurrection.*

1. MORNING breaks upon the tomb,
   Jesus scatters all its gloom;
Day of triumph through the skies—
See the glorious Saviour rise!

2. Ye, who are of death afraid,
   Triumph in the scattered shade;
· Drive your anxious cares away;
   See the place where Jesus lay!

3. Christian! dry your flowing tears,
   Chase your unbelieving fears;
Look on his deserted grave;
Doubt no more his power to save.

656.   *Confession and Entreaty.*

1. SOVEREIGN Ruler, Lord of all!
   Prostrate at thy feet I fall;
Hear, O! hear my earnest cry,
   Frown not, lest I faint and die.

2. Vilest of the sons of men—
   Chief of sinners I have been;
Oft abused thee to thy face,
   Trampled on thy richest grace.

3. Justly might thy righteous dart
   Pierce this bleeding, broken heart;
Justly might thine angry breath
Blast me in eternal death.

4. But with thee there's mercy found,
   Balm to heal my every wound :
Soothe, O! soothe the troubled breast,
   Give the weary wanderer rest.

657.   *Winning Souls.*

1. WOULD you win a soul to God?
   Tell him of a Saviour's blood,
Once for dying sinners spilt,
To atone for all their guilt.

2. Tell him how the streams did glide,
   From his hands, his feet, his side—

How his head with thorns was crowned,
   And his heart in sorrow drowned :—

3. How he yielded up his breath,
   How he agonized in death,
How he lives to intercede—
Christ, our Advocate and Head.

4. Tell him—it was sovereign grace
   Led thee first to seek his face;
Made thee choose the better part,
Wrought salvation in thy heart.

5. Tell him of that liberty,
   Wherewith Jesus makes us free;
Sweetly speak of sins forgiven,
Earnest of the joys of heaven.

658.   *The Righteous only may hope for*
            Heaven.

1. WHO, O Lord, when life is o'er,
   Shall to heaven's blest mansions soar?
Who, an ever-welcome guest,
In the holy place shall rest?

2. He whose heart thy love has warmed;
   He whose will, to thine conformed,
Bids his life unsullied run;
He whose words and thoughts are one.

3. He who shuns the sinner's road,
   Loving those who love their God;
Who, with hope and love unfeigned,
Treads the path by thee ordained ;—

4. He who trusts in Christ alone ;
   Not in aught himself has done ;—
He, great God, shall be thy care,
And thy choicest blessing share.

659.   *The Sinner warned.*

1. HASTE, O sinner! to be wise,
   Stay not for the morrow's sun;
Wisdom warns thee, from the skies,
   All the paths of death to shun.

2. Haste, and mercy now implore;
   Stay not for the morrow's sun;
Thy probation may be o'er,
   Ere this evening's work is done.

3. Haste, O sinner! now return;
   Stay not for the morrow's sun;
Lest thy lamp should cease to burn
   Ere salvation's work is done.

4. Haste, while yet thou canst be blest;
   Stay not for the morrow's sun;
Death may thy poor soul arrest,
   Ere the morrow is begun.

TIOGA. S. M.*
SLOW AND SOLEMN.

HASTINGS.

1. O where shall rest be found—Rest for the wea - ry soul?

'Twere vain the o - cean depths to sound, Or pierce to ei - ther pole.

* See also St. Bridges 284.

660. *Rest for the weary Soul.*

1. O, WHERE shall rest be found—
Rest for the weary soul ?
'Twere vain the ocean depths to sound,
Or pierce to either pole.

2. The world can never give
The bliss for which we sigh:
'Tis not the whole of life to live,
Nor all of death to die.

3. Beyond this vale of tears,
There is a life above,
Unmeasured by the flight of years;
And all that life is love.

4. There is a death whose pang
Outlasts the fleeting breath ;
O, what eternal horrors hang
Around the second death !

5. Lord God of truth and grace,
Teach us that death to shun,
Lest we be banished from thy face,
And evermore undone.

661. *The Judgment in Prospect.*

1. AND will the Judge descend ?
And must the dead arise ?
And not a single soul escape
His all-discerning eyes ?

2. How will my heart endure
The terrors of that day,

When earth and heaven before his face,
Astonished, shrink away ?

3. But ere that trumpet shakes
The mansions of the dead,
Hark ! from the gospel's cheering sound
What joyful tidings spread !

4. Ye sinners, seek his grace ;
His wrath ye can not bear ;
Fly to the shelter of his cross,
And find salvation there.

662. *Grieving the Spirit.*

1. AND canst thou, sinner ! slight
The call of love divine ?
Shall God, with tenderness invite,
And gain no thought of thine ?

2. Wilt thou not cease to grieve
The Spirit from thy breast,
Till he thy wretched soul shall leave
With all thy sins oppressed ?

3. To-day, a pardoning God
Will hear the suppliant pray,
To-day, a Saviour's cleansing blood
Will wash thy guilt away.

4. But, grace so dearly bought
If yet thou wilt despise,
Thy fearful doom with vengeance fraught
Will fill thee with surprise.

DETROIT. S. M.
AFFETTUOSO.

E. P. HASTINGS.

1. Did Christ o'er sin-ners weep, And shall our cheeks be dry!

Let floods of pen-i-ten-tial grief Burst forth from ev-ery eye.

663. *Repentance in View of Christ's Compassion.*

1. DID Christ o'er sinners weep,
And shall our cheeks be dry?
Let floods of penitential grief
Burst forth from every eye.

2. The Son of God in tears
The angels wondering see;
Be thou astonished, O my soul;
He shed those tears for thee.

3. He wept that we might weep;
Each sin demands a tear:
In heaven alone no sin is found,
And there's no weeping there.

664. *Ingratitude to Divine Goodness.*

1. Is this the kind return!
Are these the thanks we owe!
Thus to abuse eternal love,
Whence all our blessings flow!

2. To what a stubborn frame
.Has sin reduced our mind;
What strange, rebellious wretches we,
And God as strangely kind!

3. Turn, turn us, mighty God,
And mould our souls afresh;
Break, sovereign grace, these hearts of
stone,
And give us hearts of flesh.

4. Let past ingratitude
Provoke our weeping eyes;
And hourly, as new mercies fall,
Let hourly thanks arise.

665. *Submission to Christ.*

1. JESUS, I come to thee,
A sinner doomed to die;
My only refuge is thy cross;
Here at thy feet I lie.

2. Can mercy reach my case,
And all my sins remove?
Break, O my God, this heart of stone,
And melt it by thy love.

3. Too long my soul has gone
Far from my God astray;
I've sported on the brink of hell,
In sin's delusive way.

4. But, Lord, my heart is fixed,
I hope in thee alone;
Break off the chains of sin and death,
And bind me to thy throne.

5. Thy blood can cleanse my heart,
Thy hand can wipe my tears—
Oh! send thy blessèd Spirit down
To banish all my fears.

6. Then shall my soul arise,
From sin and Satan free;
Redeemed from hell and every foe,
I'll trust alone in thee.

ROMBERG. C. M.*   From the "CHORALIST."
  MODERATO, TENDERLY.

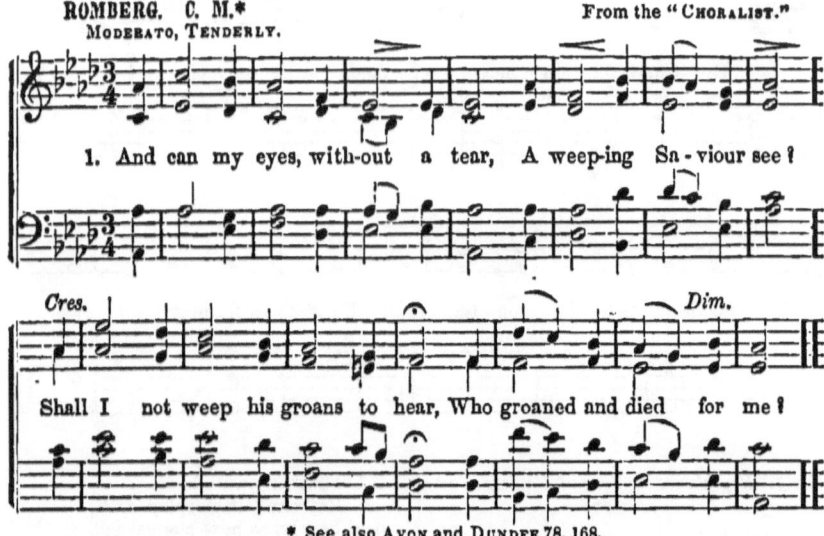

1. And can my eyes, with-out   a tear, A weep-ing Sa - viour see?

Cres.   Dim.

Shall I   not weep his groans to hear, Who groaned and died   for me?

* See also AVON and DUNDEE 78, 168.

666.   *Repentance at the Cross.*

1. AND can my eyes, without a tear,
    A weeping Saviour see?
   Shall I not weep his groans to hear
   Who groaned and died for me?

2. Blest Jesus, let those tears of thine
    Subdue each stubborn foe;
   Come, fill my heart with love divine,
    And bid my sorrows flow.

667.   *Remembering Christ.*

1. ACCORDING to thy gracious word,
    In meek humility,
   This will I do, my dying Lord!—
    I will remember thee.

2. Thy body, broken for my sake,
    My bread from heaven shall be;
   Thy testimental cup I take,
    And thus remember thee.

3. Gethsemane can I forget?
    Or there thy conflict see,—
   Thine agony and bloody sweat,
    And not remember thee?

4. When to the cross I turn mine eyes,
    And rest on Calvary,
   O Lamb of God, my sacrifice!
    I must remember thee:—

5. Remember thee, and all thy pains,
    And all thy love to me!—

Yea, while a breath, a pulse remains,
    Will I remember thee.

6. And, when these failing lips grow dumb,
    And mind and memory flee,—
   When, in thy kingdom thou shalt come,
    Jesus! remember me.

668.   *Christ our Support in Death.*

1. JESUS, the vision of thy face
    Hath overpowering charms:
   Scarce shall I feel death's cold embrace,
    While in the Saviour's arms.

2. And while ye hear my heart-strings
        break,
    How sweet the minutes roll!
   A mortal paleness on my cheek
    And glory in my soul.

669.   *Contrition and Prayer.*

1. OH! for that tenderness of heart,
    That bows before the Lord;
   That owns how just and good thou **art,**
    And trembles at thy word.

2. Oh! for those humble, contrite tears,
    Which from repentance flow;
   That sense of guilt, which, trembling,
        fears
    The long-suspended blow!

3. Oh! fill my soul with faith and love,
And strength to do thy will;
Raise my desires and hopes above,—
Thyself to me reveal.

670. *The Soul casting itself on Christ.*

1. APPROACH, my soul! the mercy-seat,
Where Jesus answers prayer;
There humbly fall before his feet,
For none can perish there.

2. Thy promise is my only plea,
With this I venture nigh:
Thou callest burdened souls to thee,
And such, O Lord! am I.

3. Bowed down beneath a load of sin,
By Satan sorely pressed,
By wars without, and fears within,
I come to thee for rest.

4. Be thou my shield and hiding-place,
That, sheltered near thy side,
I may my fierce accuser face,
And tell him, thou hast died.

5. Oh! wondrous love, to bleed and die,
To bear the cross and shame,
That guilty sinners, such as I,
Might plead thy gracious name!

671. *Love to our Neighbor.*

1. FATHER of mercies! send thy grace
All-powerful from above,
To form, in our obedient souls,
The image of thy love.

2. Oh! may our sympathizing breasts
That generous pleasure know,
Kindly to share in others' joy,
And weep for others' woe.

3. When the most helpless sons of grief,
In low distress, are laid,
Soft be our hearts their pain to feel,
And swift our hands to aid.

4. So Jesus looked on dying men,
When throned above the skies;
And, mid th' embraces of thy love,
He felt compassion rise.

5. On wings of love the Saviour flew,
To raise us from the ground;
And gave his own most precious blood,
A balm for every wound.

672. *Indwelling Sin lamented.*

1. WITH tears of anguish I lament,
Here at thy cross, my God,

My passion, pride, and discontent,
And vile ingratitude.

2. Sure there was ne'er a heart so base,
So false as mine has been;
So faithless to its promises,
So prone to every sin!

3. How long, dear Saviour, shall I feel
This warfare in my breast?
In mercy bow this stubborn will,
And give my spirit rest.

4. Break, sovereign grace, O break the charm,
And set the captive free;
Reveal, almighty God, thine arm,
And haste to rescue me.

673. *Various Influences desired*

1. ETERNAL Spirit—God of truth,
Our contrite hearts inspire;
Kindle a flame of heavenly love,
And feed the pure desire.

2. 'Tis thine to soothe the sorrowing mind,
With guilt and fear oppressed;
'Tis thine to bid the dying live,
And give the weary rest.

3. Subdue the power of every sin,
Whate'er that sin may be;
That we in singleness of heart,
May worship only thee.

4. Then with our spirits witness bear,
That we 're the sons of God;
Redeemed from sin, and death, and hell,
Through Christ's atoning blood.

674. *Peace returning.*

1. Oh speak that gracious word again,
And cheer my drooping heart!
No voice but thine can soothe my pain,
And bid my fears depart.

2. And wilt thou still vouchsafe to own
A worm so vile as I?
And may I still approach thy throne,
And Abba, Father, cry?

3. My Saviour, by his powerful word,
Hath turned my night to day;
And all those heavenly joys restored,
Which I had sinned away.

4. Dear Lord! I wonder and adore;
Thy grace is all divine:
O keep me, that I sin no more
Against such love as thine.

EMERALD.   8s & 7s. Double.*   PLYMOUTH COLL."

1. { Si - lently   the shades of evening   Gath-er round   my   low - ly   door; }
   { Si - lently   they bring before   me   Fa - ces I   shall see   no   more: }

O,   the lost,   the   un - for - got - ten, Tho'   the world be   oft   for - got;

O,   the shrouded   and   the   lone-ly,   In   our   hearts they per-ish   not.

* See also PANTING SOUL 248.

675.   *The Departed.*

1. SILENTLY the shades of evening
      Gather round my lowly door,
   Silently they bring before me
      Faces I shall see no more ;
   O, the lost, the unforgotten,
      Though the world be oft forgot ;
   O, the shrouded and the lonely,
      In our hearts they perish not.

2. Living in the silent hours,
      Where our spirits only blend,
   They, unlinked with earthly trouble,
      We still hoping for its end.
   How such holy memories cluster,
      Like the stars when storms are past,
   Pointing up to that far heaven
      We may hope to gain at last.

676.   *Christ's Presence in the Evening of*
                Life.

1. TARRY with me, O my Saviour,
      For the day is passing by ;

   See, the shades of evening gather,
      And the night is drawing nigh.

2. Many friends were gathered round me
      In the bright days of the past,
   But the grave has closed above them,
      And I linger here at last.

3. Deeper, deeper grow the shadows,
      Paler now, the glowing west,
   Swift the night of death advances,
      Shall it be the night of rest ?

4. Feeble, trembling, fainting, dying,
      Lord, I cast myself on thee ;
   Tarry with me through the darkness,
      While I sleep, still watch by me.

5. Tarry with me, O my Saviour,
      Lay my head upon thy breast,
   Till the morning, then awake me—
      Morning of eternal rest.

[*For the fifth stanza, repeat from second strain.*]

WEBER. 8s & 7s. Single.*　　　　VON WEBER.

1. In this world of sin and sor - row, Compassed round with every care,

From e - ter - ni - ty we bor-row Hope that ban - ish - es des - pair.

* See also "Parting Soul" 248.

677.　　*Eternity.*

1. In this world of sin and sorrow,
　Compassed round with every care;
From eternity we borrow
　Hope that banishes despair.

2. Thee, triumphant God and Saviour!
　In the glass of faith we see,
Oh! assist each faint endeavor,
　Raise our earth-born souls to thee.

3. Bring that awful scene before us,
　Of the last tremendous day,
When to life thou wilt restore us;—
　Lingering ages! haste away.

4. Then this vile and sinful nature
　Incorruption shall put on;
Life-renewing, glorious Saviour!
　Let thy gracious will be done.

678.　　*Decease of a Pastor.*

1. Pastor, thou art from us taken
　In the glory of thy years,
As the oak, by tempests shaken,
　Falls ere time its verdure sears.

2. Pale and cold we see thee lying
　In God's temple, once so dear,
And the mourner's bitter sighing
　Falls unheeded on thine ear.

3. All thy love and zeal, to lead us
　Where immortal fountains flow,

And on living bread to feed us,
　In our fond remembrance glow.

4. May the conquering faith that cheered
　thee
When thy foot on Jordan pressed,
Guide our spirits while we leave thee
　In the tomb that Jesus blessed.

679.　　*The Christian in Death.*

1. Why lament the Christian dying?
　Why indulge in tears or gloom?
Calmly on the Lord relying,
　He can greet the opening tomb.

2. What if death, with icy fingers,
　All the fount of life congeals?
'Tis not there thy brother lingers,
　'Tis not death his spirit feels.

3. Though for him thy soul is mourning,
　Though with grief thy heart is riven,
While his flesh to dust is turning,
　All his soul is filled with heaven!

4. Scenes seraphic, high and glorious,
　Now forbid his longer stay;
See him rise o'er death victorious,
　Angels beckon him away.

5. Hark! the golden harps are ringing,
　Sounds of rapture fill his ear;
Millions, now in heaven singing,
　Greet his joyful entrance there.

WATCH AND PRAY. C. L. M.*   SPIRITUAL SONGS.

1. Go, watch and pray, thou canst not tell How near thine hour may be;

Thou canst not know, how soon   the bell   May toll   its   notes   for thee:

Death's countless snares beset   thy way; Frail child of dust! go, watch and pray.

* See also the tune, " HOW CALM."14.

680. *"Take heed, watch and pray; for ye know not when the time is."*

1. Go, watch and pray, thou canst not tell
     How near thine hour may be;
   Thou canst not know how soon the bell
     May toll its notes for thee:
   Death's countless snares beset thy way;
   Frail child of dust! go, watch and pray.

2. Fond youth, while free from blighting
     care,
   Does thy firm pulse beat high?
   Do hope's glad visions, bright and fair,
     Dilate before thine eye?
   Soon these must change—must pass
     away;
   Frail child of dust! go, watch and pray.

3. Thou aged man! life's wintry storm
     Hath seared thy vernal bloom;
   With trembling limbs, and wasting form,
     Thou 'rt bending o'er the tomb;

And can vain hope lead *thee* astray?
Go, weary pilgrim! watch and pray.

4. Ambition, stop thy panting breath!
     Pride, sink thy lifted eye!
   Behold the caverns, dark with death,
     Before you open lie;
   The heavenly warning now obey;
   Ye sons of pride, go, watch and pray.

681.   *Submission in Trials.*

1. WHEN I can trust my all with God,
     In trial's fearful hour,
   Bow, all resigned, beneath his rod,
     And bless his sparing power:
   A joy springs up amid distress,
   A fountain in the wilderness.

2. Oh! to be brought to Jesus' feet,
     Though trials fix me there,
   Is still a privilege most sweet;
     For he will hear my prayer:
   Though sighs and tears its language be
   The Lord is nigh to answer me.

3. Then blessèd be the hand that gave,
  Still blessèd when he takes;
Blessèd be he who smites to save,
  Who heals the heart he breaks:
Perfect and true are all his ways,
  Whom heaven adores, and death obeys.

682. *A Song of Deliverance.*

1. I LOVE the Lord, whose gracious ear
  Was open to my cry;
He bade me, in the time of fear,
  Upon his grace rely:
Long as I live I'll trust his care,
To him address my fervent prayer.

2. Death's sorrows had encompassed me,
  I felt the pains of hell;
On every side was misery,
  My woes no tongue could tell·
Then I broke forth, without control,
"Lord, I beseech thee, save my soul!"

3. Tender and gracious is his name;
  Our God is ever kind;
The meek shall his protection claim,
  The humble, mercy find:
Unto thy rest, my soul, return,
The bounties of thy God discern.

4. The Lord hath kept my soul from death,
  Preserved my eyes from tears;
My feet from falling, where beneath
  Were spread the fowler's snares:
Living, I'll walk before the Lord;
His name for ever be adored.

683. *At the Communion.*

1. FORGET thyself, Christ bade thee come
  To think upon his love,
Which could reverse the sinner's doom,
  And write his name above;
Bid the returning rebel live,
And freely all his sins forgive.

2. Forget thyself, and think what pain,
  What agony he bore,
To wash away each guilty stain,
  To bless thee evermore:
To fit thee for his high abode,
The temple of the living God.

3. Forget thyself, but let thy soul
  With memories o'erflow,
Rejoice in his supreme control,
  And seek his will to know.
With thankful heart approach the feast,
And thou wilt be a welcome guest.

684. *Heavenly Anticipations.*

1. PRISONERS of hope, we're passing thro'
  Hard scenes of toil and care;
But heavenly mansions are in view,
  And we shall soon be there:
Before the eye of faith there stand
The palaces at God's right hand.

2. As, one by one, we end the race,
  And lay our armor down,
Our bodies find a resting-place,
  Our souls a heavenly crown:
We enter life as yet unknown,
Where songs of praise surround the
  throne.

3. Our sainted friends have gone before,
  While we are lingering here,
To dwell with joy for evermore
  In heaven's exalted sphere:
With quickening steps we follow on
To the blest realm where they have gone

4. Not yet, not yet, my struggling soul,
  Hast thou obtained the prize;
Conflicts will come, and troubles roll,
  And foes unseen arise:
But God's right arm shall still prevail,
His love can never, never fail.

685. *The Glory of God in Nature.*

1. SINCE o'er thy footstool here below
  Such radiant gems are strown,
O, what magnificence must glow,
  Great God! about thy throne!
So brilliant here these drops of light—
There the full ocean rolls, how bright!

2. If night's blue curtain of the sky—
  With thousand stars inwrought,
Hung like a royal canopy
  With glittering diamonds fraught—
Be, Lord, thy temple's outer vail,
What splendor at the shrine must dwell

3. The dazzling sun, at noonday hour—
  Forth from his flaming vase,
Flinging o'er earth the golden shower,
  Till vale and mountain blaze—
But shows, O Lord, one beam of thine,
What, then, the day where thou dost
  shine!

4. O, how shall these dim eyes endure
  That noon of living rays!
Or how our spirits, so impure,
  Upon thy glory gaze!
Anoint, O Lord, anoint our sight,
And fit us for that world of light.

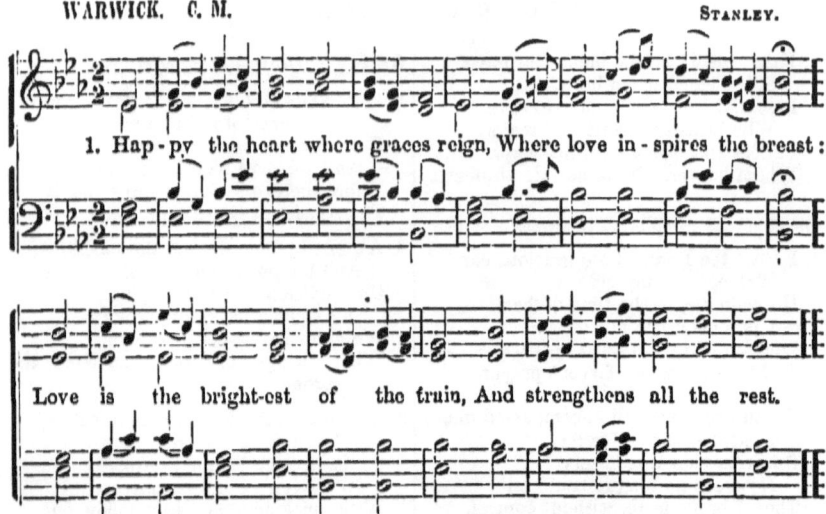

1. Hap-py the heart where graces reign, Where love in-spires the breast:

Love is the bright-est of the train, And strengthens all the rest.

---

686. *Love to God.*

1. HAPPY the heart where graces reign,
Where love inspires the breast:
Love is the brightest of the train,
And strengthens all the rest.

2. Knowledge, alas! 'tis all in vain,
And all in vain our fear;
Our stubborn sins will fight and reign,
If love be absent there.

3. This is the grace that lives, and sings,
When faith and hope shall cease;
'Tis this shall strike our joyful strings
In the sweet realms of bliss.

4. Before we quite forsake our clay,
Or leave this dark abode,
The wings of love bear us away,
To see our smiling God.

687. *Worship of God in his Temple.*

1. PRAISE waits in Zion, Lord, for thee;
There shall our vows be paid;
Thou hast an ear when sinners pray;
All flesh shall seek thine aid.

2. O Lord, our guilt and fears prevail;
But pardoning grace is thine,
And thou wilt grant us power and skill
To conquer every sin.

3. Blest are the men whom thou wilt choose
To bring them near thy face;
Give them a dwelling in thy house,
To feast upon thy grace.

4. In answering what thy church requests,
Thy truth and terror shine;
And works of dreadful righteousness
Fulfill thy kind design.

5. Thus shall the wondering nations see
The Lord is good and just;
And distant islands fly to thee,
And make thy name their trust.

688. *Thirsting after God.*

1. As pants the hart for cooling streams,
When heated in the chase,
So longs my soul, O God! for thee,
And thy refreshing grace.

2. For thee, my God, the living God!
My thirsty soul doth pine!
Oh! when shall I behold thy face,
Thou Majesty divine!

3. I sigh to think of happier days,
When thou, O Lord! wast nigh;
When every heart was tuned to praise
And none more blessed than I.

4. Why restless, why cast down my soul?
Trust God, and thou shalt sing
His praise again, and find him still
Thy health's eternal spring.

PENIEL. C. M.*   HASTINGS.

1. My God! the spring of all my joys, The life of my de-lights;

Choir.   *Congregation.*

The glo - ry of my bright - est days, And com-fort of my nights.

* See also LAIGHT STREET 246.

689. *God's Presence is Light in Darkness.*

1. My God! the spring of all my joys,
The life of my delights ;
The glory of my brightest days,
And comfort of my nights.

2 In darkest shades, if he appear,
My dawning is begun ;
He is my soul's sweet morning star,
And he my rising sun.

3. The opening heavens around me shine,
With beams of sacred bliss,
While Jesus shows his heart is mine,
And whispers—I am his.

4. My soul would leave this heavy clay,
At that transporting word ;
Run up with joy the shining way,
T' embrace my dearest Lord.

5. Fearless of hell and ghastly death,
I'd break through every foe ;
The wings of love, and arms of faith,
Should bear me conqueror through.

690. *Love to Christ desired.*

1. Thou lovely Source of true delight,
Whom I unseen adore !
Unveil thy beauties to my sight,
That I may love thee more.

2. Thy glory o'er creation shines ;
But, in thy sacred word,
I read in fairer, brighter lines,
My bleeding, dying Lord.

3. 'Tis here, whene'er my comforts droop,
And sin and sorrow rise,
Thy love, with cheering beams of hope,
My fainting heart supplies.

4. But ah ! too soon the pleasing scene
Is clouded o'er with pain ;
My gloomy fears rise dark between,
And I again complain.

5. Jesus, my Lord, my life, my light !
Oh ! come with blissful ray ;
Break radiant through the shades of
night,
And chase my fears away.

6. Then shall my soul with rapture trace
The wonders of thy love ;
But the full glories of thy face
Are only known above.

Doxology.

To praise the Father, and the Son,
And Spirit, all divine,
The One in Three, and Three in One,
Let saints and angels join.

PSALM 146. L. P. M.
BOLD.   Arranged from " MANHATTAN COLL "

1. I 'll praise my Mak - er with my breath ; And, when my voice is lost in

death, Praise shall employ my nobler powers : { My days of praise shall ne'er be past, }
{ While life, and thought, and being last, }

Or im - mor-tal - i - ty en - dures, Or im - mor-tal - i - ty en - dures.

691. *Praise to God for his Goodness and Mercy.*

1. I'LL praise my Maker with my breath,
And, when my voice is lost in death,
    Praise shall employ my nobler powers :
My days of praise shall ne'er be past,
While life, and thought, and being last,
    Or immortality endures.

2. Happy the man, whose hopes rely
On Israel's God ;—he made the sky,
    And earth, and seas, with all their train :
His truth for ever stands secure ;
He saves th' oppressed, he feeds the poor;
    And none shall find his promise vain.

3. He loves his saints—he knows them well,
But turns the wicked down to hell :
    Thy God, O Zion ! ever reigns ;

Let every tongue, let every age,
In this exalted work engage :
    Praise him in everlasting strains.

4. I 'll praise him while he lends me breath
And, when my voice is lost in death,
    Praise shall employ my nobler powers
My days of praise shall ne'er be past,
While life, and thought, and being last,
    Or immortality endures.

692. *The Excellency of the Scriptures.*

1. I LOVE the volumes of thy word ;
What light and joy these leaves afford
    To souls benighted and distrest !
Thy precepts guide my doubtful way,
Thy fear forbids my feet to stray,
    Thy promise leads my heart to rest.

2. From the discoveries of thy law
The perfect rules of life I draw:
These are my study and delight!
Not honey so invites the taste,
Nor gold that has the furnace past,
Appears so pleasing to the sight.

3. Thy threatenings wake my slumbering
eyes,
And warn me where my danger lies;
But 'tis thy blesséd gospel, Lord,

That makes my guilty conscience clean,
Converts my soul, subdues my sin,
And gives a free, but large reward.

4. Who knows the errors of his thoughts?
My God, forgive my secret faults,
And from presumptuous sins restrain;
Accept my poor attempts at praise,
That I have read thy book of grace,
And book of nature, not in vain.

"TO-DAY THE SAVIOUR CALLS." 6s & 4s. · Alternate. SPIRITUAL SONGS.

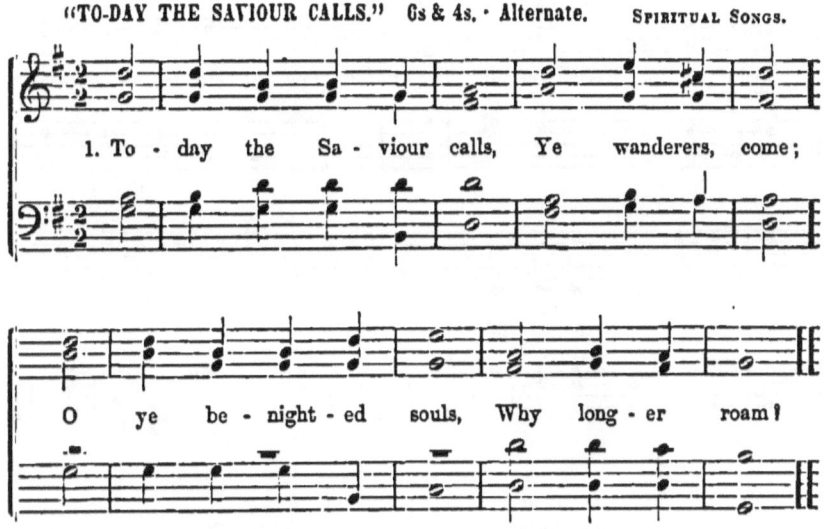

1. To - day the Sa - viour calls, Ye wanderers, come;

O ye be - night - ed souls, Why long - er roam!

693. Heb. iii. 15.

1. To-DAY the Saviour calls,
Ye wanderers, come;
O ye benighted souls,
Why longer roam?

2. To-day the Saviour calls,
O listen now:
Within these sacred walls
To Jesus bow.

3. To-day the Saviour calls,
For refuge fly:
The storm of vengeance falls—
Ruin is nigh.

4. The Spirit calls to-day,
Yield to his power:

O grieve him not away,
'Tis mercy's hour.

694. *A heavenly Portion.*

1. WHAT though the moments fly?
Mourn not their speed:
Sweet shall thy portion be
Whither they lead.

2. Though sorrow count the hours,
Hoping the last,
Sweet shall thy portion be
Ere they be past.

3. Smile when the moments fly—
Smile when they stay—
Life's longest, shortest night
Closes in day.

FREDERICK. 11s.   KINGSLEY. By permission.

1. I would not live al - way; I ask not to stay Where storm af -ter storm ris - es dark o'er the way; The few lu - cid morn - ings that dawn on us here Are fol-lowed by gloom, or be - cloud-ed with fear.

695.   *Longing for Heaven.*

1. I WOULD not live alway; I ask not to stay
Where storm after storm rises dark o'er the way;
The few lucid mornings that dawn on us here
Are followed by gloom, or beclouded with fear.

2. I would not live alway thus fettered by sin—
Temptation without and corruption within;
E'en the rapture of pardon is mingled with fears,
And the cup of thanksgiving with penitent tears.

3. I would not live away; no—welcome the tomb:
Since Jesus hath lain there, I dread not its gloom:
There, sweet be my rest, till he bid me arise
To hail him in triumph descending the skies.

4. Who, who would live alway away from his God—
Away from yon heaven, that blissful abode,
Where rivers of pleasure flow o'er the bright plains,
And the noontide of glory eternally reigns?

5. There saints of all ages in harmony meet,
Their Saviour and brethren transported to greet;
While anthems of rapture unceasingly roll,
And the smile of the Lord is the feast of the soul.

Doxology.

O FATHER Almighty, to thee be addressed,
With Christ and the Spirit, one God ever blessed,
All glory and worship from earth and from heaven,
As was, and is now, and shall ever be given.

LYONS. 5s & 6s.
MAESTOSO.
HAYDN

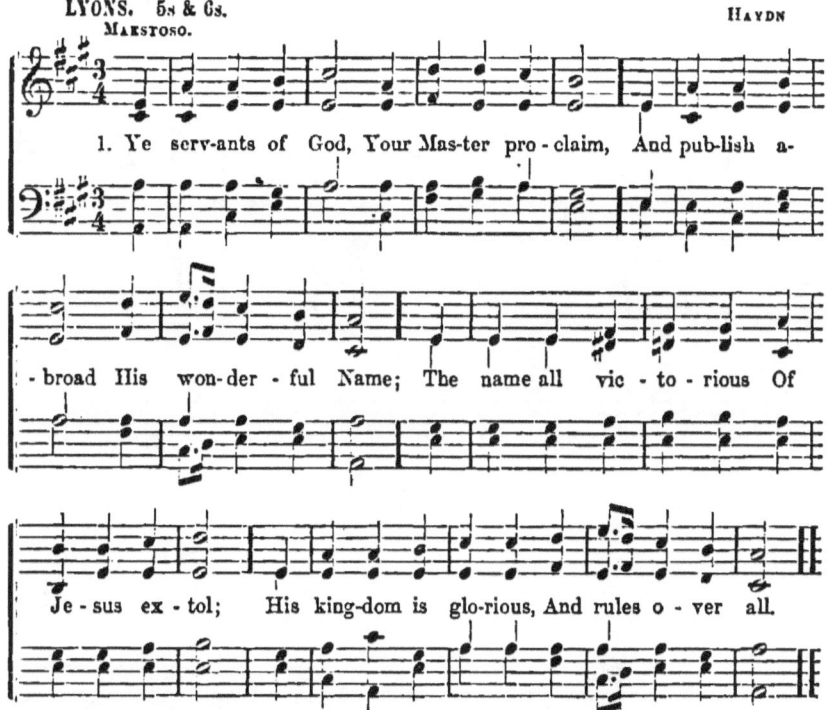

1. Ye serv-ants of God, Your Mas-ter pro - claim, And pub-lish a-broad His won-der - ful Name; The name all vic - to - rious Of Je - sus ex - tol; His king-dom is glo-rious, And rules o - ver all.

696. *God's Servants exhorted.*

1. YE servants of God,
   Your Master proclaim,
And publish abroad
   His wonderful Name;
The name all victorious
   Of Jesus extol;
His kingdom is glorious,
   And rules over all.

2. God ruleth on high,
   Almighty to save;
And still he is nigh,
   His presence we have:
The great congregation
   His triumph shall sing,
Ascribing salvation
   To Jesus, our King.

3. Salvation to God,
   Who sits on the throne ·
Let all cry aloud,
   And honor the Son;
Immanuel's praises
   The angels proclaim;
Fall down on their faces
   And worship the Lamb.

4. Then let us adore,
   And give him his right;
And glory and power,
   And wisdom and might:
All honor and blessing
   With angels above;
And thanks never ceasing,
   And infinite love.

1. On the mountain's top ap-pear-ing, Lo, the sa-cred herald stands,

Welcome news to Zi-on bear-ing, Zi-on, long in hos-tile lands;

Mourn-ing cap-tive! God him-self will loose thy bands,

Mourn-ing cap-tive! God him-self will loose thy bands.

697. *The Heralds of Salvation.*

1. On the mountain's top appearing,
Lo! the sacred herald stands;
Welcome news to Zion bearing,—
Zion long in hostile lands:
Mourning captive!
God himself will loose thy bands,

2. Has thy night been long and mournful,
Have thy friends unfaithful proved?
Have thy foes been proud and scornful,
By thy sighs and tears unmoved?
Cease thy mourning;—
Zion still is well-beloved.

3. God, thy God, will now restore thee,
He himself appears thy Friend ;
All thy foes shall flee before thee,
Here their boasts and triumphs end ;
Great deliverance—
Zion's King will quickly send.

4. Peace and joy shall now attend thee,
All thy warfare now is past,
God, thy Saviour, shall defend thee,
Peace and joy are come at last ;
All thy conflicts
End in everlasting rest.

698. *The Gladness of the Righteous.*

1. FAR from us be grief and sadness,
Farther still unhallowed mirth :
Zion's sons may sing, with gladness,
Theirs are joys of heavenly birth :
Jesus owns them,—
Jesus, Lord of heaven and earth.

2. All the worldling's mirth is madness,
All his labor fruitless toil :
'Tis the saints that taste of gladness,
Though the world their choice revile :
Sweet their portion ;—
Life is in the Saviour's smile.

3. Worlds would seem as nothing to us,
Balanced with a Saviour's love :
Since the Lord in mercy drew us,
Drew our souls to things above,
Earthly objects
Can no longer greatly move.

4. Once the world was all our treasure ;
Then the world our hearts possessed ;
Now we taste sublimer pleasure,
Since the Lord has made us blest ;
We can witness,—
Jesus gives his people rest.

699. *God, the Pilgrim's Guide.*

GUIDE me, O thou great Jehovah !
Pilgrim through this barren land ;
I am weak ; but thou art mighty ;
Hold me with thy powerful hand :
Bread of heaven !
Feed me till I want no more.

2. Open, Lord ! the crystal fountain,
Whence the healing waters flow ;
Let the fiery, cloudy pillar
Lead me all my journey through :
Strong Deliverer !
Be thou still my strength and shield.

3. When I tread the verge of Jordan,
Bid my anxious fears subside ;
Death of death, and hell's destruction !
Land me safe on Canaan's side :
Songs of praises—
I will ever give to thee.

700. *Appeal from the Cross.*

1. HARK, from yonder mount arise
Notes of sadness—Jesus dies !
On the cross the Lord of lords
Love for guilty man records :
Sinner, sinner !
Hear your dying Saviour's words.

2. "Mortal, for your guilt I die,
Guilt that dared your God defy,
Blood for you I freely give,
Death I taste that you may live :
Will you, sinner,
Free salvation now receive ?"

701. *Departure of Missionaries.*

1. MEN of God, go, take your stations ;
Darkness reigns throughout the earth ;
Go, proclaim among the nations
Joyful news of heavenly birth ;
Bear the tidings
Of the Saviour's matchless worth.

2. When exposed to fearful dangers,
Jesus will his own defend ;
Borne afar 'midst foes and strangers,
Jesus will appear your Friend ;
And his presence
Shall be with you to the end.

702. *Dawning of the Latter-Day.*

1. LOOK, ye saints ! the day is breaking ;
Joyful times are near at hand ;
God, the mighty God, is speaking
By his word in every land ;
Day advances,—
Darkness flies at his command.

2. While the foe becomes more daring,
While he enters like a flood,
God, the Saviour, is preparing
Means to spread his truth abroad :
Every language
Soon shall tell the love of God.

3. God of Jacob, high and glorious !
Let thy people see thy power :
Let the gospel be victorious,
Through the world for evermore ;
Then shall idols
Perish, while thy saints adore.

LENOX. H. M.* EDSON.

1. Ye tribes of Adam, join With heaven, and earth, and seas, And offer notes di-

- vine To your Creator's praise. Ye holy throng Of angels bright, Ye

Ye holy throng Of angels bright, Ye holy throng Of

ho - ly throng Of an-gels bright, In worlds of light, Be - gin the song.

an-gels bright, In worlds of light, Be - gin the song.

* See also Ruine 234.

703. *Praise from all Creatures.*

1. Ye tribes of Adam, join
   With heaven, and earth, and seas,
   And offer notes divine
   To your Creator's praise.
Ye holy throng | In worlds of light,
Of angels bright, | Begin the song.

2. Thou sun with dazzling rays,
   And moon that rules the night,
   Shine to your Maker's praise,
   With stars of twinkling light.
His power declare, | And clouds that fly
Ye floods on high, | In empty air.

3. The shining worlds above
   In glorious order stand,
   Or in swift courses move,
   By his supreme command.
He spake the word, | From nothing came
And all their frame | To praise the Lord.

4. Let all the nations fear
   The God that rules above;
   He brings his people near,
   And makes them taste his love:
While earth and sky | His saints shall raise
Attempt his praise, | His honors high.

704. *Christian Effort.*

1. Rise, gracious God! and shine
   In all thy saving might:
   And prosper each design,
   To spread thy glorious light:
Let healing streams of mercy flow,
That all the earth thy truth may know.

2. Put forth thy glorious power!
   The nations then will see,
   And earth present her store
   In converts born of thee:
God, our own God, his church will bless,
And earth shall yield her full increase.

705. *Jesus rising and reigning.*

1. YES, the Redeemer rose;
The Saviour left the dead!
And o'er our hellish foes
High raised his conquering head.
In wild dismay, | Fall to the ground,
The guards around, | And sink away.

2. Lo! th' angelic bands
In full assembly meet,
To wait his high commands,
And worship at his feet;
Joyful they come, | From realms of day
And wing their way | To Jesus' tomb.

3. Then back to heaven they fly,
The joyful news to bear;
Hark! as they soar on high,
What music fills the air!
Their anthems say, | Hath left the dead;
"Jesus who bled, | He rose to-day."

4. Ye mortals, catch the sound,
Redeemed by him from hell;
And send the echo round
The globe, on which you dwell;
Transported, cry | Hath left the dead,
"Jesus, who bled, | No more to die."

5. All hail, triumphant Lord,
Who sav'st us with thy blood!
Wide be thy name adored,
Thou rising, reigning God!
With thee we rise, | And empires gain
With thee we reign, | Beyond the skies.

706. *Praise to the Trinity.*

1. WE give immortal praise
For God the Father's love—
For all our comforts here,
And better hopes above:
He sent his own eternal Son
To die for sins that we had done.

2. To God the Son belongs
Immortal glory, too,
Who bought us with his blood
From everlasting woe:
And now he lives, and now he reigns,
And sees the fruit of all his pains.

3. To God, the Spirit's name,
Immortal worship give,
Whose new-creating power
Makes the dead sinner live:
His work completes the great design,
And fills the soul with joy divine.

4. Almighty God, to thee
Be endless honors done,
The undivided Three,
The great and glorious One:
Where reason fails, with all her powers,
There faith prevails, and love adores.

707. *The Shepherd's Voice.*

1. I LOVE my Shepherd's voice,
His watchful eye shall keep
My wandering soul among
The thousands of his sheep:
He feeds his flock, he calls their names,
His bosom bears the tender lambs.

2. Be Thou the counselor,
My pattern, and my guide;
And through this desert land
Still keep me near thy side:
Oh, let my feet ne'er run astray,
Nor rove, nor seek the crooked way.

708. *Opening a Place of Worship.*

1. IN sweet, exalted strains,
The King of glory praise;
O'er heaven and earth he reigns,
Through everlasting days;
He, at his will, the world controls,
Sustains, or sinks, the distant poles.

2. To earth he bends his throne—
His throne of grace divine;
Wide is his bounty known,
And wide his glories shine;
Fair Salem, still his chosen rest,
Is with his smiles and presence blest.

3. Great King of glory! come,
And, with thy favor crown
This temple as thy dome—
This people as thine own:
Beneath this roof, O! deign to show
How God can dwell with men below.

4. Here may thine ears attend
Thy people's humble cries,
And grateful praise ascend,
All-fragrant, to the skies:
Here may thy word melodious sound,
And spread celestial joys around.

5. Here may th' attentive throng
Imbibe thy truth and love;
And converts join the song
Of seraphim above;
And willing crowds surround thy board,
With sacred joy and sweet accord.

1. The Lord my Shep-herd is,   I   shall   be   well   sup-plied:

Since he   is   mine, and   I   am   his,   What can   I   want be-side!

* See also STATE STREET 268.

709.   *The good Shepherd.*

1. THE Lord my Shepherd is,
   I shall be well supplied:
Since he is mine, and I am his,
   What can I want beside ?

2. He leads me to the place,
   Where heavenly pasture grows,
Where living waters gently pass,
   And full salvation flows.

3. If e'er I go astray,
   He doth my soul reclaim;
And guides me in his own right way,
   For his most holy name.

4. While he affords his aid,
   I can not yield to fear ;
Though I should walk through death's
      dark shade,
   My Shepherd 's with me there.

5. Amid surrounding foes,
   Thou dost my table spread,
My cup with blessings overflows,
   And joy exalts my head.

6. The bounties of thy love
   Shall crown my following days;
Nor from thy house will I remove,
   Nor cease to speak thy praise.

710.   *Salvation by Christ.*

1. SEE, what a living stone
   The builders did refuse:
Yet God hath built his church thereon,
   In spite of envious Jews.

2. The scribe and angry priest
   Reject thine only Son ;
Yet on this rock shall Zion rest,
   As the chief corner-stone.

3. The work, O Lord! is thine,
   And wondrous in our eyes ;
This day declares it all divine ;
   This day did Jesus rise.

4. This is the glorious day,
   That our Redeemer made:
Let us rejoice, and sing, and pray;
   Let all the church be glad.

5. Hosanna to the King,
   Of David's royal blood ;
Bless him, ye saints!—he comes to **bring**
   Salvation from your God.

6. We bless thy holy word,
   Which all his grace displays ;
And offer, on thine altar, Lord!
   Our sacrifice of praise.

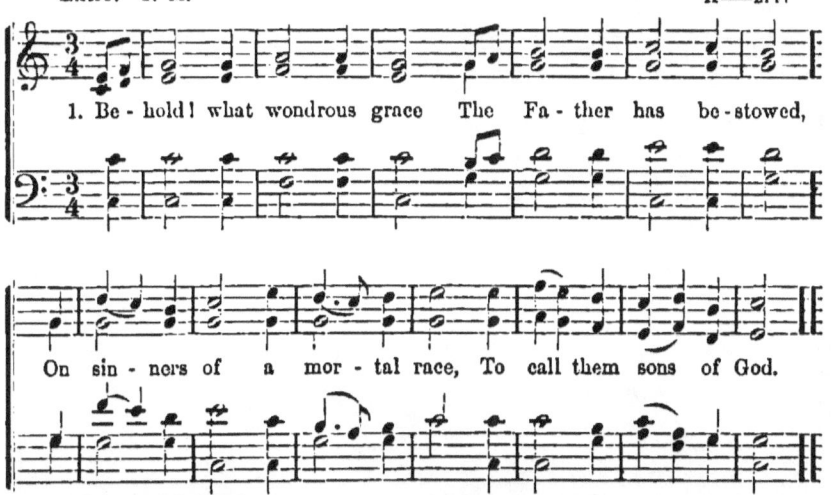

1. Be - hold! what wondrous grace The Fa - ther has be - stowed,

On sin - ners of a mor - tal race, To call them sons of God.

711.   *Adoption.*

1. BEHOLD! what wondrous grace
    The Father has bestowed,
On sinners of a mortal race,
    To call them sons of God.

2. 'Tis no surprising thing,
    That we should be unknown;
The Jewish world knew not their King—
    God's everlasting Son.

3. Nor doth it yet appear
    How great we must be made;
But, when we see our Saviour here,
    We shall be like our Head.

4. A hope, so much divine,
    May trials well endure;
May purge our souls from sense and sin,
    As Christ, the Lord, is pure.

5. If, in my Father's love,
    I share a filial part,
Send down thy Spirit, like a dove,
    To rest upon my heart.

6. We would no longer lie,
    Like slaves, beneath the throne;
Our faith shall—"Abba, Father!"—cry,
    And thou the kindred own.

712.   *Christ's Intercession.*

1. YES, the Redeemer's gone,
    T' appear before our God;

To sprinkle o'er the flaming throne
    With his atoning blood.

2. No fiery vengeance now,
    No burning wrath comes down;
If justice calls for sinner's blood,
    The Saviour shows his own.

3. Before his Father's eye
    Our humble suit he moves;
The Father lays his thunder by,
    And looks, and smiles, and loves.

4. Now may our joyful tongues
    Our Maker's honors sing;
Jesus, the Priest, receives our songs,
    And bears them to the King.

5. We bow before his face,
    And sound his glories high·
Hosanna to the God of grace,
    That lays his thunder by

6. On earth thy mercy reigns,
    And triumphs all above:
But, Lord, how weak our mortal strains
    To quench immortal love.

Doxology.

YE angels round the throne,
    And saints that dwell below,
Worship the Father, praise the Son,
    And bless the Spirit, too.

1. Re-joice—the Lord is King! Your God and King a-dore; Mor-

-tals, give thanks, and sing, And tri-umph ev-er-more: Lift up the

heart, lift up the voice, Re-joice a-loud, ye saints, re-joice.

713. *The Kingdom of Christ.* Phil. iv. 4.

1. REJOICE—the Lord is King!
   Your God and King adore;
   Mortals, give thanks and sing,
   And triumph evermore;
   Lift up the heart, lift up the voice,
   Rejoice aloud, ye saints, rejoice.

2. His kingdom can not fail;
   He rules o'er earth and heaven;
   The keys of death and hell
   Are to our Jesus given:
   Lift up the heart, lift up the voice,
   Rejoice aloud, ye saints, rejoice.

3. He all his foes shall quell,
   Shall all our sins destroy;
   And every bosom swell,
   With pure, seraphic joy;

   Lift up the heart, lift up the voice,
   Rejoice aloud, ye saints, rejoice.

4. Rejoice, in glorious hope;
   Jesus the Judge shall come—
   And take his servants up
   To their eternal home:
   We soon shall hear th' archangel's voice:
   The trump of God shall sound—rejoice'

714. *Mission of Christ.*

1. COME, every pious heart,
   That loves the Saviour's name!
   Your noblest powers exert,
   To celebrate his fame;
   Tell all above, and all below,
   The debt of love to him you owe.

2. He left his starry crown,
   And laid his robes aside;
On wings of love, came down,
   And wept, and bled, and died:
What he endured, no tongue can tell,
To save our souls from death and hell.

3. From the dark grave he rose,—
   The mansion of the dead;
And thence his mighty foes
   In glorious triumph led;
Up through the sky the conqueror rode,
And reigns on high, the Saviour God.

4. From thence he 'll quickly come,—
   His chariot will not stay,—
And bear our spirits home
   To realms of endless day:
There shall we see his lovely face,
And ever be in his embrace.

715. *The Jubilee proclaimed.*

1. BLOW ye the trumpet!—blow,—
   The gladly solemn sound!
Let all the nations know,
   To earth's remotest bound,—
The year of jubilee is come;
Return, ye ransomed sinners! home.

2. Exalt the Lamb of God,—
   The sin-atoning Lamb;
Redemption by his blood,
   Through all the world proclaim:
The year of jubilee is come;
Return, ye ransomed sinners! home.

3. Ye slaves of sin and hell!
   Your liberty receive;
And safe in Jesus dwell,
   And blest in Jesus live;
The year of jubilee is come;
Return, ye ransomed sinners! home.

4. The gospel trumpet hear,
   The news of pardoning grace:
Ye happy souls! draw near,
   Behold your Saviour's face:
The year of jubilee is come;
Return, ye ransomed sinners! home.

5. Jesus, our great High-Priest,
   Has full atonement made!
Ye weary spirits! rest,
   Ye mourning souls! be glad:
The year of jubilee is come;
Return, ye ransomed sinners! home.

716. *Rejoicing in a Revival.*

1. O ZION! tune thy voice,
   And raise thy hands on high;
Tell all the earth thy joys,
   And boast salvation nigh;
Cheerful in God | While rays divine
Arise and shine, | Stream all abroad.

2. He gilds thy mourning face,
   With beams that can not fade;
His all-resplendent grace
   He pours around thy head;
The nations round | With lustre new,
Thy form shall view, | Divinely crowned.

3. In honor to his name,
   Reflect that sacred light;
And loud that grace proclaim,
   Which makes thy darkness bright;
Pursue his praise, | In worlds above,
Till sovereign love, | The glory raise

4. There, on his holy hill,
   A brighter sun shall rise,
And, with his radiance, fill
   Those fairer, purer skies;
While, round his throne, | In nobler spheres,
Ten thousand stars, | His influence own.

717. *God reigns.*

1. THE Lord Jehovah reigns,
   His throne is built on high:
The garments he assumes,
   Are light and majesty;
His glories shine with beams so bright,
No mortal eye can bear the sight.

2. The thunders of his hand
   Keep the wide world in awe;
His wrath and justice stand,
   To guard his holy law;
And where his love resolves to bless,
His truth confirms and seals the grace.

3. Through all his perfect work,
   Surprising wisdom shines;
Confounds the powers of hell,
   And breaks their cursed designs:
Strong is his arm—and shall fulfill
His great decrees, his sovereign will.

4. And can this mighty King
   Of glory condescend—
And will he write his name,
   My Father and my Friend!
I love his name, I love his word;
Join, all my powers, and praise the Lord.

DEPARTURE. S. L. M.
MODERATO AFFETTUOSO.

Arranged from "SPIRITUAL SONGS."

1. Friend af - ter friend de-parts: Who hath not lost a friend? There is no u - nion here of hearts That finds not here an end: Were this frail world our fi - nal rest, Liv-ing or dy - ing, none were blest.

718. *Friends separated by Death.*

1. FRIEND after friend departs;
Who hath not lost a friend?
There is no union here of hearts
That finds not here an end:
Were this frail world our final rest,
Living or dying, none were blest.

2. Beyond the flight of time,
Beyond the reign of death,
There surely is some blessèd clime
Where life is not a breath,
Nor life's affections transient fire,
Whose sparks fly upward and expire.

3. There is a world above,
Where parting is unknown;
A long eternity of love,
Formed for the good alone;
And faith beholds the dying here
Translated to that glorious sphere.

4. Thus star by star declines,
Till all are passed away;
As morning high and higher shines,
To pure and perfect day;
Nor sink those stars in empty night,
But hide themselves in heaven's own light.

719. *The Death-Bed of the Righteous.*

1. THIS place is holy ground;
World! with thy cares, away!
Silence and darkness reign around;
But lo! the break of day!
What bright and sudden dawn appears,
To shine upon this scene of tears!

2. Behold the bed of death,—
This pale and lovely clay!
Heard ye the sob of parting breath?
Marked ye the eyes' last ray?—
No!—life so sweetly ceased to be,
It lapsed in immortality.

3. Could tears revive the dead,
Rivers should swell our eyes:
Could sighs recall the spirit fled,
We would not quench our sighs,
Till love relumed this altered mien,
And all th 'embodied soul were seen.

4. Bury the dead,—and weep,
In stillness, o'er the loss;
Bury the dead,—in Christ they sleep,
Who bore on earth his cross,
And, from the grave, their dust shall rise
In his own image to the skies.

PLEADING. H. M.*

Choir. QUICK, YET TENDER.

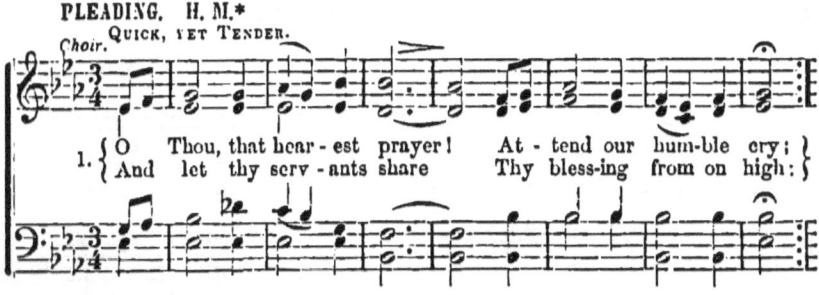

1. { O Thou, that hear - est prayer! At - tend our hum-ble cry; }
   { And let thy serv - ants share Thy bless-ing from on high: }

Congregation.
mf   Dim.

We plead the promise of thy word; Grant us thy Ho - ly Spi - rit, Lord!

* See also CULLODEN 126.

---

720. *Pleading the Promise of the Spirit.*

1. O THOU, that hearest prayer!
    Attend our humble cry;
    And let thy servants share
    Thy blessing from on high;
    We plead the promise of thy word;
    Grant us thy Holy Spirit, Lord!

2. If earthly parents hear
    Their children when they cry;
    If they, with love sincere,
    Their varied wants supply:
    Much more wilt thou thy love display,
    And answer when thy children pray.

3. Our Heavenly Father, thou;—
    We, children of thy grace:
    Oh! let thy Spirit now
    Descend, and fill the place:
    So shall we feel the heavenly flame,
    And all unite to praise thy name.

4. Oh! send thy Spirit down
    On all the nations, Lord!
    With great success to crown
    The preaching of thy word,
    Till heathen lands shall own thy sway,
    And cast their idol-gods away.

---

721. *The Wonders of Grace.*

1. GIVE thanks to God most high,—
    The universal Lord,—
    The sovereign King of kings;
    And be his grace adored:
    Thy mercy, Lord! | And ever sure
    Shall still endure; | Abides thy word.

2. He sent his only Son
    To save us from our woe,
    From Satan, sin, and death,
    And every hurtful foe:
    His power and grace | And let his name
    Are still the same; | Have endless praise

3. Give thanks aloud to God,
    To God, the heavenly King;
    And let the spacious earth
    His works and glories sing:
    Thy mercy, Lord! | And ever sure
    Shall still endure; | Abides thy word

Doxology.

To God the Father's throne
    Your highest honors raise;
Glory to God the Son;
    To God the Spirit, praise;
With all our powers | Thy name we sing,
Eternal King, | While faith adores.

ROCKINGHAM. L. M.*   L. MASON.

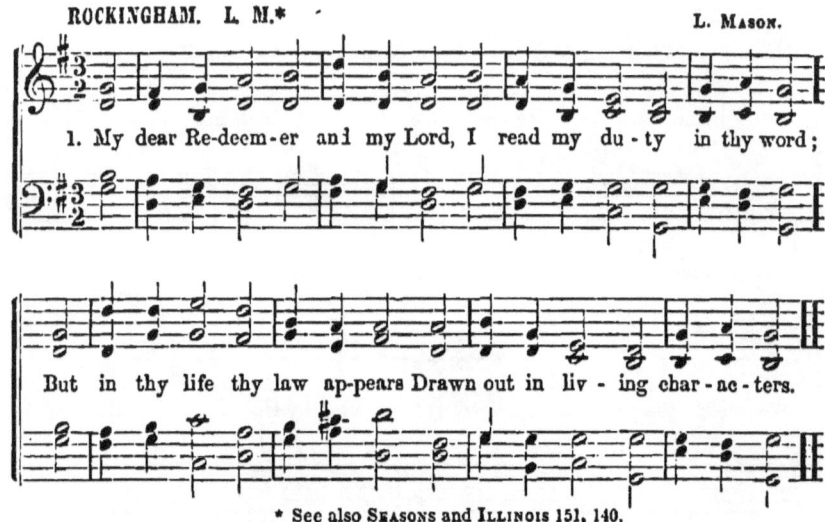

1. My dear Re-deem-er and my Lord, I read my du-ty in thy word;

But in thy life thy law ap-pears Drawn out in liv-ing char-ac-ters.

* See also SEASONS and ILLINOIS 151, 140.

722. *The Example of Christ.*

1. My dear Redeemer and my Lord,
   I read my duty in thy word;
   But in thy life thy law appears
   Drawn out in living characters.

2. Such was thy truth, and such thy zeal,
   Such deference to thy Father's will,
   Such love, and meekness so divine,
   I would transcribe, and make them mine.

3. Cold mountains, and the midnight air,
   Witnessed the fervor of thy prayer;
   The desert thy temptation knew,
   Thy conflict, and thy victory, too.

4. Be thou my pattern; make me bear
   More of thy gracious image here;
   Then God, the Judge, shall own my name
   Among the followers of the Lamb.

723. *The Lord's Supper instituted.*

1. 'T WAS on that dark—that doleful night,
   When powers of earth and hell arose,
   Against the Son of God's delight,
   And friends betrayed him to his foes.—

2. Before the mournful scene began,
   He took the bread, and blessed, and
       brake:
   What love through all his actions ran!
   What wondrous words of grace he
       spake!

3. "This is my body, broke for sin;
       Receive and eat the living food:"
   Then took the cup, and blessed the wine—
   "'Tis the new covenant in my blood."

4. "Do this," he cried, "till time shall end,
       In memory of your dying Friend;
   Meet, at my table, and record
       The love of your departed Lord."

5. Jesus! thy feast we celebrate;
       We show thy death, we sing thy name,
   Till thou return, and we shall eat
       The marriage supper of the Lamb.

724. *Prayer for Light and Guidance.*

1. COME, gracious Spirit! heavenly Dove!
   With light and comfort from above;
   Be thou our guardian, thou our guide,
   O'er every thought and step preside.

2. To us the light of truth display,
   And make us know and choose thy way
   Plant holy fear in every heart,
   That we from God may ne'er depart.

3. Lead us to holiness—the road
   That we must take to dwell with God
   Lead us to Christ, the living way,
   Nor let us from his precepts stray.

4. Lead us to God, our final rest,
   In his enjoyment to be blest:
   Lead us to heaven, the seat of bliss,
   Where pleasure in perfection is.

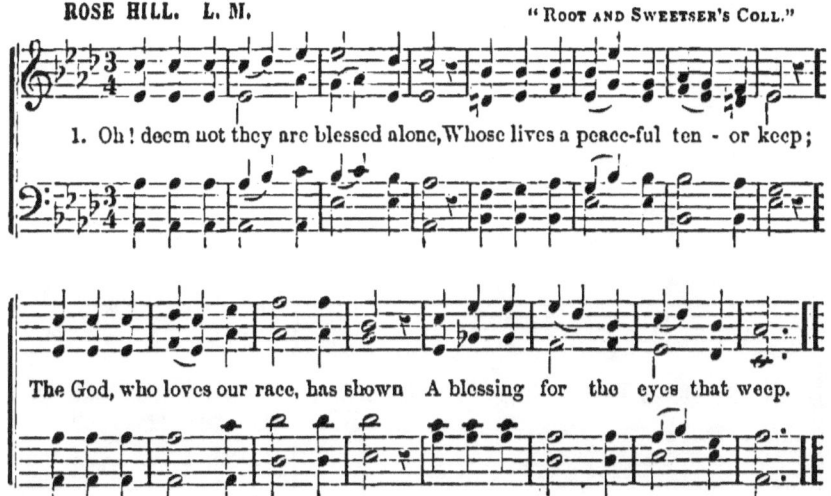

ROSE HILL. L. M.   "Root and Sweetser's Coll."

1. Oh! deem not they are blessed alone, Whose lives a peace-ful ten - or keep;

The God, who loves our race, has shown A blessing for the eyes that weep.

725. *"Blessed are they that mourn."*

1. Oh! deem not they are blessed alone,
Whose lives a peaceful tenor keep;
The God, who loves our race, has shown
A blessing for the eyes that weep.

2. The light of smiles shall fill again
The lids that overflow with tears,
And weary hours of woe and pain
Are earnests of serener years.

3. O, there are days of sunny rest
For every dark and troubled night!
Grief may abide, an evening guest,
But joy shall come with early light.

4. And thou, who o'er thy friend's low bier
Sheddest the bitter drops like rain,
Hope that a brighter, happier sphere
Will give him to thine arms again.

5. For God hath marked each anguished day,
And numbered every secret tear;
And heaven's long age of bliss shall pay
For all his children suffer here.

726. *Attraction of the Cross.*

1. Mysterious influence, divine,
That found my soul astray so far,
And o'er it bade the radiance shine
Of Bethlehem's "bright and morning
Star."

2. O, whence came love so full and free,
The precious ransom who has paid?

Is mercy bought with agony?
Is God's own Son the sufferer made?

3. Oh, love divine! my soul can sing
With exultation now the strain,
That makes heaven's echoing arches ring,
"Worthy the Lamb that once was
slain!"

4. My central Sun, thy power reveal,
To win my love from earthly dross;
Through life, in death, to make me feel
The sweet attraction of the Cross

727. *One Thing needful.*

1. Why will ye waste, on trifling cares,
That life which God's compassion spares?
While, in the various range of thought,
The one thing needful is forgot?

2. Shall God invite you from above?
Shall Jesus urge his dying love?
Shall troubled conscience give you pain?
And all these pleas unite in vain?

3. Not so your eyes will always view
Those objects which you now pursue;
Not so will heaven and hell appear,
When death's decisive hour is near.

4. Almighty God, thy grace impart,
Fix deep conviction on each heart;
Nor let us waste, on trifling cares,
That life which thy compassion spares.

BREMEN. L. C. M.    "MANHATTAN COLL."

1. O, could I speak the match-less worth, O, could I sound the
glo - ries forth, That in my Sa - viour shine; I'd soar and touch the
heavenly strings, And vie with Gabriel while he sings, In notes al-most di - vine.

---

728.   *Praise to the Redeemer.*

1. O, COULD I speak the matchless worth,
    O, could I sound the glories forth,
      That in my Saviour shine;
    I'd soar and touch the heavenly strings,
    And vie with Gabriel while he sings,
      In notes almost divine.

2. I'd sing the characters he bears,
    And all the forms of love he wears,
      Exalted on his throne:
    In loftiest songs of sweetest praise,
    I would, to everlasting days,
      Make all his glories known.

3. Soon the delightful day will come,
    When my dear Lord will bring me home,
      And I shall see his face:
    Then, with my Saviour, brother, friend,
    A blessed eternity I'll spend,
      Triumphant in his grace.

729.   *General Praise.*

1. BEGIN, my soul, th' exalted lay,
    Let each enraptured thought obey,
      And praise th' Almighty name:
    Lo! heaven and earth, and seas and
        skies,
    In one melodious concert rise,
      To swell th' inspiring theme.

2. Thou heaven of heavens, his vast abode—
    Ye clouds, proclaim your Maker, God;
      Ye thunders, speak his power;
    Lo! on the lightning's fiery wing,
    In triumph walks th' eternal King:
      The astonished worlds adore.

3. Ye deeps, with roaring billows rise,
    To join the thunders of the skies—
      Praise him who bids you roll:
    His praise in softer notes declare,
    Each whispering breeze of yielding air,
      And breathe it to the soul.

4. Wake, all ye soaring throng, and sing;
Ye feathered warblers of the spring,
Harmonious anthems raise
To him who shaped your finer mould,
Who tipped your glittering wings with
gold,
And tuned your voice to praise.

5. Let man, by nobler passions swayed,
Let man, in God's own image made,
His breath in praise employ:
Spread wide his Maker's name around,
Till heaven shall echo back the sound,
In songs of holy joy.

730. *Religious Song.*

1. THE songs of Zion oft impart,
To this poor, laboring, care-worn heart,
The balm of heavenly peace ;
They chase away each boding fear,
They turn to joy each sorrowing tear,
And bid the tumult cease.

2. O Thou, who fill'st the heavenly throne,
'Tis not in melody alone
To set the spirit free ;
Without the breathings of thy love
The sweetest strains will powerless
prove,
Nor comfort bring to me.

3. But if the Spirit of the Lord
His hallowed influence will afford,
The soul will upward rise
On wings of song with love divine,
Till heavenly light around me shine,
Beneath the bending skies.

4. If Thou the gracious influence lend,
The charms of song will sweetly blend
With pure devotion's flame ;
Will melt the heart, the mind employ,
And fill the soul with holy joy,
At mention of thy name.

5. Give me that music of the lyre
That bids each earthly wish expire,
And lifts the thoughts on high :
That fills the soul with heavenly love,
And bids her a rich foretaste prove
Of treasures in the sky.

731. *Longing to forsake the World.*

1. THE mind was formed to mount sublime
Beyond the narrow bounds of time,
To everlasting things :
But earthly vapors dim her sight,
And hang with cold, oppressive weight
Upon her drooping wings.

2. Bright scenes of bliss, unclouded skies,
Invite my soul: O could I rise,
Nor leave a thought below.
I'd bid farewell to anxious care,
And say, to every tempting snare,
Heaven calls, and I must go.

3. Heaven calls, and can I yet delay?
Can aught on earth engage my stay ?
Ah, wretched, lingering heart !
Come, Lord, with strength, and life, and
light,
Assist and guard my upward flight,
And bid the world depart.

732. *Monthly Concert of Prayer.*

1. GOD of the nations, bow thine ear,
And listen to our fervent prayer
Through thy belovéd Son ;
Build up the kingdom of his grace
Amid the millions of our race,
And make thy wonders known.

2. Send forth the heralds in his name,
Bid them a Saviour's love proclaim
With every fleeting breath ;
Till distant lands shall hear the sound,
And send the joyful echoes round,
Amid the shades of death.

3. O let the nations rise, and bring
Their offerings to th' Almighty King,
And trust in him alone ;
Renounce their idols, and adore
The God of gods for evermore,
Upon his lofty throne.

4. The dying millions thus shall prove
The matchless power of bleeding love,
And feel their sins forgiven ;
Shall join the converts' joyful throng,
And raise on high redemption's song,
Along the path to heaven.

Doxology.

To Father, Son, and Holy Ghost,
Be praise amid the heavenly host,
And in the church below ;
From whom all creatures draw their
breath,
By whom redemption blessed the earth,
From whom all comforts flow.

THE GARDEN. 7s. 6 lines.*   See WILLIS' STUDIES.

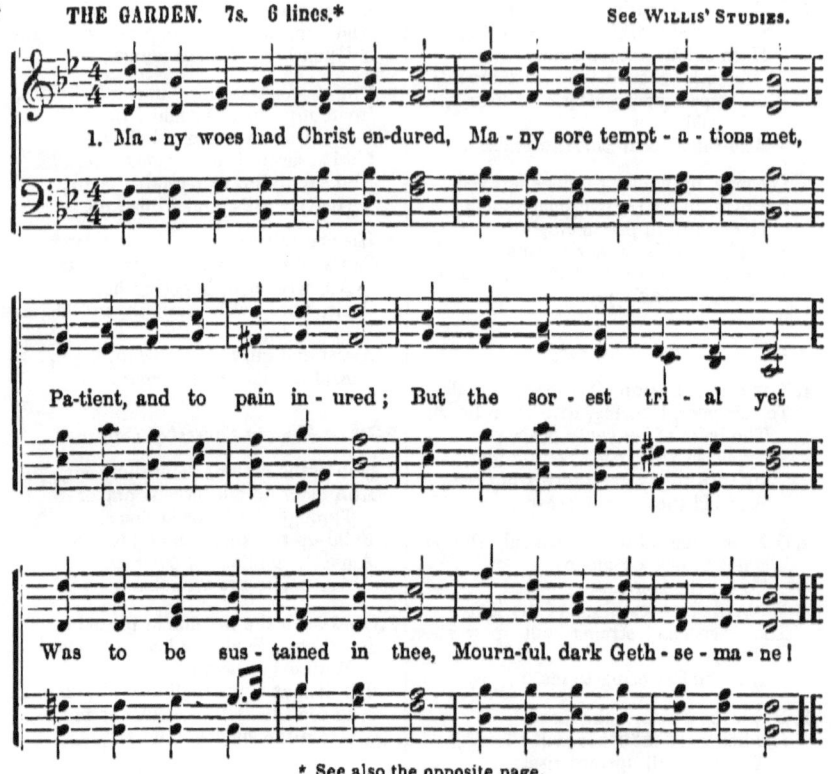

1. Ma-ny woes had Christ en-dured, Ma-ny sore tempt-a-tions met,

Pa-tient, and to pain in-ured; But the sor-est tri-al yet

Was to be sus-tained in thee, Mourn-ful, dark Geth-se-ma-ne!

* See also the opposite page.

733.   *Gethsemane.*

1. MANY woes had Christ endured,
Many sore temptations met,
Patient, and to pain inured;
   But the sorest trial yet
Was to be sustained in thee,
Mournful, dark Gethsemane!

2. Came at length the dreadful night,
   Vengeance, with its iron rod,
Stood, and with collected might
   Bruised the harmless Lamb of God.
See, my soul, thy Saviour see,
Prostrate in Gethsemane!

3. O, what wonders love has done,
   But how little understood,
God well knows, and God alone,
   What produced that sweat of blood.
None can penetrate through thee,
Doleful, dread Gethsemane!

4. There, my God bore all my guilt,
   This through grace can be believed,
But the horrors that he felt
   Are too vast to be conceived:
Who can thy deep mystery see,
Wonderful Gethsemane?

5. Sins against a holy God,
   Sins against his righteous laws,
Sins against his love, his blood,
   Sins against his name and cause,
Sins immense as is the sea—
Hide me, O Gethsemane.

734.   *Adoption.*

1. FATHER, let thy light divine
Brightly o'er my pathway shine;
Bid the shadows disappear,
Banish every sinful fear;
Guide me in the narrow way
To the realms of endless day.

2. Canst thou own a little child,
One so oft by sin defiled?
Canst thou fit me, by thy grace,
To behold thy dwelling-place?
Trembling, Lord, I would believe;
Let me not myself deceive.

3. But if I am all thy own,
Let me live for thee alone;
Let the honor of thy name
All my inmost soul inflame;
Let thy holy Spirit move,
Till my heart is filled with love.

HAWES. 7s. 6 lines.   GERMAN.

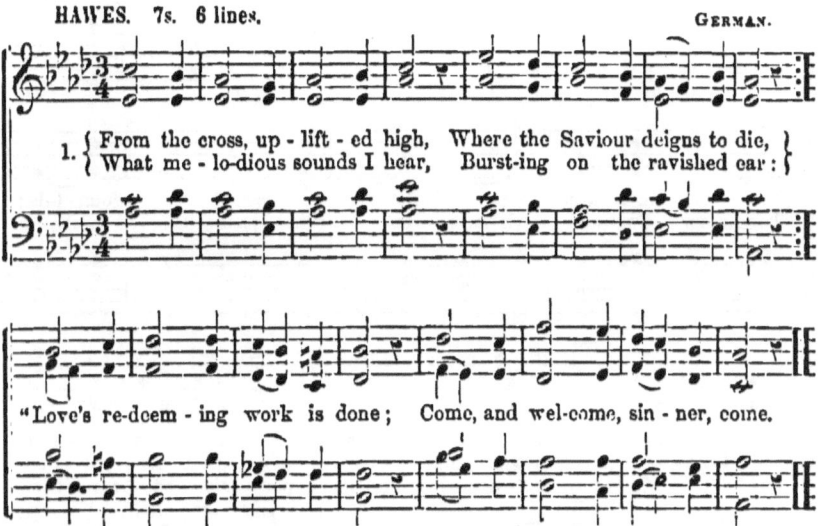

1. { From the cross, up-lift-ed high, Where the Saviour deigns to die, }
   { What me-lo-dious sounds I hear, Burst-ing on the ravished ear: }

"Love's re-deem-ing work is done; Come, and wel-come, sin-ner, come.

735.   *Come, and welcome.*

1. FROM the cross uplifted high,
Where the Saviour deigns to die,
What melodious sounds I hear,
Bursting on the ravished ear!—
"Love's redeeming work is done;
Come, and welcome, sinner, come.

2. "Sprinkled now with blood the throne,
Why beneath thy burdens groan?
On My pierced body laid,
Justice owns the ransom paid;
Bow the knee, and kiss the Son:
Come, and welcome, sinner, come.

3. "Spread for thee, the festal board,
See, with richest dainties stored;
To thy Father's bosom pressed,
Yet again a child confessed,
Never from his house to roam,
Come, and welcome, sinner, come.

4. "Soon the days of life shall end;
Lo! I come, your Saviour, Friend,
Safe your spirits to convey

To the realms of endless day,
Up to my eternal home;
Come, and welcome, sinner, come."

736.   *" Teach us to pray."*

1. HOLY Lord, our hearts prepare
For the work of solemn prayer;
Grant, that while we bend the knee,
All our thoughts may turn to thee;
Let thy presence here be found
Breathing peace and joy around.

2. While we come around thy throne,
Make thy power and glory known;
As thy children, may we call
On our Father, Lord of all,
And with confidence and fear,
At thy footstool now appear.

3. Teach us, while we breathe our woes,
On thy promise to repose;
All thy tender love to trace
In the Saviour's work of grace;
Let us all, in faith, depend
On a gracious God and Friend.

"THE VOICE OF FREE GRACE."   12s.   Or 12s & 11s.*   Dr. Clarke.

1st hymn. The   voice   of   free   grace cries, "Es-cape   to   the moun-tain;"
2d hymn. Thou art gone   to   the   grave, but we will   not de-plore thee,

For   Ad-am's   lost   race   Christ hath   o-pened   a   foun-tain;
Though sor-row   and   dark-ness   en - com-pass   the   tomb,

For   sin   and   un - clean-ness, and   ev-ery trans-gres-sion,
Cho. Halle-lu-jah   to the   Lamb, who hath pur-chased our   par-don,
The   Sa - viour   hath passed through its   por-tals   be - fore thee,

His   blood flows most free-ly   in   streams of   sal - va-tion,
We'll praise him   a - gain   when we pass   o - ver   Jor-dan,
And the lamp   of   his   love   is   thy   guide through the   gloom,

Repeat for the first hymn only.
FIRST TIME.   SECOND TIME.

His   blood flows most free-ly,   in   streams of   sal - va - tion.
We'll praise him   a - gain,   When we pass   o - ver   Jor-dan.
And the lamp of   his   love   is thy guide thro' the   gloom.

* By using, or omitting slurs.

737. *Free Grace.*

1. THE voice of free grace cries, " Escape to the mountain,"
For Adam's lost race Christ hath opened a fountain;
For sin and uncleanness, and every transgression,
His blood flows most freely in streams of salvation.
CHORUS.*—Hallelujah to the Lamb, who hath purchased our pardon,
We'll praise him again, when we pass over Jordan.

2. Ye souls that are wounded! O flee to the Saviour;
He calls you in mercy—'tis infinite favor;
Your sins are increasing—escape to the mountain—
His blood can remove them—it flows from the fountain.

3. O, Jesus! ride onward, triumphantly glorious,
O'er sin, death and hell, thou art more than victorious;
Thy name is the theme of the great congregation,
While angels and men raise the shout of salvation.

4. With joy shall we stand, when escaped to the shore;
With harps in our hands, we will praise him the more;
We'll range the sweet plains on the banks of the river,
And sing of salvation for ever and ever!

738. *Farewell to a Friend departed.*

1. THOU art gone to the grave; but we will not deplore thee,
Though sorrows and darkness encompass the tomb;
The Saviour has passed through its portals before thee,
And the lamp of his love is thy guide through the gloom.

2. Thou art gone to the grave; we no longer behold thee,
Nor tread the rough paths of the world by thy side;
But the wide arms of mercy are spread to enfold thee,
And sinners may hope, since the Saviour hath died.

3. Thou art gone to the grave; and, its mansion forsaking,
Perchance thy weak spirit in doubt lingered long;
But the sunshine of heaven beamed bright on thy waking,
And the sound thou didst hear, was the seraphim's song.

4. Thou art gone to the grave; but we will not deplore thee;
Since God was thy Ransom, thy Guardian, thy Guide;
He gave thee, he took thee, and he will restore thee;
And death has no sting, since the Saviour hath died.

739. *Christ in the Storm.*

1. WHEN through the torn sail the wild tempest is streaming,
When o'er the dark wave the red lightning is gleaming,
Nor hope lends a ray the poor sailors to cherish,
They fly to their Master, " Save, Lord, or we perish."

2. O, Jesus, once rocked on the breast of the billow,
Aroused by the shriek of despair from thy pillow,
Now, seated in glory, the poor sinner cherish,
Who cries in his anguish, " Save, Lord, or we perish."

3. And, O, when the whirlwind of passion is raging,
When sin in our hearts its wild warfare is waging,
Then send down thy grace, thy redeeméd to cherish,
Rebuke the destroyer; " Save, Lord, or we perish."

To be sung generally at the CLOSE of the hymn only.

1. Come, ye that love the Sa - viour's name, And joy to make it known! The Sov - ereign of your hearts pro - claim, And bow be - fore the throne, And bow be - fore the throne.

* See also DENMAN 102.

740. *King of Saints.*

1. COME, ye that love the Saviour's name,
   And joy to make it known!
   The Sovereign of your hearts proclaim,
   And bow before the throne.

2. Behold your King, your Saviour crowned
   With glories all divine;
   And tell the wondering nations round,
   How bright those glories shine.

3. Infinite power and boundless grace
   In him unite their rays:
   Ye that have e'er beheld his face,
   Can ye forbear his praise?

4. When in his earthly courts we view
   The glories of our King,
   We long to love as angels do,
   And wish like them to sing.

5. And shall we long and wish in vain?
   Lord, teach our songs to rise:
   Thy love can animate the strain,
   And bid it reach the skies.

741. *The Morning of the Lord's Day.*

1. EARLY, my God, without delay,
   I haste to seek thy face;
   My thirsty spirit faints away,
   Without thy cheering grace.

2. So pilgrims, on the scorching sand,
   Beneath a burning sky,
   Long for a cooling stream at hand;
   And they must drink or die.

3. I've seen thy glory and thy power
   Through all thy temple shine;
   My God, repeat that heavenly hour,
   That vision so divine.

4. Not life itself, with all its joys,
   Can my best passions move,
   Or raise so high my cheerful voice,
   As thy forgiving love.

5. Thus, till my last expiring day,
   I'll bless my God and King;
   Thus will I lift my hands to pray,
   And tune my lips to sing.

742. *Delight in the Law.*

1. Oh how I love thy holy law:
'Tis daily my delight:
And thence my meditations draw
Divine advice by night.

2. My waking eyes prevent the day,
To meditate thy word!
My soul with longing melts away
To hear thy gospel, Lord.

3. How doth thy word my heart engage,
How well employ my tongue!
And in my tiresome pilgrimage,
Yields me a heavenly song.

4. Am I a stranger, or at home,
'Tis my perpetual feast;
Not honey dropping from the comb
So much allures the taste.

5. When nature sinks, and spirits droop,
Thy promises of grace
Are pillars to support my hope,
And there I write thy praise.

743. *Christ's Commission.*

1. Come, happy souls! approach your God,
With new, melodious songs:
Come, render to almighty grace
The tribute of your tongues.

2. So strange, so boundless was the love,
That pitied dying men,
The Father sent his equal Son
To give them life again.

3. Thy hands, dear Jesus! were not armed
With a revenging rod;
No hard commission to perform
The vengeance of a God.

4. But all was mercy, all was mild,
And wrath forsook the throne,
When Christ, on the kind errand, came,
And brought salvation down.

5. Here, sinners! you may heal your wounds,
And wipe your sorrows dry;
Trust in the mighty Saviour's name,
And you shall never die.

6. See, dearest Lord! our willing souls
Accept thine offered grace;
We bless the great Redeemer's love,
And give the Father praise.

744. *The Incarnation.*

1. Awake—awake the sacred song
To our incarnate Lord!

Let every heart, and every tongue,
Adore th' eternal Word.

2. Then shone almighty power and love,
In all their glorious forms,
When Jesus left his throne above,
To dwell with sinful worms.

3. Adoring angels tuned their songs,
To hail the joyful day;
With rapture, then, let human tongues
Their grateful homage pay.

745. *Dawn of the Sabbath.*

1. Again, the Lord of life and light
Awakes the kindling ray,
Dispels the darkness of the night,
And pours increasing day.

2. Oh! what a night was that which wrapt
A sinful world in gloom!
Oh! what a sun, which broke this day,
Triumphant from the tomb!

3. This day be grateful homage paid,
And loud hosannas sung;
Let gladness dwell in every heart,
And praise on every tongue.

4. Ten thousand thousand lips shall join
To hail this welcome morn,
Which scatters blessings from its wings,
To nations yet unborn.

746. *Christ receiving Children.*

1. See Israel's gentle Shepherd stand,
With all-engaging charms;
Hark! how he calls the tender lambs,
And folds them in his arms.

2. "Permit them to approach," he cries,
"Nor scorn their humble name;
For 'twas to bless such souls as these
The Lord of angels came."

3. We bring them, Lord, in thankful hands,
And yield them up to thee;
Joyful that we ourselves are thine,
Thine let our offspring be.

4. Ye little flock, with pleasure hear:
Ye children, seek his face;
And fly with transports to receive
The blessings of his grace.

5. If orphans they are left behind,
Thy guardian care we trust:
That care shall heal our bleeding hearts,
If weeping o'er their dust.

PARTING SOUL.   8s & 7s.   Single.*   GERMAN.

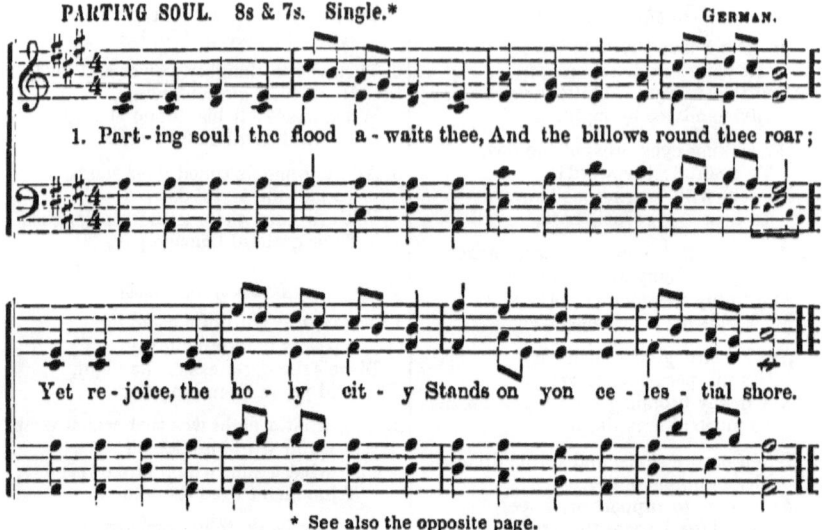

1. Part - ing soul! the flood a - waits thee, And the billows round thee roar;

Yet re - joice, the ho - ly cit - y Stands on yon ce - les - tial shore.

* See also the opposite page.

747. *The Spirit of a dying Christian.*

1. PARTING soul! the flood awaits thee,
    And the billows round thee roar;
Yet, rejoice—the holy city
    Stands on yon celestial shore.

2. There are crowns, and thrones of glory,
    There the living waters glide;
There the just, in shining raiment,
    Standing by Immanuel's side.

3. Linger not—the stream is narrow,
    Though its cold, dark waters rise;
He, who passed the flood before thee,
    Guides thy path to yonder skies.

748. *The dying Saint comforted.*

1. HAPPY soul! thy days are ending—
    All thy mourning days below:
Go, the angel guards attending—
    To the sight of Jesus go!

2. Waiting to receive thy spirit,
    Lo! the Saviour stands above;
Shows the fullness of his merit—
    Reaches out the crown of love.

3. For the joy he sets before thee,
    Bear a momentary pain;
Die—to live a life of glory;
    Suffer—with the Lord to reign:

4. Struggle, through thy latest passion,
    To thy dear Redeemer's breast—
To his uttermost salvation—
    To his everlasting rest.

749. *Weep not for the departed Saint.*

1. O, YE mourners! cease to languish
    O'er the grave of those ye love!
Pain and death, and night and anguish,
    Enter not the world above.

2. While in darkness ye are straying,
    Lonely in the deepening shade,
Glory's brightest beams are playing
    Round th' immortal spirit's head.

3. O, ye mourners! cease to languish
    O'er the grave of those ye love!
Far removed from pain and anguish,
    They are chanting hymns of love.

4. Light and peace at once deriving
    From the hand of God most high:
In his glorious presence living,
    They shall never, never die.

Doxology.

PRAISE the Father, earth and heaven,
    Praise the Son, the Spirit praise,
Everlasting praise be given,
    Glory through eternal days.

SICILIAN. 8s & 7s. Single.

1. Sa-viour, who thy flock art feed-ing With the shepherd's kindest care,

All the fee-ble gen-tly lead-ing, While the lambs thy bo-som share.

750. *Christ the Shepherd.*

1. SAVIOUR, who thy flock art feeding
   With the shepherd's kindest care,
   All the feeble gently leading,
   While the lambs thy bosom share—

2. Now, these little ones receiving,
   Fold them in thy gracious arm;
   There, we know—thy word believing—
   Only there, secure from harm.

3. Never, from thy pasture roving,
   Let them be the lion's prey;
   Let thy tenderness, so loving,
   Keep them all life's dangerous way.

4. Then, within thy fold eternal,
   Let them find a resting-place;
   Feed in pastures ever vernal,
   Drink the rivers of thy grace.

751. *Anniversary Hymn.*

1. GOD of mercy, do thou never
   From our offering turn away,
   But command a blessing ever
   On the memory of this day.

2. Light and peace do thou ordain it;
   O'er it be no shadow flung:
   Let no deadly darkness stain it,
   And no clouds be o'er it hung.

3. May the song this people raises,
   And its vows to thee addressed,
   Mingle with the prayers and praises
   That thou hearest from the blest.

4. When the lips are cold that sing thee,
   And the hearts that love thee dust,
   Father, then our souls shall bring thee
   Holier love, and firmer trust.

752. *In Sorrow.*

1. GENTLY, Lord, O gently lead us,
   Pilgrims in this vale of tears,
   Through the trials yet decreed us,
   Till our last great change appears.

2. When temptation's darts assail us,
   When in devious paths we stray,
   Let thy goodness never fail us—
   Lead us in thy perfect way.

3. In the hour of pain and anguish,
   In the hour when death draws near,
   Suffer not our hearts to languish,
   Suffer not our souls to fear.

4. And, when mortal life is ended,
   Bid us in thine arms to rest,
   Till, by angel bands attended,
   We awake among the blest.

CROSS AND CROWN. C. M.*

WESTERN MELODY.

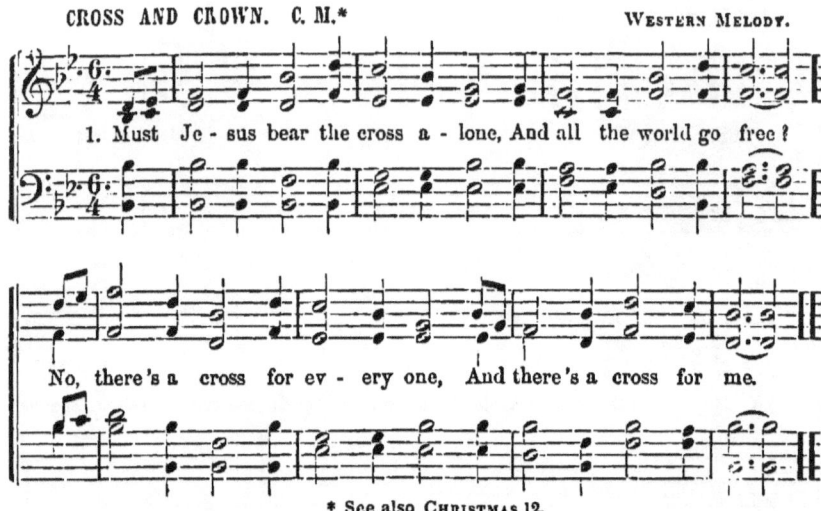

1. Must Je - sus bear the cross a - lone, And all the world go free ?

No, there's a cross for ev - ery one, And there's a cross for me.

* See also CHRISTMAS 12.

753.　　*Cross and Crown.*

1. MUST Jesus bear the cross alone,
　And all the world go free ?
No, there's a cross for every one,
　And there's a cross for me.

2. How happy are the saints above,
　Who once were sorrowing here !
But now they taste unmingled love,
　And joy without a tear.

3. The consecrated cross I'll bear,
　Till death shall set me free;
And then go home, my crown to wear,
　For there's a crown for me.

754.　　*The new Creation.*

1. SPIRIT of power and might, behold
　A world by sin destroyed:
Creator Spirit, as of old,
　Move on the formless void.

2. Give thou the word—that healing sound
　Shall quell the deadly strife;
And earth again, like Eden crowned,
　Produce the tree of life.

3. If sang the morning stars for joy,
　When nature rose to view,
What strains shall angel-harps employ,
　When thou shalt all renew !

4. And if the sons of God rejoice
　To hear a Saviour's name,
How will the ransomed raise their voice,
　To whom that Saviour came !

5. So every kindred, tongue, and tribe,
　Assembling round the throne,
Thy new creation shall ascribe
　To sovereign love alone.

755.　　*The Joys which are unseen.*

1. NOR eye hath seen, nor ear hath heard,
　Nor sense nor reason known,
What joys the Father hath prepared
　For those who love the Son.

2. But the good Spirit of the Lord
　Reveals a heaven to come:
The beams of glory in his word
　Allure and guide us home.

3. Pure are the joys above the sky,
　And all the region peace;
No wanton lip, nor envious eye,
　Can see or taste the bliss.

4. Those holy gates for ever bar
　Pollution, sin and shame;
None shall obtain admission there
　But followers of the Lamb.

756. *Lot of the Righteous and the Wicked*

1. THAT man, in life wherever placed,
　Has happiness in store,
Who walks not in the wicked's way,
　Nor learns their guilty lore.

2. Nor from the seat of scornful pride
Casts forth his eyes abroad,
But with humility and awe
Still walks before his God.

3. That man shall flourish like the trees
Which by the streamlet grow,
Whose fruitful top is spread on high,
And firm the root below.

4. But he whose blossom buds in guilt
Shall to the ground be cast,
And like the rootless stubble tossed
Before the sweeping blast.

5. For God, that God the good adore,
Will give them peace and joy:
But all the hopes of wicked men
Will utterly destroy

757. *" They who sow in tears,"* &c.

1. THERE is an hour of hallowed peace
For those with cares oppressed,
When sighs and sorrowing tears shall
cease,
And all be hushed to rest.

2. 'Tis then the soul is freed from fears,
And doubts which here annoy;
Then they, who oft have sown in tears,
Shall reap again in joy

3. There is a home of sweet repose,
Where storms assail no more ;
The stream of endless pleasure flows
On that celestial shore.

4. There smiling peace, with love appears,
And bliss without alloy ;
There they, who oft have sown in tears,
Now reap eternal joy.

158. *The unseen and blessed World.*

'. FAR from these narrow scenes of night,
Unbounded glories rise,
And realms of infinite delight,
Unknown to mortal eyes.

2. Fair, distant land ! could mortal eyes
But half its charms explore,
How would our spirits long to rise,
And dwell on earth no more !

3. No cloud those blissful regions know—
Realms ever bright and fair ;
For sin, the source of mortal woe,
Can never enter there.

4. Oh ! may the heavenly prospect fire
Our hearts with ardent love,

Till wings of faith and strong desire
Bear every thought above.

5. Prepare us, Lord ! by grace divine,
For thy bright courts on high ;
Then bid our spirits rise and join
The chorus of the sky.

759. *Charitable Appropriations.*

1. JESUS, our Lord ! how rich thy grace !
Thy bounties—how complete !
How shall we count the wondrous sum,
Or pay 'he mighty debt ?

2. High on a throne of radiant light
Dost thou exalted shine ;
What can our poverty bestow,
Since all the world is thine ?

3. But thou hast brethren here below,
The children of thy grace,
Whose humble names thou wilt confess,
Before thy Father's face.

4. In them may'st thou be clothed and fed,
Be visited and cheered ;
And, in their accents of distress, .
The Saviour's voice be heard.

5. Whate'er our willing hands can give,
Lord ! at thy feet we lay ;
Grace will the humble gift receive,
And grace at length repay.

760. *Ministers watch for Souls.*

1. LET Zion's watchmen all awake,
And take th' alarm they give ;
Now let them, from the mouth of God,
Their awful charge receive.

2. 'Tis not a cause of small import,
The pastor's care demands ;
But what might fill an angel's heart—
It filled a Saviour's hands.

3. They watch for souls, for which the Lord
Did heavenly bliss forego ;
For souls, that must for ever live,
In raptures, or in woe.

4. All to the great tribunal haste,
Th' account to render there ;
And should'st thou strictly mark our
faults,
Lord ! how should we appear ?

5. May they that Jesus, whom they preach,
Their own Redeemer, see ;
And watch thou daily o'er their souls,
That they may watch for thee

WARFARE. L. M.*
BOLD.
HASTINGS.

1. Stand up, my soul! shake off thy fears, And gird the gos - pel
ar - mor on; March to the gates of end - less joy, Where Je - sus
thy great Cap - tain's gone, Where Je - sus thy great Cap - tain's gone.

Final.

* See also PARK STREET 74.

761. *The Christian Warfare.*

1. STAND up, my soul! shake off thy fears,
And gird the gospel armor on;
March to the gates of endless joy,
Where Jesus thy great Captain's gone.

2. Hell and thy sins resist thy course,—
But hell and sin are vanquished foes;
Thy Jesus nailed them to the cross,
And sung the triumph, when he rose.

3. Then, let my soul march boldly on,
Press forward to the heavenly gate;
There peace and joy eternal reign,
And glittering robes for conquerors wait.

4. There shall I wear a starry crown,
And triumph in almighty grace;
While all the armies of the skies
Join in my glorious Leader's praise.

762. *"Labor on."*

1. Go, labor on, spend, and be spent—
Thy joy to do the Father's will,

It is the way the Master went,
Should not the servant tread it still.

2. Go, labor on, while it is day,
The world's dark night is hastening on;
Speed, speed thy work, cast sloth away:
It is not thus that souls are won.

3. Men die in darkness at your side,
Without a hope to cheer the tomb;
Take up the torch and wave it wide,
The torch that lights time's thickest gloom.

4. Toil on, faint not, keep watch and pray·
Be wise the erring soul to win;
Go forth into the world's highway,
Compel the wanderer to come in.

5. Toil on, and in thy toil rejoice;
For toil comes rest, for exile, home;
Soon shalt thou hear the Bridegroom's voice,
The midnight peal, behold, I come!

763. *Zion encouraged.*

1. ZION! awake, thy strength renew,
Put on thy robes of beauteous huo;
And let th' admiring world behold
The King's fair daughter clothed in gold.

2. Church of our God! arise and shine,
Bright with the beams of truth divine:
Then shall thy radiance stream afar,
Wide as the heathen nations arc.

3. Gentiles and kings thy light shall view;
All shall admire and love thee, too;—
Shall come, like clouds across the sky,
Or doves that to their windows fly.

764. *The heavenly Race.*

1. AWAKE, our souls; away, our fears,
Let every trembling thought be gone;
Awake, and run the heavenly race,
And put a cheerful courage on.

2. True, 'tis a strait and thorny road,
And mortal spirits tire and faint;
But they forget the mighty God,
Who feeds the strength of every saint;

3. The mighty God, whose matchless power
Is ever new and ever young,
And firm endures, while endless years
Their everlasting circles run.

4. From thee, the overflowing spring,
Our souls shall drink a full supply;
While those who trust their native strength
Shall melt away, and droop, and die.

5. Swift as an eagle cuts the air,
We 'll mount aloft to thine abode;
On wings of love our souls shall fly,
Nor tire amid the heavenly road.

765. *The Hosanna of the Children.*

1. ALMIGHTY Ruler of the skies!
Thro' the wide earth thy name is spread,
And thine eternal glories rise
O'er all the heavens thy hands have
made.

2. To thee the voices of the young
A monument of honor raise;
And babes, with uninstructed tongue,
Declare the wonders of thy praise.

3. Thy power assists their tender age
To bring proud rebels to the ground;
To still the bold blasphemer's rage,
And all their policies confound.

4. Children amidst thy temple throng,
To see their great Redeemer's face;
The Son of David is their song,
And young hosannas fill the place.

766. *Security of the Saints.*

1. WHO shall the Lord's elect condemn?—
'Tis God who justifies their souls;
And mercy, like a mighty stream,
O'er all their sins divinely rolls.

2. Who shall adjudge the saints to hell?—
'Tis Christ, who suffered in their stead,
And, the salvation to fulfil,
Behold him, rising from the dead!

3. He lives!—he lives, and reigns above,
For ever interceding there;
Who shall divide us from his love?—
Or what shall tempt us to despair?

4. Not all that men on earth can do,
Nor powers on high, nor powers below,
Shall cause his mercy to remove,
Or wean our hearts from Christ, our love.

767. *Prayer on opening a Church Edifice*

1. WITHIN thy house, O Lord our God!
In glorious majesty appear;
Make this a place of thine abode,
And shed thy choicest blessings here.

2. When we thy mercy-seat surround,
Thy Spirit, with thy word, impart;
And let thy gospel's joyful sound,
With power divine, reach every heart.

3. Here, let the blind their sight obtain,
Here, give the broken spirit rest;
Let Jesus here triumphant reign,—
Enthroned in every yielding breast.

4. Here, let the voice of sacred joy
And humble supplication, rise,
Till higher strains our tongues employ,
In realms of bliss, beyond the skies.

768. *The coming Reign of Christ.*

1. ASCEND thy throne, almighty King!
And spread thy glories all abroad;
Let thine own arm salvation bring,
And be thou known the gracious God

2. Let millions bow before thy seat,—
Let humble mourners seek thy face;
Bring daring rebels to thy feet,
Subdued by thy victorious grace.

3. Oh! let the kingdoms of the world
Become the kingdoms of the Lord;
Let saints and angels praise thy name,—
Be thou through heaven and earth
adored.

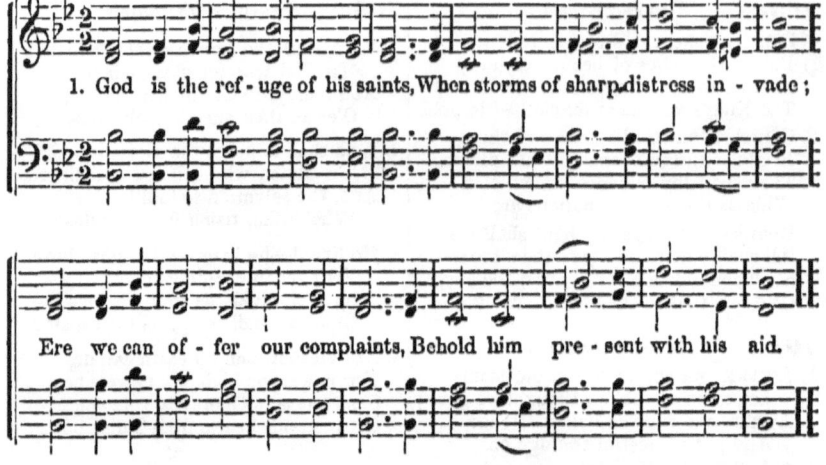

1. God is the ref - uge of his saints, When storms of sharp distress in - vade;

Ere we can of - fer our complaints, Behold him pre - sent with his aid.

769. *God the Refuge and Portion of his People.*

1. GOD is the refuge of his saints,
   When storms of sharp distress invade;
   Ere we can offer our complaints,
   Behold him present with his aid.

2. Loud may the troubled ocean roar;
   In sacred peace our souls abide,
   While every nation, every shore,
   Trembles and dreads the swelling tide.

3. There is a stream whose gentle flow
   Supplies the city of our God;
   Life, love, and joy, still gliding through,
   And watering our divine abode.

4. That sacred stream, thy holy word,
   Supports our faith, our fear controls;
   Sweet peace thy promises afford,
   And give new strength to fainting souls.

5. Zion enjoys her Monarch's love,
   Secure against a threatening hour:
   Nor can her firm foundation move,
   Built on his truth, and armed with power.

770. *Secret Self-Examination.*

1. RETURN, my roving heart, return,
   And chase those shadowy forms no more
   Now seek in solitude to mourn,
   And thy forsaken God implore.

2. O thou great God, whose piercing eye
   Distinctly marks each deep recess:
   In these sequestered hours draw nigh,
   And with thy presence fill the place.

3. Through all the windings of my heart,
   My search let heavenly wisdom guide,
   And still its radiant beams impart,
   Till all be cleansed and purified.

4. O with the visits of thy love,
   Vouchsafe my inmost soul to cheer;
   Till every grace shall join to prove
   That God has fixed his dwelling here.

771. *At the Communion.*
1 Cor. xi. 24; Luke xxii, 19.

1. DRAW near, O Holy Dove, draw near,
   With peace and gladness on thy wing;
   Reveal the Saviour's presence here,
   And light, and life, and comfort bring.

2. Eat, O my friends—drink, O beloved,—
   We hear the Master's voice exclaim:
   Our hearts with new desire are moved,
   And kindled with a heavenly flame.

3. No room for doubt, no room for dread,
   Nor tears, nor groans, nor anxious sighs
   We do not mourn a Saviour dead,
   But hail him living in the skies:

4. While this we do, remembering thee,
   Dear Saviour, let our graces prove
   We have thy blessed company,
   Thy banner over us is love.

772. *Christ is mine.*

1. JESUS, whom angel-hosts adore,
Became a man of griefs for me ;
In love, though rich, becoming poor,
That I through him enriched might be.

2. Though Lord of all, above, below,
He went to Olivet for me ;
There drank my cup of wrath and woe,
When bleeding in Gethsemane.

3. The ever-blessèd Son of God
Went up to Calvary for me ;
There paid my debt, there bore my load,
In his own body on the tree.

4. Jesus, whose dwelling is the skies,
Went down into the grave for me ;
There overcame my enemies,
There won the glorious victory.

5. In love the whole dark path he trod,
To consecrate a way for me ;
Each bitter footstep marked with blood,
From Bethlehem to Calvary.

6. 'Tis finished all ; the vail is rent,
The welcome sure, the access free ;—
Now then we leave our banishment,
O Father, to return to thee !

773. *Christ, the only Refuge.*

1. THOU only Sovereign of my heart,
My Refuge, my almighty Friend !
And can my soul from thee depart,
On whom alone my hopes depend ?

2. Whither, ah ! whither shall I go,
A wretched wanderer from my Lord ?
Can this dark world of sin and woe
One glimpse of happiness afford ?

3. Eternal life thy words impart,
On these my fainting spirit lives ;
Here sweeter comforts cheer my heart
Than all the round of nature gives.

4. Let earth's alluring joys combine ;
While thou art near, in vain they call ;
One smile—one blissful smile of thine—
My dearest Lord ! outweighs them all.

5. Low at thy feet my soul would lie,—
Here safety dwells, and peace divine ;
Still let me live beneath thine eye,
For life—eternal life—is thine.

774. *Hope in the Covenant.*

1. HOW oft have sin and Satan strove,
To rend my soul from thee, my God !
But everlasting is thy love,
And Jesus seals it with his blood.

2. The oath and promise of the Lord
Join to confirm the wondrous grace ;
Eternal power performs the word,
And fills all heaven with endless praise

3. Amid temptations, sharp and long,
My soul to this dear refuge flies ;
Hope is my anchor, firm and strong,
While tempests blow, and billows rise.

4. The gospel bears my spirit up ;
A faithful and unchanging God
Lays the foundation for my hope,
In oaths, and promises, and blood.

775. *The Sufferings of Christ.*

1. DEEP in our hearts, let us record
The deeper sorrows of our Lord ;
Behold the rising billows roll,
To overwhelm his holy soul !

2. Yet, gracious God ! thy power and love
Have made the curse a blessing prove ;
Those dreadful sufferings of thy Son
Atoned for sins that we had done.

3. The pangs of our expiring Lord
The honors of thy law restored ;
His sorrows made thy justice known,
And paid for follies not his own.

4. Oh ! for his sake, our guilt forgive,
And let the mourning sinner live :
The Lord will hear us in his name,
Nor shall our hope be turned to shame

776. *Christ present with his People.*

1. HOW sweet to leave the world awhile,
And seek the presence of our Lord !
Dear Saviour ! on thy people smile,
And come, according to thy word.

2. From busy scenes we now retreat,
That we may here converse with thee
Ah ! Lord ! behold us at thy feet ;—
Let this the "Gate of heaven" be.

3. " Chief of ten thousand !" now appear,
That we by faith may see thy face :
Oh ! speak, that we thy voice may hear,
And let thy presence fill this place.

WEBB. 7s & 6s.*
ALLEGRO.

G. J. WEBB.

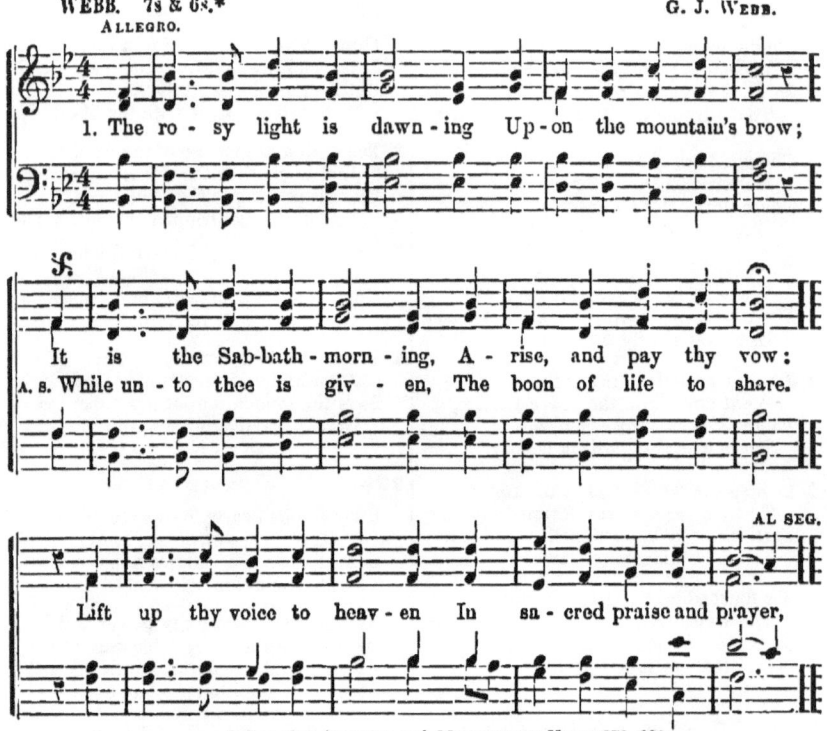

1. The ro - sy light is dawn - ing Up - on the mountain's brow;

It is the Sab-bath - morn - ing, A - rise, and pay thy vow:
A. s. While un - to thee is giv - en, The boon of life to share.

AL SEG.

Lift up thy voice to heav - en In sa - cred praise and prayer,

* See also SAXONY and MISSIONARY HYMN 272, 122.

777. *A bright Sabbath Morning.*

1. THE rosy light is dawning
   Upon the mountain's brow ;
   It is the Sabbath morning,
   Arise and pay thy vow:
Lift up thy voice to heavén
   In sacred praise and prayer,
While unto thee is givén,
   The boon of life to share.

2. The landscape, lately shrouded
   By evening's paler ray,
   Smiles beauteous and unclouded
   Before the eye of day:
So let our souls, benighted
   Too long in folly's shade,
By thy kind smiles be lighted
   To joys that never fade.

3. O, see those waters streaming
   In crystal purity,
While earth, with verdure teeming,
   Gives rapture to the eye!

Let rivers of salvation
   In larger currents flow,
Till every tribe and nation
   Their healing power shall know.

778.   *Reflections at Sunset.*

1. THE mellow eve is gliding
   Serenely down the west ;
So, every care subsiding,
   My soul would sink to rest.
The woodland hum is ringing
   The daylight's gentle close ;
May angels, round me singing,
   Thus hymn my last repose.

2. The evening star has lighted
   Her crystal lamp on high ;
So, when in death benighted,
   May hope illume the sky.
In golden splendor dawning,
   The morrow's light shall break ·
O, on the last bright morning
   May I in glory wake !

779. *Praise to the Saviour.*

1. To thee, my God and Saviour,
   My soul exulting, sings;
   Rejoicing in thy favor,
   Almighty King of kings;
   I'll celebrate thy glory,
   With all thy saints above—
   And tell the joyful story
   Of thy redeeming love.

2. Soon as the morn with roses
   Bedecks the dewy east,
   And when the sun reposes
   Upon the ocean's breast;
   My voice in supplication,
   My Saviour, thou shalt hear:
   O grant me thy salvation,
   And to my soul draw near.

3. By thee, through life supported,
   I pass the dangerous road,
   With heavenly hosts escorted,
   Up to their bright abode:
   Then cast my crown before thee,
   And, all my conflicts o'er,
   Unceasingly adore thee;
   What could an angel more?

780. *Autumn.*

1. The leaves, around me falling,
   Are preaching of decay;
   The hollow winds are calling,
   "Come, pilgrim, come away."
   The day, in night declining,
   Says I must, too, decline;
   The year, its bloom resigning,
   Its lot foreshadows mine.

2. The light, my path surrounding,
   The loves to which I cling,
   The hopes within me bounding,
   The joys that round me wing—
   All, all, like stars at even,
   Just gleam, and shoot away,
   Pass on before to heaven,
   And chide at my delay.

3. The friends gone there before me
   Are calling from on high,
   And happy angels o'er me
   Tempt sweetly to the sky;
   "Why wait," they say, "and wither,
   'Mid scenes of death and sin?
   O, rise to glory, hither, .
   And find true life begin"

4. I hear the invitation,
   And fain would rise and come,
   A sinner, to salvation,
   An exile, to his home;
   But while I here must linger,
   Thus, thus, let all I see
   Point on, with faithful finger,
   To heaven, O Lord, and thee.

781. *A Christian Family.*

1. What sight on earth more blissful
   Than that domestic scene,
   Where union, pure and peaceful
   As sunlit clouds at e'en,
   Each kindred heart enlightens
   With many a heaven-born ray,
   Which ever shines and brightens
   Unto the perfect day.

2. There discord is a stranger,
   There strife can never come,
   And many a snare and danger
   Are exiled from that home;
   While indolence and folly
   Are banished, with their train,
   And converse, pure and holy,
   Exerts her gentle reign.

3. And there, how sweet and precious
   The grateful song to raise,
   To him, so kind and gracious,
   Who claims the highest praise:
   With glad, harmonious voices,
   Parents and children join;
   While every heart rejoices
   In blessings so divine.

4. In such a habitation
   May we be ever found,
   Where waters of salvation
   In healing streams abound;
   Affection's voice to chide us,
   Whene'er we go astray;
   And mercy's hand to guide us
   Along the narrow way.

Doxology.

To Father, Son and Spirit,
Eternal praise be given,
By all that earth inherit,
And all that dwell in heaven—
Thou Triune God, before thee,
Our inmost souls adore,
Who art and hast been worthy,
And shalt be evermore.

AMITY STREET. S. M.*   "CHORALIST." By permission.

1. The Saviour kind - ly calls Our chil-dren to his breast,

He holds them in his gra-cious arms:—Him - self de - clares them blest.

* See also BOYLSTON 52.

782.   *Christ blessing Children.*

1. THE Saviour kindly calls
   Our children to his breast;
   He holds them in his gracious arms:—
   Himself declares them blest.

2. "Let them approach," he cries,
   "Nor scorn their humble claim;
   The heirs of heaven are such as these,—
   For such as these I came."

3. With joy we bring them, Lord!
   Devoting them to thee,
   Imploring, that, as we are thine,
   Thine may our offspring be.

783.   *The Mercy-Seat.*

1. How charming is the place
   Where my Redeemer God
   Unveils the glories of his face,
   And sheds his love abroad!

2. Not the fair palaces
   To which the great resort,
   Are once to be compared with this,
   Where Jesus holds his court.

3. Here, on the mercy-seat,
   With radiant glory crowned,
   Our joyful eyes behold thee sit,
   And smile on all around.

4. To thee, our prayers and cries
   Each humble soul presents:
   O listen to our broken sighs,
   And grant us all our wants.

5. Give us, O Lord, a place
   Within thy blest abode;
   Among the children of thy grace,
   The servants of our God.

784.   *Christ our Sacrifice.*

1. NOT all the blood of beasts
   On Jewish altars slain,
   Could give the guilty conscience peace,
   Or wash away the stain.

2. But Christ, the heavenly Lamb,
   Takes all our sins away;
   A sacrifice of nobler name,
   And richer blood than they.

3. My faith would lay her hand
   On that dear head of thine;
   While like a penitent I stand,
   And there confess my sin.

4. My soul looks back to see
   The burdens thou didst bear,
   When hanging on the cursèd tree,
   And hopes her guilt was there.

5. Believing, we rejoice
   To see the curse remove;
   We bless the Lamb with cheerful voice,
   And sing his bleeding love.

OLMUTZ. S. M.   Arr. from a Greg. Chant, by L. MASON.

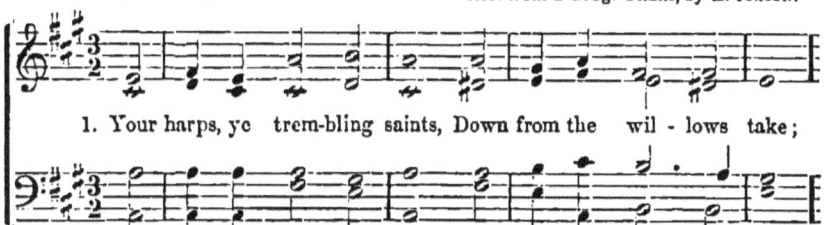

1. Your harps, ye trem-bling saints, Down from the wil - lows take;

Loud, to the praise of love di - vine, Bid ev - ery string a - wake.

785.   *Trust in God.*

1. YOUR harps, ye trembling saints,
   Down from the willows take;
Loud, to the praise of love divine,
   Bid every string awake.

2. Though in a foreign land,
   We are not far from home;
And, nearer to our house above,
   We every moment come.

3. His grace will, to the end,
   Stronger and brighter shine;
Nor present things, nor things to come,
   Shall quench this spark divine.

4. When we in darkness walk,
   Nor feel the heavenly flame,
Then will we trust our gracious God,
   And rest upon his name.

5. Soon shall our doubts and fears
   Subside at his control:
His loving-kindness shall break through
   The midnight of the soul.

6. Blest is the man, O God!
   That stays himself on thee:—
Who waits for thy salvation, Lord!
   Shall thy salvation see.

786.   *The Light of the World.*

1. How heavy is the night
   That hangs upon our eyes,
Till Christ, with his reviving light,
   Over our souls arise!

2. Our guilty spirits dread
   To meet the wrath of heaven;
But, in his righteousness arrayed,
   We see our sins forgiven.

3. Unholy and impure
   Are all our thoughts and ways;
His hands infected nature cure,
   With sanctifying grace.

4. The powers of hell agree
   To hold our souls in vain;
He sets the sons of bondage free,
   And breaks the cursèd chain.

5. Lord! we adore thy ways
   To bring us near to God;
Thy sovereign power, thy healing grace,
   And thine atoning blood.

Doxology.

YE angels round the throne,
   And saints that dwell below,
Worship the Father—love the Son,
   And bless the Spirit, too.

"SAFELY THROUGH." 7s. 6 lines.   Dr. L. Mason.

1. Safe-ly through an-oth-er week, God has brought us on our way; Let us now a blessing seek, Waiting in his courts to-day: Day of all the week the best, Emblem of e-ternal rest, Day of all the week the best, Emblem of e-ter-nal rest.

787. *The Sabbath in the Sanctuary.—No. 1.*

1. SAFELY through another week
    God has brought us on our way;
  Let us now a blessing seek,
    Waiting in his courts to-day :
  Day of all the week the best,
  Emblem of eternal rest.

2. While we seek supplies of grace,
    Through the dear Redeemer's name :
  Show thy reconciling face—
    Take away our sin and shame ;
  From our worldly cares set free,
  May we rest this day in thee.

3. Here we come, thy name to praise ;
    Let us feel thy presence near ;
  May thy glory meet our eyes,
    While we in thy house appear ;
  Here afford us, Lord, a taste
  Of our everlasting feast.

4. May the gospel's joyful sound
    Conquer sinners—comfort saints,

Make the fruits of grace abound,
    Bring relief from all complaints :
  Thus let all our Sabbaths prove,
  Till we join the church above.

[*Above is the hymn in its usual form. Origin-
ally it was written for Saturday evening. See
Olney Hymns.*]

788.   *Saturday Evening.—No. 2.*

1. SAFELY through another week
    God has brought us on our way;
  Let us now a blessing seek,
    On th' approaching Sabbath day ;
  Day of all the week the best,
  Emblem of eternal rest.

2. While we pray for pardoning grace,
    Through the blest Redeemer's name,
  Show us, Lord, thy smiling face,
    And remove our guilt and shame :
  Thus from every care set free,
  May we rest this night with thee.

3. When the morn shall bid us rise,
  May we feel thy presence near;
  May thy glory meet our eyes,
  When we in thy courts appear :
  There in spirit may we taste
  Fruits of heaven's eternal rest.

4. May the gospel's joyful sound,
  Conquer sinners, comfort saints ;
  Bid the fruits of grace abound,
  Bring relief for all complaints :
  Thus may every Sabbath prove,
  Till we join the church above.

MOORE. L. C. M.*   GERMAN.

1. My God, thy boundless love I praise; How bright on high its glories blaze! How sweetly

bloom below! { In streams from thy eter - nal throne; } Thro' heaven its joys for ever run, { And o'er the earth they flow.

* See also BREMEN 240.

789.   *The Love of God.*

1. My God, thy boundless love I praise;
  How bright on high its glories blaze !
  How sweetly bloom below !
  It streams from thy eternal throne;
  Through heaven its joys for ever run,
  And o'er the earth they flow.

2. 'Tis love that paints the purple morn,
  And bids the clouds, in air upborne,
  Their genial drops distill ;
  In every vernal beam it glows,
  And breathes in every gale that blows,
  And glides in every rill.

3. But in the gospel it appears
  In sweeter, fairer characters,
  And charms the ravished breast;
  There love immortal leaves the sky,
  To wipe the drooping mourner's eye,
  And give the weary rest.

4. Then let the love that makes me blessed,
  With cheerful praise inspire my breast,
  And ardent gratitude ;

And all my thoughts and passions tend
  To thee, my Father and my Friend,
  My soul's eternal good.

790.   *Songs in the Night.*

1. Songs in the night full oft are given,
  Soft breathings from the air of heaven,
  Sweet zephyrs to the soul ;
  The pilgrim's lonely heart to cheer,
  And bring celestial glories near
  By their divine control.

2. Songs in the night kind Heaven supplies,
  When cares and trials round us rise,
  Our comfort to destroy ;
  They bid the tempter far retire,
  And fill the soul with holy fire,
  Celestial peace and joy.

3 Songs in the night of sorrow's power,
  Affliction's tempest, death's dark hour,
  The pilgrim yet will sing ;
  He'll shout with faith's uplifted eye,
  "O grave, where is thy victory !
  O death, where is thy sting !"

AMERICA, 6s & 4s,*   HANDEL.

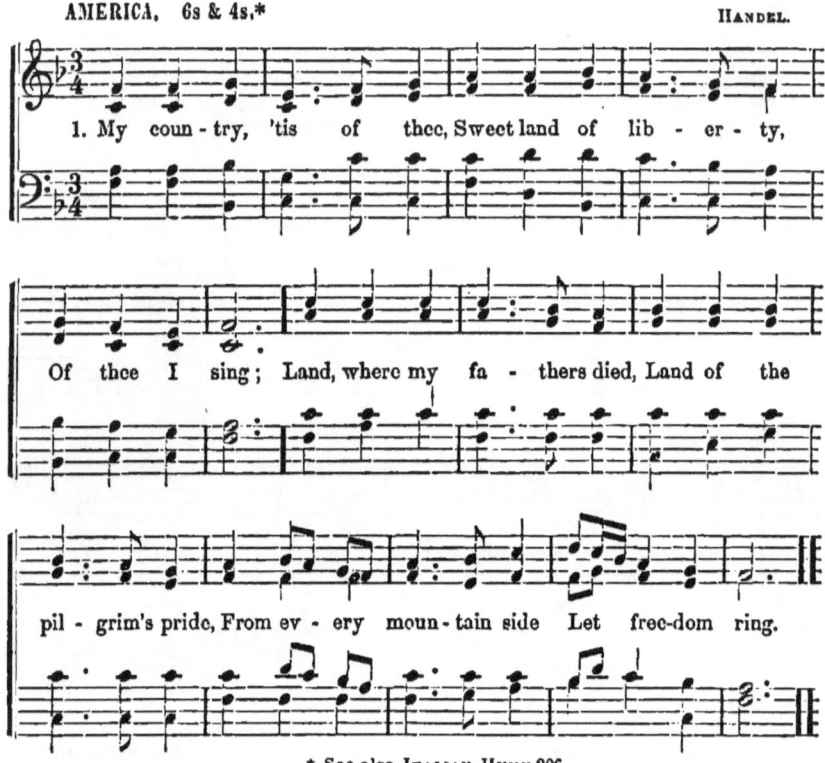

1. My coun - try, 'tis of thee, Sweet land of lib - er - ty,

Of thee I sing; Land, where my fa - thers died, Land of the

pil - grim's pride, From ev - ery moun - tain side Let free-dom ring.

* See also ITALIAN HYMN 206.

791.   *National Hymn.*

1. MY country, 'tis of thee,
Sweet land of liberty,
Of thee I sing;
Land, where my fathers died,
Land of the pilgrim's pride,
From every mountain side
Let freedom ring.

2. My native country, thee—
Land of the noble free—
Thy name I love;
I love thy rocks and rills,
Thy woods, and templed hills;
My heart with rapture thrills
Like that above.

3. Let music swell the breeze,
And ring from all the trees
Sweet freedom's song:
Let mortal tongues awake;

Let all that breathe partake;
Let rocks their silence break—
The sound prolong.

4. Our fathers' God, to thee,
Author of liberty,
To thee we sing:
Long may our land be bright
With freedom's holy light;
Protect us by thy might,
Great God, our King.

792.   *Thanksgiving Hymn.*

1. THE God of harvest praise;
In loud thanksgiving raise
Hand, heart, and voice;
The valleys smile and sing,
Forests and mountains ring,
The plains their tribute bring,
The streams rejoice.

2. Yea, bless his holy name,
And purest thanks proclaim
Through all the earth
To glory in your lot
Is duty—but be not
God's benefits forgot,
Amidst your mirth.

3. The God of harvest praise;
Hands, hearts, and voices raise,
With sweet accord;
From field to garner throng,
Bearing your sheaves along,
And in your harvest song
Bless ye the Lord.

CORONATION. C. M.*

HOLDEN. Arranged.

1. All hail the power of Je-sus' name, Let an-gels prostrate fall;

Bring forth the ro-yal di-a-dem, And crown him—Lord of all; Bring

forth the ro-yal di-a-dem, And crown him—Lord of all.

* See also HARBOROUGH 113.

793. *Coronation of Christ.*

1. ALL hail the power of Jesus name!
Let angels prostrate fall;
Bring forth the royal diadem,
And crown him—Lord of all.

2. Crown him—ye morning stars of light!—
Who formed this floating ball:
Now hail the strength of Israel's might,
And crown him—Lord of all.

3. Ye chosen seed of Israel's race—
Ye ransomed from the fall!

Hail him, who saves you by his grace,
And crown him—Lord of all.

4. Sinners! whose love can ne'er forget
The wormwood and the gall—
Come, spread your trophies at his feet,
And crown him—Lord of all.

5. Let every kindred, every tribe,
On this terrestrial ball,
To him all majesty ascribe,
And crown him—Lord of all.

IMMORTALITY. 7s & 5s.

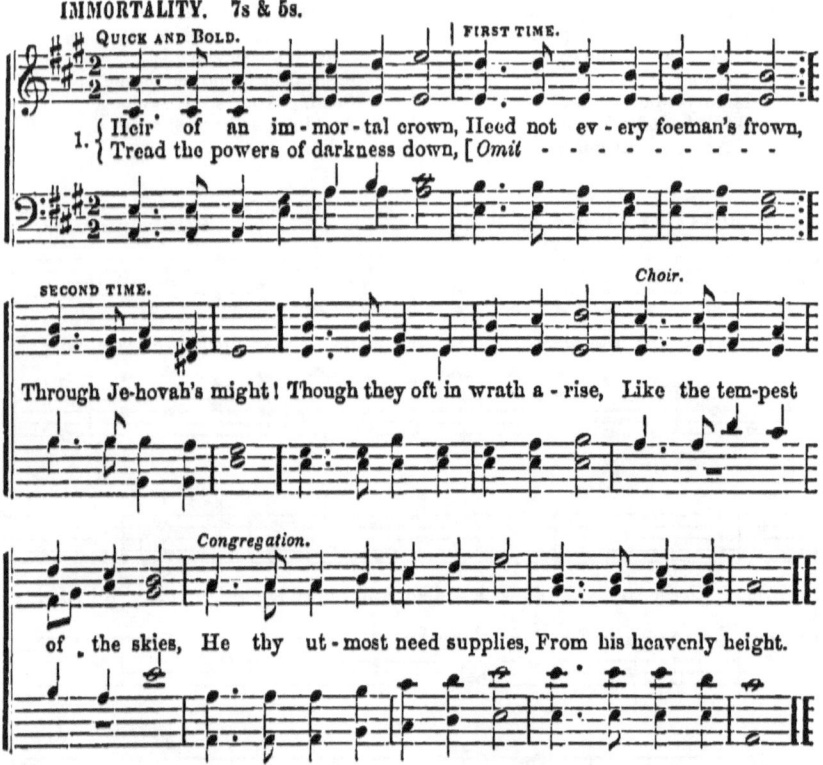

1. Heir' of an im-mor-tal crown, Heed not ev-ery foeman's frown,
Tread the powers of darkness down, [*Omit* - - - - - - - - -
Through Je-hovah's might! Though they oft in wrath a-rise, Like the tem-pest
of the skies, He thy ut-most need supplies, From his heavenly height.

794. *The Conflict.*

1. Heir of an immortal crown,
Heed not every foeman's frown,
Tread the powers of darkness down,
    Through Jehovah's might!
Though they oft in wrath arise,
Like the tempest of the skies,
He thy utmost need supplies,
    From his heavenly height.

2. Soldier in the tented field,
Ply thy heav'n-wrought sword and shield,
Till the line of battle yield,
    And before thee flee:
In thine armor ever stand,
Girded by Jehovah's hand,
Till within the promised land
    He shall set thee free.

795. *A Favored Land.*

1. Children of a free-born race,
Happy in your dwelling-place,

As your blessings ye retrace,
    Think from whence they flow:
Think of that Creative Hand,
Author of the sea and land,
By whose power the nations stand,
    In their weal or woe.

3. Here are freedom, health, and peace,
Here oppression's surges cease,
Streams of knowledge here increase,
    Deepening far and wide:
Science here her tribute pours,
Industry collects her stores,
Wealth flows in from foreign shores,
    Like a swelling tide.

3. Here religion undefiled,
With an influence pure and mild,
Reaches to the humblest child,
    E'en from door to door:
Let us then our off'rings bring,
Thanks unto the heavenly King,
From the heart his praises sing,
    Now and evermore.

796. *Trust in God.*

1. CHILD of sorrow, child of care,
Wouldst thou learn thy griefs to bear,
And escape from every snare,
Trust in God alone:
Human strength is weak and vain,
Let not sin its power regain;
Humbly ask and help obtain
From thy Father's throne.

2. Know'st thou in this vale of tears,
Gloomy doubts, distracting fears,
Painful months and sorrowing years?
To the Saviour fly:
He that drank the bitter cup,
Bids thee in his mercy hope;
Let thy prayer be lifted up
To his throne on high.

CLARKSON. 5s & 8s. "MANHATTAN COLL."
BOLD.

1. Re - joice in the Lord, Be - lieve in his word, Con - fide in his mer - cy and grace; His throne shall en-dure, His promise is sure, In him shall the righteous have peace, In him shall the right-eous have peace.

797. *Joy in God.*

1. REJOICE in the Lord,
Believe in his word,
Confide in his mercy and grace;
His throne shall endure,
His promise is sure,
In him shall the righteous have peace.

2. Thrice happy are they
Who his precepts obey,
Who delight in the law of their God;
Their joys shall increase,
And their trials shall cease,
As they enter the heavenly abode.

3. What scenes will arise,
As they pass through the skies,
What raptures their bosoms will fill,
As their harps they employ,
In the fullness of joy,
On the height of some heavenly hill!

4. Rejoice in the Lord,
Believe in his word,
Confide in his mercy and grace;
His throne shall endure,
His promise is sure,
In him shall the righteous have peace.

HARWELL.   8s & 7s.   Double.   L. MASON.

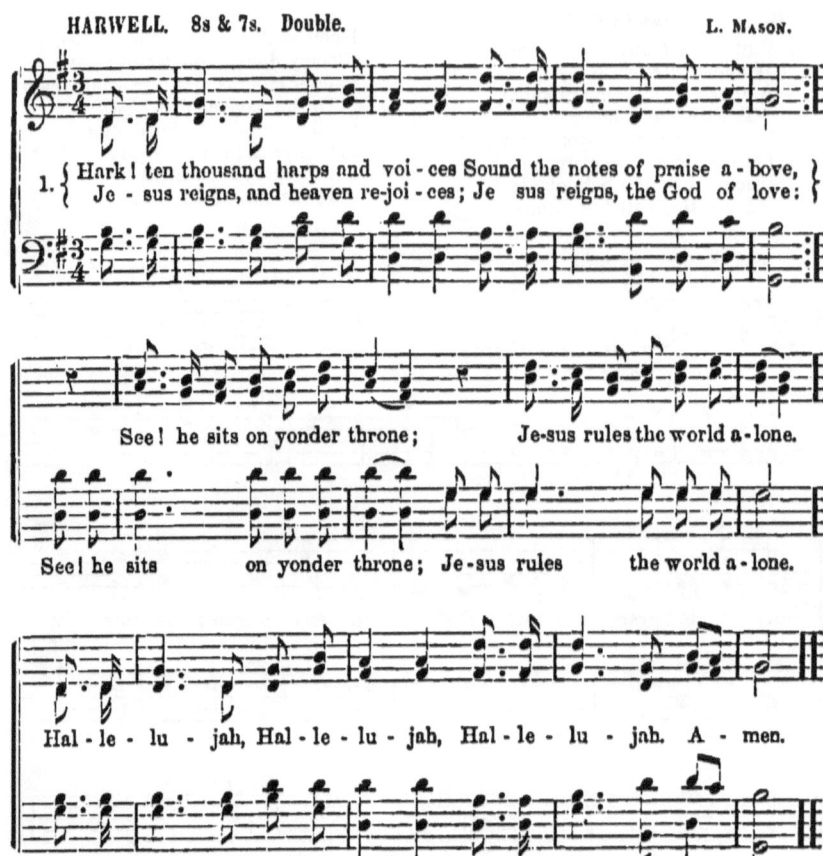

1. { Hark! ten thousand harps and voi-ces Sound the notes of praise a-bove, }
   { Je-sus reigns, and heaven re-joi-ces; Je sus reigns, the God of love: }

See! he sits on yonder throne;   Je-sus rules the world a-lone.

See! he sits   on yonder throne; Je-sus rules   the world a-lone.

Hal-le-lu-jah, Hal-le-lu-jah, Hal-le-lu-jah. A-men.

798. *Christ, the Lamb, enthroned and wor-shiped.*

1. HARK!—ten thousand harps and voices
   Sound the notes of praise above,
   Jesus reigns, and heaven rejoices;—
   Jesus reigns, the God of love:
   See! he sits on yonder throne;
   Jesus rules the world alone.
   Hallelujah, etc.

2. Jesus! hail! whose glory brightens
   All above, and gives it worth;
   Lord of life! thy smile enlightens,
   Cheers, and charms thy saints on earth:
   When we think of love like thine,
   Lord! we own it love divine.
   Hallelujah etc

3. King of glory! reign for ever—
   Thine an everlasting crown;
   Nothing, from thy love, shall sever
   Those whom thou hast made thine
   own;
   Happy objects of thy grace,
   Destined to behold thy face.
   Hallelujah, etc.

4. Saviour! hasten thine appearing;
   Bring—Oh! bring the glorious day,
   When, the awful summons hearing,
   Heaven and earth shall pass away;—
   Then, with golden harps, we 'll sing—
   "Glory, glory to our King."
   Hallelujah, etc.

799. *Christ, the Saviour, born.*

1. HAIL, thou long-expected Jesus!
   Born to set thy people free;
   From our sins and fears release us,
   Let us find our rest in thee.

2. Israel's strength and consolation,
   Hope of all the saints, thou art;
   Long-desired of every nation,
   Joy of every waiting heart.

3. Born, thy people to deliver—
   Born a child, yet God our King—
   Born to reign in us for ever—
   Now thy gracious kingdom bring.

4. By thine own eternal Spirit,
   Rule in all our hearts alone;
   By thine all-sufficient merit
   Raise us to thy glorious throne.

AQUILA. 8s & 7s. Single. ZINGARELLI.

1. Hark! what mean those lamen-ta-tions, Roll - ing sad - ly thro' the sky!

'Tis the cry of hea - then na-tions—" Come, and help us, or we die.

800. *The Heathen crying for Help.*

1. HARK! what mean those lamentations,
   Rolling sadly through the sky?
   'Tis the cry of heathen nations—
   "Come and help us, or we die!"

2. Hear the heathens' sad complaining,
   Christians! hear that dying cry:
   And, the love of Christ constraining,
   Haste to help them, ere they die.

801. *Days of Worship.*

1. WELCOME, days of solemn meeting!
   Welcome, days of praise and prayer!
   Far from earthly scenes retreating,
   In your blessings we would share.

2. Be thou near us, blessèd Saviour,
   Still at morn and eve the same,
   Give us faith that can not waver;
   Kindle in us heaven's own flame.

3 When the fervent prayer is glowing,
   Holy Spirit, hear that prayer;

When the song of praise is flowing,
   Let that song thine impress bear.

802. *The Church in the Desert*

1. ZION, dreary, and in anguish,
   In the desert hast thou strayed?
   O, thou weary, cease to languish,
   Jesus shall lift up thy head.

2. Still lamenting and bemoaning,
   'Mid thy follies and thy woes?
   Soon repenting, and returning,
   All thy solitude shall close.

3. Though benighted and forsaken,
   Though afflicted and oppressed,
   His Almighty arm shall waken,
   Zion's King shall give thee rest.

4. Cease thy sadness, unbelieving,
   Soon his glory shalt thou see,
   Joy, and gladness, and thanksgiving,
   And the voice of melody.

STATE STREET. S. M.*   WOODMAN

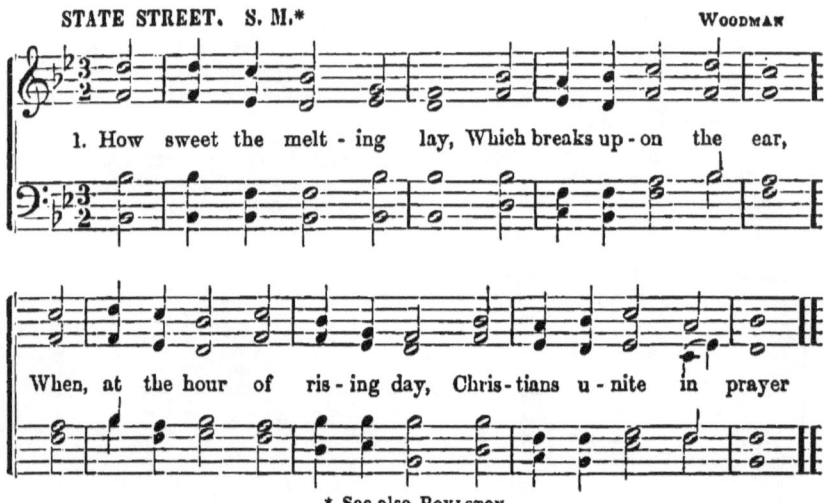

1. How sweet the melt-ing lay, Which breaks up-on the ear,

When, at the hour of ris-ing day, Chris-tians u-nite in prayer

* See also BOYLSTON.

803. *Morning Prayer Meeting.*

1. How sweet the melting lay,
    Which breaks upon the ear,
When, at the hour of rising day,
    Christians unite in prayer.

2. The breezes waft their cries
    Up to Jehovah's throne;
He listens to their bursting sighs,
    And sends his blessings down.

3. So Jesus rose to pray,
    Before the morning light;
Once on the chilling mount did stay,
    And wrestle all the night.

4. Glory to God, on high,
    Who sends his blessings down,
To rescue souls condemned to die,
    And make his people one.

804. *Convicting and sanctifying Influence.*

1. COME, Holy Spirit! come,
    Let thy bright beams arise;
Dispel the sorrow from our minds,
    The darkness from our eyes.

2. Convince us of our sin,
    Then lead to Jesus' blood;
And, to our wondering view, reveal
    The secret love of God.

3. 'Tis thine to cleanse the heart,
    To sanctify the soul,
To pour fresh life in every part,
    And new-create the whole.

4. Revive our drooping faith;
    Our doubts and fears remove;
And kindle in our breasts the flame
    Of never-dying love.

805. *The accepted Time.*

1. Now is th' accepted time,
    Now is the day of grace;
O, sinners, come, without delay,
    And seek the Saviour's face.

2. Now is th' accepted time,
    The Saviour calls to-day;
To-morrow it may be too late,
    Then why should you delay?

3. Now is th' accepted time,
    The gospel bids you come;
And every promise in his word
    Declares there yet is room.

4. Lord, draw reluctant souls,
    And melt them by thy love:
Then will the angels speed their flight,
    To bear the news above.

806. *Communion with Christ and with Saints.*

1. JESUS invites his saints
To meet around his board;
Here pardoned rebels sit, and hold
Communion with their Lord.

2. This holy bread and wine
Maintain our fainting breath,
By union with our living Lord,
And interest in his death.

3. Our heavenly Father calls
Christ and his members one;
We, the young children of his love,
And he, the first-born Son.

4. Let all our powers be joined
His glorious name to raise:
Pleasure and love fill every mind,
And every voice be praise.

807. *Prayer and Praise.*

1. I HEAR thy word with love,
And I would fain obey;
Send thy good Spirit from above,
To guide me, lest I stray.

2. Oh! who can ever find
The errors of his ways?
Yet, with a bold, presumptuous mind,
I would not dare transgress.

3. Warn me of every sin,
Forgive my secret faults?
And cleanse this guilty soul of mine,
Whose crimes exceed my thoughts.

4. While, with my heart and tongue,
I spread thy praise abroad,
Accept the worship and the song,
My Saviour and my God!

808. *Saturday Evening.*

1. THE hours of evening close;
Its lengthened shadows, drawn
O'er scenes of earth, invite repose,
And wait the Sabbath dawn.

2. So let its calm prevail
O'er forms of outward care;
Nor thought for "many things" assail
The still retreat of prayer.

3. Our guardian Shepherd near
His watchful eye will keep ;
And, safe from violence and fear,
Will fold his flock to sleep.

4. So may a holier light,
Than earth's, our spirits rouse,
And call us, strengthened by his might,
To pay the Lord our vows.

809. *Christ will hear Prayer.*

1. JESUS, who knows full well
The heart of every saint,
Invites us, all our grief to tell,
To pray and never faint.

2. He bows his gracious ear—
We never plead in vain ;
Then let us wait till he appear,
And pray, and pray again.

3. Jesus, the Lord, will hear
His chosen when they cry ;
Yes, though he may a while forbear,
He 'll help them from on high.

4. Then let us earnest cry,
And never faint in prayer ;
. He sees, he hears, and from on high
Will make our cause his care.

810. *Prayer for all Lands.*

1. O GOD of sovereign grace !
We bow before thy throne;
And plead, for all the human race,
The merits of thy Son.

2. Spread through the earth, O Lord !
The knowledge of thy ways;
And let all lands, with joy, record
The great Redeemer's praise.

811. *Coming boldly to the Throne of Grace.*

1. BEHOLD the throne of grace !
The promise calls us near;
There Jesus shows a smiling face,
And waits to answer prayer.

2. That rich, atoning blood,
Which sprinkled round we see,
Provides, for those who come to God,
An all-prevailing plea.

3. Thine image, Lord ! bestow,
Thy presence and thy love;
We ask to serve thee here below
And reign with thee above.

4. Teach us to live by faith,
Conform our will to thine ;
Let us victorious be in death,
And, then, in glory shine

5. If thou these blessings give,
And wilt our portion be,
All worldly joys we 'll cheerful leave,
And find our heaven in thee.

QUICK, BUT GENTLE.

1. The Lord is my Shepherd, his kind-ness I know, My wants will be ev - er sup-plied; He makes me re - pose where the green pas - tures grow, And wa - ters in gen - tle - ness glide.

812. Psalm xxiii.

1. THE Lord is my Shepherd, his kindness I know,
   My wants will be ever supplied;
   He makes me repose where the green pastures grow,
   And waters in gentleness glide.

2. My wandering affections, so often astray,
   His kindness and care will reclaim;
   To wisdom and holiness point me the way
   To the praise of his glorious name.

3. What though I walk through the dark valley of death,
   No evil my spirit will fear:
   My Shepherd is with me, his arm is beneath,
   His love and his comfort are near.

4. The hand of his bounty my table supplies,
   My cup of enjoyment o'erflows;
   He keeps me in safety when troubles arise,
   Nor yields to th' assaults of my foes.

5. His goodness and mercy around me are poured,
   His love shall for ever endure;
   For ever I 'll dwell in the house of the Lord,
   His word of salvation is sure.

813. *Thanksgiving and Praise in the Sanctuary.*

1. Be joyful in God, all ye lands of the earth!
 Oh! serve him with gladness and fear;
 Exult in his presence with music and mirth,
 With love and devotion draw near.

2. Jehovah is God, and Jehovah alone,
 Creator and Ruler o'er all:
 And we are his people, his sceptre we own;
 His sheep, and we follow his call.

3. Oh! enter his gates with thanksgiving and song,
 Your vows in his temple proclaim;
 His praise with melodious accordance prolong,
 And bless his adorable name.

4. For good is the Lord, inexpressibly good,
 And we are the work of his hand;
 His mercy and truth from eternity stood,
 And shall to eternity stand.

GOSHEN. 11s.   German

1. How cheering the thought that the spi - rits in bliss Should bow their bright

a. s. To breathe o'er our

wings to a world such as this! And leave the sweet songs of the mansions above,
bosom some mes- sage of love.

814. *The Ministry of Angels.*

1. How cheering the thought that the spirits in bliss
 Should bow their bright wings to a world such as this!
 And leave the sweet songs of the mansions above,
 To breath o'er our bosom some message of love.

2. They come—on the wings of the morning they come,
 To convoy the stranger in peace to his home;
 The pilgrim to waft from this stormy abode,
 And lay him to rest in the arms of his God.

3. They come when we wander, they come when we pray,
 In mercy to guard us wherever we stray:
 A glorious cloud their bright witness is given;
 Encircling us here are these angels of heaven.

SAXONY. 7s & 6s. Peculiar.*   CHANTS CRETIENS.

1. Go, for the Mas-ter calls thee, Shed not one bit-ter tear;
   No earth-ly care en-thralls thee, Nor hast thou aught to fear.

To him we now com-mend thee, Who rules a-bove the skies; His

bless-ing will at-tend thee, Wher-e'er thy path-way lies.

* See also MISSIONARY HYMN 122.

815.   *Departure of a Missionary.*

1. Go, for the Master calls thee,
   Shed not one bitter tear;
   No earthly care enthralls thee,
   Nor hast thou aught to fear:
   To him we now commend thee,
   Who rules above the skies;
   His blessing will attend thee,
   Where'er thy pathway lies.

2. Go, in the midst of dangers,
   Declare a Saviour's love,
   Till distant heathen strangers
   His willing subjects prove;
   Till many a crowd assembling,
   Shall hearken to thy voice;
   Confess their guilt with trembling,
   And in his name rejoice.

3. Go, for the Master calls thee,
   Far from thy native home;
   Whatever there befalls thee,
   Whatever ills may come,

He is thy strong salvation,
His presence thou shalt share;
He 'll aid thy supplication,
And hearken to thy prayer.

816.   *Gospel Banner.*

1. Now be the gospel banner
   In every land unfurled,
   And be the shout, Hosanna!
   Re-echoed through the world:
   Till every isle and nation,
   Till every tribe and tongue,
   Receive the great salvation,
   And join the happy throng.

2. What though th' embattled legions
   Of earth and hell combine?
   His power, throughout their regions,
   Shall soon resplendent shine:
   Ride on, O Lord, victorious,
   Immanuel, Prince of Peace!
   Thy triumph shall be glorious,
   Thy empire still increase!

3. Yes, thou shalt reign for ever,
 O Jesus, King of kings!
Thy light, thy love, thy favor,
 Each ransomed captive sings:
The isles for thee are waiting,
The deserts learn thy praise,
The hills and valleys greeting,
 The song responsive raise.

817. *Christ's Reign upon earth as the Son
 of David.* Psalm lxxii.

1. HAIL to the Lord's anointed,
 Great David's greater Son!
Hail, in the time appointed,
 His reign on earth begun!
He comes to break oppression,
 To set the captive free;
To take away transgression,
 And rule in equity.

2. He comes, with succor speedy,
 To those who suffer wrong;
To help the poor and needy,
 And bid the weak be strong;
To give them songs for sighing,
 Their darkness turn to light,
Whose souls, condemned and dying,
 Were precious in his sight.

3. He shall come down like showers,
 Upon the fruitful earth;
And love and joy, like flowers,
 Spring, in his path, to birth;
Before him, on the mountains,
 Shall peace, the herald, go;
And righteousness, in fountains,
 From hill to valley flow.

4. For him shall prayer unceasing,
 And daily vows ascend;
His kingdom still increasing,
 A kingdom without end:
The tide of time shall never
 His covenant remove;
His name shall stand for ever,
 That name to us is Love.

818. *God our Refuge.*

1. THERE is a peaceful river
 Descending from on high,
Whose streams are pure for ever,
 Whose waters can not dry:
No waves of tribulation
 Disturb their gladd'ning course;
The Rock of our salvation
 Is their unfailing source.

2. God in the midst is dwelling,
 Mount Zion shall not move;
The streams of grace are swelling,
 A tide of boundless love:
Her foes, so oft conspiring,
 Tumultuous in noise,
Like angry waves retiring,
 Have melted at his voice.

3. The Lord of Hosts is with us,
 The God of Jacob near;
With his strong arm beneath us
 Our souls shall never fear!
Our Refuge is most glorious!
 Be still, for he is God:
His cause shall be victorious,
 Earth trembles at his nod.

819. *Confidence in God.*

1. GOD is my strong salvation;
 What foe have I to fear?
In darkness and temptation,
 My light, my help, is near:
Though hosts encamp around me,
 Firm in the fight I stand;
What terror can confound me,
 With God at my right hand?

2. Place on the Lord reliance;
 My soul, with courage wait;
His truth be thine affiance,
 When faint and desolate;
His might thy heart shall strengthen,
 His love thy joy increase;
Mercy thy days shall lengthen;
 The Lord will give thee peace.

820. *Universal Hallelujah.*

1. WHEN shall the voice of singing
 Flow joyfully along?
When hill and valley, ringing
 With one triumphant song,
Proclaim the contest ended,
 And him, who once was slain,
Again to earth descended,
 In righteousness to reign?

2. Then from the craggy mountains,
 The sacred shout shall fly,
And shady vales and fountains
 Shall echo the reply:
High tower and lowly dwelling
 Shall send the chorus round,
The hallelujah swelling
 In one eternal sound.

ZELL.   8s & 7s.   Single.*
CHEERFUL.   BOST, of Switzerland.

1. Hark, what mean those ho - ly voi - ces   Sweet- ly sound-ing

through the   skies!   Lo!   th' an - gel - ic   host   re - joi - ces;

CODA—*Last verse.*

Heavenly hal - le - lu - jahs rise.   [Glo - ry   be   to   God   most high.]

* See also HARWELL—Repeating from 2d strain for 5th stanza 266.

821.   *The Song of Angels.*

1. HARK, what mean those holy voices
     Sweetly sounding through the skies!
   Lo! th' angelic host rejoices;
     Heavenly hallelujahs rise.

2. Listen to the wondrous story
     Which they chant in hymns of joy:
   " Glory in the highest, glory!
     Glory be to God most high.

3. " Peace on earth, good will from heaven,
     Reaching far as man is found,
   Souls redeemed, and sins forgiven;
     Loud our golden harps shall sound.

4. " Christ is born, the great Anointed,
     Heaven and earth his praises sing!
   O receive whom God appointed,
     For your Prophet, Priest, and King.

5. " Hasten, mortals, to adore him;
     Learn his name, and taste his joy;
   Till in heaven ye sing before him,
     Glory be to God most high."

822.   *The Incarnation.*

1. SHEPHERDS! hail the wondrous stranger;
     Now to Bethle'm speed your way;
   Lo! in yonder humble manger,
     Christ, the Lord, is born to-day :

2. Christ, by prophets long-predicted,
     Joy of Israel's chosen race;
   Light to Gentiles long-afflicted,
     Lost in error's darkest maze.

3. Bright the star of your salvation,
     Pointing to his rude abode!
   Rapturous news for every nation:
     Mortals! now behold your God!

4. Glad, we trace th' amazing story,
     Angels leave their bliss to tell;
   Theme sublime, replete with glory—
     Sinners saved from death and hell.

5. Love eternal moved the Saviour
     Thus to lay his radiance by;
   Blessings on the Lamb for ever—
     Glory be to God on high!

ROBINSON, 8s & 7s.- Double.   "MANHATTAN COLL." Arranged.

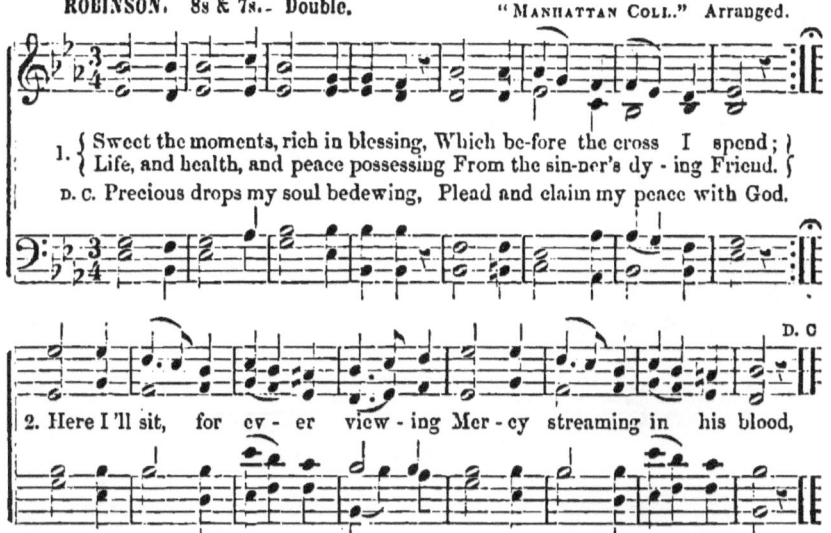

1. { Sweet the moments, rich in blessing, Which be-fore the cross I spend; }
   { Life, and health, and peace possessing From the sin-ner's dy - ing Friend. }

D. C. Precious drops my soul bedewing, Plead and claim my peace with God.

2. Here I 'll sit, for ev - er view - ing Mer - cy streaming in his blood,

D. C

[*For the fifth stanza, of the following hymns repeat from second strain.*]

823.   *Redemption.*

1. SWEET the moments, rich in blessing,
   Which before the cross I spend:
   Life, and health, and peace possessing
   From the sinner's dying Friend.
2. Here I 'll sit for ever viewing
   Mercy streaming in his blood,
   Precious drops my soul bedewing,
   Plead and claim my peace with God.
3. Here it is I find my heaven,
   While upon the cross I gaze ;
   Love I much ! I 've much forgiven—
   I 'm a miracle of grace.
4. Love and grief my heart dividing,
   Gazing here I 'd spend my breath ;
   Constant still in faith abiding,
   Life deriving from his death.
5. Lord, in ceaseless contemplation,
   Fix my heart and eyes on thine,
   Till I taste thy whole salvation,
   Where, unveiled, thy glories shine.

824.   *Redeeming Love.*

1. COME, thou Fount of every blessing !
   Tune my heart to grateful lays ;
   Streams of mercy, never ceasing,
   Call for songs of loudest praise.
2. Teach me some melodious measure,
   Sung by raptured saints above ;
   Fill my soul with sacred pleasure,
   While I sing redeeming love.
3. Jesus sought me when a stranger,
   Wandering from the fold of God ;
   He, to save my soul from danger,
   Interposed his precious blood.
4. Oh ! to grace how great a debtor
   Daily I 'm constrained to be !
   Let thy grace, Lord ! like a fetter,
   Bind my wandering heart to thee.
5. Prone to wander,—Lord ! I feel it ;
   Prone to leave the God I love ;
   Here 's my heart, Oh ! take and seal it,
   Seal it from thy courts above.

[*For the following hymn omit the repeat.*]

825.   *An Evening Offering.*

1. THROUGH the day thy love has spared us
   Now we lay us down to rest ;
   Through the silent watches guard us,
   Let no foe our peace molest ;
   Jesus ! thou our Guardian be,
   Sweet it is to trust in thee.

2. Pilgrims here on earth, and strangers,
   Dwelling in the midst of foes,—
   Us and ours preserve from dangers,
   In thine arms let us repose,
   And, when life's short day is past,
   Rest with thee, in heaven, at last.

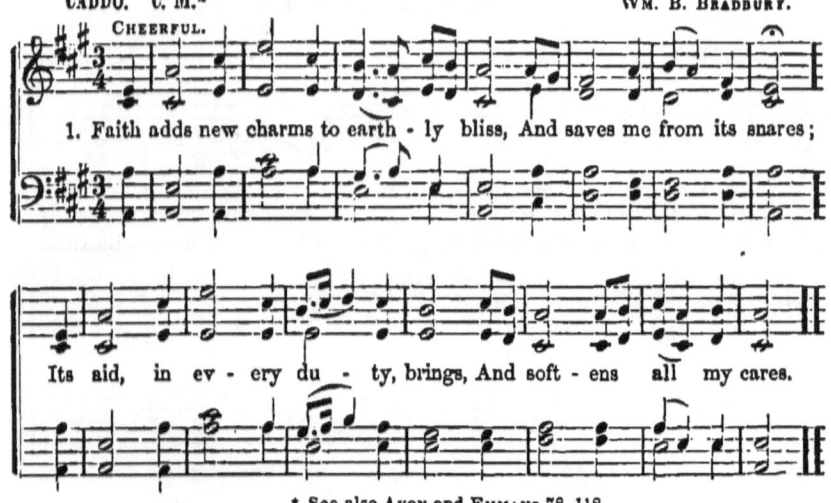

CHEERFUL.

1. Faith adds new charms to earth - ly bliss, And saves me from its snares;

Its aid, in ev - ery du - ty, brings, And soft - ens all my cares.

* See also AVON and EMMAUS 78, 118.

826. *The Power of Faith.*

1. FAITH adds new charms to earthly bliss,
And saves me from its snares;
Its aid, in every duty, brings,
And softens all my cares.

2. The wounded conscience knows its power
The healing balm to give;
That balm the saddest heart can cheer,
And make the dying live.

3. Wide it unveils celestial worlds,
Where deathless pleasures reign;
And bids me seek my portion there,
Nor bids me seek in vain.

4. It shows the precious promise sealed
With the Redeemer's blood;
And helps my feeble hope to rest
Upon a faithful God.

5. There—there unshaken would I rest,
Till this vile body dies;
And then, on faith's triumphant wings,
To endless glory rise.

827. *The Sovereignty of God.*

1. THY way, O God, is in the sea;
Thy paths I can not trace;
Nor comprehend the mystery
Of thy redeeming grace.

2. Here the dark veils of flesh and sense
My captive soul surround;

Mysterious deeps of Providence
My inward thoughts confound.

3. As through a glass, I dimly see
The wonders of thy love:
How little do I know of thee,
Or of the joys above!

4. Though but in part I know thy will,
I bless thee for the sight;
When will thy love the rest reveal
In glory's clearer light?

5. In rapture shall I then survey
Thy providence and grace;
And spend an everlasting day
In wonder, love, and praise.

828. *Invocation.*

1. COME, Holy Ghost, my soul inspire—
This one great gift impart—
What most I need—and most desire,
An humble, holy heart.

2. Bear witness that I'm born again,
My many sins forgiven:
Nor let a gloomy doubt remain
To cloud my hope of heaven.

3. More of myself grant I may know,
From sin's deceit be free,
In all the Christian graces grow,
And live alone to thee.

EVAN. C. M. From "HALLELUJAH." By permission.

1. How are thy servants blessed, O Lord! How sure is their de - fense!

E - ter - nal wis-dom is their guide, Their help, Om - ni - po - tence.

829. *Servants of God safe.*

1. How are thy servants blessed, O Lord!
   How sure is their defense!
   Eternal wisdom is their guide,
   Their help, Omnipotence.

2. In foreign realms, and lands remote,
   Supported by thy care,
   Through burning climes they pass unhurt,
   And breathe in tainted air.

3. When, by the dreadful tempest borne,
   High on the broken wave,
   They know thou art not slow to hear,
   Nor impotent to save.

4. The storm is laid—the winds retire
   Obedient to thy will;
   The sea, that roars at thy command,
   At thy command is still.

5. In midst of dangers, fears, and deaths,
   Thy goodness we'll adore;
   We'll praise thee for thy mercies past,
   And humbly hope for more.

830. *Heaven on Earth.*

1. WHILE thro' this changing world we roam,
   From infancy to age,
   Heaven is the Christian pilgrim's home,
   His rest at every stage.

2. Thither, his raptured thought ascends,
   Eternal joys to share:
   There his adoring spirit bends,
   While here, he kneels in prayer.

3. From earth his freed affections rise,
   To fix on things above,
   Where all his hope of glory lies—
   Where all is perfect love.

4. There, too, may we our treasure place,
   There let our hearts be found;
   That still, where sin abounded, grace
   May more and more abound.

5. Henceforth, our conversation be
   With Christ, before the throne;
   Ere long we, eye to eye, shall see,
   And know as we are known.

831. *Summer and Harvest.*

1. To praise the ever-bounteous Lord,
   My soul, wake all thy powers:
   He calls—and at his voice came forth
   The smiling harvest hours.

2. His covenant with the earth he keeps
   My tongue, his goodness sing;
   Summer and winter know their time,
   The harvest crowns the spring.

3. Well pleased the husbandmen behold
   The waving, yellow crop;
   With joy they bear the sheaves away,
   And sow again in hope.

4. Thus teach me, gracious God, to sow
   The seeds of righteousness;
   Smile on my soul, and with thy beams
   The ripening harvest bless.

WARNING VOICE. L. C. M.* HASTINGS.

1. That warning voice, O sin-ner, hear, And while sal-va-tion lin-gers near, The heavenly call o-bey: Flee from de-struction's downward path, Flee from the threat'ning storm of wrath, That ris-es o'er thy way!

* See also the opposite page.

832. *A Voice of Warning.*

1. THAT warning voice, O sinner, hear,
And while salvation lingers near,
  The heavenly call obey:
Flee from destruction's downward path,
Flee from the threatening storm of wrath,
  That rises o'er thy way!

2. Soon night comes on, with thickening
    shade,
The tempest hovers round thy head,
  The winds their fury pour:
The lightnings rend the earth and skies,
The thunders roar, the flames arise—
  What terror fills that hour!

3 That warning voice, O sinner, hear,
Whose accents linger on thine ear,
  Thy footsteps now retrace:
Renounce thy sins, and be forgiven;
Believe, become an heir of heaven,
  And sing redeeming grace

4. Then, while a voice of pardon speaks,
The storm is hushed, the morning breaks,
  The heavens are all serene:
Fresh verdure clothes the beauteous fields,
Joy echoes from the distant hills,
  New wonders fill the scene.

833. *Present and future Realities.*

1. Lo! on a narrow neck of land,
Between two boundless seas I stand,
  Yet how insensible!
A point of time—a moment's space—
Removes me to yon heavenly place,
  Or—shuts me up in hell!

2. O God, my inmost soul convert,
And deeply on my thoughtless heart
  Eternal things impress;
Give me to feel their solemn weight,
And save me, ere it be too late—
  Wake me to righteousness.

3. Before me place, in bright array,
The pomp of that tremendous day
When thou, with clouds, shalt come,
To judge the nations at thy bar;—
And tell me, Lord, shall I be there,
To meet a joyful doom?

4. Be this my one great business here,
With holy trembling, holy fear,
To make my calling sure;
Thine utmost counsel to fulfill,
And suffer all thy righteous will,
And to the end endure.

MERIBAH. L. C. M.

L. MASON.

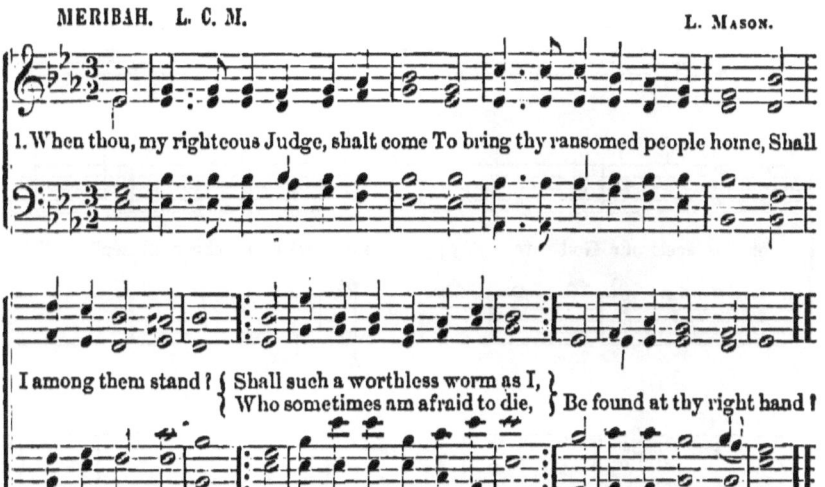

1. When thou, my righteous Judge, shalt come To bring thy ransomed people home, Shall I among them stand? { Shall such a worthless worm as I, Who sometimes am afraid to die, } Be found at thy right hand?

834. *The Saint at Christ's right Hand.*

1. WHEN thou, my righteous Judge! shalt come
To bring thy ransomed people home,
Shall I among them stand?
Shall such a worthless worm as I,
Who sometimes am afraid to die,
Be found at thy right hand?

2. Blest Saviour! grant it by thy grace;
Be thou my only hiding-place,
In this, th' accepted day;
Thy pardoning voice, Oh! let me hear,
To still my unbelieving fear,
Nor let me fall, I pray.

3. Among thy saints let me be found,
Whene'er th' archangel's trump shall sound,
To see thy smiling face;
Then, filled with rapture, shall I sing,
While heaven's resounding mansions ring
With shouts of sovereign grace.

835. *The new Birth.*

1. AWAKED by Sinai's awful sound,
My soul in bonds of guilt I found,
And knew not where to go:
One solemn truth increased my pain—
The sinner "must be born again,"
Or sink to endless woe.

2. I heard the law its thunders roll,
While guilt lay heavy on my soul—
A vast, oppressive load:
All creature aid I saw was vain;—
The sinner "must be born again,"
Or drink the wrath of God.

3. The saints I heard with rapture tell,
How Jesus conquered death and hell
To bring salvation near:
Yet still I found this truth remain—
The sinner "must be born again,"
Or sink in deep despair!

4. But, while I thus in anguish lay,
The bleeding Saviour passed that **way,**
My bondage to remove:
The sinner once by justice slain,
Now by his grace is born again,
And sings redeeming love.

DALSTON. S. P. M.   A. WILLIAMS,

1. How pleased and blessed was I,   To   hear the peo-ple   cry, "Come,

let us seek our God to - day;"   Yes, with a cheer-ful zeal, . We'll

haste to Zi - on's hill, And there our vows and hon - ors pay.

836. *Delight in public Worship.*

1. How pleased and blessed was I,
   To hear the people cry,—
"Come, let us seek our God to-day;"
   Yes, with a cheerful zeal
   We'll haste to Zion's hill,
And there our vows and honors pay.

2. Zion, thrice happy place,
   Adorned with wondrous grace,
And walls of strength embrace thee
        round;
   In thee our tribes appear,
   To pray, and praise, and hear
The sacred gospel's joyful sound.

3. May peace attend thy gate,
   And joy within thee wait,
To bless the soul of every guest;

The man that seeks thy peace,
   And wishes thine increase,
A thousand blessings on him rest.

4. My tongue repeats her vows—
   "Peace to this sacred house,"
For here my friends and kindred dwell;
   And since my glorious God
   Makes thee his blessed abode,
My soul shall ever love thee well.

837. *Assimilation to Christ.* 2 Cor. iii. 18.

1. How blessed indeed are they,
   Who keep their shining way,
Sustained by precious thoughts of God:
   The soul that he approves,
   Is formed to what it loves,
And made the Spirit's fair abode.

2. Grant us the mind, O Lord,
   To search thy holy Word,
Thy glorious beauty there to see;
   So, by transforming grace,
   Our hearts shall bear the trace
Of thine own image, stamped by thee.

3. And when above the skies,
   Thou shalt unveil our eyes,
And doubt and shadows all depart,
   Like thee we shall appear,
   Whose worthy name we bear,
For we shall see thee as thou art.

COME, YE DISCONSOLATE.

Arranged.

1. Come, ye dis-con-solate, where-e'er ye lan-guish; Come to the
mer-cy-seat, fer-vent-ly kneel; Here bring your wounded hearts,
here tell your an-guish, Earth has no sorrows that Heaven can not heal.

838. *Consolation at the Mercy-Seat.*

1. COME, ye disconsolate, where'er ye languish,
   Come to the mercy-seat, fervently kneel;
   Here bring your wounded hearts, here tell your anguish,
   Earth has no sorrows that Heaven can not heal.

2. Joy of the comfortless, light of the straying,
   Hope of the penitent, fadeless and pure;
   Here speaks the Comforter, tenderly saving—
   Earth has no sorrows that Heaven can not cure.

3. Here see the Bread of Life; see waters flowing
   Forth from the throne of God, pure from above;
   Come to the feast prepared—come, ever knowing
   Earth has no sorrows but Heaven can remove.

AUTUMN. 8s & 7s. Double.*   SPANISH.

1. Je-sus, I my cross have taken, All to leave, and fol-low thee;

Naked, poor, despised, for-sak-en, Thou, from hence, my all shalt be.
A. s. Yet how rich is my con-di-tion, God and heaven are still my own.

Perish, ev-ery fond am-bi-tion, All I've sought, or hoped, or known;

* See also ABERDEEN 120.

839.   *Taking up the Cross.*

1. JESUS, I my cross have taken,
     All to leave, and follow thee;
Naked, poor, despised, forsaken,
     Thou, from hence, my all shalt be.
Perish, every fond ambition,
     All I've sought, or hoped, or known;
Yet how rich is my condition,
     God and heaven are still my own!

2. Let the world despise and leave me;
     They have left my Saviour, too;
Human hearts and looks deceive me—
     Thou art not, like them, untrue;
Oh! while thou dost smile upon me,
     God of wisdom, love, and might,
Foes may hate, and friends disown me,
     Show thy face, and all is bright.

3. Perish, earthly fame and treasure,
     Come, disaster, scorn, and pain:
In thy service, pain is pleasure;
     With thy favor, life is gain:
Oh! 'tis not in grief to harm me,
     While thy love is left to me;
Oh! 't were not in joy to charm me,
     Were that joy unmixed with thee.

840.   *Jesus, exalted to the Throne.*

1. JESUS! hail! enthroned in glory,
     There for ever to abide;
All the heavenly host adore thee,
     Seated at thy Father's side.
2. There, for sinners, thou art pleading,
     There thou dost our place prepare;
Ever for us interceding,
     Till in glory we appear.

3. Worship, honor, power, and blessing,
   Thou art worthy to receive;
   Loudest praises, without ceasing,
   Meet it is for us to give.
4. Help, ye bright, angelic spirits!
   Bring your sweetest, noblest lays;
   Help to sing our Saviour's merits—
   Help to chant Immanuel's praise.

841.   *Missionaries charged.*

1. ONWARD, onward, men of heaven;
   Bear the gospel banner high;
   Rest not till its light is given—
   Star of every pagan sky:
   Send it where the pilgrim stranger
   Faints beneath the torrid ray;
   Bid the hardy forest-ranger
   Hail it, ere he fades away.

2. Where the Arctic ocean thunders,
   Where the tropics fiercely glow,
   Broadly spread its page of wonders,
   Brightly bid its radiance flow:
   India marks its lustre stealing;
   Shivering Greenland loves its rays;
   Afric, 'mid her deserts kneeling,
   Lifts the untaught strain of praise.

3. Rude in speech, or wild in feature,
   Dark in spirit, though they be,
   Show that light to every creature—
   Prince or vassal, bond or free:
   Lo! they haste to every nation;
   Host on host the ranks supply:
   Onward! Christ is your salvation,
   And your death is victory.

842.   *In Sadness.*

1. SUMMER'S mildest breeze is blowing
   Through the meadow and the grove,
   And her purest fragrance flowing,
   To inspire the heart with love:
   All creation wakes to gladness,
   Bids us in her music share:
   But this heart is filled with sadness,
   And disturbed by anxious care.

2. Why, my soul, this sad emotion?
   Why this self-tormenting pain?
   Light the fires of pure devotion,
   And thy wonted peace regain:
   If thy wanderings are forgiven,
   Be not anxious for the rest;
   Leave thy cause alone with Heaven,
   And in Christ be ever blest.

843.   *False and true Pleasures.*

1. TELL us, wanderer! wildly roving
   From the path that leads to peace,
   Pleasure's false enchantment loving—
   When will thy delusion cease?
2. Once, like thee, by joys surrounded,
   We could kneel at pleasure's shrine;
   Then our brightest hopes were bounded
   By delights as false as thine.
3. But those visions never blessed us—
   Soon their fleeting day was o'er;
   Then the world, that had caressed us,
   Charmed us with its smiles no more.
4. Such is pleasure's transient story;
   Lasting happiness is known
   Only in the path to glory—
   In the Saviour's love alone.

844.   *Protection and Success are from God.*

1. VAINLY through night's weary hours,
   Keep ye watch, lest foes alarm;—
   Vain our bulwarks, and our towers,
   But for God's protecting arm.
2. Vain were all our toil and labor,
   Did not God that labor bless;
   Vain, without his grace and favor
   Every talent we possess.
3. Vainer still the hope of heaven,
   That on human help relies;
   But to him shall help be given,
   Who in humble faith applies.
4. Seek we, then, the Lord's Anointed,
   He will grant us peace and rest;
   Ne'er was suppliant disappointed,
   Who thro' Christ his prayer addressed.

845.   *Sowing and reaping.*

1. HE that goeth forth with weeping,
   Bearing precious seed in love,
   Never tiring, never sleeping,
   Findeth mercy from above:
   Soft descend the dews of heaven,
   Bright the rays celestial shine;
   Precious fruits will thus be given,
   Through an influence all divine.

2. Sow thy seed, be never weary,
   Let no fears thy soul annoy;
   Be the prospect ne'er so dreary,
   Thou shalt reap the fruits of joy.
   Lo, the scene of verdure brightening!
   See the rising grain appear;
   Look, again! the fields are whitening,
   For the harvest time is near.

ST. BRIDGES. S. M.   DR. HOWARD.

QUICK AND EARNEST.

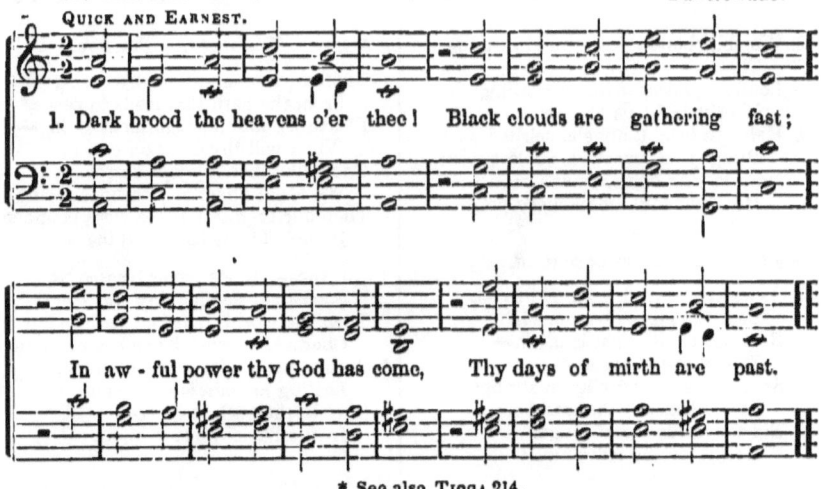

1. Dark brood the heavens o'er thee! Black clouds are gathering fast;

In aw - ful power thy God has come, Thy days of mirth are past.

*See also TIOGA 214.

846. *A Vision of Judgment.*

1. DARK brood the heavens o'er thee!
   Black clouds are gathering fast;
In awful power thy God has come,
   Thy days of mirth are past.

2. Dark brood the heavens o'er thee!
   Red flames are bursting round;
Bright lightnings flash, loud thunders roar,
   How shakes the trembling ground!

3. Dark brood the heavens o'er thee!
   Behold the Judge appears;
Unnumbered millions throng around,
   Raised from the dust of years.

4. Dark brood the heavens o'er thee!
   Soon thou wilt hear thy doom;
Destruction opens wide for thee,
   Thy chosen, final home.

5. Yet stay—the vision lingers;
   Why, sinner, wilt thou die?
Dark brood the heavens, but mercy waits,
   This hour to Jesus fly.

847. *The last Account.*

1. I SAW, beyond the tomb,
   The awful Judge appear,
Prepared to scan, with strict account,
   The blessings wasted here.

2. His wrath, like flaming fire,
   In hell for ever burns;
And, from that hopeless world of woe,
   No fugitive returns.

3. Ye sinners! fear the Lord,
   While yet 'tis called to-day;
Soon will the awful voice of death
   Command your souls away.

4. Soon will the harvest close,
   The summer soon be o'er;
O, sinners! then your injured God
   Will heed your cries no more.

848. *Death and the Resurrection.*

1. AND must this body die?—
   This mortal frame decay?
And must these active limbs of mine
   Lie mouldering in the clay?

2. God, my Redeemer, lives,
   And, often from the skies,
Looks down and watches all my dust,
   Till he shall bid it rise.

3. Arrayed in glorious grace,
   Shall these vile bodies shine,
And every shape, and every face,
   Look heavenly and divine.

4. These lively hopes we owe
   To Jesus' dying love;
We would adore his grace below,
   And sing his praise above.

5. Dear Lord! accept the praise
   Of these, our humble songs;
Till tunes of nobler sound we raise,
   With our immortal tongues.

BOYLE. S. M.

WM. B. BRADBURY.

1. Ye mes - sen - gers of Christ! His sove - reign voice o - bey;

A - rise, and fol - low where he leads, And peace at - tend your way.

849. *Missionaries encouraged.*

1. YE messengers of Christ!
His sovereign voice obey;
Arise, and follow where he leads,
And peace attend your way.

2. The Master, whom you serve,
Will needful strength bestow;
Depending on his promised aid,
With sacred courage go.

3. Go, spread the Saviour's name;
Go, tell his matchless grace;
Proclaim salvation, full and free,
To Adam's guilty race.

4. Mountains shall sink to plains,
And hell in vain oppose;
The cause is God's—and will prevail
In spite of all his foes.

850. *The Death of an aged Minister.*

1. SERVANT of God! well done!
Rest from thy loved employ:
The battle fought—the victory won—
Enter thy Master's joy."

2. The voice at midnight came,
He started up to hear;
A mortal arrow pierced his frame,
He fell—but felt no fear.

3. Tranquil amid alarms,
It found him on the field,
A veteran, slumbering on his arms,
Beneath his red-cross shield.

4. The pains of death are past—
Labor and sorrow cease:
And, life's long warfare closed at last,
His soul is found in peace.

5. Soldier of Christ! well done!
Praise be thy new employ;
And, while eternal ages run,
Rest in thy Saviour's joy.

851. *Man condemned before God.*

1. AH! how shall fallen man
Be just before his God?
If he contend in righteousness,
We fall beneath his rod.

2. If he our ways should mark,
With strict, inquiring eyes,
Could we, for one of thousand faults,
A just excuse devise?

3. All-seeing, powerful God!
Who can with thee contend?
Or who, that tries th' unequal strife,
Shall prosper in the end?

4. The mountains, in thy wrath,
Their ancient seats forsake;
The trembling earth deserts her place,
Her rooted pillars shake.

5. Ah! how shall guilty man
Contend with such a God?
None—none can meet him and escape,
But through the Saviour's blood.

LOUVAN. L. M.*

V. C. TAYLOR.

1. Thou whom my soul ad-mires a-bove All earthly joy, and earth-ly love,—

Tell me, dear Shepherd, let me know—Where do thy sweetest pastures grow?

* See also UXBRIDGE 66.

852. *The Good Shepherd.*

1. THOU! whom my soul admires above
All earthly joy, and earthly love,—
Tell me, dear Shepherd! let me know—
Where do thy sweetest pastures grow?

2. Where is the shadow of that rock,
That from the sun defends thy flock?
Fain would I feed among thy sheep,—
Among them rest, among them sleep.

3. Why should thy bride appear like one
That turns aside to paths unknown?
My constant feet would never rove,—
Would never seek another love.

4. The footsteps of thy flock I see;
Thy sweetest pastures here they be;
A wondrous feast thy love prepares,
Bought with thy wounds, and groans,
and tears.

5. His dearest flesh he makes my food,
And bids me drink his richest blood:
Here to these hills my soul will come,
Till my belovéd leads me home.

853. *Infant Baptism.*

1. O LORD encouraged by thy grace,
We bring our infants to thy throne;
Give them within thy heart a place,
Let them be thine, and thine alone.

2. Wash them from every stain of guilt,
And let them all be sanctified;
Lord, thou canst cleanse them if thou wilt,
And all their native evils hide.

3. We ask not for them earthly bliss,
Or earthly honors, wealth, or fame:
The sum of our request is this,
That they may love and fear thy name.

4. These infants we by faith commit
To thy kind love and guardian care;
We lay them at the Saviour's feet,
He will not let them perish there.

854. *Living Waters.*

1. HO! every one that thirsts! draw nigh;
'Tis God invites the fallen race;
Mercy and free salvation buy,
Buy wine, and milk, and gospel grace.

2. Ye nothing in exchange can give,—
Leave all ye have and are behind;
Freely the gift of God receive,
Pardon and peace in Jesus find.

3. Come to the living waters, come;
Sinners! obey your Maker's voice;
Return, ye weary wanderers! home,
And in redeeming love rejoice.

ST. EDMUND'S. L. M.

TENDERLY.

Theme by HAYDN.

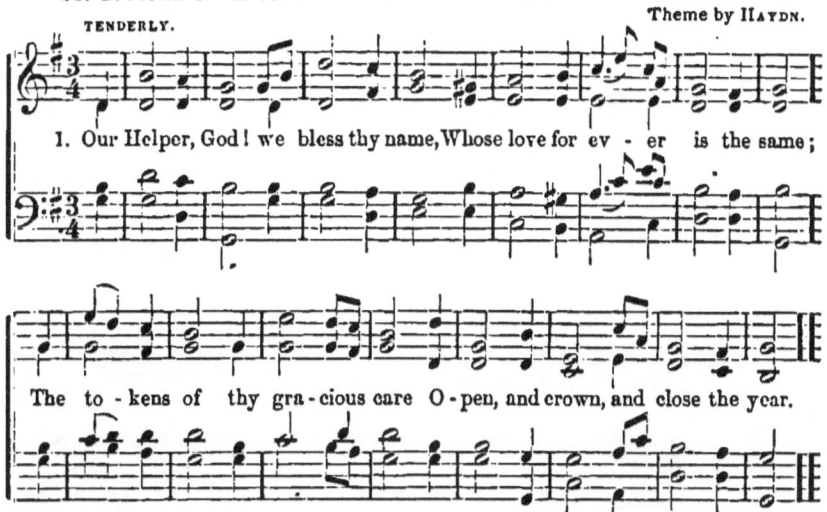

1. Our Helper, God! we bless thy name, Whose love for ev - er is the same;

The to - kens of thy gra - cious care O - pen, and crown, and close the year.

855. *New Year: God, our Helper.*

1. OUR Helper, God! we bless thy name,
   Whose love for ever is the same;
   The tokens of thy gracious care
   Open, and crown, and close the year.

2. Amid ten thousand snares we stand,
   Supported by thy guardian hand;
   And see, when we review our ways,
   Ten thousand monuments of praise.

3. Thus far thine arm has led us on;
   Thus far we make thy mercy known;
   And, while we tread this desert land,
   New mercies shall new songs demand.

4. Our grateful souls, on Jordan's shore,
   Shall raise one sacred pillar more;
   Then bear, in thy bright courts above,
   Inscriptions of immortal love.

856. *Men mortal—the Church safe.*

1. IT is the Lord our Saviour's hand
   Weakens our strength amidst the race;
   Disease and death, at his command,
   Arrest us, and cut short our days.

2. Spare us, O Lord! aloud we pray,
   Nor let our sun go down at noon;
   Thy years are one eternal day,
   And must thy children die so soon?

3. Yet, in the midst of death and grief,
   This thought our sorrow should as-
      suage; —

"Our Father and our Saviour live:
   Christ is the same through every age."

4. The starry curtains of the sky,
   Like garments shall be laid aside;
   But still thy throne stands firm and high;
   Thy church for ever must abide.

5. Before thy face, thy church shall live,
   And on thy throne thy children reign;
   This dying world shall they survive,
   And the dead saints be raised again.

[*For the following hymn repeat the first strain.*]

857. *Christ All, and in All.*

1. JESUS, thou source of calm repose,
   All fullness dwells in thee divine;
   Our strength, to quell the proudest foes
   Our light, in deepest gloom to shine;
   Thou art our fortress, strength, and tower,
   Our trust and portion, evermore.

2. Jesus, our Comforter thou art;
   Our rest in toil, our ease in pain;
   The balm to heal each broken heart,
   In storms our peace, in loss our gain;
   Our joy, beneath the worldling's frown;
   In shame, our glory and our crown;—

3. In want, our plentiful supply;
   In weakness, our almighty power;
   In bonds, our perfect liberty;
   Our refuge in temptation's hour;
   Our comfort, 'midst all grief and thrall;
   Our life in death, our all in all.

HELMSLEY. 8s, 7s & 4s.*

OLD SCOTTISH.

1. Lo! he comes, in clouds de-scend-ing, Once for fa-vored

sin-ners slain; Thou-sand thou-sand saints, at-tend-ing,

Swell the tri-umph of his train: Hal-le-lu-jah,

Hal-le-lu-jah, Hal-le-lu-jah! Je-sus shall for ev-er reign.

* See also FARLAND 154.

858. *Christ coming to Judgment.*

1. Lo! he comes, in clouds descending,
Once for favored sinners slain ;
Thousand thousand saints, attending,
Swell the triumph of his train :
Hallelujah!
Jesus shall for ever reign.

2. Every eye shall now behold him,
Robed in dreadful majesty ;
Those who set at nought, and sold him,
Pierced and nailed him to the tree,
Deeply wailing,
Shall the great Messiah see.

3. Every island, sea, and mountain,
Heaven, and earth, shall flee away;
All who hate him, must, confounded,
Hear the trump proclaim the day;
Come to judgment!—
Come to judgment,—come away.

4. Now the Saviour, long expected,
See, in solemn pomp, appear!
All his saints, by man rejected,
Now shall meet him in the air.
Hallelujah!
See the day of God appear.

859. *Saints and Sinners judged.*

1. DAY of judgment! day of wonders!
Hark!—the trumpet's awful sound,
Louder than a thousand thunders,
Shakes the vast creation round:
How the summons
Will the sinner's heart confound!

2. See the Judge, our nature wearing,
Clothed in majesty divine!
You, who long for his appearing,
Then shall say,—"This God is mine!"
Gracious Saviour!
Own me in that day for thine.

3. At his call, the dead awaken,
Rise to life from earth and sea:
All the powers of nature, shaken
By his looks, prepare to flee:
Careless sinner!
What will then become of thee?

4. But to those who have confessed,
Loved and served the Lord below,
He will say,—"Come near, ye blessed!
See the kingdom I bestow!
You for ever
Shall my love and glory know."

"STAR OF PEACE."

From a MS. of G. E. P. Arranged.

1. Star of Peace, to wand'rers wea-ry, Bright the beams that smile on me;

Cheer the pi-lot's vis-ion drear-y, Far, far at sea.

860. *Seamen's Song.*

1. STAR of Peace, to wanderers weary,
Bright the beams that smile on me;
Cheer the pilot's vision dreary,
Far, far at sea.

2. Star of Hope, gleam on the billow,
Bless the soul that sighs for thee;
Bless the sailor's lonely pillow,
Far far at sea.

3. Star of Faith, when winds are mocking
All his toil, he flies to thee;
Save him, on the billows rocking,
Far, far at sea.

4. Star Divine! O, safely guide him—
Bring the wanderer home to thee;
Sore temptations long have tried him,
Far, far at sea.

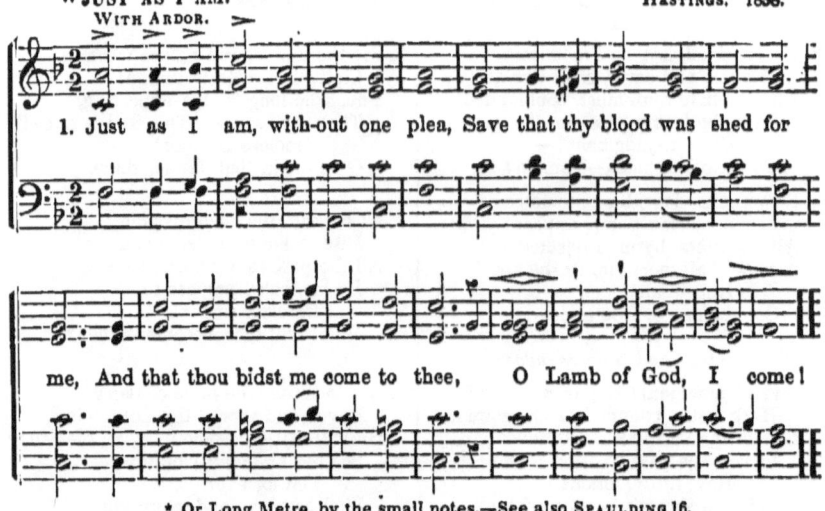

1. Just as I am, with-out one plea, Save that thy blood was shed for

me, And that thou bidst me come to thee, O Lamb of God, I come!

* Or Long Metre, by the small notes.—See also SPAULDING 16.

861.   John vi. 39.

1. JUST as I am, without one plea,
Save that thy blood was shed for me,
And that thou bidst me come to thee,
O Lamb of God, I come!

2. Just as I am, and waiting not
To rid my soul of one dark blot,
To thee, whose blood can cleanse each
spot,
O Lamb of God, I come!

3. Just as I am, though tossed about
With many a conflict, many a doubt,
With fears within, and foes without,
O Lamb of God, I come!

4. Just as I am, poor, wretched, blind,
Sight, riches, healing of the mind,
Yea, all I need, in Thee to find,
O Lamb of God, I come!

5. Just as I am—thou wilt receive,
Wilt welcome, pardon, cleanse, relieve;
Because thy promise I believe—
O Lamb of God, I come!

6. Just as I am—thy love unknown
Has broken every barrier down;
Now to be thine, yea, thine alone—
O Lamb of God, I come!

862.   *The Wanderer reclaimed.*

1. THE wanderer no more will roam,
The lost one to the fold hath come;
The prodigal is welcomed home,
O Lamb of God, in thee.

2. Though clad in rags, by sin defiled,
The Father hath embraced his child,
And I am pardoned, reconciled,
O Lamb of God, in thee.

3. It is the Father's joy to bless;
His love provides for me a dress—
A robe of spotless righteousness—
O Lamb of God, in thee.

4. Now shall my famished soul be fed;
A feast of love for me is spread;
I feed upon the children's bread,
O Lamb of God, in thee.

5. Yea, in the fullness of his grace,
He puts me in the children's place,
Where I may gaze upon his face,
O Lamb of God, in thee.

6. I can not half his love express;
Yet, Lord, with joy my lips confess
This blessèd portion I possess,
O Lamb of God, in thee.

7. It is *thy* precious name I bear,
It is *thy* spotless robe I wear;
Therefore the Father's love I share,
O Lamb of God, in thee.

SLOW.

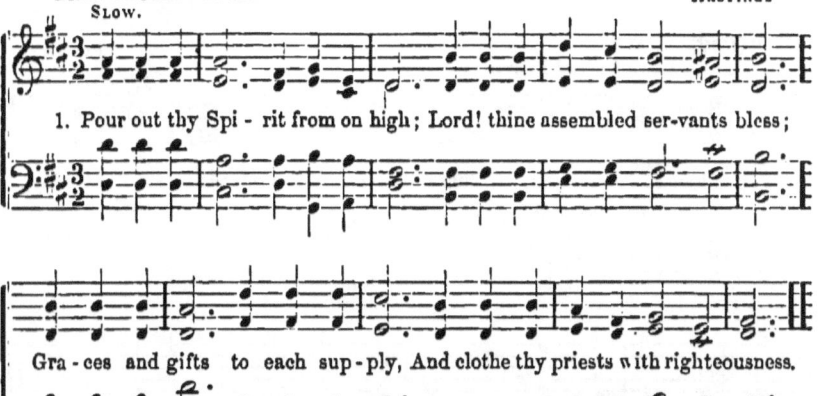

1. Pour out thy Spi - rit from on high; Lord! thine assembled ser-vants bless;

Gra - ces and gifts to each sup - ply, And clothe thy priests with righteousness.

* See also HAMBURGH 28.

863. *Meeting of Ministers.*

1. POUR out thy Spirit from on high;
Lord! thine assembled servants bless;
Graces and gifts to each supply,
And clothe thy priests with righteousness.

2. Within thy temple where we stand,
To teach the truth as taught by thee,
Saviour! like stars, in thy right hand,
The angels of the churches be!

3. Wisdom, and zeal, and faith impart,
Firmness with meekness from above,
To bear thy people on our hearts,
And love the souls whom thou dost love :—

4. To watch, and pray, and never faint;
By day and night strict guard to keep:
To warn the sinner, cheer the saint,
Nourish thy lambs, and feed thy sheep.

5. Then, when our work is finished here,
In humble hope, our charge resign :
When the chief Shepherd shall appear,
O God! may they and we be thine.

864. *Divine Protection amid Dangers.*

1. HE that hath made his refuge, God,
Shall find a most secure abode ;
Shall walk all day beneath his shade,
And there, at night, shall rest his head.

2. Then will I say,—"My God! thy power
Shall be my fortress and my tower ;
I, who am formed of feeble dust,
Make thine almighty Arm my trust."

3. Thrice happy man! thy Maker's care
Shall keep thee from the fowler's snare
Satan, the fowler, who betrays
Unguarded souls a thousand ways.

4. If burning beams of noon conspire
To dart a pestilential fire ;
God is thy life,—his wings are spread
To shield thee with a healthful shade,

865. *Hindrances to Prayer.*

1. WHAT various hindrances we meet
In coming to a mercy-seat !
Yet who that knows the worth of prayer
But wishes to be often there ?

2. Restraining prayer, we cease to fight;
Prayer makes the Christian's armor bright ;
And Satan trembles when he sees
The weakest saint upon his knees.

3. Have you no words ? Ah, think again
Words flow apace when you complain,
And fill a fellow-creature's ear
With the sad tale of all your care.

4. Were half the breath thus vainly spent
To heaven in supplication sent,
Our cheerful song would oftener be,
"Hear what the Lord hath done for me."

BARBY. C. M.*   TANSUR.
Quick, *but with varied Expression.*

1. Plunged in   a   gulf   of   dark de-spair,   We wretched   sin - ners lay,

With - out   one   cheer - ful   beam   of   hope,   Or spark   of glimmering day.

* See also LAIGHT STREET, and LATOUR 246, 32.

866.   *Praise to the Redeemer.*

1. PLUNGED in a gulf of dark despair,
   We wretched sinners lay,
   Without one cheerful beam of hope,
   Or spark of glimmering day.

2. With pitying eyes the Prince of grace
   Beheld our helpless grief;
   He saw, and—Oh! amazing love!—
   He ran to our relief.

3. Down from the shining seats above,
   With joyful haste he fled,
   Entered the grave in mortal flesh,
   And dwelt among the dead.

4. Oh! for this love let rocks and hills
   Their lasting silence break;
   And all harmonious human tongues
   The Saviour's praises speak.

5. Angels! assist our mighty joys;
   Strike all your harps of gold;
   But when you raise your highest notes,
   His love can ne'er be told.

867.   *Christ, the Way, the Truth, and the Life.*

1. THOU art the Way;—to thee alone
   From sin and death we flee;
   And he, who would the Father seek,
   Must seek him, Lord! in thee.

2. Thou art the Truth;—thy word alone
   True wisdom can impart;

Thou only canst instruct the mind,
   And purify the heart.

3. Thou art the Life;—the rending tomb
   Proclaims thy conquering arm;
   And those who put their trust in thee
   Not death nor hell shall harm.

4. Thou art the Way, the Truth, the Life;—
   Grant us to know that Way,
   That Truth to keep, that Life to win,
   Which lead to endless day.

868.   *Holy Fear, and Tenderness of Conscience.*

1. WITH my whole heart I've sought thy face;
   O, let me never stray
   From thy commands, O God of grace,
   Nor tread the sinner's way.

2. Thy word I've hid within my heart,
   To keep my conscience clean,
   And be an everlasting guard
   From every rising sin.

3. My heart with sacred reverence hears
   The threatenings of thy word;
   My flesh, with holy trembling, fears
   The judgments of the Lord.

4. My God, I long, I hope, I wait,
   For thy salvation still;
   Thy holy law is my delight,
   And I obey thy will.

ALLEN. S. M.

WITH VARIED EXPRESSION.

HASTINGS.

1. My soul! re-peat his praise, Whose mer-cies are so great;

Cres. — — — — — *Dim.*

Whose an-ger is so slow to rise, So rea-dy to a-bate.

869. *Mercy in the Midst of Judgment.*

1. My soul! repeat his praise,
   Whose mercies are so great;
Whose anger is so slow to rise,
   So ready to abate.

2. High as the heavens are raised
   Above the ground we tread,
So far the riches of his grace
   Our highest thoughts exceed.

3. His power subdues our sins;
   And his forgiving love,
Far as the east is from the west,
   Doth all our guilt remove.

4. The pity of the Lord,
   To those who fear his name,
Is such as tender parents feel;
   He knows our feeble frame.

5. Our days are as the grass,
   Or like the morning flower;
If one sharp blast sweep o'er the field,
   It withers in an hour.

6. But thy compassions, Lord!
   To endless years endure,
And children's children ever find
   Thy words of promise sure.

870. *Affliction blessed.*

1. How tender is thy hand,
   O thou beloved Lord!
Afflictions come at thy command,
   And leave us at thy word.

2. How gentle was the rod
   That chastened us for sin!
How soon we found a smiling God,
   Where deep distress had been!

3. A Father's hand we felt,
   A Father's heart we knew;
With tears of penitence we knelt,
   And found his word was true.

4. We told him all our grief,
   We thought of Jesus' love;
A sense of pardon brought relief,
   And bade our pains remove.

5. Now we will bless the Lord,
   And in his strength confide;
For ever be his name adored;
   For there is none beside

Doxology.

YE angels round the throne,
   And saints that dwell below,
Worship the Father, love the Son,
   And bless the Spirit, too.

HARVEST PAST. 11s & 8s.   L. MASON. Arr. from "Spir. Songs."
WITH ARDOR.

1. When the har-vest is past, and the summer is gone, And sermons and
   When the beams cease to break of the sweet Sabbath morn, And Je-sus in-

prayers shall be o'er;
- vites thee no more; When the rich gales of mer-cy no long-er shall

blow, The gos-pel no mes-sage de-clare; Sin-ner, how canst thou

bear the deep wail-ings of woe? How suf-fer the night of de-spair!

871.   *Harvest Past.*   Jer. viii. 20.

1. When the harvest is past, and the summer is gone,
   And sermons and prayers shall be o'er;
   When the beams cease to break of the sweet
   Sabbath morn,
   And Jesus invites thee no more;
   When the rich gales of mercy no longer shall blow,
   The gospel no message declare;
   Sinner, how canst thou bear the deep wailings
   of woe?
   How suffer the night of despair?

2. When the holy have gone to the regions of
   peace,
   To dwell in the mansions above;
   When their harmony wakes, in the fullness of
   bliss,
   Their song to the Saviour they love:
   Say, O sinner, who livest at rest and secure,
   Who fearest no trouble to come;
   Can thy spirit the swellings of sorrow en-
   dure?
   Or bear the impenitent's doom?

INDEX OF TUNES.*

*The tunes credited to Messrs. MASON and BRADBURY, and other living composers, must be understood as here inserted by permission.

METRICAL INDEX.

INDEX

FIRST LINES OF THE PSALMS AND HYMNS.

———————◆———————

* By Rev. J. W. Alexander, D.D.

INDEX OF SUBJECTS

The figures refer to the Hymns.

INDEX OF PSALMS.

INDEX OF SCRIPTURES.

ADDITIONAL TUNES.

ALL SAINTS. L. M. "O HAPPY DAY," &c. **No. 461.** KNAPP.

AYLESBURY. S. M. "AND MUST THIS BODY," &c. **No. 848.** DR. GREEN.

BENEVENTO. 7s, Double. "SINNERS TURN." &c. **No. 14.**
Slow.

DOVER. S. M. "The Lord my Shepherd is," &c. No. 709.

FRANCONIA. 6s & 5s. "Why that look." &c. No. 636. Kl—ff.

GOLDEN HILL. S. M. "Blest be the tie." &c. No. 408.

LATHROP. S. M. "How sweet the melting." &c. No. 803. L. Mason.

LUTON. L. M. "WITH ALL MY POWERS," &c. No. 147. BURDER.

MARLOW. C. M. "LET EVERY MORTAL," &c. No. 251.

. MEAR. C. M. "O FOR A SHOUT," &c. No. 450.

334 NAZARETH. L. M. "What sinners value," &c. No. 175. S. Webbe.

NORWICH. 7s, Single. "Haste, O sinner," &c. No. 659.

PETERBOROUGH. C. M. "Once more, my soul," &c. No. 93.

RIVINGTON. H. M. "To spend one sacred," &c. No. 388. Hastings.

ROCHESTER. C. M. "God, my supporter," &c. No. 558.

335

SILVER STREET. S. M. "Come, sound his praise," &c. No. 136. I. Smith.

WINCHESTER. L. M. "Life is the time," &c. No. 570. German.

ZEBULON. H. M. "Lord of the worlds," &c. No. 383.

1.   **L. M.**

PRAISE God, from whom all blessings flow,
Praise him, all creatures here below;
Praise him above, ye heavenly host;
Praise Father, Son, and Holy Ghost.

2.   **L. M.**

To God the Father, God the Son,
And God the Spirit, three in one,
Be honor, praise, and glory given,
By all on earth and all in heaven.

3.   **C. M.**

LET God the Father, and the Son,
  And Spirit, be adored,
Where there are works to make him known,
  Or saints to love the Lord.

4.   **C. M.**

To Father, Son, and Holy Ghost,
  One God, whom we adore,
Be glory as it was, is now,
  And shall be evermore.

5.   **C. M.—*Double.***

THE God of mercy be adored,
  Who calls our souls from death;
Who saves by his redeeming word,
  And new creating breath.
To praise the Father and the Son,
  And Spirit, all divine—
The One in Three, and Three in One,
  Let saints and angels join.

6.   **S. M.**

YE angels round the throne,
  And saints who dwell below,
Worship the Father, praise the Son,
  And bless the Spirit too.

7.   **H. M.**

To God the Father's throne
Perpetual honors raise;
Glory to God the Son!
  To God the Spirit praise!
    With all our powers,
    Eternal King,
    Thy name we sing,
  While faith adores.

8.   **7s.—*Single.***

To the Father, to the Son,
To the Spirit, three in one,
Glory be for ever given,
By the hosts of earth and heaven.

9.   **7s.—6 lines.**

FATHER, Son, and Holy Ghost,
  One in three, and three in one,
As by the celestial host,
  Let thy will on earth be done:
Praise by all to thee be given,
Glorious Lord of earth and heaven.

10.   **7s.—*Double.***

FATHER, Son, and Holy Ghost,
  One in three, and three in one,
As by the celestial host,
  Let thy will on earth be done;
Sing we to our God above
Praise eternal as his love;
Praise by all to thee be given,
Glorious Lord of earth and heaven.

11.   **8s and 7s.—*Single.***

PRAISE the Father, earth and heaven,
  Praise the Son, the Spirit praise,
Everlasting praise be given,
  Glory through eternal days.

12.   **8s and 7s.—*Double.***

MAY the grace of Christ our Saviour,
  And the Father's boundless love,
With the Holy Spirit's favor,
  Rest upon us from above.
Thus may we abide in union
  With each other and the Lord,
And possess, in sweet communion,
  Joys which earth cannot afford.

13.   **8s, 7s, and 4s.**

GREAT Jehovah, we adore thee,
  God the Father, God the Son,
God the Spirit, joined in glory
  On the same eternal throne:
    Endless praises
  To Jehovah, three in one.

14.   **7s and 6s.—*Peculiar.***

To Father, Son, and Spirit,
  Eternal praise be given,
By all that earth inherit,
  And all that dwell in heaven;
Thou Triune God, before thee
  Our inmost souls adore,
Who art and hast been worthy,
  And shalt be evermore.

15.   **6s and 4s.**

To the great One in Three,
The highest praises be,
  Hence evermore;
His sovereign majesty
May we in glory see,
And to eternity
  Love and adore.